POLICY AND GOVERNMENT
IN NORTHERN IRELAND

Policy and Government in Northern Ireland

LESSONS OF DEVOLUTION

Derek Birrell
and
Alan Murie

GILL AND MACMILLAN
BARNES & NOBLE BOOKS

First published 1980 by
Gill and Macmillan Ltd
15/17 Eden Quay
Dublin 1
with associated companies in
London, New York, Delhi, Hong Kong,
Johannesburg, Lagos, Melbourne,
Singapore, Tokyo

Published in the USA 1980 by
Barnes & Noble Books
SBN 7171 0890 2 (Gill and Macmillan)
ISBN 0–389–20019–0 (Barnes & Noble)
Library of Congress Catalog Number LC 79–53791

Printed in Great Britain by
Bristol Typesetting Co. Ltd, Barton Manor, St Philips, Bristol

Contents

Introduction

THIS book presents a study of Northern Ireland's institutions of government and the policy processes in both the period of fully devolved government and the subsequent period of British government intervention. The Government of Ireland Act, 1920, established a system of legislative devolution which was unique in the United Kingdom. Constitutionally the Northern Ireland government and parliament were subordinate to the Westminster government, but in practice they evolved with increasing powers and with a substantial degree of autonomy. Northern Ireland's relationship with Westminster showed the difficulty in making a clear distinction between federal and devolved status.

A major aim of the book is to describe the system of devolution that operated in Northern Ireland and make some comment on its effectiveness and value. This involves consideration of a number of features: the constitutional and financial relationship with Great Britain; the adoption of the Westminster system of cabinet and parliamentary government and associated conventions; the operation of the major institutions, including the effect of devolution on the role of the Civil Service, local government authorities and pressure groups; and the policy outputs of the system. Consideration of these topics requires some analysis of the background to policy-making in terms of political attitudes and behaviour and of social and economic needs and problems. The political system was characterised by the dominance of one party and by the emphasis on ideological values. A study of social and economic policy facilitates an assessment of the value of devolution in dealing with key regional problems. The major developments in the powers of the Stormont government and parliament after 1921 were in the social and economic fields, and Northern Ireland chose to develop policies differently from Britain in some areas, although constrained in other areas by the principle of parity.

The book concentrates on the operation of the system of government, and it is not within its scope to provide an analysis of all aspects of the 'Northern Ireland problem', the historical background to the establishment of Northern Ireland, or the nature of conflict and violence.

The Northern Ireland experience of devolution is also of general relevance to the whole issue of devolution. The major arguments in favour of devolution emphasise the advantages of accessibility and the value of gearing policies to suit local needs or reflect local attitudes. Did the Stormont model of devolution realise these ends? And are these ends to be valued? Northern Ireland's experience of legislative devolution is also relevant to the discussion of devolution for Scotland and Wales. It has been argued that Northern Ireland's experience of devolution is of little relevance because of its peculiar political problems. However, many aspects of the practical functioning of devolution are relevant to the likely working of devolution in other areas; among the most important of these aspects are finance, administration, use of economic powers, local government, and the discussion of regional affairs at Westminster.

Devolution in Northern Ireland operated over a considerable period of time, and the rate of development of political institutions and the nature of policy processes varied. Patterns do emerge over time: the period of gradual and cautious evolution of institutions from 1921 to 1943; a period of administrative and policy innovations from 1943 to 1948; a period of relative stagation from 1948 to 1963; a period of policy rationalisation, the development of economic and regional planning and further reform and change in the machinery of government from 1963 to 1972; and more recently the period of Westminster intervention and direct rule. While our study is not a history of Northern Ireland, it does analyse the major events and developments in its system of government since its inception.

Since 1972 the devolved institutions have ceased to operate, and apart from the brief duration of the Northern Ireland Assembly and Executive in 1974 Northern Ireland has been governed by the system of direct rule. In effect the province is still governed under the Northern Ireland Constitution Act, 1973, but British government ministers in Northern Ireland hold executive power and Northern Ireland legislation is passed at Westminster. The system of administrative devolution through Northern Ireland Civil Service departments has remained. These developments have led to a complete reassessment of devolved government. In political terms the British government has accepted the need for a more broadly based system of government and an end to Unionist Party domination. The range of functions of a new devolved system of government and the mechanisms of Westminster control are also key issues. This study ends by assessing the problems of devolved institutions and examining the prospects for a new system of devolved government appropriate for Northern Ireland. The period of direct rule is also of interest in that it enables comparisons to be made between the government of Northern Ireland through devolved institutions and its government directly from Westminster; such comparisons provide further evidence about the merits, values and problems of devolution.

1

The Stormont–Westminster Relationship

THE Northern Ireland government and parliament was established by an act of the Westminster parliament, the Government of Ireland Act, 1920. These institutions were established not in response to demands within the six north-eastern counties of Ireland for a form of regional self-government but as part of the British government's general settlement of the Irish problem.

The 1920 act provided for separate parliaments in Northern and Southern Ireland as a solution to the Home Rule controversy. The act came into operation only in Northern Ireland, where the first meeting of the regional parliament was held in June 1921. The 1920 act never came into effect in Southern Ireland, and in December 1921 the British government agreed that the whole of Ireland, North and South, was to become a self-governing dominion. Northern Ireland, however, was given the alternative option of retaining its status under the Government of Ireland Act, 1920, and within a month this option was exercised. The Irish Free State (Consequential Provisions) Act, 1922, made certain modifications to the 1920 act in the light of this decision. It created the office of Governor of Northern Ireland, established a Privy Council of Northern Ireland, and made a number of adjustments to the financial provisions of the earlier act. The exact boundaries of Northern Ireland were not confirmed until the passage of the Ireland Act, 1925, following a tripartite conference which resolved previous disagreements. Northern Ireland was then left with a Home Rule constitution which few, if any, politicians in the province had demanded. The Ulster Unionists accepted it as the only means of preserving the Union with Great Britain.

The system of government that was established can best be described as a system of legislative devolution in which a range of responsibilities was devolved from Westminster to Stormont. It was therefore a devolved system, not a federal system. Northern Ireland's system of government could be amended or abolished by an act of the Westminster parliament, and Westminster had overall responsibility. Constitutionally the Northern Ireland government was subordinate in powers and status to Westminster, not co-ordinate as would have been the case in a federal system.

The Northern Ireland government operated with a written constitution[1] comprising the Government of Ireland Act, 1920, and subsequent amendments. These constitutional documents laid down the basic lines on which the devolved system was to operate, specified the financial arrangements that were to apply, and defined precisely the roles and powers of the governments at Stormont and Westminster. Northern Ireland's system of government thus had two focuses: an internal one which covered the working of the parliamentary and cabinet system, and an external one which covered the relationship with the Westminster government. This chapter concentrates on the external relationship, while the following two chapters deal with the internal aspects.

The Division of Powers

The 1920 act gave the new parliament the general power to pass legislation for the peace, order and good government of Northern Ireland, subject to certain limitations. The act then set out the subjects which were excluded from its powers, classified as 'excepted' and 'reserved' services. 'Excepted' services were matters which concerned the United Kingdom as a whole and included the Crown, armed forces, foreign relations, external trade, naturalisation, coinage, aerial navigation, wireless telegraph, weights and measures, and patent rights. The 'reserved' matters were fewer and included the Post Office, reserved taxation, saving banks, designs for stamps, registration of deeds, land purchase, and the Supreme Court of Northern Ireland. It was originally intended that the subjects which were reserved by Westminster would be transferred eventually to an all-Ireland parliament or a Council of Ireland when the Northern and Southern Ireland parliaments set up under the 1920 act reached an agreement. A three-tier system of government was thus envisaged for Ireland.

Responsibility for all services other than the excepted and reserved services was transferred to Northern Ireland. The authors of the original act could not have envisaged the growth of the welfare state and the economic functions of government and did not foresee that legislation on such important matters would come under the category of devolved powers.

The powers of the Northern Ireland parliament were limited not only by the list of excepted and reserved services but also by some important general restrictions. Section 5 of the 1920 act expressly forbade the making of laws which directly or indirectly endowed any religion, restricted the free exercise of religion, or gave preference, advantage or privilege, or imposed any disadvantages, on account of religious belief or status. While this clause prohibited legislation which discriminated on religious grounds, it did not make illegal the administration or application of legislation on a discriminatory basis. Section 5 also contained a provision prohibiting the taking of property without compensation, although this was removed in 1962. Section 4 of the act imposed a territorial limitation so that the parliament of Northern Ireland could not legislate except in respect of matters exclusively relating to that part of Ireland within its jurisdiction. However, the most important limitation was that of Section 75 of the 1920 act which preserved 'the supreme authority of the parliament of the United Kingdom over all persons, matters, and things in Northern Ireland'. It is generally accepted that this preserved the overall power of the United Kingdom parliament and its right to amend or suspend the constitution of Northern Ireland. It referred to the supremacy of the Westminster parliament as the source of the Northern Ireland constitution, but it did not specifically give the government of the United Kingdom any authority over devolved matters.

The development of the constitution did not see any diminution in the powers of the Northern Ireland government. Various Westminster statutes amending the 1920 act conferred further powers on Stormont to deal with matters which were originally excluded from its functions, for example civil defence, the registration of deeds, land purchase, and certain matters concerning the Supreme Court. Section 1 of the Northern Ireland Act, 1947, removed territorial restrictions to enable Stormont to legislate and enter into agreement with the government of the Irish Republic concerning cross-border schemes for electricity, drainage and transport. In 1962 Northern Ireland was given the power to deal with such matters as the regulations for the export of agricultural produce. In most cases amendments were of a technical nature and were concerned with overcoming restrictions which interfered with the proper administration of transferred services.

There have been remarkably few problems arising out of the complex division of responsibilities. As McBirney (1967) noted, 'Careful observance by both governments of the general rule— United Kingdom matters for Westminster, Northern Ireland matters for Stormont—have maintained the properly balanced exercise of powers, and ensured harmonious relations between the two parliaments.'[2] When difficulties arose Westminster always appeared willing to extend the area of Stormont's jurisdiction. All the constitutional amendments took place either at the request of Stormont or with its agreement. Nothing happened in the fifty years of the Stormont government's existence to restrict its legislative powers. This tolerant attitude to the powers of a subordinate parliament may be partly explained by a desire to make the experiment in devolution work, and partly by an unwillingness to get involved too deeply in Ulster affairs. At any rate it is clear that Stormont's powers were interpreted in London in a generous fashion.

This raises the question of the significance of the powers granted to Stormont and its degree of independence. Most commentators have taken one of two approaches to this question. The first approach involves an examination of the legal provisions of the 1920 act and subsequent constitutional practices; and this does seem to indicate a Stormont with a significant degree of autonomy. Thus Newark (1953) has stated that 'Apart from the excluded and reserved matters, the Northern Ireland parliament is a sovereign parliament.'[3] And Donaldson (1955) has claimed that 'The combined effect of the constitutional practices is that Northern Ireland has control over its own affairs. Over the years there has evolved a convention which gives the local parliament an exclusive jurisdiction which would otherwise be concurrent.'[4] The second approach has emphasised Stormont's financial dependence on Great Britain as a major restriction on Stormont's independence. Thus Rose (1971) has written: 'The institutional arrangements linking Stormont and Westminster were simple and slight because prior to 1969 there was little inclination on the part of London to intervene when the financial aspect was of minor importance.'[5] And it has been argued by Lawrence (1956) that 'It is difficult for a subordinate parliament and government to act independently except in fields that do not involve financial and economic considerations.'[6]

An assessment of Stormont's independence has to be based on a consideration of the whole range of controls available to Westminster and the extent to which they have been utilised formally or informally. It is therefore useful to examine in some detail some of the major methods of control: legislative, political, financial, economic, administrative, and judicial.

Legislative Controls

The Westminster parliament retained supreme legislative power; technically it was even free to legislate for Northern Ireland on transferred matters over the head of Stormont. In practice the parliament of the United Kingdom refrained from legislating on matters with which the parliament of Northern Ireland could deal, except at the request of or with the consent of the government of Northern Ireland. This principle became a well-established convention and led Jennings (1959) to declare that 'It would be un-constitutional for parliament to exercise its legal power of legislation in the matters delegated to the parliament of Northern Ireland, except with the consent of that parliament.'[7] And in fact the United Kingdom government never imposed its legislative will upon Northern Ireland against the opposition of the Stormont government. There is some evidence that the threat to legislate over Stormont's head was used occasionally to force Stormont to enact legislation.[8]

The British government kept a degree of supervision over the legislative process at Stormont, as it was the practice to hold consultations between the two governments, or, more precisely, between the Cabinet Office in Northern Ireland and the Home Office in London, on all legislative proposals going before both parliaments.[9] This scrutiny and consultation was primarily concerned with the constitutional propriety of the legislation, not its political desirability. This kind of formal communication was often necessary in respect of international treaties, agreements and conventions, since these may have involved matters which in Northern Ireland were the responsibility of its own parliament. For example, Stormont's powers were extended to allow it to amend its legislation on the adoption of children so that the United Kingdom could comply with the 1965 Hague Convention.

The British government had also a clear power of legislative veto, as all Stormont legislation had to receive the assent of the Governor of Northern Ireland. He was obliged to give or withhold assent according to instructions received from the Home Secretary. In 1922 the royal assent was refused to a local government bill altering the electoral system and abolishing the existing proportional representation system, a change which would benefit the Unionist Party. But after strong representation from Northern Ireland, including the threat by the government to resign, the assent was finally given. The British cabinet took the view that the vetoing of a measure clearly within the powers delegated to the Northern Ireland parliament would constitute a dangerous precedent. The Governor's veto was not used on any subsequent occasion to thwart Stormont's legislative proposals, and a possible crucial instrument of Westminster control thus lapsed into disuse.

It is clear that there was very little direct control over legislative powers which had been transferred to Stormont. Yet it might be argued that there was to a large extent an indirect form of legislative control in that the Northern Ireland government felt obliged to follow whatever legislation was introduced at Westminster.

There is nevertheless evidence to show that Stormont used its powers to introduce legislative proposals and policies which diverged considerably from legislation on similar matters in Great Britain. This tendency is clearly revealed in an analysis of legislation at Stormont during the period 1965–70 which was carried out for the benefit of the Kilbrandon Commission on the constitution. Three main categories of legislation were distinguished: (A) parity legislation; (C) legislation peculiar to Northern Ireland; and (B) legislation falling between categories A and C. In addition, there was a further category for technical legislation, for example the Appropriation Acts and Consolidated Fund Acts, which differ in content and in form from Westminster Supply Bills. The findings of the survey are given in Table 1.

Table 1: Degree of Similarity of Northern Ireland and United Kingdom Legislation

	1965	1966	1967	1968	1969	Up to 5 Feb. 1970	Total	%
(A) Parity legislation	6	13	5	3	9	–	36	19
(B) Legislation falling between categories A and C	8	11	15	14	12	2	62	33
(C) Legislation peculiar to Northern Ireland	8	17	16	14	15	6	76	40
Technical acts	3	3	4	3	3	–	16	8
Total	25	44	40	34	39	8	190	100

Differences in legislation covered a wide range of matters, including the highly controversial areas of political rights, personal freedom, trade union affairs, the legal system and, most significantly, the social services. Substantial differences in social policies have often been overlooked. The social services have been described as an area where the 'step-by-step' policy prevailed. Barritt and Carter (1962) have written that 'The social services are for the most part copied from those in Great Britain.'[10] Rose similarly stated that 'A policy of step-by-step legislation in welfare matters meant the Northern Ireland regime adopted British welfare programmes shortly after the Westminster parliament approved such measures for Great Britain.'[11] It is undeniably a declared policy that Northern Ireland should enjoy the same standard of social services as the rest of the United Kingdom; yet this principle of parity is a very general one and (apart from social security and the health service) has been subject to varying interpretations. Legislation and policies in

Northern Ireland concerning the major social services, education, housing and children's welfare were markedly different from those obtaining in the rest of the United Kingdom.

It may be concluded that Westminster exercised very little direct control over legislation which came under the heading of devolved matters and that Stormont had a great deal of freedom to choose whether to follow Westminster's legislation or not. Consequently wide divergences developed from British legislation on important social and political matters.

Political Controls

While overall responsibility for Northern Ireland rested with the British government, the latter rarely chose to intervene politically. The formal channels of political control were little used. These were the Home Office, parliament and the Governor. The official channel of communication between Stormont and Westminster was through the Cabinet Office at Stormont and the Home Office. The province was not directly one of the Home Secretary's major concerns; it was the responsibility of the General Department, which looked after anything which did not fit into any of the principal departments of the Home Office. The General Department was concerned with such matters as liquor licensing and British Summer Time, and one of its divisions dealt with the Channel Islands, the Isle of Man, the Charity Commission and Northern Ireland. This group of subjects was under the control of a staff of seven, of whom only one was a member of the administrative class.[12] In 1968 the Home Office had no civil servants devoting full-time attention to Northern Ireland affairs. In 1967 Mr Callaghan on his first day in office as Home Secretary was given a dispatch box full of documents on the major concerns of his department, but there was not a word about Northern Ireland.[13] The Home Office was occasionally forced to take decisions about Northern Ireland, for example when the Northern Ireland government requested an amendment to the 1920 act. In 1945 there occurred a rare example of a Home Secretary giving a direct political refusal to the Northern Ireland government concerning the possibility of an amendment to Section 5 of the 1920 act to make legal provisions compelling teachers paid with public funds to give Bible instruction. The Home Secretary pointed out that there would be great objection to an enabling act which could be represented as impairing safeguards in the 1920 act for the toleration and protection of minorities.[14] Normally, however, there was no Home Office interest in devolved matters, and Stormont's contact with the Home Office was mainly about minor matters such as constitutional points about legislation or visits of diplomats.

In the past there was very little discussion of Northern Ireland matters in the British House of Commons. This was partly because Ulster affairs were of little interest to members of parliament, but also because a convention was established that the House of Commons should not debate matters which were the responsibility of Stormont. Obviously it was not easy to determine on what matters there was no responsibility at Westminster, and it was left to the Speaker to decide what was permissible for discussion and debate. As regards parliamentary questions, unless there was clearly no ministerial responsibility, the practice was to allow the question and leave it to the minister to whom it was addressed to determine the basis of his responsibility in his answer.[15] The principle that ministerial responsibility for transferred matters rested solely at Stormont was a strongly established convention, and it was not broken until the debates following the disturbances of 1968–69.

The third possible channel of formal political control was through the office of Governor. The Governor performed his duties as the representative of the Crown. His functions included the summoning, proroguing and dissolution of parliament and the granting of the royal assent to legislation, and he was responsible for convening joint meetings of the House of Commons and the Senate if there was a dispute between them. The Governor's position was not, however, used to supervise or veto Stormont's activities. It appears that it was originally intended to use the Governor's power as a veto on legislation and matters of policy. But after the British government retracted on its decision to use the Governor's power to refuse assent to a local government bill in 1922 there was little further 'political' use of the Governor. By 1936 Mansergh felt justified in stating that 'A precedent of non-interference in internal affairs has been established by the Crown.'[16] The Governor played a minor role in constitutional relationships. In 1970 some Opposition MPs petitioned the Governor to withhold the royal assent to a Public Order Bill. This petition was rejected after the Governor had consulted the Home Office. Rose has argued that the narrow construction of the Governor's power was maintained by the appointment to the post of men who had no wish to exercise an independent influence upon Stormont.[17] It is clear that the British government has been responsible for choosing not to utilise this office as a method whereby it could exert influence over Stormont.

It appears that successive British governments saw no reason why they should try to exercise any political controls. They had no wish to become embroiled in Irish affairs, and at Westminster there was simply a lack of interest in the internal politics of Northern Ireland.

Northern Ireland Prime Ministers did have occasional meetings with the British Prime Minister or Home Secretary, but these were largely courtesy visits. Terence O'Neill (1972) gives an account of several of these meetings between 1963 and 1968, including a meeting with Harold Macmillan, the British Prime Minister, in 1963 shortly after Captain O'Neill became Prime Minister, when Macmillan was surprised that the Northern Ireland premier should want to talk about anything other than the weather.[18] Callaghan (1973) has noted that O'Neill on his part showed very little enthusiasm for visits to Northern Ireland by Home Secretaries.[19]

Successive Northern Ireland governments strove to avoid political conflict with Westminster governments. Periods of office by Labour governments provided some anxious moments for the Unionist regime. This was particularly true in the post-war period when a Labour government embarked on the implementation of the welfare state and increased intervention in the economy. The Unionist cabinet at Stormont faced criticism for its adoption of socialist measures passed at Westminster. This led to considerable discussion at cabinet and party level on the possibility of Northern Ireland recovering greater constitutional freedom through dominion status. The Northern Ireland Prime Minister's argument prevailed in the debate. He declared there was 'no practical alternative to co-operation with the government at Westminster' and added:

> I suggest we should not lay undue emphasis on the administrative convenience of following closely United Kingdom legislative measures. When we have decided to introduce bills on lines similar to those of imperial acts we should endeavour to avoid identity of phraseology and title and incorporate such modifications as may be possible.[20]

Northern Ireland did introduce welfare state legislation similar to Britain, and relationships with the Attlee government remained cordial.

In a situation where a parliament operates with a subordinate one it might be expected that there should be clear and formal channels of control and supervision. Yet none existed beyond the provision of Section 75 of the 1920 act, which preserved the supreme authority of the Westminster parliament but did not give the government at Westminster any direct means of authority over transferred matters. Rose comments that 'Westminster has the blockbuster power of abolishing the Stormont regime but few other formal powers.'[21] This rather anomalous position was accepted by British ministers when they were first faced with demands for political intervention in Northern Ireland's affairs in 1967. Mr Roy Jenkins, the Home Secretary, reminded the House of Commons:

We cannot simply put aside the constitution of Northern Ireland. Under the constitution certain powers and responsibilities are vested in the parliament and government of Northern Ireland. Successive governments have refused to take any steps which inevitably cut away not only the authority of the Northern Ireland government, but also the constitution of the province.[22]

The disturbances in August 1969 and the intervention of British troops brought about a fundamental change in the relationship between the British government and the government of Northern Ireland. It was obvious that the Westminster government would have to assume a close interest both in the policies and actions of the Northern Ireland government. Harold Wilson (1971) has stated that he saw the necessity for a political directive and declaration to govern relationships between the Westminster and Stormont governments.[23] This declaration, the Downing Street Declaration of 19 August 1969, stated that

> The Northern Ireland Government have reaffirmed their intention to take into the fullest account at all times the views of Her Majesty's Government in the United Kingdom, especially in relation to matters affecting the status of citizens of that part of the United Kingdom and their equal rights and protection under the law.[24]

Callaghan saw this as a momentous passage, with Northern Ireland acknowledging for the first time since 1922 that the British government's views on civil and other rights must be listened to.[25]

It was quite clear that the period following the disturbances of 1969 saw direct Westminster intervention and control. The constitutional powers of Stormont were still preserved in appearance, as the reform programme was presented in public statements as originating at Stormont and carrying the endorsement and approval of Westminster and all the legislative proposals went through Stormont as government legislation. Many of the most important reform proposals were not presented directly by Westminster to the Northern Ireland cabinet but came through intermediary bodies such as the joint working parties or advisory committees, for example the Hunt Committee on the police.[26] This was a technique which cloaked the reality of outright political direction from Westminster. Stormont had little choice but to accept the proposals of the British government and the recommendations of independent bodies which it had set up. The alternative was a direct clash with the British government, resulting in a full-scale constitutional crisis.

While Westminster chose to exercise power informally, it can be

argued that its political control and supervision became institutionalised or formalised in at least three ways: firstly, through the issuing
of joint declarations of policy; secondly, through the creation of
joint working parties of officials of both governments in which the
Westminster side had a dominant role; and thirdly, through the
appointment of a United Kingdom representative attached to the
Cabinet Office. The first incumbent of this post was Oliver Wright
from the Foreign Office. Callaghan has described his role as
follows: 'It was decided that he would sit in a room next to
Chichester-Clark's [the Prime Minister] at Stormont Castle and that
his job would be to explain British policy to Chichester-Clark and
warn him where he was likely to get into difficulties with us.'[27] In
practice his task was that of acting as watchdog over the progress
of the reform programme, reporting on events in Northern Ireland
directly to the cabinet at Westminster, and serving as a channel of
communication for various political groups in Northern Ireland in
making their representations to the Westminster government. Westminster control and interference existed on this *ad hoc* and largely
informal basis until the introduction of direct rule in March 1972.

Financial Controls

The financial arrangements laid down in the 1920 act were based
on the principle that Northern Ireland would be able to finance its
own services and make a substantial contribution towards the cost
of services still provided by the British government.[28] Under these
financial provisions Northern Ireland derived its revenue from two
sources. The first of these was transferred revenue, which was
controlled by the Northern Ireland government and included minor
taxes (motor vehicle duties, stamp duties, betting duties, entertain-
ments tax, certain excise duties, mineral rights duty, and (from
1966) selective employment tax) plus certain non-tax revenue from
land annuities, interest on advances, and some other minor items.
The second main source of revenue was the province's share of
reserved taxes, which were controlled by the United Kingdom
Treasury. These included the main taxes for which Great Britain
and Northern Ireland formed a single fiscal unit: income tax,
purchase tax, capital gains tax, customs and excise duties,
corporation tax, etc. Northern Ireland was then given its appropriate
share of this reserved revenue which was estimated to have been
raised from taxpayers in Northern Ireland. Before this was paid
over two amounts were deducted and retained by the United
Kingdom government: the costs of certain reserved services operated in Northern Ireland such as revenue collection and the
Supreme Court, and the 'imperial contribution'. This latter payment

was Northern Ireland's contribution towards the costs of defence expenditure, national debt charges and United Kingdom representation overseas. The remainder of the reserved revenue was given back to Northern Ireland for expenditure on transferred services (see Table 3). These amounts were determined by the United Kingdom Treasury and the Northern Ireland Ministry of Finance, and the financial arrangements were supervised by a statutory Joint Exchequer Board which consisted of one representative each from the Treasury and the Ministry of Finance and an independent chairman.

These arrangements were intended to confer on Northern Ireland a very large measure of financial independence. The method of financing was on a revenue basis whereby Northern Ireland was given certain predetermined sources of revenue and had to finance the devolved services out of the proceeds, as opposed to an expenditure basis in which expenditure requirements would be measured first and Northern Ireland given the income necessary to meet them. There was no question of its relying on negotiable grants from the central government, or of central control over its expenditure. The 1920 act also laid down that the imperial contribution and the cost of certain reserved services was a first charge on Northern Ireland's income and that the transferred services were to be wholly financed out of what was left. The standards of services were not specifically related to standards in Great Britain. It was felt that such disparities were justified by differences in prices, wages and conventional standards.

This financial system ran into difficulties soon after its inception. It was not long before expenditure began to outstrip revenue. The first major crisis came with a large deficit on the Unemployment Insurance Fund. Northern Ireland's unemployment rate of 24 per cent (compared with 11 per cent in Britain) resulted in a decrease in taxation revenue and an increase in expenditure on unemployment relief. This specific problem was solved by an Unemployment Insurance Agreement in 1926 providing that if in any year the payment by the Northern Ireland Exchequer to its Unemployment Fund exceeded, per head of population, the corresponding payment by the British government, then the British Exchequer would pay three-quarters of the excess.

Throughout the 1930s the province's financial difficulties increased, and the imperial contribution dwindled from £6.6 million in 1923–24 to a token sum of £24,000 in 1934–35. There were three alternatives for reducing the problem of financing the transferred services. The first alternative was to increase transferred taxes; however, this would not have raised much additional revenue.

Northern Ireland had also the power to impose new taxes, but the low tax-paying capacity of the population ruled this out. The second alternative was to cut public expenditure and allow the standard of services to fall further below British standards. This was unacceptable on political grounds, and it would also have raised complaints of Northern Ireland people paying the same rates of taxes as people in Britain but receiving lower benefit and much poorer services. Northern Ireland therefore had to abandon the position of financial autonomy and adopt the remaining alternative of seeking increasing financial support from the British Exchequer in order to maintain services at a similar standard to Britain.

In 1938 a memorandum embodying a new financial agreement was issued in the Westminster parliament by the Chancellor of the Exchequer, Sir John Simon, which stated that if a deficit occurred in the Northern Ireland budget which was not the result of a higher degree of expenditure or a lower degree of taxation, means would be found to make good this deficit and to ensure that Northern Ireland would have the same social standards and services as in Britain. In 1945 the planned post-war expansion of the social services was extended to Northern Ireland in the form of a British government commitment that there would be special Exchequer assistance to lift underdeveloped services to Britain's level. Following negotiations between the Stormont government and the post-war Labour government, the scheme was implemented through a series of agreements which laid down the basis for financing Northern Ireland's social services and which continued in similar form up to 1972. Northern Ireland expenditure was the subject of a general Treasury agreement in which the guiding principles were that there should be parity of services and taxation between Great Britain and Northern Ireland. The Northern Ireland budget, together with any proposed divergence from parity standards, would be agreed each year between the Treasury and the Ministry of Finance for submission to the Joint Exchequer Board. The Ministry of Finance had to consult with the Treasury in advance in respect of any new items of expenditure outside the principle of parity estimated to exceed £50,000 in amount.[29] Secondly, there was a National Insurance Agreement which ensured that the Northern Ireland National Insurance Fund was in parity with the British fund, parity being defined by reference to the proportion which the Northern Ireland insured population bears to the total insured population. For several reasons, including the higher incidence of unemployment and sickness, payments to Northern Ireland have been required each year. This agreement also covered industrial injuries and (from 1965) redundancy payments. The agreement was a reciprocal one, and in fact transfers have been made from Northern Ireland to Britain in the case of the Industrial Injuries and Redundancy Funds, although involving small amounts.[30] Thirdly, there was a Social Services Agreement which covered national assistance, family allowances, pensions and the health services. This provided that if the cost of these services was more than 2½ per cent of the total United Kingdom cost, then the British Exchequer would pay 80 per cent of the excess.

The principle of parity was a flexible one which altered in the course of time, and in 1955 the Joint Exchequer Board laid down a wider definition of its scope. This stressed four principles: firstly, that there should be parity of social services in Great Britain and Northern Ireland; secondly, that there should be a general parity of standards as between Northern Ireland and comparable areas of Great Britain; thirdly, that it was necessary to incur additional expenditure in Northern Ireland in order to make up the substantial leeway in various services such as housing, schools and hospitals; and fourthly, that there was a need for special expenditure in Northern Ireland to offset the economic disadvantage from which it suffered in comparison with Great Britain as a whole by reason of its geographical separation. At the same time the board reaffirmed the principle that the level of taxation in Northern Ireland should be similar to that obtaining in Britain.[31]

Northern Ireland's financial dependence on Britain continued to grow. The basic problem was that Northern Ireland had lower incomes and higher unemployment than the national averages, as well as a large child population; there was thus a lower tax revenue per head of population and a greater need for social services than in Britain. The flow of funds from the United Kingdom increased substantially from 1966 onwards. In 1966 the amount paid over to Northern Ireland as the residuary share of reserved taxes was increased by allocation of a population proportion of 2.7 per cent of the received customs and excise duties. In 1967 it was recognised that the cost of the selective and regional employment premium could not be borne by the Northern Ireland Exchequer, and the Treasury agreed to pay to Northern Ireland the whole cost. In 1971 the Westminster government cut the income tax rates; this, with other reductions, would have meant a substantial loss of revenue to Northern Ireland. New arrangements were therefore introduced to make it possible for Northern Ireland to receive extra funds for the social services. For family allowances and supplementary benefits an amount up to the whole cost of the services could be paid to Northern Ireland; this scheme was later extended to include Family Income Supplement, constant attendance allowances, and pensions for the over-eighties. There was also a new separate Health Services Agreement providing for increased payments on the basis of 90 per cent of the excess over a 2 per cent proportion instead of 80 per cent of the excess cost over a $2\frac{1}{2}$ per cent proportion.

Table 2: Financial Arrangements[32]

	1966–67	1967–68	1968–69	1969–70	1970–71	1971–72
	£m	£m	£m	£m	£m	£m
1. Social services (including health until 1971–72)	10	10	19	16	24	40
2. Health services	–	–	–	–	–	20
3. Regional employment premium	–	4	9	10	11	11
4. Remoteness grant (agriculture)	2	2	2	2	2	2
5. Agricultural subsidies paid by Ministry of Agriculture, Fisheries and Food	25	30	31	31	37	31
6. National insurance	15	17	13	15	14	22
	52	63	74	74	88	126

Table 3: Northern Ireland Revenue, 1971–72

	£m
Share of United Kingdom reserved taxes	269
Less Imperial contribution	1
Cost of reserved services	4
Residuary share of reserved taxes	264
Revenue from transferred taxes	45
Revenue from transferred non-tax sources	43
Total revenue under Government of Ireland Act	352
Extra payments from United Kingdom	74
Total	426

These tables illustrate that financial subsidisation from Britain increased rapidly from 1966 onwards and that the imperial contribution became a nominal sum. In 1944–45 the imperial contribution had reached a maximum of £36 million.

Northern Ireland has also received substantial agricultural payments from the United Kingdom, which since the 1930s has borne the cost of Northern Ireland's agricultural support and guarantee system. There have also been other specific Exchequer payments, for example to assist industrial development and shipbuilding.

Although it has usually been assumed that the extent of financial support from Westminster greatly restricted the independence of Stormont, certain aspects of the financial relationship suggest that Northern Ireland had a substantial degree of freedom.

The main responsibility for the financial arrangements did not rest with either parliament but with officials of the United Kingdom Treasury and the Northern Ireland Ministry of Finance. It has been argued that Westminster exercised no oversight over the Treasury's role in the negotiations for Northern Ireland's annual budget.[33] The effective powers of decision rested with senior civil servants. The Joint Exchequer Board was originally given the power to determine the final arrangements, but in practice it met only once a year and automatically accepted a joint memorandum agreed by the Ministry of Finance and the Treasury beforehand, although it had a residual role in deciding any dispute between these two bodies. It appears that there was very little if any governmental or parliamentary supervision of the discussions held between the two groups of officials and the decisions made by them. Payments to Northern Ireland under the 1920 act and the various supplementary agreements were covered by permanent statutory authority, and the annual approval of parliament was not required.

In practice Stormont had some control over revenue and taxation. In its handling of transferred taxation it was able to make several departures from British practice. For many years the scale of estate duty had special regard to the relatively large number of small private companies. Owing to the greater reliance on road transport in Northern Ireland, the rate of tax on commercial vehicles was lower than in Great Britain. When selective employment tax became a transferred tax there was some variation from Britain in the amount of refund in recognition of the high unemployment rate. Such differences in transferred taxes were designed not to raise additional revenue but to provide special treatment for certain groups. Major variations in transferred rate of taxation were discouraged by the principle of the parity of taxation.

Stormont's control over the raising of only about 11 per cent of its revenue contrasts significantly with its responsibility for administering about 90 per cent of public expenditure. Thus while Northern Ireland was financially dependent on the Treasury for revenue, it still had a considerable degree of freedom in determining expenditure. Such Treasury control over expenditure as did exist was based on the principle of parity, with the provision that excess expenditure might be necessary to bring services in Northern Ireland up to British standards. Policies with substantial spending implications had to have Treasury approval. An account of the relationship with the Treasury was given in the evidence to the Kilbrandon Commission on the constitution in 1971 by senior civil servants. The general position was described as follows by the Permanent Secretary at the Ministry of Finance in 1970:

> It is necessary to decide in relation to any Northern Ireland expenditure whether it is in parity or not, or whether there is a special case for accepting it as a charge against reserved revenue. If an item is clearly within parity, we normally do not approach the Treasury about it. Under this system every item of expenditure is liable to scrutiny by the Treasury, but in practice it becomes a matter of judgement when not to refer items for Treasury approval. If the Treasury refused to approve an item of expenditure, it would simply be saying in effect that expenditure could not be charged against reserved revenue, not that it would not be incurred at all.[34]

Further comment on the relationship indicates that there was very little detailed control over approved expenditure, or even of special payments, and that Ministry of Finance officials were given a fairly free rein.

The evidence seems to show that the Northern Ireland government had a much wider area of discretion over public expenditure than has often been imagined, while Treasury policy has frequently seemed distinctly *laissez-faire*. For example, during the period 1965–70 Northern Ireland spent roughly one and a half times as much on roads as was spent in Great Britain. There seemed no problem in gaining Treasury approval for this expenditure despite the fact that Northern Ireland had a good road system and the 'leeway' principle was hardly applicable. The motorway building programme seemed extravagant to many economists and was criticised in the 1970–75 Development Programme.[35]

Captain O'Neill recounts that when Minister of Finance he had no difficulty in persuading the Treasury to let Northern Ireland have its own Ulster Development Bonds.[36] The Treasury attitude appears to have been conditioned by the fact that Northern Ireland had its own parliament, whose demands, it was felt, should be facilitated whenever possible. The Kilbrandon Report, in discussing the Treasury's attitudes, also refers to the view that there was much to be said for the quiet adoption of administrative devices to allow

Northern Ireland to solve its problems in the way it thought best, and to the fact that proposals to meet Northern Ireland's particular difficulties commended sympathetic attention. Whatever Northern Ireland proposed, it would not cost very much by United Kingdom standards. Moreover, the guidelines on parity were open to interpretation, as was the 'leeway' that Northern Ireland had to make up on services.

Another significant aspect of Treasury approval is that while it was required for proposed expenditure on services which was higher than that in Great Britain, it was not necessary to seek it if the proposed expenditure was lower than in Great Britain. In such a situation not only was there no Treasury control over Stormont's proposal, but there was no political or parliamentary control from Westminster. There were no formal procedures for supervision of Stormont's policies, and only informal pressure could be applied to persuade Stormont to raise expenditure. In practice no such pressures were applied, and in areas such as the social services expenditure has been proportionately lower than in Great Britain until very recently.[37]

It is therefore possible to conclude that the Stormont parliament had a wide area of freedom in determining priorities and expenditure levels on nearly all the public services provided in Northern Ireland. And it is doubtful whether the Treasury's overall financial power was a significant restriction on Stormont's freedom to distribute its financial resources.

Economic Controls

The power of the Northern Ireland government to take decisions on economic policies was limited both by the constitutional arrangements and by its economic integration with Great Britain. Constitutionally Northern Ireland could not make use of the techniques which sovereign countries use to sustain economic independence. It was prohibited from establishing separate tariffs and legislation for external trade. It had no power to follow an independent monetary or fiscal policy, and it had few effective powers of taxation.[38] The major decisions affecting the economy were taken as part of the common policy for the United Kingdom as a whole. These determined the general level of economic activity, the standard of living, wage rates and private investments. At the same time the responsibility for the details of economic affairs rested with Stormont. In some cases Stormont chose not to exercise its powers because of practical difficulties that might arise, and United Kingdom legislation was thus applied, for example, to monopolies and restrictive trade practices. Nevertheless, Stormont was responsible for formulating and implementing policies on an important range of economic matters. These included industrial development, regional planning, promotion of employment, trade and commerce and public investment. There was practical co-operation between the two governments in the field of economic planning and industrial development. However, the policies of the two governments often differed. There were many instances of Northern Ireland following policies distinctly different from those of Great Britain in industrial and commercial affairs. Northern Ireland's range of incentives for new industry was different in form and wider in scope than those provided in Great Britain. Stormont had also the power to nationalise private industry. As long ago as 1935 it decided that road transport, both passenger and freight services, should be nationalised in order to ensure the proper co-ordination between road and rail; and the Ulster Transport Authority, which was established in that year, had a monopoly of all public transport until it was terminated in 1964. Northern Ireland was also responsible for industrial relations, and its legislation on trade unions and various issues affecting labour differed from British law.

Responsibility for general economic planning and development rested primarily at Stormont. The government commissioned a number of economic reports, including two five-year plans, and accepted their recommendations as the basis for its overall development policy embracing physical planning, industrial development and investment programmes. There was little indication of any direct involvement by the British government in the formulation of these policies, although the authors of the reports and the Stormont government constantly took wider national economic interests into consideration when devising policies. It is clear that within the limitations of the need for Treasury approval for special expenditure Stormont had complete responsibility for economic policy and the development programme. Treasury approval was forthcoming in the 1960s for a large-scale physical development programme, including a motorway scheme and a new city project, neither of which were very realistic either economically or politically. As Simpson (1971) has noted in discussing Stormont's economic powers, 'Northern Ireland has managed over the years to move the power from Whitehall by securing a commitment that Whitehall will find the finance for approved expenditure.'[39] Stormont had the responsibility for initiating its own policies for economic progress and development, and it was thus able to follow an independent and distinctive line without interference from Westminster.

Administrative Controls

With the existence of two separate administrations, it became necessary to develop channels of communication and co-operation. Formal communication on administrative matters between the two governments was the responsibility of the Cabinet Office at Stormont and the Home Office at Whitehall. It consisted primarily of correspondence concerning international agreements, visits by representatives of foreign governments, and appointments to United Kingdom advisory bodies. The business of liaison between the Cabinet Office and the Home Office was literally a daily affair,[40] although owing to the routine nature of the communications the Home Office did not need to have a full-time civil servant dealing solely with Northern Ireland affairs before 1969. However, since 1940 an assistant secretary from the Cabinet Office had been seconded for service in the Home Office and was available for consultation with officials there.

The nature and extent of links between Northern Ireland government departments and their Whitehall opposite numbers varied with subject and department. Social security legislation and levels of payment were the same in Northern Ireland as in Britain, and consequently there was close liaison between the departments concerned. Uniformity of standards in the public health service was also maintained, and this again necessitated regular and detailed consultation. The team of officials which determined the agricultural support prices in London and negotiated with the farmers' union representatives included civil servants from the Northern Ireland Ministry of Agriculture. There was also close liaison between the departments concerned with industrial development. On the other hand, a greater number of Northern Ireland departments, for example Education, had very few contacts with their counterparts in London.

It was sometimes thought desirable that any government activity which was a reserved function should be administered locally, and accordingly Section 63 of the Government of Ireland Act permitted Northern Ireland departments to act as agents of Whitehall departments. Agency arrangements were more convenient than having United Kingdom ministries create their own machinery in Northern Ireland. Thus the Northern Ireland Department of Agriculture acted as agent for the department in London in the administration of a range of grants. The Northern Ireland permanent secretary was responsible to his opposite number in London rather than to his own minister for schemes of this kind.

Agency relationships also operated to a lesser degree in the reverse direction. Services which were the responsibility of Northern Ireland government departments were administered by British government departments in Northern Ireland on an agency basis. These included the collection of certain licence duties by the Customs and Excise Department, the printing and production of maps and other services by the United Kingdom Ordnance Survey Department, the manufacture and distribution of certain licences by the Inland Revenue Department, and certain services performed by the Post Office for the Ministry of Finance.

There were regular consultations between the Treasury and the Ministry of Finance on questions of revenue and expenditure. The Northern Ireland budget was worked out in collaboration with the Treasury as described above, and the existence of the Joint Exchequer Board as an independent arbitrator ensured that the Ministry of Finance did not have to occupy a totally subordinate status. Any expenditure which was not obviously justifiable as parity was fully discussed. The Treasury itself recognised that parity was a complex concept and that its working out in practice depended on a multitude of individual decisions which involved elements of give and take on both sides.

Northern Ireland departments had to work within certain guidelines concerning parity of expenditure. Although every item of expenditure could be scrutinised by the Treasury, in practice only major items of expenditure were referred. And for major items such as subsidy in the agricultural field or substantial expenditure on roads, hospitals and schools, there was normally consultation with the Treasury and a detailed cross-examination of the project. If there was any doubt about whether an item was in parity, Treasury advice was sought. This frequently resulted in a day-to-day process of consultation.[41] In the event of a dispute, senior civil servants in the relevant Northern Ireland department, together with Ministry of Finance officials, would refer the matter to Treasury officials and perhaps officials from the corresponding department in Whitehall. Treasury control did exist as a constraint on Northern Ireland departments, but it was not as tight or as detailed a control as was exercised over departments in Whitehall; and the Ministry of Finance was thus able to perform many Treasury functions in relation to Northern Ireland departments. Some examples of Treasury refusals have been documented, such as the rejection in 1943 of a demand for specific finance and materials to be allocated for wartime housing in Northern Ireland.[42] But by and large the Treasury tended to look at Northern Ireland's proposals on broad lines, paying due regard to general policy considerations and total expenditure but without the detailed 'value for money' scrutiny that it applied to United Kingdom departments.[43]

The Northern Ireland administration was completely separate from the British central administration, and its departments were in no way subordinate to those in Whitehall. Although consultation was frequent, joint projects by civil servants were rare. In 1961 a joint working party was set up to report on factors causing persistent high unemployment, and in 1969 joint working parties were established to produce proposals for reform. Generally, however, the existence of a separate system of central administration and a separate Civil Service was an important factor in contributing to the independence and autonomy of the Stormont government.

Judicial Controls

The Northern Ireland parliament derived its powers from Westminster statutes, and it was possible for the United Kingdom courts to rule on the validity of laws enacted at Stormont and the actions of authorities on which it had conferred powers. There were, however, only a small number of cases where enactments passed by Stormont were challenged in the United Kingdom courts.[44] These cases have been of two types: those relating to situations where it was claimed that Stormont was exceeding its powers in regard to excepted and reserved matters, and those where it was alleged to have infringed one of the general restrictions imposed by the 1920 act. What is immediately evident is that most of these cases were devoid of direct political implications, since the points at issue were mainly technical and concerned with commercial activities. There was also a special provision made in Section 51 of the 1920 act for determining constitutional questions. This section had been incorporated within the act in order to provide a method of getting a speedy and definite decision on the validity of legislation. It established a procedure by which any Northern Ireland act or bill could be referred by either the Governor of Northern Ireland or the Home Secretary to the Judicial Committee of the Privy Council for a decision on its validity. There was only one such action, in 1937, when Belfast Corporation presented a petition to the Governor, who forwarded it to the Home Secretary, who then made the necessary referral. This particular case concerned the power of Stormont to require local authorities to levy a rate for educational expenditure. Controversy over the constitutionality of education bills in 1925 and in 1945 led to discussions in the British and Northern Ireland cabinets about the possibility of referring the bills to the Judicial Committee, but these attempts proved abortive.[45] The wording of Section 51 also appeared to empower the Judicial Committee to rule on whether executive acts of the Northern

Ireland government were within its lawful authority, but this doubtful right was never invoked.

There has been an insufficient number of cases for it to be claimed that a body of constitutional law and doctrines evolved determining the relationship between Westminster and Stormont. This is surprising, given the complexity of the division of powers and the imaginable difficulties in interpreting a constitution drawn up in the contemporary situation of 1920. There are a number of reasons for the lack of cases. Bills at Stormont were thoroughly scrutinised as regards their constitutionality at the draft stage and received a certificate of validity from the Northern Ireland Attorney-General. Also enablements extending the powers of the Stormont parliament settled questions which might otherwise have led to litigation. Donaldson (1959) has argued that this *ad hoc* extension of powers reduced to a minimum the area of potential constitutional dispute.[46] The same writer has also pointed out that a further explanation for the paucity of constitutional cases may be that since constitutional questions were comparatively novel, they simply may not have occurred to potential litigants as possible subjects for judicial decision.[47] This point may also be applicable in explaining the legal profession's reluctance in pursuing constitutional cases. Palley (1972) has also referred to 'an unawareness of the opportunities court machinery creates for manipulation of the political process, and the general tendency on the part of the political opposition to dismiss the courts as manifestations of the Unionist establishment and as therefore unlikely to deliver judgements adverse to the interests of that establishment'.[48] In cases which went before the courts it was usual for the court to attempt to uphold the validity of challenged legislation; and in interpreting Northern Ireland statutes they were therefore apt to rule that, provided the pith and substance of the disputed item was within the powers of Stormont, it would not be held *ultra vires* because incidentally or in some slight degree it went beyond the competence of the local parliament. An actual case illustrates how this doctrine was applied. A milk producer in Co. Donegal who crossed the border to sell his milk was convicted of trading without a licence under a prohibition in a Milk Act of 1934. The producer argued that this act was outside the powers of Stormont because it interfered with 'international' trade. The case eventually went to the House of Lords, where it was ruled that the nature and character of the act, the pith and substance, was to protect the health of the inhabitants of Northern Ireland. It had not been enacted primarily in respect of trade, although it might incidentally affect cross-border trade.

Westminster chose not to define strictly the limit on the powers

B

of Stormont and did not encourage the courts to adjudicate on constitutional relationships. Some of Northern Ireland's problems might in fact have been solved by greater use of the courts in interpreting the constitution, and it can be argued that some sections of the constitution could have been interpreted to prohibit actions of the government which allegedly discriminated on religious grounds. Judicial review did not really operate as a technique of control on the powers and actions of Stormont or determine Stormont's relations with Westminster.

Conclusion

The 1920 act gave the Northern Ireland parliament and government a very wide range of powers which could be used to pursue policies separate and different from the rest of the United Kingdom. Since 1921 a process of the preservation and growth of the powers of the regional legislature was made possible through lack of interference from Westminster. This was a consequence not only of a lack of interest and a desire not to interfere on the part of British politicians, but also of the absence of adequate channels through which the subordinate parliament could be subjected to governmental or parliamentary control from London.

The 1920 act also gave Northern Ireland a large measure of financial freedom, comparable to that which might be enjoyed by a province in a federal system. It was to be self-financing, with no question of grants from central government or central control over its expenditure. In practice these arrangements soon collapsed, and Northern Ireland decided to forgo its financial independence and entered into agreements with Westminster to accept financial subsidies to ensure parity of standards and services. This inevitably resulted in the United Kingdom Treasury controlling and supervising revenue and expenditure, although it still left Northern Ireland with a large area of discretion over public expenditure.

While remaining firmly within the United Kingdom, Northern Ireland thus developed with many of the characteristics of an independent state. Although it received continued and increasing financial and economic support from Westminster, it retained its own parliament, its own Civil Service and its own security forces, and it was able to pursue policies distinctly different from Britain in many politically controversial areas. Westminster supervision was slight, and while the ultimate supreme power of the United Kingdom parliament under Section 75 of the Government of Ireland Act, 1920, had to be acknowledged, it is arguable that in practice the status of the Stormont government was closer to the federal model than the devolution model—that is, that the two governments were almost co-ordinate in powers with each other, each with its own sphere of influence. (The usual relationship in a devolved system is that the regional government is subordinate to the central government.)

When the British government tried to intervene politically after 1968 it found it difficult to reduce Stormont's role to a subordinate one. Attempted dictation, informal pressures and persuasion, control of the army, the sending of a representative to oversee Stormont and the placing of senior Whitehall civil servants in key positions, all proved unsatisfactory means of ruling Northern Ireland from Westminster in co-operation with the government of Northern Ireland. The Westminster government was faced with the recurrent problem of securing political supervision through informal channels.

Cabinet Government at Stormont

THE Government of Ireland Act, 1920, laid down that Northern
Ireland government departments should be headed by ministers.
The act also stated that the persons who were ministers should
form an executive committee of the Privy Council of Northern
Ireland, to be called the Executive Committee of Northern Ireland,
to aid and advise the Governor of Northern Ireland in the exercise
of executive power in relation to Irish services in Northern Ireland.[1]
There was no specification of an office of Prime Minister. But the
expectation was that these outlines would be filled out with the
substance of British constitutional practice, thus enabling a system
of executive government similar to that of the United Kingdom.[2]
In practice the Executive Committee became the Northern Ireland
cabinet. Thus a system of executive government was established
with the same conventions governing the relationship between the
Governor (representing the Crown), the Prime Minister, the cabinet
and parliament as existed in Britain.

The Size of the Cabinet

The cabinet grew from seven members in 1921 to fifteen in 1971.
In 1921 the cabinet consisted of the Prime Minister and the Ministers of Finance, Home Affairs, Labour, Education, Agriculture
and Commerce (the last two departments sharing a minister until
1925). The Ministry of Health and Local Government was added
in 1944. Two ministries were created for short periods, both with
ministers of cabinet rank: the Ministry of Public Security from
1940 to 1944, and the Ministry of Community Relations from 1969
to 1972. Also after 1944 the Leader of the Senate had a cabinet
seat, and in 1966 a new cabinet post of Minister and Leader of the
House of Commons was created in response to the increasing workload of the House of Commons. The minister as well as taking
responsibility for the legislative programme and business of the
House, also kept a general oversight over the Whip's Office. Increasing work was also the reason for the creation of new cabinet-
rank posts of ministers of state in 1969. By 1971 there were four
such posts: at Development to assist with new planning pro-

grammes, at the Department of the Prime Minister to assist with community relations, at Home Affairs, and at Finance. These developments led to the substantial increase in the size of the cabinet. In 1971 it had fifteen members, which was not far short of the size of the British cabinet, which consisted of eighteen members in 1970.

Occasionally ministers have held responsibility for two departments, but this tended to be a temporary arrangement in response to an emergency.

As well as cabinet ministers, there were also junior ministers outside the cabinet. There were always parliamentary secretaries in two departments. The Parliamentary Secretary at the Department of the Prime Minister was the Prime Minister's representative in the Senate and assisted with government business there. The Ministry of Finance generally had two or three parliamentary secretaries who were also government whips. As this was not a very difficult or time-consuming task, they also helped with government business in the House of Commons. The total number of parliamentary secretaries was usually between five and seven, but there was little consistency in their actual allocation among the ministries. The official reason for the appointment of a parliamentary secretary related to the amount of work of the department concerned; for example, in 1963 a Parliamentary Secretary to the Minister of Health and Local Government was appointed because of the government's acceptance of the Matthew Report which created a wide range of new planning responsibilities. In spite of the *ad hoc* basis of most of these appointments, it was rare to find a parliamentary secretary ever returning to the backbenches. He tended to remain at his post until he was made a minister or became a parliamentary secretary in another department. Quite a number of parliamentary secretaryships lapsed on the promotion of their occupants to ministerial posts. It was also not uncommon for one person to hold two posts, either because the work was insufficient for two persons or in an attempt to keep the number of ministers down. Mr William Fitzsimmons was Parliamentary Secretary to both the Ministry of Commerce and Ministry of Home Affairs in 1963–64, and Parliamentary Secretary to Commerce and Health and Local Government in 1964–65.

There was one further government post, that of Attorney-General. He was always a member of the House of Commons, but (unlike his counterpart in the Republic of Ireland) did not have a seat in the cabinet. Most Northern Ireland Attorney-Generals went on to occupy senior posts in the judiciary, and a number of ministers with aspirations in this direction, including several Ministers of

Home Affairs, gave up their cabinet posts to become Attorney-General.

The total number of government posts varied between fifteen and eighteen. This presented a problem of balance between the size of the government and the number of government backbenchers.

Table 4: Number of Government Posts held by Members of the House of Commons

	Cabinet ministers	Parliamentary secretaries	Attorney-General	Government posts	Speaker & Chairman of Ways & Means	Government backbenchers	Opposition members
1930	7	7	1	(15)	2	20	15
1940	8	8	1	(17)	2	20	13
1950	9	4	1	(14)	2	21	15
1960	9	5	1	(15)	2	20	15
1966	11	4	1	(16)	2	18	16
1971	15	4	1	(20)	2	16	15

Table 4 shows clearly the state of imbalance resulting from the fact that so many members of parliament, out of a total of fifty-two, were either members of the cabinet or parliamentary secretaries or held other paid positions. Between a third and a quarter of the total membership held posts in the government, and nearly half the Unionist MPs held government offices or paid parliamentary posts. In 1971 there were more Unionists in the government than on the backbenches. The high proportion of MPs in the government helped to strengthen the power of the executive against a small legislature. It meant that the number of government backbenchers was relatively small and thus reduced the amount of criticism that would emanate from that source. It also ensured that revolts by government backbenchers could have little impact unless they had the support of some government ministers. There was a relatively small pool of backbenchers from which to select future ministers, and it might be thought unreasonable to expect one-third to one-half of the government MPs to possess ministerial abilities or potential.

The Appointment of Cabinet Ministers

The appointment of ministers was a matter for the Prime Minister.

Generally the office of parliamentary secretary provided a training ground for potential cabinet ministers. Excluding the members of the first cabinet (none of whom had any previous experience of government office apart from the Prime Minister, Sir James Craig, and the Minister of Education, Lord Londonderry), of forty-one Northern Ireland cabinet ministers only fourteen came straight into the cabinet with no experience of junior office. Out of a total of fifty parliamentary secretaries, twenty-seven went on to become cabinet ministers. Most MPs spent quite a long spell on the back-benches before promotion to ministerial level, the average period of time being about six years. Very few backbenchers gained quick promotion; only two ministers took up office within one year of their election to parliament, while others had spent sixteen or seventeen years on the backbenches before being promoted.

Senators were eligible to become ministers, but little use was made of them for ministerial appointments apart from two posts connected with Senate, the Leader of the Senate and the Parliamentary Secretary to the Prime Minister's Department. The first four Ministers of Education were senators, but this tradition was dropped later. It may seem surprising that so few senators were cabinet ministers, especially as they were permitted to attend the House of Commons, answer questions, take part in debates and introduce legislation; and greater use of senators would also have helped reduce the imbalance between the government and back-benchers. The lack of ministerial appointments is to be explained by the age structure of the Senate, the calibre of senators and the Senate's low status. This last feature of the Senate is illustrated by the fact that five senators resigned specifically in order to take seats in the Commons and become ministers.

It was also possible for ministers to hold office for a maximum period of six months without being a member of either House. This procedure was not used until 1971, when it was brought into operation to enable the appointment of two non-Unionists to the cabinet: Mr David Bleakley, a former Labour MP, who became Minister of Community Relations in March, and Dr Gerard B. Newe, a Roman Catholic, who was appointed minister of state in the Prime Minister's Department in October. Until the two 1971 appointments the only other non-Unionist to serve as a minister was Mr Harold Midgley, a former member of the Northern Ireland Labour Party who in 1942 formed a Commonwealth Labour Party to emphasise the constitutional link with Great Britain. In 1944 Sir Basil Brooke, in forming his new administration, appointed Mr Midgley as Minister of Public Security as a small gesture to the notion of coalition government in wartime.[3] Mr Midgley joined the

Unionist Party in 1949. Apart from these three exceptions, the Unionist Party, with its substantial parliamentary majority, has dominated all cabinet positions.

It is usual to look upon cabinet posts as forming a hierarchical structure of senior posts and less important posts, thus enabling a process of promotion within the cabinet to be identified. In the Northern Ireland cabinet the office of Minister of Finance was second in seniority to the Prime Minister, its occupant usually holding the position of Deputy Prime Minister. Two Prime Ministers had been Minister of Finance before their appointment as premier. Home Affairs ranked third in importance, although the careers of occupants of this office were somewhat different from those of other ministers. Relatively few ministers moved sideways within the cabinet to Home Affairs: out of the twelve Ministers of Home Affairs, six had no previous ministerial experience and four others had experience only as parliamentary secretaries. Nine out of the twelve ministers had a legal background. Three Ministers of Home Affairs resigned to become Attorney-General, and two others resigned to take up senior judicial positions. Thus the Ministry of Home Affairs (like the post of Attorney-General) was for some of its occupants a stepping-stone on a professional legal career rather than a political career.

There is little to indicate that the other ministries can be ranked, although it is noticeable that the occupants of the Ministry of Commerce have usually played a fairly prominent role in the workings of the cabinet. The remaining ministries appear to have held equal lower ranking, with the exception of the Ministry of Labour, which was the most junior post in the cabinet. Only one of its nine occupants moved from another ministry (the wartime Ministry of Public Security), three were promoted from parliamentary secretaryships, and five from the backbenches. It can be concluded that appointment to Finance or Home Affairs indicated promotion; otherwise it is not easy to generalise. Only Captain O'Neill progressed through what has been regarded as the top three positions, from Minister of Home Affairs to Minister of Finance to Prime Minister.

It is perhaps even more difficult to find any pattern of demotions. Ministers tended to retire, move out of politics or take up judicial appointments rather than move downwards to a less important ministerial post. Mr J. L. O. Andrews moved from Ministry of Finance to become Leader of the Senate in 1964—a case of being pushed upwards to accommodate cabinet changes by the new Prime Minister. In 1966 Mr Brian McConnell was moved from Home Affairs to the minor post of minister of state at Development after permitting the Rev. Ian Paisley to hold a demonstration at a meeting of the General Assembly of the Presbyterian Church and then attending the Assembly to apologise.

Government reshuffles were much less common and more restricted than at Westminster. Cabinet changes tended to be a reaction to individual resignations by ministers. There were few reshuffles for reasons of ministerial inefficiency, or to give ministers experience of other departments, or as part of political manoeuvring. The small number of people in the cabinet and the parliamentary party made sackings difficult.

Even incoming Prime Ministers did not drastically alter the existing cabinet—with one notable exception. This followed Sir Basil Brooke's accession to the premiership in 1943 after the resignation of Mr J. M. Andrews, which had resulted from a great deal of criticism of the performance of the cabinet and also of its age. Apart from the new Prime Minister, only one member of the old cabinet was included in the new government. Lord Glentoran was offered the post of Minister of Agriculture which he had held in Andrews's administration but turned it down. Three out of five new ministers had been parliamentary secretaries in the old administration.

When other Prime Ministers took office there were no radical changes. When Andrews became Prime Minister in 1940 he asked the existing ministers to continue in their offices; and Captain O'Neill, on taking up office in 1963, brought in Mr William Craig as Minister of Home Affairs, probably in response to Mr Craig's support as Chief Whip during soundings within the party on the successor to Lord Brookeborough. Other changes were geared to a new policy emphasis on economic and regional development; hence Mr Brian Faulkner's appointment to Commerce in 1963 and Mr Craig's appointment to the new Ministry of Development in 1964. When Major Chichester-Clark became Prime Minister in 1969 his main aim in selecting his cabinet was to try to heal party divisions and at the same time maintain some continuity and stability. Prominent supporters of Captain O'Neill in the cabinet remained in office, while Mr Faulkner, who had resigned from the cabinet four months earlier and had been a contender for the premiership, came back into the cabinet as Minister of Development. When Faulkner himself became Prime Minister in 1971 the question of balance and party unity was again a dominating factor in the selection of the cabinet. Two former supporters of Captain O'Neill, Mr Phelim O'Neill and Dr Robert Simpson, were dropped from the cabinet, but Mr Robin Bailie from the liberal wing of the party became Minister of Commerce, and cabinet posts were offered to Mr

B*

Bleakley of the Labour Party and later to Dr Newe as a step towards creating a broader based government.[4] At the same time Mr Harry West from the right wing of the party came back into the cabinet as Minister of Agriculture. Thus a broad spectrum of opinion was represented in the cabinet of 1971–72.

Ministers tended not to move frequently between offices, only one minister ever holding as many as four cabinet positions. Mr Brian Maginess held the posts of Minister of Labour, Commerce, Home Affairs and Finance between 1946 and 1956 and was also Attorney-General from 1956 to 1964. Out of a total of forty-nine cabinet ministers, ten held three different posts, thirteen two posts, and the remainder only one post. Ministers were rarely in danger of having their ministerial careers ended or interrupted by defeat at an election. During the period 1921–72 the average length of time that ministers spent in a department was about three and a half years, higher than the United Kingdom average of two years. This overall average figure is somewhat misleading, as it is possible to identify three distinct sub-periods between which there were considerable variations in the length of ministerial service. Firstly, from 1921 to 1943 the average length of time was eight years, and many cabinet ministers retained their posts for much longer periods. In 1943 Sir Richard Dawson Bates had been Minister of Home Affairs for twenty-two years, Mr J. M. Andrews had been twenty-two years in the cabinet, and Mr James Milne Barbour eighteen years. Secondly, between 1943 and 1968 the average period was about four years, although the Minister of Agriculture, the Rev. Robert Moore, held the post for seventeen years from 1943 to 1960. Thirdly, in the period of political turmoil within the Unionist Party from 1968 to 1972 there were some thirty changes in the cabinet and the average length of time in a department was reduced to less than a year. Given the small number of persons of ministerial ability available, the average length of a ministerial career (about eight years) does not seem unduly long.

Resignations and Dismissals

Resignations from the cabinet took place for a number of reasons and are classified in Table 5 along with the number of ministers dropped when an incoming Prime Minister was forming a new administration. (Sometimes, of course, there have been discrepancies between the publicly stated reasons for resignations and what have been later found to be the true reasons.)

There are only four clear examples of ministers having been dismissed from the cabinet. Lord Brookeborough dismissed two

Table 5: Reasons Stated for Leaving the Cabinet

Dismissed by Prime Minister	4
Resigned for political reasons	6
Dropped by incoming Prime Minister	6
On taking up judicial appointment	6
Ill-health	2
Other reasons (retirement, etc.)	10
Died in office	7

Note: These figures do not include the resignation of the entire cabinet on 23 March 1972.

Ministers of Education amid considerable controversy over education legislation. In May 1943 Professor William Corkey, a Presbyterian clergyman, was appointed Minister of Education, a controversial action in itself as there had been a prolonged dispute between the government and the churches on provisions for teaching religious instruction in schools. An act in 1930 had satisfied the demands of the Protestant churches by compelling teachers to give Bible instruction. In 1944, when the Minister of Education was preparing a new Education Bill, there was a proposal to remove this compulsion. The minister made it clear that he would oppose any attempt to repeal the settlement of 1930, and in February 1944 the Prime Minister asked for his resignation.[5] However, the reason given by the Prime Minister for Corkey's dismissal was that he had not devoted sufficient time to his post, in particular neglecting his duty of visiting his department's headquarters in Portrush.[6] Corkey claimed that this was only an excuse for dispensing with his services.

Professor Corkey's successor, Lieutenant-Colonel Samuel Hall-Thompson, suffered much the same fate in 1949. He was involved in considerable controversy and criticism over the Education Bill, 1947, which increased grants to Catholic voluntary schools. Then in 1949 he introduced a bill to allow the government to pay the employers' proportion of teachers' national insurance contribution in voluntary schools, which produced a strong backbench opposition on the grounds that it extended the principle of grants to voluntary schools. Following meetings of the cabinet and the Unionist Party and consultation with the Grand Orange Lodge, it was announced that the minister had resigned and that as a compromise the bill would be introduced for a short period pending a final arrangement.[7] Hall-Thompson was dismissed in order to restore party unity and appease opponents of the bill even though his measure was a government bill supported by the Prime Minister and most of the cabinet. This is the only example of a cabinet dismissal forced by backbenchers and extra-parliamentary forces.

The other two instances of dismissal occurred during Captain O'Neill's premiership. In April 1967 Mr Harry West, the Minister of Agriculture, was sacked as a result of his involvement in certain land transactions in Co. Fermanagh; it was alleged that in his purchase and sale of land Mr West had infringed a code of ministerial conduct introduced by Captain O'Neill. Mr West argued that he was really being dismissed on political grounds. He stated: 'I deeply regret that the Prime Minister in his apparent desire to dispense of my services as a member of his administration should come to the Dispatch Box with charges which were not justified.'[8] Mr West was one of several cabinet ministers who had disagreed with some of the Prime Minister's actions, but Captain O'Neill has asserted that his sole aim was to see that his code of conduct was not defied.[9] In December 1968 Captain O'Neill also dismissed the Minister of Home Affairs, Mr William Craig, for his public statements criticising the Prime Minister's policies. Mr Craig had made a number of speeches attacking the programme of reforms and the intervention by the British government, and he was dismissed after criticising a televised speech by Captain O'Neill to rally support for his reforms.

Resignations for political reasons were rare. In April 1965 Mr Ivan Neill, the Minister of Finance, resigned in protest against Captain O'Neill's decision to relieve him of his post as Leader of the House of Commons. Many Unionist backbenchers were apparently dissatisfied with the way Mr Neill fulfilled his functions as Leader of the House.[10] In more recent times resignations not only indicated deep divisions in the cabinet, but were also employed as a tactic to oust the Prime Minister. After a long period of disagreement Mr Brian Faulkner resigned in January 1969 in protest against the lack of strong government by Captain O'Neill's administration, followed closely by Mr William Morgan, the Minister of Health and Social Services. Both resignations undermined the Prime Minister's position. The resignation of Major Chichester-Clark on 23 April 1969 constituted the final blow to O'Neill's leadership.

The Background of Cabinet Ministers

The infrequency of cabinet changes up until the late 1960s was reflected in the age structure of cabinet ministers. The average age on appointment was forty-eight, and about one-fifth were over sixty. Only four ministers, Mr Faulkner, Mr Craig, Mr John Taylor

Table 6: Age of Cabinet Ministers[11]

	N. Ireland 1921–72	Rep. of Ireland 1922–65
Under 39	4	25
40–49	23	21
50–59	13	16
Over 60	11	2

and Mr Robin Bailie, were under forty when first appointed. This forms a marked contrast with the practice in the Republic of Ireland, where the tendency has been to appoint ministers at a much younger age (see Table 6).

The level of educational attainment of ministers has changed over the years, but a much lower proportion than in Britain have had a university education. Only twenty-one out of fifty-one cabinet ministers had a university degree. Four members of the Northern Ireland cabinet in 1970 had university degrees, whereas in Britain in 1970 sixteen out of the eighteen members of the Conservative government had degrees, and eighteen out of twenty-one in the Labour government which succeeded them had degrees.

Table 7: Socio-Economic Status of Ministers[12]

	N. Ireland 1921–72		Rep. of Ireland 1922–65	British Conservative cabinet 1970
	Number	%	%	%
Employers, managers, company directors	17	33	20	22
Barristers, solicitors	13	25	32	33
Other professional	6	12	26	17
Farmers, landowners	11	22	8	17
Skilled manual	2	4	5	–
Other	2	4	9	11
		100	100	100

Cabinet ministers were drawn from three main occupational groups: businessmen, large farmers, and barristers and solicitors. There has been a higher proportion of businessmen and farmers in the Northern Ireland cabinet than in the Republic of Ireland cabinet. These occupations were also more strongly represented than in the 1970 Conservative cabinet in Britain. It is also noticeable that professional groups were not very strongly represented except for the legal profession. Given the lack of members of parliament with professional qualifications, those with such qualifications had good prospects for a ministerial career.

The occupation of ministers was significant, as cabinet posts were treated for a long time as part-time appointments and ministers were thus able to continue with their ordinary jobs. Many ministers were in business and commerce and held directorships which raised the questions of possible conflicts of interest. The British convention of ministers giving up directorships on taking office was not followed. It was left to a minister's own discretion to decide whether any directorship was likely to involve a conflict with his public duties. It was argued that it was important to attract members of the business community into government and also that cabinet ministers had sufficient time to carry out their cabinet duties and look after their business interests. Indeed, it was also argued that there was not sufficient work in any department for a full-time cabinet minister. As one backbencher put it, 'Can anyone really suggest that an establishment of eight full-time ministers is required to run a country of this size?'[13] However, by the 1960s the amount of ministerial work had increased. Shortly after Captain O'Neill came to power he drew up a code of conduct for ministers. It laid down the basic principle that no minister should place himself in such a position that his private interest might conflict with his public duty. The code emphasised that the application of the principles in any case was the final responsibility of the Prime Minister. This code did not prohibit ministers from holding directorships, but a list of these was published in Hansard at the beginning of each session; about half the cabinet appeared in this list. Captain O'Neill's code also included the principle that a minister should avoid any outside interest which made such demands upon his time and energy that it became difficult for him to discharge the responsibilities of his public office. After 1963 cabinet office became much more like a full-time occupation.

The Appointment of the Prime Minister

The office of Prime Minister was not mentioned in the Government of Ireland Act, 1920, but it was established as an integral part of the system of cabinet government, and the British convention was accepted that the leader of the party with the majority in the Northern Ireland House of Commons would be asked by the Governor to form a government and would therefore become Prime Minister. The first Prime Minister, Sir James Craig, was directly invited by the standing committee of the Unionist Party to submit himself for appointment to the post[14] and he was unanimously elected leader of the Unionist Party in succession to Sir Edward Carson in February 1921. After the first general election to the Northern Ireland parliament he was invited to form a government in May 1921.

The Unionist Parliamentary Party, like the British Conservative Party, had no formal procedure for the election of a new leader in the event of the resignation or death of the current leader. As in the Conservative Party, the name of the new leader was expected to emerge from intra-party discussions. This procedure presented some difficulties for the Governor, for it was not always clear whom he should send for to form a new administration. He was expected to consult the outgoing leader and the party whips for advice. It is known that Lord Craigavon (formerly Sir James Craig) had hoped that Sir Basil Brooke would succeed him,[15] but Mr J. M. Andrews, the Minister of Finance, emerged as the popular choice of the cabinet and probably also of the parliamentary party.[16] When Andrews resigned in 1943 he advised the Governor to invite Sir Basil Brooke, who had been the leader of the group critical of him, to form a new administration.

The most confused succession followed the resignation of Lord Brookeborough (formerly Sir Basil Brooke) in 1963. The complications arose partly from the death in 1962 of Mr William May, the Minister of Education, who had emerged as a favourite to succeed Brookeborough, and partly from the apparent refusal of Brookeborough to express any clear views on who his successor should be. There were three main candidates, Captain O'Neill, Mr Faulkner and Mr Andrews, the son of the previous Prime Minister. The final decision rested with the Governor; and when he told Brookeborough that he intended to send for Captain O'Neill, the retiring Prime Minister again refused an opinion.[17] O'Neill's candidature was supported by Mr Craig, the Chief Whip, who was responsible for taking soundings inside the party and informing the Governor.[18] The situation was further complicated by the fact that backbenchers claimed to have been given a guarantee by Brookeborough that his successor would be selected at a full meeting of the Unionist Party.[19] As a consequence of this confusion, procedures were drawn up for the election of future leaders by the parliamentary party. There was to be an election between candidates and a simple majority was to determine the result. In May 1969, following the resignation of Captain O'Neill, Major Chichester-Clark was elected leader by a majority of one (18 to 17) over Mr Faulkner. There was another election in March 1971 after Chichester-Clark's resignation, when Faulkner defeated Craig by 26 votes to 4. The Governor on each occasion automatically invited the new elected leader to form a government.

The Prime Minister, the Cabinet and the Unionist Parliamentary Party

The relationships between the Prime Minister, the cabinet and the Unionist Parliamentary Party were fairly close. The small size of the parliamentary party meant that any dissension in the cabinet was likely to be reflected in the parliamentary party, and vice versa.

There is evidence that all Northern Ireland's Prime Ministers, apart from Lord Craigavon, who died in office, were subject to pressure which forced them to resign. Craigavon was the only Prime Minister who really dominated his cabinet and party. He had a reputation for acting on his own initiative and paying more attention to the Orange Order and the extra-parliamentary Unionist Party than to the parliamentary party.[20]

Andrews's resignation is the clearest example of a Prime Minister being forced out of office. There was a growing dissatisfaction among the party with the performance of Andrews's administration in controlling unemployment and in wartime production, and at the age and lack of vigour of his government. The defeats of two Unionists in Stormont by-elections in Belfast and the victory of a Labour candidate in a Westminster by-election in West Belfast in February 1943 showed that the discontent was spreading to the public, particularly over the government's handling of industrial disputes. Eventually Sir Basil Brooke and three junior ministers offered their resignations. They demanded that Andrews should either convince the dissident members of the parliamentary party they were wrong, or failing to do this, that he should resign.[21] Andrews did gain the support of the Ulster Unionist Council, but subsequently five junior members of the government and one cabinet minister made it clear they would withdraw support unless he yielded to demands for changes. Two other cabinet members offered to resign if it would solve the crisis.[22] Following meetings of the cabinet and the parliamentary party, Andrews saw that he had lost the support of the latter body and resigned.

Sir Basil Brooke (later Lord Brookeborough) was an astute manager of his cabinet. When disputes in the cabinet arose he frequently instructed the ministers concerned to get together to work out a solution, for example when a dispute arose in 1947 between the Ministers of Home Affairs, Health and Local Government and Finance over which department should be responsible for delinquent children.[23] The most serious division in the cabinet occurred between 1944 and 1947 over proposed increases in grants to voluntary schools. The proposal by the Minister of Education, Colonel Hall-Thompson, to increase grants met with opposition from some cabinet ministers and backbenchers. At a decisive cabinet meeting on 11 November 1946 the Prime Minister, while acknowledging the strength of the agitation against increased grants, supported the Minister of Education; and the cabinet agreed that if the government was defeated on this point in the House, it would resign.[24] Several ministers reserved their positions. Mr Grant, the Minister of Health and Local Government, who, with Mr Maginess, the Minister of Labour, had been most vocal in opposition to the proposal in the cabinet, declared that he would stand by his colleague if a crisis arose, but felt that if he had to fight an election, he must be free to state his opposition to the proposal. The Rev. Robert Moore, the Minister of Agriculture, thought that the government should resign if it did not have the majority of the party with it, while Sir Roland Nugent, the Minister of Commerce, said that if the government went out of office, he must reserve his right to criticise any new administration. The Prime Minister and his Minister of Education managed to get this contentious proposal through a divided cabinet, but in 1949, when faced with similar criticism of educational policy, Brookeborough retreated and dismissed his minister to preserve party unity.

The influence of party pressures in forcing the resignation of four of Northern Ireland's Prime Ministers is least marked in the case of Lord Brookeborough. In 1963 he was becoming increasingly incapacitated by ill-health, and there was a feeling among Unionist Party members that he should be replaced by a younger and more energetic man. A note asking for his resignation was accordingly drawn up and signed by ten backbenchers. It was withdrawn when it was learned that the Prime Minister was about to enter hospital, but apparently he was aware of its existence and it may have influenced his decision to resign.[25]

The most open examples of conflict between a Prime Minister, cabinet ministers and members of parliamentary party occurred during Captain O'Neill's premiership. O'Neill's method of succession caused resentment among some members of the cabinet and the parliamentary party. His style of leadership in taking controversial decisions without consulting his cabinet was also a source of discontent. This was particularly true of his decision to invite the Prime Minister of the Irish Republic, Mr Seán Lemass, to Stormont in 1965. O'Neill informed the Minister of Finance the day before the visit, and the rest of his cabinet on the day of the visit itself.[26] Although the cabinet's immediate reaction was to give its collective assent to the visit of Mr Lemass, some ministers were later to publicly express reservations. One Unionist MP claimed that a stunned cabinet was forced to accept the position or resign.[27] Following the North–South visits, Captain O'Neill received a vote of confidence from the parliamentary party but had to give an assurance that no decisions relating to Ulster's constitutional position would be taken without prior consultation with the cabinet. O'Neill's view was that 'There are occasions when a Prime Minister must take a step forward on his authority. That is the nature of leadership.'[28]

Captain O'Neill's policies and his style of leadership provoked strong opposition, and there appear to have been several attempts to remove him from office. In 1966, when Captain O'Neill was in England, news of a rebellion leaked out. A list of signatures asking for O'Neill's resignation had been gathered among the parliamentary party. Captain O'Neill returned to face his cabinet, and after Major Chichester-Clark, the Chief Whip, issued a statement supporting O'Neill the rebellion crumbled. Captain O'Neill later alleged that Mr Faulkner and Mr West, both ministers at the time, were involved in the rebellion.[29] Mr Faulkner has revealed that although the list of dissidents amounted to only one less than half of the total membership of the parliamentary party, Captain O'Neill refused to resign and contest the leadership when asked to do so.[30] The dismissal of Mr West in 1967 apparently led to further crisis when Mr Ivan Neill, the minister who had resigned in 1965, was asked if he would make his services available in the event of an outright challenge to Captain O'Neill's premiership.[31] Eventually the opposition within the cabinet became more pronounced. The dismissal of Mr Craig in December 1968 and the resignation of Mr Faulkner and Mr Morgan in January 1969 showed the extent of the deep divisions. The exchange of letters between Captain O'Neill and Mr Faulkner after the latter's resignation were particularly bitter, with O'Neill accusing Faulkner of not giving him the loyalty and support that should be expected of the Deputy Prime Minister,[32] a charge denied by Mr Faulkner. Captain O'Neill remained in office sustained by several votes of confidence from the parliamentary party. In January 1969 a group of twelve dissident Unionist MPs signed a document asking for a change of leadership. The crucial vote for O'Neill in the parliamentary party came in April 1969 on the issue of 'one man one vote' in local government elections. O'Neill and the government won the vote by 28 to 22, but this included the votes of senators. Within the parliamentary party the majority was only three. The Prime Minister was now clearly in a very weak position. As long as he had been backed up by strong support within the parliamentary party, he had felt able to deal with the dissidents in the cabinet. But he had now lost the support of almost half the party on a fundamental plank of his policy, and he duly resigned.

It was not long before O'Neill's successor, Major James Chichester-Clark, had also to face criticism from sections of the parliamentary party. In March 1970 five MPs, Messrs West, Craig, Boal, McQuade and Laird, refused to support a motion of confidence in the government, but the Prime Minister felt strong enough to expel them from the parliamentary party and to announce that he would not resign for as long as he had the support of the parliamentary party.[33] Eventually, when he felt unable to satisfy the demands of the party on security, he did resign in March 1971.

Another important influence on the cabinet relationships in recent years has been the extra-parliamentary Unionist Party (particularly its central committee), the Ulster Unionist Council, and its standing committee and executive committee. This has not always been the case. The support of party organisations had not saved Andrews in 1943. While facing a rebellion in the parliamentary party he had been re-elected Unionist Party leader, and the Ulster Unionist Council had expressed its confidence in him. But his parliamentary opponents were able to ignore this support. Lord Brookeborough later wrote that 'To my mind the MPs were the only people that mattered in this dispute, and... votes of confidence from other bodies, no matter how Unionist, would not convince MPs that they were wrong.'[34] However, in more recent times party bodies have been used as platforms to undermine the position of Prime Ministers. The opposition to Captain O'Neill repeatedly used the central party organisations in attempts to bring him down. In March 1969, after the general election, the Unionist Party's standing committee met and confirmed O'Neill's leadership by 183 votes to 116, and a short time later a vote of confidence was passed at a meeting of the Ulster Unionist Council by only seventy-five votes (338 to 263), which undoubtedly weakened O'Neill's position. In 1970 a vote of no confidence in the law-and-order policies of Major Chichester-Clark was passed at a poorly attended meeting of the Unionist Party's executive committee. In January 1971 a demand for the Prime Minister's resignation, signed by 170 mem-

bers of the Ulster Unionist Council, was handed in at party headquarters. Votes at Unionist Party level were also to be crucial in
undermining Mr Faulkner's position in 1974 as head of the Executive.

These extra-parliamentary organisations of the Unionist Party had
an influence on cabinet and parliamentary relationships which is
largely unknown among the corresponding institutions of British
political parties, where the central party machinery has a solely
organisational function. Long years in office led Unionist leaders
to neglect maintaining control over the party machinery. During
the period 1968–74 it was relatively easy for dissidents in the party
to call meetings to harass and embarrass the leadership and the
government with votes of no confidence.

The Work of the Cabinet

The work of the cabinet was to determine the major items of government policy, draw up the legislative programme, and generally
co-ordinate the work of the government. The cabinet generally met
once a week and tended to work as a whole, i.e. without a system
of cabinet committees, although committees existed from time to
time on an *ad hoc* basis. The largest number of committees operating at one time appears to have been four in the period of post-war
reconstruction, when there were cabinet committees on post-war
policy, building, transport and publicity; each of these committees
consisted of four ministers,[35] and the Prime Minister was a member
of all but one of them. In the early 1950s there was a cabinet committee on employment,[36] and a cabinet security committee was in
operation during 1966. This latter committee was reactivated in
1969, when its membership comprised the Prime Minister and the
Ministers of Home Affairs, Agriculture and Development.[37]

A cabinet secretariat serviced the cabinet and any committees. It
also acted as a liaison body between the cabinet and government
departments by receiving and circulating memoranda on matters
which ministers wished to bring before the cabinet, by following
up cabinet decisions to see that they were carried out by departments, and, on occasions, by playing an active role in resolving
interdepartmental disputes.[38] The Cabinet Office was part of the
Prime Minister's Department, and the principal officials of the
cabinet secretariat were appointed by the Prime Minister and had
an important role as his personal advisers. During Captain O'Neill's
premiership some important decisions at the initial stage involved
his personal advisers rather than the members of the cabinet.
O'Neill's team of Sir Cecil Bateman, the Cabinet Secretary, his

deputy, Mr Ken Bloomfield, and his private secretary, Mr Jim Malley, were involved in the discussions preceding the visit of Mr Lemass from which the cabinet were excluded.[39] It was also members of this group who carried out the negotiations leading to the recognition of the Northern Ireland Committee of the Irish Congress of Trade Unions. This close-knit group of Civil Service advisers has been described as a 'hidden cabinet' and as 'the presidential advisers'.[40]

Mr Faulkner did not involve the whole cabinet closely in the decision to introduce internment in August 1971. A member of the cabinet has written that Faulkner was reluctant to discuss details in any meaningful way with his cabinet colleagues and that only rarely was the whole cabinet given an opportunity to have a full-scale discussion on the subject.[41] From what is known about cabinet government in Northern Ireland, there is little evidence of an 'inner cabinet' of senior ministers. There is evidence that some ministers did emerge as important figures in the political sense because of their standing with the party or the public. Thus in 1968 the Prime Minister, Captain O'Neill, was accompanied by Mr Craig, Minister of Home Affairs, and Mr Faulkner, Minister of Commerce—both aspirants to the leadership—to meetings with Mr Harold Wilson in Downing Street. While these were the senior political personalities in the cabinet, they did not form an inner cabinet for policy-making purposes. On the contrary, O'Neill has disclosed that his confidants within the cabinet were other ministers who supported his policies.

Apart from performing their parliamentary duties, taking legislation through parliament, replying to parliamentary questions and taking part in debates, the main work of cabinet ministers concerned the running of their departments and preparing memoranda on policy and legislation for the cabinet. The type of work varied somewhat between ministries. Health and Social Services required a mainly administrative approach where most legislation simply followed Westminster examples. Other departments required more executive decisions and the promotion of new policies; for example, the Minister of Commerce had the task of attracting new industry, and the Minister of Development was concerned with promoting growth centres, including a large new urban complex, and encouraging mobility. Decisions were more politically controversial in ministries such as Home Affairs and Education. Otherwise the work of ministers lay primarily in the field of public relations, attending functions, opening buildings, etc. It is also worth noting that cabinet ministers travelled abroad and were received by foreign governments as having the status of government ministers of a sovereign state. Prime Ministers travelled widely and were received by heads of state, foreign ministers or other representatives, for example in Germany, France, the United States and Canada.

The Principles of Cabinet Government

Northern Ireland's system of cabinet government was modelled on the Westminster example and was therefore based essentially on the key principles of ministerial responsibility and collective responsibility.

Ministerial responsibility meant that ministers were responsible for the actions of their departments and accountable to parliament. This accountability was enforced mainly through the minister's obligation to answer questions. Since 1921 it has been the general practice in Northern Ireland legislation to confer powers, duties and functions upon the impersonal ministry rather than upon the minister. In 1953 the Attorney-General ruled that, regardless of whether the power was conferred upon the minister or the ministry, the minister was responsible in parliament for the actions of the ministry.[42]

In Britain the doctrine of ministerial responsibility also required that a minister should be personally answerable for mistakes made by his department and, if a serious issue is involved, that he should resign. This doctrine is not really operative any longer in Britain, owing to the growth of government activity and the larger size of departments. There have been no cases of ministers resigning in Northern Ireland in this kind of situation. One of the few times the issue came up was over the 'Seenozip' case, when a company which had been set up with large amounts of public finance went bankrupt soon afterwards. The Minister of Commerce had been acquainted with the matter and stated that he was in close touch with the problem when the ministry was taking various decisions.[43]

The other key doctrine of the cabinet government in Britain is collective responsibility, which means, in essence, that all ministers have to support cabinet decisions. The implications are that if a minister disagrees with the government's policy to the point of wishing to criticise it in public, then he must resign. It was intended to apply this principle to the Northern Ireland cabinet, but Captain O'Neill in particular had difficulty in enforcing it. The clearest example arose as a result a series of speeches made by Mr Craig, the Minister of Home Affairs, in which the minister criticised the programme of reforms approved by the cabinet in 1968. Mr Craig did not resign and was eventually dismissed. There were other statements by ministers which were critical of government policy, for example on issues like North–South co-operation, the reform programme and the dismissal of Mr West; yet in spite of the principle of collective responsibility, there was no question of resignations. Captain O'Neill was later to write to Mr Faulkner after his resignation stating: 'If on these earlier occasions to which you refer you took issue with me on some vital points of principle, you should surely have resigned.'[44] Mr Faulkner's view that 'We are there to implement the policies of the Unionist Party, and so long as Captain O'Neill sticks to these policies so long will I support him'[45] obviously implied difficulties for the practical exercise of collective responsibility. On occasions ministers were publicly reprimanded for expressing public criticism of government policy, as in 1971 when Mr Taylor was called to order by Major Chichester-Clark. Generally the doctrine of collective responsibility was somewhat loosely interpreted at Stormont.

Conclusion

Northern Ireland had a system of cabinet government operating largely on the British model, but a number of features characterised the system and distinguished it from the Westminster system. Firstly, ministers had a light workload. Up until the mid-1960s ministerial office was very much a part-time occupation, but from that period onwards the Stormont government did appear to generate sufficient work to make it a full-time job. A second distinguishing feature was the strong influence of the extra-parliamentary party organisations on the questions of leadership and policy within the cabinet. A third feature was the imbalance in the size of the cabinet *vis-à-vis* the number of the government backbenchers. Fourthly, there were grounds for doubts about the calibre of at least some of Northern Ireland's ministers. There was a relatively small pool of ministerial talent. Fifthly, the doctrine of collective responsibility was loosely interpreted. Finally, the Northern Ireland cabinet as a devolved institution was not faced with taking major decisions, particularly with regard to finance. The area of executive decision-making where the cabinet had to work out policies for itself was naturally much smaller than in a cabinet in a sovereign state. James Callaghan, in assessing his series of meetings with the Northern Ireland cabinet, wrote: 'I found it difficult to take seriously the idea that the Northern Ireland cabinet and Prime Minister had any resemblance to what we in Britain understood by these offices.'[46]

3

The Stormont Parliament

THROUGHOUT the fifty-one years of its existence the Northern Ireland parliament adopted the procedures and precedents of the Westminster parliament.[1] The House of Commons with fifty-two members became operative as a miniature Westminster House of Commons. In the original proposals of the Government of Ireland Act, 1920, there was no provision for a second chamber, but a Senate was created by means of an amendment initiated in the House of Lords in order to provide a counterbalance to the power of the House of Commons. The operation of parliament can be assessed under three headings: its legislative role, its financial functions, and its role of scrutinising and criticising the actions of the government.

The Legislative Role

The legislative process mirrored Westminster practice very closely. All legislation had three readings in the House of Commons and three in the Senate. The first reading was the formal introduction of the bill. The second reading was the occasion for a debate on the bill's general principles. The bill then went through a committee stage where it could be examined in detail and amended. Following this, the bill was reported back to the House at the report stage, after which there was a final third reading. This process was then repeated in the Senate; and if there were Senate amendments, the bill was returned to the Commons so that MPs could debate them. After approval by both Houses the bill went to the Governor of Northern Ireland to receive the royal assent.

The committee stage was the only part of the process where procedure differed from Westminster. There was no system of standing committees such as have existed at Westminster since 1945 to examine legislation in detail and discuss amendments. There were insufficient numbers of MPs at Stormont to establish a parallel system. Instead the committee stage of all Stormont bills was taken in a committee of the whole House, at which all MPs were eligible to attend. Consequently all legislation was examined in detail and amendments discussed and voted upon in the House of Commons, where an atmosphere of political tension was more readily engendered. The atmosphere in committee rooms would have been more informal and probably more conducive to compromise and mutual concession between government and Opposition. Discussion would have attracted less public attention, co-operation between politicians might have been easier, and there would have been more convenient access to specialist background information from civil servants.

Table 8 shows that it was fairly unusual in the committee stage for the Opposition or government backbenchers to have amendments accepted by the minister in charge of the bill.

Table 8: Amendments by Opposition and
Government Backbenchers[2]

	Proposed by Opposition				Proposed by government backbenchers			
	Proposed	Withdrawn	Rejected	Accepted	Proposed	Withdrawn	Rejected	Accepted
1950–51	–	–	–	–	28	12	6	10
1956	1	1	–	–	2	–	–	2
1961–62	97*	12	83	2	32	6	19	7
1966	29	3	20	6	52	13	21	18
1968	56	4	47	5	11	–	4	7

* About two-thirds of this number concerned an Electoral Reform Bill.

The Opposition appeared to be largely inactive in proposing amendments until the 1960s, and even then it had little success in making any significant alterations to legislation. This can be illustrated by reference to the examples enumerated for 1966 and 1968 in Table 8. In 1966 out of the six amendments accepted one concerned a private member's bill and the other five concerned one minor issue in relation to a Dogs Bill. In 1968 three concerned the formula for calculating compensation for criminal injuries, one a change in procedure in showing evidence to accused persons, and one the composition of the Youth Employment Board.

Government backbenchers had more amendments accepted, but the majority of these were fairly minor alterations. Occasionally

Unionist backbenchers were able to convince a minister of the value of a more substantial amendment; for example, in 1966 amendments were successfully moved for revising the definition of a dwelling-house for rating purposes and for reducing government control over eel-fishing in response to backbench fears of a move towards nationalisation.

Between one-third and one-half of the bills went through parliament with no amendments, and these bills often went through the committee stage, report stage and third reading at the same time and with no comment whatsoever. The report stage was automatic and largely superfluous, as it involved the same MPs accepting what they had just decided in committee. This repetitiveness was also found between the second reading and committee stages, since there was a tendency for members to deal with committee points during the second-reading debate, which was supposed to be devoted to discussion of the principles underlying the bill.[3] Only very controversial legislation led to amendments being proposed at the later stages, e.g. during the third readings of the Criminal Justice Bill, 1966, and the Education Bill, 1968.

While no committees existed to deal with ordinary legislation, there were a number of legislative select committees concerned with specialist bills. The Joint Committee on Consolidated Bills examined all bills consolidating existing acts of parliament and revising statute law. This committee was composed of members of the House of Commons and the Senate. Its reports clearly show the advantages of committees studying bills in detail, as they reveal a thorough investigation of issues, detailed questioning of civil servants on background information, and a harmonious method of discussion with few votes on amendments. References in some of the reports to the difficulties experienced in obtaining a quorum of members, resulting in delays in completing consideration of bills and the misuse of members' and civil servants' time, provide a further illustration of the difficulties encountered in operating Westminster procedure at Stormont.[4]

Local bills at Stormont were the equivalent of private bills at Westminster and were promoted mainly by local authorities or other public bodies seeking to acquire extra powers or by private bodies wishing to acquire land or property. They were presented to parliament in the form of petitions after having been scrutinised by the Examiner of Petitions for Private Bills to see that standing orders had been complied with. If they had not been complied with, the bill then went to a Local Bills Standing Orders Joint Committee. This was a rare occurrence; indeed, the committee met for the first time in twenty-seven years in 1967 to examine the Down County Council (Strangford Lough Ferry) Bill. Local bills went through the same procedure as public bills, but at the committee stage they were dealt with by a special Joint Committee on Unofficial Bills, a small committee of four, which would consider the bill in detail. This committee operated in a very thorough manner, and it was its custom to take extensive evidence from government departments. The report on the Londonderry Corporation Bill, 1969, was 114 pages long, and the report on the Allied Irish Banks Bill, 1971, 124 pages. On the rare occasion that a local bill was opposed by a counter-petition an *ad hoc* joint committee was established to take the committee stage and hear evidence for and against. In 1969 such a joint select committee was appointed to examine the Magee University College, Londonderry, Bill, which proposed the integration of the college into the New University of Ulster, after a petition opposing the bill was presented by the Presbyterian Church. This dispute was finally resolved without the select committee having to adjudicate.[5] This complex committee system again followed Westminster practice, but local bills

Table 9: Type of Legislation

	Government bills		Local bills		Private members' bills	
	Introduced	Passed	Introduced	Passed	Introduced	Passed
1926	31	30	2 (1)*	1	–	–
1930	29	26	5 (2)	3	–	–
1935–36	36	33	7 (6)	7	2 opp.†	–
1940–41	26	25	2	1	1 opp.	–
1946–47	31	30	2	–	1 opp.	–
1951–52	28	26	3	3	1 opp.	–
1955–56	31	30	–	–	–	–
1960	21	19	–	–	2 backb.	–
1965–66	43	39	2	2	3 opp.	–
					1 backb.	1
					1 joint	1
1968	39	31	1	–	5 opp.	–
					1 joint	1
1970–71	50	50	2	–	3 opp.	–
					1 joint	1

* ( ) refers to Divorce Bills
† Code: opp. = opposition; backb. = government backbenchers; joint = jointly sponsored

took up a very small proportion of the parliamentary timetable, as is shown in Table 9.

The Westminster practice of allowing backbenchers to introduce legislative proposals as private members' bills was also followed. The number of private members' bills introduced each session has been small, and although it increased from the mid-1960s, the greatest number introduced in any session was eight in 1966–67. The number of successful bills has never been more than one or two a year. The majority of private members' bills were introduced by the Opposition and were defeated by the government majority, not unexpectedly perhaps, as most dealt with such controversial political issues as electoral reform, trade unions, human rights, reform of rent law, and an ombudsman. In the 1960s several Opposition bills were introduced repeatedly and were always defeated at the second reading. A Human Rights Bill was introduced each year between 1965 and 1968. A Public Defenders Bill to establish an ombudsman was introduced five times between 1961 and 1968 by Nationalist members. An MP sponsoring a bill required at least tacit government support to have his bill enacted, and this was not forthcoming for legislative proposals suggested by Opposition members. Even uncontroversial proposals were rejected, for example a bill to establish a Department of Physical Culture and Recreation in 1966 and a bill to remove the disqualification of teachers from being elected to local government in 1968. There was hardly any incentive for Opposition members to produce bills other than as a means of making a political gesture.

A few successful private members' bills were introduced by government backbenchers with government approval. Most concerned relatively unimportant matters and often appeared to be a response to requests from particular groups, for example the Driving of Invalid Carriages Bill, 1965, to reduce the age limits for driving invalid carriages, the Roads (Liability of Road Authorities for Neglect) Bill, 1966, to require local authorities to complete and repair roads, and the Consumers' Protection Bill, 1965. There were also a few examples of successful bills sponsored jointly by a government backbencher and a member of the Opposition. Among these was the Matrimonial Law (Reports) Bill, 1966, which prohibited publication of parts of the proceedings in divorce cases in the press. The Business Tenancies Amendment Bill, 1968, was prepared by Mr Roderick O'Connor, a Nationalist, and Mr John Dobson, a Unionist, and was introduced in the Commons by Mr O'Connor and in the Senate by the leader of the Nationalist Opposition there, Mr Gerard Lennon.

In a regional parliament where there was little pressure on time it might have been expected that backbenchers would have had more scope for devising legislative proposals and obtaining support for them or that the Opposition would be encouraged to initiate legislative ideas in this manner. The rigidity of political divisions and the dominance of certain issues were the main reasons preventing this. There is no example of a private member's bill sponsored solely by the Opposition being accepted. The Wild Birds Act, 1931, a measure for the protection of wild birds, has been cited as the only example;[6] but although the bill was introduced in the Senate and the Commons by a Nationalist member, it was also sponsored by Unionist backbenchers. At Westminster private members' bills have been used as a method of introducing legislation of a controversial nature involving moral or religious issues and allowing a free vote, for example on abortion and divorce. But as most moral and religious issues have strong party-political connotations in Northern Ireland, private members' bills have rarely been used this way. In 1970 a jointly sponsored bill to abolish live hare coursing was passed in the House of Commons on a free vote, with voting crossing the party lines. It was also the custom to allow free voting when debating capital punishment.

Financial Functions

The financial functions of the Northern Ireland parliament were similarly modelled on Westminster practice. The House of Commons had the traditional functions of granting supplies, authorising expenditure and checking on spending. The financial procedures at Westminster have come to be recognised as increasingly obsolescent, but they were copied closely at Stormont. The House of Commons formed itself into the Committee of Supply to consider the Estimates and each minister explained the annual Estimates of his own department. Following the traditional Westminster principle of 'redress of grievances before granting supply', discussion on the revised Estimates could extend over a wide range of issues. One important divergence from Westminster practice was the absence of an Estimates Committee to probe the details of expenditure proposals. Westminster procedures were also followed, though with no great justification, with regard to the budget and the annual Finance Bill. The Northern Ireland budget was presented after the Westminster budget and always followed Westminster policy on the major items of taxation. The Minister of Finance had the power to control only the transferred taxes, and even here the general principle of parity of taxation with Britain usually applied. As general fiscal and monetary policy was determined at Westminster, the Minister of Finance tended to confine his budget speech to a statement on the general economic situation, the level of government spending and borrowing, and the negotiations with the Joint Exchequer Board. The debate on the budget generally did not last a full day and sometimes did not even attract a quorum (ten members present). A Finance Bill incorporating the budget proposals followed and usually failed to generate any debate or amendments—again in sharp contrast to the experience at Westminster, where the Finance Bill is usually highly contentious and may take up to fifteen days of discussion.

The House of Commons exercised control over expenditure through the accounting process. Again following Westminster practice, this task was performed by a Comptroller and Auditor-General and a Commons Select Committee on Public Accounts. The Public Accounts Committee consisted of seven MPs. It is traditional at Westminster for a member of the Opposition to serve as its chairman, but this practice was not followed at Stormont.

The Public Accounts Committee was the most powerful parliamentary committee at Stormont. Its task was to report to the House of Commons on any items in the accounts which appeared to involve waste or extravagance or raised issues of principle in financial procedures. It worked on the basis of the report of Comptroller and Auditor-General, who had the job of certifying the accounts and reporting upon them. The Comptroller and Auditor-General attended the meetings of the Public Accounts Committee, and the committee could question the relevant accounting officers for each department.

The Public Accounts Committee did find several instances of waste or inefficiency.[7] Its reports present details of building projects abandoned after substantial expenditure and professional services; various schemes which substantially exceeded the estimated cost; improper payments under Agricultural Grants Schemes; and incorrect use of funds from the Industrial Enterprise Fund in 1970. The committee tended to note past errors or misjudgements (in its view) and made recommendations for future changes in procedures; for example, it advised that government departments should adopt new methods for the placing of contracts for building and civil engineering work. In 1966 the committee made a detailed study of the awarding of a motorway contract to a tender which was not the lowest. Opposition MPs had alleged political favouritism in this case. The committee made no findings regarding this particular matter, but it was critical of the way negotiations between government departments and the county council involved were conducted and the failure to apply the correct procedural rules.

On other occasions the committee made recommendations to

ensure better value for money or small savings; for example, the report for 1968–69 argued that there could be price advantages in bulk central purchasing rather than the local purchasing of hospital supplies. Detailed proposals of this type were made in every area of public expenditure: the committee's recommendations ranged from calling a halt to what it considered to be unnecessary new government office accommodation to suggesting new ways for collecting unpaid parking meter fines and increasing the receipts from advertisements in government publications.

It was not possible for the Public Accounts Committee to begin its work until about a year after the close of a financial year, and it therefore had to consider numerous payments which had been made from one to two years before and for which commitments may have been entered into much earlier. Thus the committee itself maintained that one of its primary functions was to frame its conclusions in such a way as to ensure that the lessons of the past were applied in the future, and that it was accordingly doing more than shutting the stable door after the horse had gone.[8] Nevertheless, it appeared on the scene long after the vital decisions had been taken, and it had few sanctions to enforce its recommendations. The parliamentary debates on its reports tended to be fairly brief, and the reports themselves only occasionally attracted press coverage. One of the most important consequences of the reports was the publication by the Ministry of Finance of a memorandum commenting on the recommendations and criticisms and detailing what action would be taken or, alternatively, giving reasons for the ministry's disagreement with the committee's findings. To some extent, then, the Public Accounts Committee ensured economy and efficiency in the use of public money and also acted as a check on the bureaucracy.

A major defect in the financial process was the lack of detailed scrutiny of the Estimates. It is desirable to make economies when the money is being asked for rather than discover wastage or inefficiency in the accounting process. The Public Accounts Committee itself recommended an Estimates Committee,[9] but the government's view was that the thirteen days devoted to the parliamentary discussion of supplies provided ample opportunity to debate all expenditure in detail. There was also the difficulty of manning another committee. The arrangements at Stormont for parliamentary scrutiny of expenditure did not change between 1921 and 1972, despite the increase in the amount of government expenditure from £8 million in 1922 to £200 million in 1966 and £440 million in 1970–71. Westminster procedures have been found to be unsatisfactory in Great Britain, and in 1969 the Estimates Committee was replaced by an Expenditure Committee responsible for examining

projected expenditure for five-year periods. But the financial procedures adopted by the Northern Ireland parliament were preserved
unreformed and were clearly increasingly inappropriate to the needs
of a regional parliament with a relatively small budget, few direct
powers of taxation and particular regional economic problems.

The Role of Scrutiny and Criticism

Given the fact that the government was firmly in control of both
the legislative and financial processes (apart from the proviso
that many important financial decisions were taken by Westminster),
the task of scrutinising and criticising the actions of the government
offered the best opportunity for parliament to play an effective role.
There were three main methods by which this role was carried out:
by parliamentary questions, by debates, and by the use of select
committees to inquire into certain matters.

Parliamentary Questions

Question time at Stormont was one of the more useful devices
adopted from Westminster practice. The small number of MPs
meant that there was adequate time for dealing with questions. Up
until the 1950s the average number of questions per day was
between five and eight; during the 1960s it increased to between
eight and ten; and in the 1970–71 session it reached fourteen.
Ministers were on call each day to answer questions about matters
concerning their departments. Questions were usually answered by
ministers rather than by junior ministers, and nearly all of them
were put down for oral answers. There was little pressure on MPs
to be content with written answers, as at Westminster.

With adequate time available and with oral questions predominat-
ing, it was easy and customary to put supplementary questions. On
occasions a fairly lengthy discussion ensued, with a number of MPs
joining in. The parliamentary question was a simple and effective
device for obtaining information from government ministers, bringing matters to a minister's attention, or eliciting an immediate
response from the government. It was also a method for raising
constituents' individual grievances. Parliamentary questions relating
to allegations of discrimination in housing and employment by local
authorities and complaints about social security benefits were
numerous. The police, courts and the administration of justice also
constituted a popular subject area.

Once a question had been submitted, it was guaranteed some kind
of investigation and reply. Thus parliamentary questions helped to
act as a check on the bureaucracy, and the potential threat of a
question probably meant that departments paid close attention to

MPs' letters concerning constituents' grievances. The constituency interests of MPs were reflected in the relatively high proportion of questions on such topics as hospital facilities, agricultural subsidies, fishing, industrial development, improvement of roads, and tourism. Others concerned more detailed local issues which might have been thought out of place in a national parliament but which might be considered particularly suitable for useful discussion in a regional parliament. There were frequent questions on recreational facilities, local playgroups, roads, traffic accidents, efficiency of bus services, local drainage, and water supplies. However, it would be incorrect to say that most questions fell into the category of trivial or local matters; the majority did concern the policy and administration of a regional government.

Table 10 shows that Opposition members made most use of question time. Opposition members accounted for some 75 per cent of questions, except in the 1950s when the proportion fell to about 65 per cent. The contribution of government backbenchers varied a great deal. Some members pursued a particular interest with a large number of questions, for example in the 1960s Mr Phelim O'Neill on agriculture and Dr S. Nixon on health. Others did not put down any questions during a session; for example, in 1965–66 eleven out of twenty government backbenchers did not ask any questions.

Parliamentary question time was one of the more successful parliamentary institutions at Stormont and, as such, was indicative

Table 10: Parliamentary Questions

	Total questions	Written questions	Put by Opposition	Put by govern-ment backbenchers
1926	218	–	186	32
1935	324	10	223	101
1946–47	500	23	373	127
1951–52	241	24	147	94
1955–56	247	10	160	87
1960–61	558	10	381	177
1965–66	699	35	512	187
1967	889	64	616	273
1968	663	73	489	174
1970–71	1,832	286	1,342	489

c

of the value of regional government. It ensured a degree of parliamentary control over the administration and activity of government ministers. Furthermore, it proved to be an extremely useful device for airing constituents' grievances.

Debates

Debating procedure also followed Westminster practice, but there were greater opportunities at Stormont for backbenchers to both initiate and participate in debates. Debates on adjournment motions tended to concern matters of immediate interest on which a member wished to hold a short debate. They were also commonly used to express a member's dissatisfaction with the answer given to his parliamentary question. Adjournment motions covered a very wide range of matters from school crossings to entry into the EEC. It was also open to MPs to put down a private member's motion, and generally time would be allocated for such a debate. Throughout the 1960s there was a very substantial increase in the number of private members' motions. They were useful for getting publicity for an issue and for testing reactions among other MPs and the government.

Motions were also used as a technique to allow debates on matters which were reserved to Westminster. The Northern Ireland parliament could not discuss reserved matters directly, even though decisions on them affected the internal affairs of Northern Ireland. However, a ruling was eventually made by the Speaker that it was in order to put down motions asking the government of Northern Ireland to make representations to the United Kingdom government on matters arising out of legislative or government action at Westminster, e.g. on entry into the EEC. Motions of censure, in accordance with Westminster tradition, were used sparingly. The most popular subject of censure motions was the government's mishandling of the economic situation. There is little evidence that debates on motions resulted in any direct action by the government, but they did help to draw the attention of the public and the media to various problems.

Select Committees

Parliamentary questions and debates have limitations as an effective means for detailed examination of government activity. The use of select committees of backbenchers has become accepted at Westminster as an effective method for detailed scrutiny and investigation of areas of government performance. In many other countries the main work of parliament is done by committees specialising in different subjects. The Northern Ireland parliament, following Westminster practice, established a number of sessional select committees to look after the operation of parliament; the Committee of Privileges, for example, had the task of investigating allegations of breach of privilege and other procedural matters. There were two important scrutiny committees, the Public Accounts Committee and the Committee on Statutory Rules, Orders and Regulations. The latter was a joint committee of ten whose function was to examine statutory instruments (i.e. rules and orders granting delegated powers to government departments) to determine whether the special attention of parliament should be drawn to any item on the grounds that it imposed a charge, contained provisions excluding it from challenge in the courts, made an unusual use of powers, had retrospective effect, or required elucidation. The work of this committee steadily increased. The number of instruments assessed by it was 30 in 1946, 115 in 1955, 165 in 1965, 289 in 1969, and 360 in 1970–71. In the 1970–71 session it made no fewer than thirty-five separate reports. The work of this select committee was important owing to the increase in delegated legislation and the fact that such a committee was the only means of parliamentary control. The committee seems to have done its work thoroughly, and, contrary to the practice at Westminster, civil servants attended its sittings to answer questions.

Few specialist select committees were appointed to inquire into specific issues. Before 1943 a number of committees were set up to report on social and economic issues, and their reports did undoubtedly influence subsequent policy. These included select committees on the Rents Act in 1931, on road transport in 1938, on unemployment in 1940, and on the health services in 1943. After 1943 the tendency was for select committees to examine non-controversial issues where some detailed study was required, for example the committees on shop legislation in 1953, business tenancies in 1960, and a few dealing with parliamentary matters, salaries, and the disqualification of MPs. Somewhat ironically, one of the last committees to be appointed was an all-party committee on world poverty in 1967. The reasons for the relative lack of committees appear to have been the small numbers available for this kind of work, a reluctance by the government to appoint committees which might develop independent lines of thought and recommend policies unacceptable to the government, and also perhaps lack of enthusiasm or interest among backbenchers. Throughout the 1950s and 1960s the government relied much more on departmental committees or special committees of inquiry to carry out any detailed investigations it required. Opportunities to involve MPs from all parties in co-operative ventures were thereby lost. It was not until 1971 that the Northern Ireland government, in a consultative document on the future development of parliament, recognised the case for setting up functional select committees[10]

The Senate

The Senate consisted of twenty-four senators elected on the principle of proportional representation by members of the House of Commons for a term of eight years. In addition, the Lords Mayor of Belfast and Londonderry were *ex officio* senators. The Senate was an integral part of the legislative process and had two main functions. Firstly, it was responsible for the introduction and main committee work on non-controversial legislation. Up until 1967 there were only two or three such bills per year, but after this there was a sharp increase in this type of business; in 1969 there were eighteen bills of this type. Generally the Senate was permitted to do the full committee work. There were no prolonged discussions or amendments when the legislation went to the House of Commons. Only one of the eighteen bills in 1969 was amended in the Commons, and only two out of nine bills in 1970–71. In 1968 the Criminal Procedure (Commitment for Trial) Bill drew nineteen amendments in the Commons and was clearly more controversial than had been anticipated when given to the Senate to introduce.

The second major legislative function of the Senate was the revision of legislation which had passed through the Commons. But the number of bills amended was quite small, as is shown in Table 11.

Table 11:　Amendment of Bills in the Senate

	Total bills	Financial bills	Bills with no amendments proposed	Bills with amendments proposed and rejected	Amended bills
1956	29	5	21	1	2
1961–62	37	10	18	5	4
1968	26	6	9	8	3
1969	30	8	14	4	4
1970–71	45	10	19	5	11

The great majority of amendments were proposed by Opposition members of the Senate, even though they constituted a group of no more than six or seven. Very few amendments were proposed by government senators other than the senator in charge of the bill.

On controversial legislation, or when the Opposition had put down a large number of amendments, it was the custom for the minister in charge of the bill in the Commons to attend the Senate sessions, as, for example, with the Education Amendment Bill, 1968.

The traditional argument for a legislative second chamber is that it allows a second look at legislation and provides an opportunity for considered appraisal by legislators who are free from constituency pressures and less deeply involved in party politics. There is, however, little evidence of the Northern Ireland Senate operating on this basis. Unionist senators appeared to be very content to accept what the House of Commons had approved. Opposition senators tended to make the same kind of amendments as their colleagues had proposed in the Lower House, although in the 1960s one Nationalist senator, Dr P. F. Magill, did appear to subject the work of the parliamentary draftsmen to a more independent and thorough scrutiny. Any amendments approved by the Senate were such that the concurrence of the House of Commons was usually a formality.

The Senate was originally conceived as a possible blocking agent, and elaborate machinery was incorporated into the Government of Ireland Act in case of a dispute between the House of Commons and the Senate. If the Senate failed to pass a Commons bill or amendment and sent it back on two occasions, the Governor could convene a joint sitting of the two Houses. At this meeting a simple majority carried the measure, thus ensuring the dominance of the Commons. This procedure was never used, although there were a few disputes. In 1956 the Senate voted to refuse to give a second reading to a Licensing of Dogs Bill because the bill, which, among other things, increased the dog licence fee, was introduced into the Commons as a money resolution, which meant that it could not be amended by the Senate. The Senate saw this as a tactic to restrict its power and forced the government to withdraw the measure.[11] A more prolonged confrontation took place in 1969 on the Livestock (Protection from Dogs) Bill. The issue this time was the right of farmers to shoot unaccompanied dogs found on hill land. The bill was introduced initially in the Senate and was amended in the Commons. The Commons amendment was rejected by the Senate on a vote of 11 to 10, and the bill was sent back again to the Commons, who reinserted the amendment and returned it to the Senate. This time the Senate stepped down, thus avoiding the first-ever joint session.

The Senate has occasionally rejected proposals from the Commons passed through private members' legislation; for example, in 1967 a Birds Bill, sponsored by Unionist backbenchers and con-

cerning the shooting of wild birds, was defeated, and in 1970 the
Abolition of Hare Coursing Bill, which had been passed on a free
vote in the Commons, was defeated on a free vote in the Senate.
The legislation that the Senate opposed was hardly of great importance, but it is significant that the Senate chose to take an
independent line mainly on agricultural or sporting matters. This
tendency reflected the social background and interests of a majority
of senators. The small number of private members' bills originating
in the Senate also revealed the same rural preoccupations of their
sponsors, for example the Coursing of Hares Bill, 1930, and the
Game Act Amendment Bill, 1955.

The Senate was not a source of legislative initiatives or new
policy ideas. It had little prestige or status, and its proceedings
received little attention. Until the late 1960s it met very irregularly,
usually about once a week and perhaps twenty-five to thirty times
a year, and the average length of a sitting was only about one hour.
It was thought originally that the Senate might provide an opportunity for representatives of the Catholic minority to participate
and make known their views. Donaldson (1958) comments that
probably the best argument that can be advanced for the Senate
was that it could provide an effective platform for a vocal minority.[12] But given the small number of Opposition members and
the low status of the Senate, this was never a very significant
function.

Generally debates were carried on in a partisan atmosphere not
very different from that of the Lower House, and debates and
divisions tended to duplicate events in the Commons. Quite frequently alignments led to all amendments being forced to a division,
whereas the House of Lords does not regard this as the best way
of arriving at decisions. Divisions were usually on party lines; for
example, in 1961–62 only five out of eighty divisions were on non-
party lines.[13]

The Senate's most useful role, apart from assisting parliament
and the government with the legislative process, was providing
manpower to sit on joint committees. Few senators have held
office as cabinet ministers. Apart from the Leader of the Senate,
who sat in the cabinet, only four senators held ministerial office
(all as Minister of Education). The amount of non-legislative work
undertaken by the Senate was very small, despite the fact that
senators might have had ample time for such work.

Most assessments of the Senate have been critical. Sayers (1955)
states that 'The members are chosen more for party services than
for intellectual or administrative attainments, and as a consequence
the Upper House has little influence on law-making and contributes

only in a minor way to the discussion of affairs.'[14] Magill (1965) writes that it abdicated its function of criticising legislation with vigilance and independence and instead followed the same partisan approach that characterised debates in the Lower House.[15] The Senate was not a counterbalance to the Commons and played a minor role in the legislative process. Its work mostly involved the correcting of drafting errors and small improvements rather than the revision of legislation.

Conclusion

The Northern Ireland parliament had perhaps two outstanding features. The first was its attempt to follow the procedures and practices of the Westminster parliament as closely as possible in the legislative process, the financial process, debating procedure, question time, the committee system, and the relationship between the Upper and Lower Houses. This was inappropriate for several reasons. Parliament was small in comparison with Westminster, and the length of time it devoted to its deliberations was much shorter. The House of Commons met three afternoons a week, from 2.30 to 6.30 p.m. for two days and until 9.30 or 10.30 p.m. on Wednesday. Later sittings were fairly uncommon, and until the mid-1960s the House often met on only two days a week. Parliamentary sessions varied in length, but the average over a twelve-month period increased from about 45 sitting days in the 1930s to 60–65 days in the 1950s to around 86–88 days between 1965 and 1971. It could with some justification be called a part-time parliament. The adoption of Westminster parliamentary procedures on debates, divisions and voting on amendments in committee, and even a similar physical layout with front benches and Opposition benches, all served to encourage political confrontation and accentuated divisions. Westminster procedures were not appropriate to the requirements of a regional assembly which was itself subordinate to Westminster. There remained a need for detailed discussion of and control over the administration of services, and for wide-ranging, comprehensive debate on social and economic issues and financial allocations.

The second outstanding feature of the Northern Ireland parliament was the dominance of the government party. The government was always sure of a large majority and could thus afford to ignore the Opposition. This was evident in the legislative process, where the government was unwilling to accept Opposition proposals and rarely accepted amendments to legislation from the Opposition on issues of substance. This attitude was also displayed in parliamentary appointments, for example in the invariable nomination of Unionist backbenchers to the chairmanship of the Public Accounts Committee. At Westminster a member of the Opposition traditionally holds this post. In 1945 the government even objected to a proposal by the BBC for a 'Week in Stormont' radio programme because Opposition MPs would be allowed to express their views on the air.[16]

The government normally had little to fear from opposition by their own backbenchers. Research carried out by J. H. Whyte (1973) has shown that there were a few occasions when backbenchers voted against the government, but such revolts usually involved a small group of dissidents or independently minded backbenchers who were critical of the government on certain issues. The refractory MPs tended to be hardliners on the right wing of the party, voting often against government extravagance or bureaucracy or against increases in government grants to voluntary schools. In 1949 a government bill proposing to give grants for the entire insurance and superannuation contribution of teachers in voluntary schools was defeated by a backbench rebellion.[17]

There have been a number of occasions when backbench disquiet at legislative proposals led the government to drop the proposals or revise them, but this was not recorded in any divisions. For example, in 1956 a government scheme to change family allowances to benefit smaller rather than larger families was abandoned after pressure from a large number of backbenchers. A Statistics of Trade Bill, 1956, similar to Westminster legislation, was withdrawn and amended after backbench opposition on the grounds that it was a step towards nationalisation. A Housing and Farms Bill was withdrawn in 1960, as backbenchers objected to the level of grants offered to farmers. In 1961–62 a bill on planning appeals procedures was discontinued, again in response to backbench dissatisfaction. There was more substantial opposition to the Education Bill, 1947, and the Health Bill, 1947, as a result of which the government eventually gave way to backbench opinion on certain clauses; but such incidents do not justify the view that the government was under persistent pressure from backbenchers on its legislative programme.

As might be expected in the political circumstances, between 1969 and 1971 the proportion of Unionist backbenchers who voted at least once against the government was higher than in any other parliament; in fact a group of seven right-wing Unionists voted repeatedly against government policies.[18] But although the parliamentary party was divided by the beginning of 1969 into pro- and anti-O'Neill factions and split over the need for reform legislation, the Unionist government had no real trouble with its majority in parliament.

The dominant position of Unionist governments was accentuated by the lack of a large or coherent Opposition. It was only in the 1950s that the Nationalist Party fully participated in parliament and became an effective Opposition party, and it refused to become the official Opposition until 1965. Even this decision made little difference to the party's degree of participation in parliament or to its treatment by the government beyond being given the post of Deputy Chairman of Ways and Means in 1966. Since 1933 the Nationalist Party had a maximum of nine MPs; but notwithstanding its small size and the fact that its members lived mainly in the west and south of the province, and in spite of lack of encouragement from the government party, it played a very active role in debates, question time and legislative work in the Commons and, more noticeably, in the Senate, where the Nationalist members composed nearly the total Opposition. Without the co-operation of Nationalist MPs and senators the Northern Ireland parliament would have borne little resemblance to a parliament at all. The Nationalist Party placed considerable emphasis on partition and the treatment of Catholics and was usually supported in this by small groups of Republican Labour or Irish Labour MPs. The other group which played an important Opposition role was the Northern Ireland Labour Party. Its four MPs made a very large contribution to parliamentary proceedings between 1958 and 1965, and in 1958 they became the official Opposition. The position of leader of the Opposition at Stormont never had the status accorded it at Westminster. In 1958 the Speaker recognised the NILP as the official Opposition, but the government did not. The NILP representatives, together with a few Republican Labour MPs, provided a much stronger emphasis on socio-economic issues in Stormont's debates. With the help of a group of independently minded Unionist backbenchers they made parliament in the 1960s a much more active institution, as the statistics in Tables 8–10 show. At the same time the role of the Opposition members was confined largely to criticism, and they were afforded little opportunity by parliamentary procedure or by the government to contribute to policy-making.

C*

Direct Rule: Government without Stormont

THE system of government in Northern Ireland has been completely transformed in recent years. The period 1968–72 saw growing intervention by the British government, but there was an obvious reluctance to become fully embroiled in Ulster affairs, and Westminster's course of action at this stage was largely restricted to persuading the Northern Ireland Prime Minister and cabinet to introduce reforms. The area where the British government had the clearest responsibility was the army and security policy. Control over security was a particularly complex issue. In order to co-ordinate the work of the security forces and because many of the security decisions had political implications, a Joint Security Committee was created in 1971, consisting of representatives of the army, the Royal Ulster Constabulary, the Stormont cabinet and a United Kingdom government representative and chaired by the Stormont Prime Minister. Although overall responsibility for security rested with Westminster, the security committee allowed the Stormont government an influential voice in its decisions. The influence of Stormont appeared to increase in 1970 with the coming to power at Westminster of a Conservative government which was known to favour a more *laissez-faire* approach to security matters. When Mr Brian Faulkner became Prime Minister in 1971 he set up a small high-powered branch of the Cabinet Office for the co-ordination of security policy and the servicing of the Joint Security Committee.[1] Important security decisions still had to be sanctioned by the Westminster cabinet, but the initiatives in making proposals after March 1971 rested largely with Stormont, and its demands were often successful. The decisions to rearm the RUC, to crater roads across the border with the Republic of Ireland and to introduce internment in 1971 were endorsed by Westminster after strong pressure from the Northern Ireland government.

Increasing violence, the apparent failure of the internment policy, and, finally, the disaster of Bloody Sunday in Londonderry in

January 1972 convinced the British government that fundamental changes in the control of security were urgently necessary. It was the Joint Security Committee which decided how the demonstration in Londonderry was to be handled. The anomalies of divided responsibility for security was further shown by a decision of the Northern Ireland High Court in February 1972 that the army's use of power conferred on it by the Northern Ireland Special Powers Act was in fact unlawful.

British intervention since 1969 had concentrated, under the Labour government, on a programme of administrative reforms and, under the Conservative government, on security measures. Neither approach had ended the violence or satisfied Catholic demands for change, and neither had fundamentally altered the internal political structure. In 1971–72 the Conservative government yielded to the view that a major new political initiative was necessary. This became a more urgent requirement when the SDLP withdrew from the Stormont parliament in July 1971. The immediate reason was the refusal by the government to hold an inquiry into the shooting of two men in Londonderry, but the statement issued by the SDLP following its decision revealed more fundamental grievances. It argued that the position of the army, the supervision by Westminster of the reform programme, the continuing presence of the British representatives as a watchdog and the continuance of the Stormont system all created permanent political instability. The SDLP MPs believed that their withdrawal would bring home to those in authority the need for strong political action.[2]

The British government now came to accept that the transfer of responsibility for law and order was an indispensable condition for progress in finding a political solution. It would also end the existing confused lines of control and supervision. At a meeting at 10 Downing Street on 22 March 1972 the Northern Ireland Prime Minister, Mr Faulkner, found himself faced with the proposition that all statutory and executive responsibility for law and order (including police, prisons, public prosecuting power, criminal law and procedure, special powers and public order) should be vested in the United Kingdom parliament and government. The British Prime Minister, Mr Edward Heath, also proposed a move towards ending internment, the creation of a new Westminster post of Secretary of State for Northern Ireland, and open-ended talks with SDLP on a new form of government.[3]

The Northern Ireland cabinet was unable to accept these proposals, declaring that they would undermine the powers, authority and standing of the government, and on 23 March 1972 the entire cabinet agreed to sign a letter of resignation.[4] In the light of this, Mr Heath announced the suspension of the devolved institutions of government and the introduction of direct rule of Northern Ireland from Westminster. Mr Faulkner's cabinet agreed to stay on in office until the necessary legislation instituting direct rule could be passed at Westminster.

Direct Rule: The First Phase, March 1972–December 1973

Direct rule meant the assumption by Westminster of direct responsibility for government and administration in Northern Ireland and the transfer to Westminster of all legislative and executive functions. The Northern Ireland (Temporary Provisions) Act became law on 30 March, proroguing the Stormont parliament and transferring its powers for one year. A ministerial team was appointed: Mr William Whitelaw as Secretary of State, assisted by three junior ministers, of whom two were ministers of state and one a parliamentary under-secretary. Mr Whitelaw and his team assumed responsibility for the executive powers of the Northern Ireland cabinet, the work of the former Stormont cabinet ministers being divided between the three junior ministers. The United Kingdom parliament became responsible for Northern Ireland legislation.

The transfer of functions led to the creation of the Northern Ireland Office with personnel at both Whitehall and Stormont. New machinery had also to be created to carry out certain cabinet functions, particularly the co-ordination of the work of the eight different government departments. The equivalent of the cabinet procedure was a meeting held three times a week, presided over by the Secretary of State and attended by ministers who were present in Northern Ireland, by the principal civil advisers and, at least twice a week, by the heads of the security forces. These meetings also had authority to make final decisions on all matters relating to the running of the civil administration, including, for example, the resolving of interdepartmental disputes. In addition, Mr Whitelaw held daily meetings of available ministers and advisers to work on problem areas. The machinery of direct rule was completed by a central secretariat, whose duties were to co-ordinate government, to service a wide range of committees, to assist the Secretary of State and his ministers and to concentrate upon particular projects of special urgency. Lord Windlesham, a junior minister, noted that the comparative smallness of the organisation directly in contact with the Secretary of State led to a pattern of working which was much less hierarchical than in large government departments.[5]

As well as Civil Service advisers, the ministerial team had the assistance of the Northern Ireland Advisory Commission. This commission, all of whose members were residents of Northern Ireland, was set up in May 1972 to make recommendations to the Secretary of State on such matters connected with the discharge of his functions relating to the province as he might refer to it. It was also his duty to refer legislative proposals to the commission for its advice. The commission had eleven members, seven Protestants and four Roman Catholics. It met on thirty-six occasions between June 1972 and March 1973. The commission was purely advisory, and the ministers were not obliged to accept its suggestions. The idea behind the commission was to provide some channel for local opinion; but its members were not political representatives, and the role of the commission seems generally to have been a low-key one.

There was, however, no shortage of groups offering advice to the new ministers. The tradition of easy access to Stormont ministers was maintained even more rigorously under the new regime by a continuous procession of delegates representing political factions, churches and community groups.

Direct rule brought significant changes to Northern Ireland's legislative process. The Temporary Provisions Act provided that proposals formerly within the legislative competence of the Northern Ireland parliament should take the form of Orders in Council. These were laid before parliament at Westminster and required the approval of both Houses before being submitted to the Queen in Council. In cases where urgent action had to be taken the act made allowance for an Order in Council to be laid before parliament and to take immediate effect, with the proviso that it should subsequently be approved by both Houses within a period of forty days. In the period between April 1972 and May 1973 twelve Orders in Council were made under the urgent procedure and twenty-three under the normal procedure.[6]

The major problems with this system was that the orders could not be amended and there was a limited time for discussion, generally not more than one and a half hours of debate. Some of the Northern Ireland Orders in Council received only a few minutes' debate, for example a superannuation order in July 1972. A complex planning order with one hundred clauses and seven schedules was debated for only one and a half hours. A number of orders did receive more favourable treatment than the strict Order in Council procedure allowed. The order establishing area boards to deal with education and libraries received more than three and a half hours of debate, and the order introducing proportional representation for local government elections received seven hours.[7] There was a further difficulty in that Orders in Council were not taken until 10 p.m. or later, so that the majority of Northern Ireland orders were discussed late at night when attendance was low. Most of the Orders in Council in this period were not contentious, and there were divisions on only four occasions. This system was introduced as a temporary expedient, in line with the administrative arrangements of the Temporary Provisions Act; but it was also clearly designed to prevent Northern Ireland business interfering too much with the rest of business in the House of Commons.

With no opportunity provided to amend legislation, more attention was given to the pre-legislative procedures. New legislative proposals from departments were first considered by a Policy Coordinating Committee of senior officials. Draft orders were then introduced to the Northern Ireland Advisory Commission by the minister with departmental responsibility for the legislation, and the comments of that body were invited. Each order was then printed and made available to the public, together with an explanatory document including much of the information that would have been given by a minister introducing a bill at Stormont.

Direct rule resulted in an increase in Westminster's legislative workload. As well as large number of orders, there were bills passing through Westminster concerning Northern Ireland matters of the type formerly reserved to Westminster. Among important items of legislation enacted in this way were the Border Poll Act, 1972, the Northern Ireland Assembly Act, 1973, and the Northern Ireland Constitution Act, 1973. Procedures were not entirely normal in that most of the legislation had its committee stage on the floor of the House.

Apart from this category of legislation specifically connected with the political initiatives and constitutional change, the majority of measures would have gone through Stormont had it survived. Many of the Orders in Council in 1972–73 were connected with the reorganisation of local administration and had been in the pipeline already. This first phase of direct rule did not see the initiation of any new proposals at Westminster or any attempt to bring Northern Ireland legislation into line with British legislation in the many areas where differences existed.

The Westminster parliament also had to take on certain other functions of the Stormont parliament. In fourteen months of direct rule there were some 1,500 parliamentary questions, the majority concerning security matters. Ministers in both Houses made numerous statements or answered private notice questions, and there were several full-scale debates. Such was its workload that the Northern Ireland Office stood at fourth place in the House of Commons table of hours consumed in parliamentary business. Only the Departments of the Environment, Trade and Industry and the Treasury exceeded it.[8] It has been said that the volume and urgency of Northern Ireland business played havoc with the parliamentary timetable.[9]

Direct rule had a less dramatic effect on the financial arrangements. Under the 1972 act Orders in Council took the place of Appropriation Acts and Consolidated Fund Acts. The Westminster Public Accounts Committee had to take over the work of the equivalent Stormont committee. There were also some minor alterations in two items of transferred taxation, estate duty and stamp duties, to correspond to similar changes in Britain. A possible review of the whole area of financial arrangements had been under discussion at the time of the prorogation of the Northern Ireland parliament. The British government had recognised that it was increasingly necessary to supplement Northern Ireland's tax revenue with a number of special contributions. In 1973 a White Paper was published which noted that the continued rise in development expenditure and reductions in tax rates made it clear that a more comprehensive means of supplementing Northern Ireland's tax revenue was necessary.[10]

The Northern Ireland Assembly and Executive, 1 January–29 May 1974

The Formation of the Executive

Direct rule was intended to be a temporary phase until a new constitutional solution was reached. Following discussion between the Secretary of State and a wide range of interests, the government published new proposals for the constitutional future of Northern Ireland on 11 March 1973.[11] Legislation followed, the Northern Ireland Assembly Act and the Northern Ireland Constitution Act, establishing a new representative forum, the Northern Ireland Assembly, with legislative powers on a range of transferred matters. Members of the Assembly would act as heads of each government department, and these heads would collectively form an Executive. The most radical aspect of the new scheme was its acceptance of the principle of power-sharing, as contained in the proposal that the Executive should not be solely based upon any single party but should be more widely representative of the community. The constitutional proposals also envisaged an 'Irish dimension' through the mechanism of a 'Council of Ireland'.

The implementation of the new constitution and the devolution of powers to Northern Ireland institutions involved four stages.

(1) The election for the new Northern Ireland Assembly took place in June 1973 and returned 23 Official Unionists, 19 SDLP, 8 Alliance and one NILP member, all in favour of the constitutional proposals in the White Paper, and 27 Unionists and loyalists who were opposed to the proposals.

(2) The Assembly developed its own rules and procedures in accordance with broad provisions laid down in the Constitution Act. It held its first meeting on 31 July 1973 and was to spend the autumn months in an acrimonious discussion of its future standing orders.[12]

(3) Discussions took place between representatives of the Assembly and the Secretary of State to arrive at an acceptable basis for the formation of an Executive and the devolution of powers. In November 1973 agreement was reached between three parties, the Official Unionists, Alliance and the SDLP, on the shape and balance of an Executive and administration in which they would serve jointly.

(4) This made possible the nomination of an Executive-designate pending an agreement on the proposal for a Council of Ireland. This question was settled in the course of a tripartite conference between representatives of the Northern Ireland parties in the Executive-designate, the British government and the government of the Irish Republic at Sunningdale in December 1973.[13] Legislative and executive powers were accordingly devolved to the Assembly and Executive on 1 January 1974.

The New Constitution

In comparison with the 1920 constitution, there was a reduction in the legislative and executive powers of the regional assembly.

There was a tripartite division of the government's legislative functions. (1) *Excepted matters.* These were matters on which the Assembly could not legislate. Apart from the items in the 1920 list, some matters which had formerly been within the legislative capacity of the Northern Ireland parliament were excluded from the Assembly's terms of reference. These included elections, the appointment of judges and magistrates, public prosecutions, special powers, and certain taxation powers. (2) *Reserved matters.* These were matters which were to be excluded for the present from the normal legislative competence of the Assembly, but in respect of which the Assembly might exceptionally legislate with the agreement of the United Kingdom government. This category mainly covered law-and-order matters, the criminal law, the courts, penal institutions, and the police. It also included the reserved items in the 1920 act. (3) *Transferred matters.* These comprised all other matters, and the Assembly was free to legislate on these. The act also had a provision prohibiting the Assembly from making a law of a discriminatory character.

The right of the United Kingdom parliament to legislate for Northern Ireland on any matter was preserved, but it was expected that this would operate in the field of devolved powers only in exceptional circumstances or at the special request of the Northern Ireland government.

The new Executive had executive functions similar to those exercised before direct rule by the Stormont cabinet, with the exceptions of judicial appointments and certain other executive powers in relation to the police, public order and penal establishments.

The office of Secretary of State was preserved, its incumbent now having a fourfold division of responsibilities: firstly, to conduct consultations on the formation of the Executive in accord with the government's principles and to formally appoint the heads of departments; secondly, to exercise direct ministerial responsibility in relation to reserved services; thirdly, to scrutinise and approve Northern Ireland legislation passed by the Assembly; and finally, to represent Northern Ireland in the United Kingdom cabinet, particularly in relation to the allocation of financial resources.

The government's White Paper of 1973 had referred to past difficulties about the constitutional competence of the Stormont parliament to legislate and the numerous amendments, enablements and artificial drafting contrivances that had to be used to keep the 1920 constitution operating. A more flexible scheme was proposed for the Assembly which would allow Northern Ireland 'measures' to have the same force as acts of parliament, subject to appropriate Westminster ministerial control.

All measures and legislative proposals passed by the Assembly had the force of law when approved by the Queen in Council. The Secretary of State had the power to refer back to the Assembly for further consideration any measure which he considered to contain a provision dealing with an excepted or reserved matter; and if such a measure was resubmitted to the Secretary of State, he could veto it.

In December 1973 agreement was reached on a basis for setting up a Council of Ireland as part of the new constitutional arrangements.[14] The Council of Ireland was to consist of representatives from both parts of Ireland. At the outset it would comprise a council of ministers of seven members each from the Northern Ireland Executive and the government of the Republic of Ireland.

The council of ministers would provide the forum for consultation, co-operation and co-ordination of action in relation to areas of common interest in economic and social matters, including the exploration, conservation and development of natural resources, electricity generation, tourism, roads, transport, agricultural matters, cross-border planning, and work relating to the impact of the EEC. The council of ministers would act only on the basis of complete unanimity. It was envisaged that later there would also be a consultative assembly of sixty members, thirty each from the Northern Ireland Assembly and the parliament of the Irish Republic, and a transfer of certain functions from existing departments and authorities to the council of ministers.

Financial Arrangements

The 1973 Constitution Act made substantial changes in Northern Ireland's financial arrangements. The revenue required to meet the cost of devolved services would be derived from the product of taxes levied locally, firstly from the rates (about £15 million in 1973–74), secondly from locally generated non-tax revenue (about £68 million), and thirdly from the yield of the attributed taxation of Northern Ireland to be paid from the Consolidated Fund of the United Kingdom (some £301 million).

The 1973 act laid down the present method for calculating Northern Ireland's share of each tax. For income tax the Northern Ireland share is the amount which bears to the total United Kingdom proceeds of income tax the same proportion as the total income of individuals resident in Northern Ireland bears to the total income of individuals resident in the United Kingdom. For VAT and other taxes levied by the Customs and Excise Department the share is taken to be that sum which bears to the whole United Kingdom proceeds the same proportion as expenditure in Northern Ireland on the goods and services subject to these taxes bears to total expenditure in the United Kingdom on the same goods and services. For corporation tax the share is based on Northern Ireland profits as a proportion of total United Kingdom profits. For motor vehicle duty, capital gains tax, estate duty and stamp duty it is the amount actually collected in Northern Ireland.[15]

The 1973 act abolished most of the special forms of assistance and *ad hoc* agreements which had existed until that time and replaced them by a general grant-in-aid to the Northern Ireland Consolidated Fund. This grant-in-aid is estimated annually in relation to the deficiencies in Northern Ireland's revenue account compared with approved public expenditure. The Agricultural Remoteness Grant continued to be paid separately, and arrangements for national insurance, industrial injuries and redundancy payments were maintained as before. The total financial subvention was £313 million in 1973–74. The act abolished the Joint Exchequer Board and the imperial contribution, but it gave the Treasury power to make a deduction towards the cost of excepted and reserved matters from Northern Ireland's share of United Kingdom taxation.

These new arrangements meant that Northern Ireland was more integrated financially with Great Britain than had been the case previously. The overall level of public expenditure would be determined at Westminster in the light of public expenditure for the whole United Kingdom. Any special increases over ordinary requirements would have to be specially justified. However, it was argued that this new system would leave Northern Ireland with a large measure of autonomy in its choice of priorities and policies, except in relation to cash social services and assistance to industry and agriculture, where it had been necessary to place limits upon local freedom of decision.[16]

The Operation of the Executive and Assembly

There were eleven members of the Executive and four additional members of the administration, comprising seven Unionists, six SDLP members and two members of the Alliance Party. Each was head of a department, and Mr Brian Faulkner, the Unionist Party leader, himself took up the post of Chief Executive.

Minister	Post	Party
Brian Faulkner	Chief Executive	Unionist
Gerry Fitt	Deputy Chief Executive	SDLP
Herbert Kirk	Finance	Unionist
John Hume	Commerce	SDLP
Leslie Morrell	Agriculture	Unionist
Paddy Devlin	Health and Social Services	SDLP
Austin Currie	Housing, Local Government and Planning	SDLP
Roy Bradford	Environment	Unionist
Basil McIvor	Education	Unionist
John Baxter	Information	Unionist
Oliver Napier	Legal Minister and Head of the Office of Law Reform	Alliance

There were also four other ministers in the administration who were not voting members of the Executive.

Ivan Cooper	Community Relations	SDLP
Robert Cooper	Manpower Services	Alliance
Robert Hall-Thompson	Chief Whip	Unionist
Eddie McGrady	Executive Planning and Co-ordination	SDLP

The division of responsibilities reflected the interest of the SDLP in social and economic policy, on which the party would now clearly exercise an enormous influence since its representatives were in charge of health and personal social services, housing and commerce, including industrial development and employment.

The creation of an administration of fifteen members to satisfy the aspirations of the parties regarding the composition of the Executive led to a rearrangement of the areas traditionally assigned to the former Northern Ireland government departments. Thus the old Ministry of Development was split into the Department of the Environment and the Department of Housing, Local Government and Planning, and the Ministry of Health and Social Services into the Department of Health and Social Services and the Department of Manpower Services. The Departments of Law Reform, Information, Community Relations and Co-ordination all took over small sections of previously existing departments. The Department of Planning and Co-ordination appeared to be a somewhat nebulous creation. The functions of the Ministry of Home Affairs passed to the Northern Ireland Office. The Executive agreed that it would hold itself responsible to the Assembly and would be bound by the principle of collective responsibility. Although officially designated as heads of departments, the Executive members were soon to take the title of minister.

The Assembly was not really able to function as a normal parliament, as the loyalist members refused to play any part in much of the business of the Assembly and did not take up their role as an official Opposition. They did attend on several occasions to make known their opposition to the constitutional arrangement, and there were several acrimonious debates ending in disturbances in the Assembly. The other parties in the Assembly did make the system work for a short period. Ministers introduced Estimates, there were debates on social and economic policy and on reports from administrative bodies, and some three hundred questions were put to ministers during the five months of the Assembly's existence. A system of committees for each department was set up in February 1974; but the loyalist members refused to participate, and consequently the committees had only five to nine members each. As events turned out, the committees were not given sufficient time to develop their role, and the system never really got off the ground.

The legislative output of the Assembly was fairly meagre. During the five-month period only twelve measures (legislative proposals) were introduced, and only four routine measures, two of them financial measures, passed through all their stages. The only measures to reflect any kind of policy initiative were in the area of legal reform: a Department of Legal Affairs Measure, a Law Reform (Limitation of Actions) Measure, a Licensing Measure and a Solicitors Measure; none of these had great political significance. Certain other changes in policy were introduced through Orders in Council, e.g. the Rent Rebate Order and the Regional Rate Order, although these policies had been in the pipeline since 1973 and were not initiated by the Assembly.

The Assembly and the Executive have been criticised for their lack of new policies and legislation which might have improved the public standing of the new government by showing that it was actively concerned in promoting change and progress. In January 1974, shortly after its formation, the new government published a social and economic programme, *A Statement of Social and Economic Aims*, outlining its broad objectives,[17] but no legislation emerged to assist the implementation of this programme. There was not perhaps sufficient time to produce new legislation, and undoubtedly the continuing political debate both inside and outside the Assembly on the constitutional arrangements and security problems must have distracted members' attention.

Some ministers in the Executive did make some progress with their own contributions to new policies. This was particularly true of Education, where Mr McIvor produced proposals to facilitate the provision of integrated education through a shared management system; he even envisaged a number of pilot schemes along these lines. The minister later announced plans for the complete provision of nursery education over a ten-year period, a policy contained in the *Statement of Social and Economic Aims*. Mr Hume also made an impact as Minister of Commerce with a commitment to greater state participation in creating new employment projects and with his work in strengthening his department's overseas representation. The Minister of Housing, Mr Currie, proposed a major review of housing policy and strategy, although his first priorities were in dealing with emergency housing problems arising from the effects of violence.[18]

Assessments of the achievements of the Executive vary even among the participants. Mr Devlin wrote that 'It was fair to say that no single four-year session of parliament since 1921 produced a workload or performance equal to that of the Assembly during the five exciting months that business was conducted by the Executive.'[19] On the other hand, Mr Bradford, Executive Minister of the Environment, has claimed that 'The quality of the Executive's performance and the extent of the achievements have been greatly exaggerated, particularly by the SDLP.'[20]

The Fall of the Executive

The Assembly and Executive faced very hostile opposition from the loyalist representatives and also from sections of the Unionist Party. There was strong opposition to the principle of sharing power with the SDLP and to the Council of Ireland, which was perceived as an embryo all-Ireland parliament. On 4 January the Ulster Unionist Council (the central co-ordinating body of official Unionism) passed a motion rejecting the proposed all-Ireland Council by a majority of eighty votes. After this rejection of his policies Mr Faulkner resigned as leader of the Unionist Party just a few days after becoming head of the Executive. He moved the headquarters of his Unionist Assembly group, and on 22 January Mr Harry West was elected leader of the Unionist Party.

Disruption of the Assembly and opposition to the Sunningdale Agreement continued unabated. A petition with 300,000 signatures was collected to demonstrate that the agreement on the formation of the Executive had not the widespread acceptance required by the Constitution Act. The threat of more militant opposition came with the development of the Ulster Workers' Council, the lineal descendant of the Loyalist Association of Workers, a grassroots working-class organisation which had staged a widespread protest strike after the fall of Stormont in 1972. From January 1974 onwards the UWC was considering an industrial stoppage to block the Council of Ireland.

The most critical development of all for the Executive was the British general election of February 1974. The Unionist constituency associations were divided. Five official nominations went to pro-Assembly candidates but all five, plus two unofficial pro-Assembly Unionist candidates, were defeated by a United Ulster Unionist Coalition (UUUC) of anti-Assembly official Unionists and loyalists. Eleven of the coalition's twelve candidates were returned to Westminster with some 51 per cent of the vote. The pro-Assembly Unionists polled a mere 13 per cent of the vote, even though they had been proposing only qualified approval for the Council of Ireland. The SDLP polled 22 per cent, and Alliance 3 per cent. The power-sharing parties had hoped for 60 per cent of the vote. The election result was a major blow to the Executive and reflected strong Protestant opposition to the Sunningdale Agreement, although the loss of the official party machinery and official Unionist status was also a significant factor in the poor showing of those moderate Unionists who still supported Mr Faulkner. The UUUC could fairly claim that the Executive had no wide support. Moreover, at this time tensions were beginning to develop within the Executive itself.

On 14 May a loyalist motion calling for re-negotiation of all the constitutional arrangements was defeated in the Assembly, and a counter-amendment was passed which stated that if the British and Irish governments fulfilled their commitments, a system of broadly based government under the Constitution Act would enjoy the support of an overwhelming majority in the parliament of the United Kingdom and of the people of Northern Ireland. This vote was made the occasion for the Ulster Workers' Council to call a general stoppage of work. The UWC and the politicians associated with it issued a strong demand for new elections and new constitutional arrangements. The strike had nominal support during the first day, but the blocking of major roads and the support for the strike by the power workers soon had increasingly severe effects. Electricity supplies dwindled, and after a week the distribution of petrol and oil virtually ceased. Following warnings of the disastrous social consequences that were approaching, the Chief Executive and his Unionist colleagues in the Executive advocated some form of negotiation or mediation with the strikers. When the Secretary of State rejected this proposal Mr Faulkner and his Unionist colleagues resigned on 28 May. As the necessary broad basis for maintaining the Executive had been lost, the Executive was brought to an end on 29 May.

The success of the strike led to much speculation as to whether the Executive could have survived.[21] Given time to demonstrate that it could work, it might have achieved stronger support. The general election of February 1974 undoubtedly occurred at the worst possible moment for the infant government still struggling to win the trust of the public. It was also unfortunate that during its brief existence the Executive found it necessary to place more emphasis on implementing the Sunningdale Agreement than on putting its social and economic programme into operation. The SDLP perhaps pushed too strongly and too quickly on the controversial Council of Ireland proposals. The response by the Irish government on meaningful recognition of Northern Ireland's separate status and effective legal machinery for convicting fugitive offenders did little to encourage support for the Sunningdale Agreement among Protestants. On the other hand, the SDLP was of the opinion that decisive action by the army and police to clear roadblocks in the first crucial days of the agitation might have defused the strike and saved the Executive.

The principal effect of the strike was to destroy the immediate prospect of devolved institutions of government and a political settlement based on power-sharing and an Irish dimension. Direct rule from Westminster was reintroduced.

Interim Arrangements, 29 May–17 July 1974

The collapse of the Executive and the prorogation of the Assembly caused problems affecting the constitutional arrangements. Under the Northern Ireland Constitution Act, 1973, the powers devolved to the Assembly and Executive did not revert to the British government and parliament. Section 8 of the act provided a means for dealing with devolved executive powers under these circumstances by enabling the Secretary of State to appoint for up to six months ministers from outside the Assembly. Using this section, the Secretary of State appointed the two ministers of state and two parliamentary secretaries of state at the Northern Ireland Office as the political heads of the government departments. In this way the executive government of Northern Ireland could be carried on.

The government accepted that these arrangements could only be temporary, as they had two serious flaws. Firstly, the position of Westminster ministers in the Northern Ireland Office as heads of Northern Ireland departments was anomalous in that under the Constitution Act they were responsible to the Assembly which was prorogued and of which they were not members. Secondly, the legislative procedures for Northern Ireland under the Temporary Provisions Act, 1972, had lapsed since 1 January 1974. All Northern Ireland legislation subsequent to the prorogation of the Assembly would therefore have to be obtained through ordinary bills passed at Westminster. These flaws clearly showed the need for new constitutional arrangements.

Direct Rule: The Second Phase, July 1974–

The Northern Ireland Act, 1974

The procedures in this new act for the government of Northern Ireland were modelled on the 1972 act. The 1974 act made the Secretary of State responsible for devolved services, and laws for Northern Ireland were again to be made by Order in Council. The act did not repeal any part of the Constitution Act, 1973. It temporarily set aside those parts of the 1973 act dealing with the functions of the Assembly and Executive, but all its other provisions, including the financial arrangements, remained in force. The new act also enabled the dissolution of the Assembly, but it also stipulated that that body was not to be dissolved until an election for a Constitutional Convention was called. The Convention was to meet for the purposes of considering new forms of government, but it was to have no governmental functions. Apart from these provisions, the bulk of the 1974 act was concerned with the form of executive government and the legislative process.

The Machinery of Government
All power of executive government was placed under the control of the Secretary of State, who also assumed direct responsibility for the Department of Finance and the new Department of the Civil Service. Instead of two ministers and two under-secretaries holding office as heads of departments, the Secretary of State controlled all the departments with the assistance of his junior ministers. An innovation was that the ministers were also asked to have a special concern for certain matters reserved to the Secretary of State. The division of duties during 1977 was as follows.

Minister	*Departmental responsibilities*	*Areas of special concern*
Don Concannon (Minister of State)	Commerce; Manpower Services; EEC matters	Prison administration; compensation
Lord Melchett (Minister of State)	Health and Social Services; Education	Probation; training schools; penal matters; courts; civil emergencies
Raymond Carter (Under-Secretary of State)	Environment	Construction Industry Advisory Council
James Dunn (Under-Secretary of State)	Agriculture; Finance	Police administration; control of firearms and explosives

The collapse of the Executive eventually led to the Department of the Environment absorbing the Department of Housing, Local Government and Planning, and the Department of Education absorbing Community Relations, although the Department of Manpower Services remained in existence unchanged. (The division of ministerial responsibilities following the Conservative general election victory in May 1979 is given in the Appendix.)

In addition to his duties outlined above, the Secretary of State also became directly responsible for the Northern Ireland Office. Most of the divisions of the Northern Ireland Office in Belfast deal with the administration of law-and-order functions and are located separately from the divisions dealing with security and political affairs and the private office of the Secretary of State. The London office of the Northern Ireland Office now has one of three divisions dealing with financial matters. The London office has tended to concentrate on handling Northern Ireland business at Westminster and relationships with other Whitehall departments.

Co-ordination machinery in Northern Ireland was formalised through an executive committee consisting of ministers and the permanent secretaries of departments. This committee, the Secretary of State's Executive Committee (SOSEC), meets regularly and has been described by one Secretary of State as a co-ordinating committee similar to an executive or a cabinet. It oversees the general administration of transferred powers and may discuss proposals for legislation. The co-ordination machinery was further improved by the establishment of a separate post of head of the Civil Service; this official is responsible to the Secretary of State for the co-ordination of policies and programmes of all Northern Ireland departments and for advising the Secretary of State on the allocation of resources.[22] The central secretariat which had operated during the earlier period of direct rule from Westminster was re-established with identical duties.

The problem of dealing with Northern Ireland legislation on matters previously devolved has remained. Such legislation continued to be made by Order in Council, subject to the affirmative resolution procedure. The government did state, however, that wherever major legislation or sensitive issues were involved it would proceed by a normal bill rather than by an Order in Council. This arrangement has, however, proved unsatisfactory. To introduce all Northern Ireland legislative proposals as ordinary bills at Westminster would add tremendously to parliament's workload, while to introduce them as Orders in Council means inadequate discussion and amendment. In 1975 some forty orders went through parliament in two months without the possibility of amendment. Orders in Council passed during 1975–76 which might have been expected to produce lengthy debate in a Northern Ireland parliament were the Industrial Relations Order, 1976, the Northern Ireland Development Agency Order, 1976, the Firearms Order, 1976, and the Education Order, 1975 (this last item increasing capital grants for voluntary schools).

An alternative legislative method is to apply British bills to

Northern Ireland. It would not be too difficult to make special adoptions where necessary, as is sometimes done in the case of Scotland, or to amend previous Northern Ireland measures. The government has generally decided against this in accordance with its view that a system of devolved government necessitates the maintenance of a separate statute book for Northern Ireland.

In 1976 the government made two changes to try to improve the legislative process on devolved matters. The government proposed extended debates on Orders in Council in special cases. During 1977 a total of twenty hours was spent on debates on five orders, an average of four hours each compared with the normal one and a half hours. Secondly, the Northern Ireland orders, published as proposals before they were formally introduced in parliament, would be sent as a matter of course to each of the major political parties in Northern Ireland for comment. The government also proposed that the new Northern Ireland Committee (see below) could discuss draft orders at this preliminary stage.

Northern Ireland Orders in Council, in common with other statutory instruments and delegated legislation, were subject to technical scrutiny by a parliamentary Joint Committee on Statutory Instruments. The committee raised doubts about the practicality of submitting Northern Ireland orders to the kind of technical scrutiny appropriate to United Kingdom delegated legislation. It was also dissatisfied with its commission to scrutinise Orders in Council which were 'disguised' as delegated legislation but which were really primary legislation and had the form and content of bills rather than subordinate legislation. In response to these objections, Northern Ireland Orders in Council were excluded from the committee's consideration from June 1977.[23]

Legislation on reserved matters requires an ordinary Westminster bill and goes through the normal legislative procedures, for example the emergency provisions legislation of 1973 and the Administration of Justice Bill, 1973. Any measure which the government feels is very important or controversial is liable to be dealt with in this manner. The Fair Employment Bill, 1976, to outlaw religious discrimination was in this category and gave an indication of the extra business involved in the Northern Ireland legislation. The bill, which was opposed by the Unionist members, took thirty hours in committee, and the report stage in the House of Commons lasted six hours.

Direct rule has had a heavy impact on the workload of the House of Commons, involving extra legislation, a large number of debates on Orders in Council, debates on Northern Ireland subjects, ministerial statements, and a large increase in the number of parliamentary questions on Northern Ireland matters (from 140 in 1970 to over 1,000 for 1975–76). It has also increased the work of some Westminster committees. The Public Accounts Committee now covers all Northern Ireland government departments, and in 1976 its brief was extended to cover certain public bodies such as the Housing Executive, which disbursed public money directly but had not been previously subject to examination by the Public Accounts Committee. The Public Expenditure Committee now includes Northern Ireland expenditure within its scope, and in 1976 the government suggested that other select committees, particularly the Select Committee on Nationalised Industries, should include Northern Ireland within their scope.

The Northern Ireland Committee

In January 1975, as part of new arrangements to deal more adequately with Northern Ireland business, the government proposed setting up a Northern Ireland Standing Committee of MPs. The committee was established in February 1975 with the status of a standing committee and with the task of considering specific matters relating exclusively to Northern Ireland. Matters to be referred to the committee would first of all come before the House of Commons for approval, and the topics for discussion would then be agreed with the members concerned. All Northern Ireland MPs would sit on the committee as of right, with twenty other members who would be appointed separately for each debate. Unlike the Scottish and Welsh committees, its composition was not a carefully selected cross-section of the whole House. The committee was obliged to consider matters for not more than four days before preparing a report. It was also empowered to take evidence from officials.

The Northern Ireland Committee had a delayed start because the Ulster Unionist members and the government could not agree on a suitable inaugural subject. The government offered a debate on the economic situation, but the Unionists refused to participate, insisting on a debate on security. Eventually the committee did consider the economy, and its subsequent proceedings dealt with housing, health and social services and compensation laws. In 1977 the restriction on the number of sittings that the committee could hold in a parliamentary session were removed, and the government promised to facilitate discussions of legislative proposals. Subsequently three orders were debated for a total of $9\frac{3}{4}$ hours in the Northern Ireland Committee before they were laid before both Houses. As a result of this extended scrutiny, changes in draft legislation have been recommended by the committee and agreed to by the government, as, for example, in the case of the Compensation for Criminal Injuries Order, 1977, which was the subject of a five-hour debate in the committee. The functions of the Northern Ireland Committee may expand to include keeping an oversight on the work of the government departments and considering the reports of the Northern Ireland Examiner of Statutory Rules, who inspects Northern Ireland Orders in Council under delegated powers.

The Impact on Policy, 1975–79
The first period of direct rule and the first year of the second period saw little new legislation on devolved matters emanating from Westminster. Legislation on these matters was considered as something on which a future devolved government might be expected to take its own decisions.

The British government was also awaiting the outcome of the Constitutional Convention. The Convention was intended to provide a forum in which elected representatives would find some agreement on the establishment of local institutions enjoying broadly based support throughout the community. The Convention elections were duly held in May 1975, but its members failed to agree on any form of power-sharing or partnership in government. The final report represented the views of the majority United Ulster Unionist Coalition.[24] In March 1976 the British government accepted that there was no prospect of agreement between the parties, and the Convention was dissolved. With it went the likelihood of a speedy return to devolved government. The Labour government turned its attention to social and economic policies, and the Secretary of State announced that henceforward direct rule would be positive, not negative.

Legislation on industrial relations was introduced to bring Northern Ireland into line with Great Britain in such matters as the protection of workers' rights. These and similar reforms in the fields of labour and employment, and including the establishment of a Labour Relations Agency, went further than the recommendations of the Northern Ireland government's review body in 1974. Another original initiative resulted in the setting up of the Northern Ireland Development Authority for the purpose of promoting state industry. It is unlikely that a Unionist government at Stormont would have introduced such measures. Northern Ireland was also brought into line with Britain in some other areas, for example in company law and in legislation against sex discrimination. The government also produced proposals for the reorganisation of secondary education along comprehensive lines, intending to proceed eventually with legislation. The government also declared its intention of introducing legislation to conform with British law on divorce, homosexuality and children and young persons. In July 1976 the Secretary of State announced that the government would no longer hesitate in taking action in devolved areas, with the likely consequence that future developments in Northern Ireland and Great Britain would correspond even more closely.

In 1978 a proposed divorce order was introduced, but some twenty amendments put forward by the Ulster Unionists were accepted by the government. Thus the resulting legislation therefore did differ in some respects from that in England and Wales, e.g. it does not allow postal divorces. However, the main focus of Westminster legislation has been to bring Northern Ireland more into line with Britain—although a proposal to introduce the compulsory wearing of seat belts has led to claims that Northern Ireland is being used as a place for experimentation with radical new policies.

Northern Ireland is now (1979) governed directly by the Westminster government and parliament. In the absence of a devolved government and a developed system of local government, public accountability for all major public services rests at Westminster. Direct rule was introduced as an interim measure, but it now appears that it is likely to remain the form of government for Northern Ireland for some time. The British government since 1976 has moved from a passive to a positive form of direct rule which has been mainly concerned with bringing Northern Ireland into line with British policies and legislation; on the more practical level it has also initiated consultations on long-term policy changes on secondary education, on children and young persons, and on hospital reorganisation.

The defects of the machinery of direct rule are acknowledged by the British government, and some action has already been taken in four different areas. Firstly, the inadequacies of the legislative system have been reduced by the use of extended debates, but eventual incorporation of Northern Ireland into British legislation or separate Northern Ireland bills rather than Orders in Council seems most unlikely. The persistent difficulties presented by Orders in Council therefore remain : orders cannot be amended when introduced in parliament, and the time between the publication of a draft order and its introduction is not always sufficient for groups to prepare representations. Secondly, the Northern Ireland Committee of the House of Commons is now able to discuss and influence legislation at the initial stage. A Northern Ireland Committee to handle the committee stage of Northern Ireland bills is a future possibility, although the time factor is a major constraint on changing the system of legislation by Orders in Council. Thirdly, the government has decided to increase the number of Northern Ireland MPs from twelve to seventeen. Fourthly, following criticisms of Northern Ireland Office ministers concerning the lack of time they spend in Ulster, a policy of getting out and about in the province has been adopted, and in 1978 an additional junior minister was appointed.

Despite all these changes, there are few politicians in Northern Ireland who see this system as preferable to a devolved regional government and parliament.

5

The Political System

THE main characteristics of the political system in Northern Ireland may be identified as the dominance of a single party and the pronounced ideological basis to political thought and behaviour which is largely determined by religious affiliation and expressed in a close association between party and religious alignments.

A Dominant Party

In the general elections from 1921 to 1969 the official Unionist Party has always had a clear majority over all other parties, winning between 32 and 40 out of a total of 52 seats in the Northern Ireland House of Commons (see Table 12). Their proportion of the vote has ranged from 43 to 67 per cent, but has generally been around the 50 per cent mark. The party's dominant position has been clearly associated with two factors: the unity of the Unionist Party, and the fragmentation of the opposition.

There were four main opposition groups: the Independent Unionists, the Northern Ireland Labour Party (NILP), the Nationalist Party, and the small anti-partition parties. There have always been Independent Unionists outside the official party, ranging from individuals to organised groups such as the Progressive Unionists and the Democratic Unionist Party. Until 1973 they have usually won only a few seats and between 5 and 12 per cent of the vote, although there have been occasional exceptions, such as the remarkable 21 per cent which they achieved in 1933. The Northern Ireland Labour Party had also a small representation in terms of seats, between one and four, although in the early 1960s it began to win a substantial proportion of votes: 26 per cent in 1962 and 20 per cent in 1965. The Nationalist Party was the largest opposition party. It had a consistent electoral record, always winning between seven and ten seats until 1969, although the proportion of the vote it secured varied from 5 to 27 per cent. The consistency in the number of seats won by the Unionists and Nationalists in comparison with the considerable variation in votes cast is explained

Table 12: Election Results, 1921–69[1]

Number of seats won						
Year	Unionist	Independent Unionist	NI Labour	Nationalist/ Republican	Independent Labour	Others
1921	40	–	–	12	–	–
1925	32	4	3	12	–	1
1929	37	3	1	11	–	–
1933	36	3	2	11	–	–
1938	39	3	1	8	1	–
1945	33	2	2	10	3	2
1949	37	2	–	9	2	2
1953	38	1	–	9	3	1
1962	34	–	4	9	3	2
1965	36	–	4	9	2	3
1969	36	3	2	6	2	3

mainly by the number of unopposed returns, which was always quite substantial. Generally between 14 and 25 Unionists and 3 and 6 Nationalists were returned unopposed. The small anti-partition parties, Republican or Republican Labour, usually accounted for a small part of the vote and only two or three seats.

The second factor ensuring the dominance of the Unionist Party has been the monolithic character of the party and its ability to maintain electoral unity. Breakaway movements have been fairly frequent, but have had little success until recent times. For example, in 1938 the Progressive Unionists put up twelve candidates, but all were defeated by official Unionists. In the general elections of 1962 and 1965 Ulster Unionism was completely united, but by the late 1960s serious divisions appeared within Unionist ranks over the question of support for Captain O'Neill's reform programme. At the 1969 election the party split into pro- and anti-O'Neill factions. Of the 29 pro-O'Neill candidates, 24 were returned as official Unionists, as were 12 out of 15 anti-O'Neill candidates; in addition, there were 3 successful independent pro-O'Neill Unionists. The total number of official Unionists returned was exactly the same as in the previous election of 1965. A more serious fragmentation occurred in 1973 on the issue of accepting the British government's proposals for an Assembly with an Executive consisting of representatives of the Protestant and Catholic communities and for some form of a Council of Ireland. The Unionists were split into six different groups

D

at the Assembly election in June 1973. Two splinter parties, the Democratic Unionist Party and the Vanguard Unionist Progressive Party, operated in an electoral coalition. The Unionist Party was itself split over the proposals in the British government's White Paper, and the party leader decided that candidates would not be officially endorsed unless they accepted the party's pledge to support the White Paper.[2] There were 44 official Unionist Party candidates, but 4 of these did not accept the party pledge, and there were 12 other Unionists who were unpledged. The fifth group was the West Belfast Loyalist Coalition; and finally, there was a group of independent loyalist candidates. At the election 24 official Unionist candidates were returned with 27 per cent of the first-preference votes. The other Unionists won 35 per cent of the first preferences, with the Democratic Unionists winning 8 seats, Vanguard winning 7 seats, unofficial Unionists winning 8, and the West Belfast Loyalist Coalition 3.

By the time of the 1975 Convention election Mr Faulkner had resigned as leader of the Unionist Party and had formed a separate party, the Unionist Party of Northern Ireland (UPNI), leaving the Official Unionist Party composed of Unionists opposed to power-sharing. At the election the traditional Unionist vote was divided among four parties. Mr Faulkner's party did badly, winning only 5 seats and 8 per cent of first-preference votes. The Official Unionists won 19 seats, the Democratic Unionists 12 seats, and Vanguard 14 seats; these three groups won 53 per cent of first-preference rates. Some semblance of Unionist unity was re-created under the United Ulster Unionist Coalition (UUUC) umbrella, but this was mainly an electoral pact and no move was made to form a united Unionist party.

It is worth noting that the total number of 'Unionist' seats was almost exactly the same in both the Assembly and Convention elections: 49 in 1973 and 50 in 1975. The proportion of votes cast for all kinds of Unionist candidates in 1973 was 62.9 per cent; in 1975 it was 62.5 per cent. It is also interesting to note that the proportion of votes cast for Unionist candidates at the Westminster general elections in February and October 1974 was 64.2 per cent and 62.0 per cent respectively. This indicates that the total Unionist vote has remained almost unchanged despite the division of the Unionists into different factions.

The only test of electoral opinion between 1975 and 1978 was provided by the local government elections of May 1977. Involving as they did specifically local issues and a large number of non-party candidatures, such elections are not directly comparable with a Northern Ireland general election; nevertheless, the results did seem

Table 13: Election Results, 1973, 1975 and 1977

	Seats	1973 (Assembly) First-preference % votes	1975 (Convention) Seats	% votes	1977 Local gov-ernment) % votes
Official Unionist	24	29.3	19	25.8	30.2
Unofficial Unionist	8	8.5	–	–	–
Vanguard Unionist	7	10.5	14	12.7	1.5
Democratic Unionist	8	10.8	12	14.7	12.3
Other Loyalists	3	2.9	2	1.5	3.5
Unionist Party of NI	–	–	5	7.7	3.0
Alliance	8	9.2	8	9.8	15.2
NI Labour Party	1	2.6	1	1.4	1
SDLP	19	22.1	17	23.7	18.8
Republican Clubs	–	3.2	–	2.2	1.7
Others	–	1.0	10	.4	13.8

to indicate a change in Unionist voting (see Table 13). With no electoral pacts between the various Unionist parties, the Unionist vote went largely to the Official Unionists (30 per cent) and Democratic Unionists (12 per cent). In June 1977 the Official Unionist Party formally announced the end of the UUUC. The Official Unionist Party does appear to have regained its position as the largest party in Northern Ireland, but it has lost its position of overall dominance.

The Nature of the Party System: Institutional Factors

There are broadly two classes of explanation for the existence of particular types of party system. One is in terms of specific political institutions, the other in terms of the nature of the social system. The relevant political institutions are the system of government and the electoral system. It may be argued that the adoption in Northern Ireland of the parliamentary and cabinet system, whereby the party with the majority in parliament forms the government, has in itself encouraged the maintenance of a united Unionist Party whose prime objective has been to command such a majority and form a government. This has clearly been a factor in producing unity and reducing divisions within the party.

The second institutional factor was the electoral system. Election by a simple majority in single-member constituencies fostered the dominant position of the Unionist Party and was detrimental to the small parties, particularly the moderate centre parties which occupied the middle ground between the Unionist and Nationalist Parties. This argument is supported by the evidence from the first two Northern Ireland general elections in 1921 and 1925, which took place under the proportional representation system. From a comparison with later elections, it is clear that with the abolition of proportional representation the major parties gained a larger share of the seats. In the 1925 election the Unionist Party won 64 per cent of the votes and 65 per cent of the seats, whereas between 1929 and 1969 the party won, on average, 62 per cent of the votes and 69 per cent of the seats. In 1925 the Nationalist Party won 29 per cent of the votes and 25 per cent of the seats, whereas between 1929 and 1969 the averages were 15 per cent of the votes and 19 per cent of the seats.[3] Lawrence *et al.* (1975) conclude that, so far as contested elections were concerned, there can be no doubt that the substitution of the simple majority system for PR was the main cause of the tendency for the two larger parties to gain a bigger share of seats than votes.[4]

The abolition of PR made it more difficult for the smaller parties to win seats. In 1925 the Northern Ireland Labour Party won three seats, but in the 1929 election it lost two of these. In 1929 Independent Unionists gained 9 per cent of the vote and four seats, but in 1938 they gained 29 per cent of the vote and only three seats. It seems that the main reason for the abolition of PR was to help prevent the growth of independent Unionism. Announcing its abolition in 1929, Lord Craigavon pointed to the desirability of eliminating all opposition except that represented by the Nationalist Party.[5]

In the 1960s the electoral system clearly disadvantaged the Northern Ireland Labour Party. In 1962 the party polled 76,842 votes—half the number of votes cast for the Unionist Party—but won only four seats. In 1965 it polled 66,323 votes, but won only two seats. It is instructive to examine the ratio of votes to successful candidates in contested seats at these two elections. In 1962 it took 10,000 votes to elect a Unionist MP, 7,500 to elect a Nationalist, and 19,000 to elect a Labour member. In 1965 it took 8,500 to elect a Unionist, 16,500 to elect a Nationalist, and 33,000 to elect a Labour member.

Another effect of the abolition of PR was an increase in the number of uncontested seats from 1 in 1921 and 12 in 1925 to 22 in 1929 and 33 in 1933. This was due to the creation of single-member constituencies and to the fact that many of them contained an overwhelming majority of supporters of one party, usually the Unionist Party.

In 1973 the single transferable vote method of PR and a system of multi-member constituencies was reintroduced for the election to the Assembly. The British government hoped that this would reduce political polarisation by diminishing the dominance of the Unionist Party and helping the centre parties to gain greater representation. In practice the new electoral system had only a marginal effect in this direction. Generally there has been a close relationship between the proportion of votes cast for the various parties and the seats won by them. In 1973 there was a slight distortion in proportional allocation. The Official Unionists, Unofficial Unionists and Alliance were over-represented by one seat each, the SDLP by two seats. In 1975 the system operated to the advantage of the United Ulster Unionist Coalition, which won 54 per cent of the first-preference votes but gained 62 per cent of the seats. This was largely due to the voting strategy of the UUUC supporters, who kept lower preferences effectively within the UUUC grouping. The Vanguard Unionist Party, in particular, benefited from this, receiving 12.7 per cent of the total first-preference votes and winning 14 seats (18 per cent of total), while the Democratic Unionist Party received 14.7 per cent of first preferences and won 12 seats (15 per cent of total). The Official Unionists obtained almost double the proportion of Vanguard's first preferences (25.4 per cent) but won only 19 seats (23 per cent of total). The Alliance Party won 8 seats (10 per cent of total) at both elections, with 8 per cent of first preferences in 1973 and 10 per cent in 1974, whereas clearly it would have found it difficult to win one seat under the simple majority single-constituency system.

Generally the centre parties polled poorly in both elections. The expectation that the STV system would produce a large bloc of moderate opinion was not fulfilled. This was partly due to the fact that cross-voting on a large scale did not take place. In 1973 88 per cent of Unionist and loyalist transfers went to other Unionists and loyalists; only 3 per cent to centre parties, and none at all to the SDLP or Republican candidates. Similarly, 82 per cent of the SDLP and Republican transfers were mutually exchanged, 18 per cent to centre parties, and none to Unionists and loyalists. Only 0.25 per cent (848 out of a total of 308,197 transfers) crossed from one side of the sectarian divide to the other.[6] Also the centre parties, particularly the Labour Party and the Unionist Party of Northern Ireland, lost many of their lower preferences to the loyalists. In 1975 the general pattern of transfers showed the UUUC and SDLP maintaining support within their own group. In the Convention election 88 per cent of transfers to UUUC candidates came from other UUUC candidates, and 65 per cent of transfers to SDLP came from other SDLP candidates. There was again almost no transfer of votes across the sectarian divide: UUUC candidates obtained 412 transfers from SDLP, and SDLP 185 transfers from UUUC candidates.[7] Transfers between the centre parties were more frequent, although there were also substantial transfers between UPNI, NILP and UUUC candidates and between Alliance and SDLP. In 1975 there was no marked process of transfers between the three parties who had participated in the power-sharing administration, particularly between UPNI and SDLP.

Grouping together Unionists and loyalists on one side and the SDLP and Republican parties on the other, the pattern of results at PR elections was not very different from previous Stormont elections, with the exception of greater representation for the small centre parties and an end to uncontested seats. The introduction of proportional representation did not change voting behaviour, and the UUUC in 1975 was able to manipulate the system by strategic nomination and voting to secure representations in excess of proportionality. The main effect of PR may have been to diminish the dominance of the Official Unionist Party in that it encouraged the splinter Unionist groups to contest elections. The kind of electoral agreements made by the UUUC parties in allocating candidates for the multi-seat constituencies would have been much more difficult in a system of single-member constituencies. The continuance of PR may mean that Unionist divisions are more likely to be reflected electorally.

The Nature of the Party System: Societal Divisions

One of the main features of the political system has been the close identification between political preference and religious affiliation, between support for the Unionist Party and membership of a Protestant denomination, and between support for anti-partition parties (mainly the Nationalist Party) and membership of the Roman Catholic Church. Ulster's political parties have represented a politico-religious interest rather than a socio-economic interest.

Political parties may represent such an interest in three different senses. Firstly, electoral support may be drawn mainly from members of one religious group. Surveys and opinion polls have shown that this is largely true. Rose's investigation in 1968 found that 79 per cent of Protestants identified with the Unionist Party and 51 per cent of Catholics with the Nationalist Party. Catholics have been more divided in party loyalties, and the Nationalist Party operated in the rural areas rather than in Belfast, where Catholics tended to vote for Republican Labour or Northern Ireland Labour Party candidates. In 1970 the Social Democratic and Labour Party emerged to replace the Nationalist Party and quickly gained the support of a large majority of Catholics.

Secondly, political parties may be said to consist of people who belong to the respective religious groups. The Unionist Party has had an almost exclusively Protestant membership. In 1959 a suggestion that Catholics should be admitted as members of the Unionist Party received little support from the party leadership, and in 1968 a Catholic member of Queen's University Unionist Association was unsuccessful in his attempt to become an election candidate. The SDLP has a small number of Protestant members, and two of its candidates in the 1975 Convention election were Protestants. However, such cases are unusual, and although no statistics are available on the subject, it appears that membership of the main parties has been almost exclusively confined to each side of the religious divide.

Thirdly, the policies of the political parties may be said to represent religious interests. This has been true in a limited sense. The major parties have claimed to be non-sectarian in the formulation of policy and have made electoral appeals to all sections of the community. In practice party policy can be said to reflect the ideals and interests of the communities they represent on political, social and moral issues which often have religious undertones; but specific religious values relating to such matters as Sunday observance obtrude only occasionally. The dominant issue in Northern Ireland party politics—the question of partition and the constitutional status of the province—is one on which the two religious groups have conflicting views. Heslinga (1971) expresses this forcefully: 'If for an Irish Roman Catholic his nationality is hardly separable from his religion, the same is broadly true of the Ulster Protestant.'[8] He declares the driving force of both Irish nationalism and Ulster Unionism to be religion. The major political parties can thus be said to represent the interests and aspirations of the two religious groups.

The influence of religion and politics is shown by the weakness of the Northern Ireland Labour Party and the failure of its attempt to acquire working-class support across religious lines. Appeals addressed to socio-economic groups and policies based on social and economic premises or socialist principles have attracted little interest in an area with a large farming community, a small trade union movement, a tradition of small family businesses, and a conservative church influence. The NILP has also had difficulty in making up its mind on the issue of partition. In 1945 the party chose to identify itself with the Union with Great Britain, largely on the grounds that the standard of living of workers could best be improved by Northern Ireland's continued membership of the United Kingdom. The party was attempting to unite Protestant and Catholic workers in calling for more socialist policies within the context of the existing constitutional arrangement. Party membership was mainly Protestant, and the party's stand on the constitution led to the creation of a rival Republican Labour Party in Belfast. During the period 1958–62 the NILP began to make some headway on social and economic platforms in working-class constituencies of Belfast and won four Stormont seats in the 1962 general election. Since 1966, however, the increase in community polarisation and sectarianism and the formation of new parties have proved disastrous for the NILP. Most of its Catholic support was lost to the new Social Democratic and Labour Party, and much of its radical middle-class support switched to the Alliance Party. The party has performed very poorly in recent elections, receiving only 1.4 per cent of first preferences in the 1975 Convention election.

In contrast to its exclusive appeal to a single religious grouping, the Unionist Party has sought support across class lines, and its membership and support covers a wide spectrum of Protestant society. A prominent Unionist politician has called the party an umbrella, a common stand, a great crusading cause.[9] Party membership was drawn from all levels of society. Sayers (1955) refers to the party as representing a fusion of classes brought about by a common loyalty to country and religion.[10] The party sought to cover a wide range of social and economic interests, although the leadership was largely in the hands of the old landed families and wealthy businessmen. There was an Ulster Unionist Labour Association to foster the identification of working men with Unionism. This, however, was hardly necessary as the Protestant working class seldom deviated from its wholehearted support of the Unionist Party.

Class tensions have come to the fore at various times. There was a long tradition of Independent Unionists representing working-class constituencies in Belfast. Most of these independents were ultra-Protestant and ultra-loyalist in their views but to the left of the party on social and economic issues. There have also been specific movements such as the Progressive Unionist Party of the 1930s, which tried to promote a programme of social and economic reform but had no electoral success. It has been argued that a decision after 1946 to reform the structure of the Unionist Party and open its institutions to a wider range of membership in terms of social class resulted in the decline of independents.[11] It is only in more recent years that class tensions have again emerged within the party. The growth of the Protestant Unionists and later the Democratic and Vanguard Unionist movements have been interpreted as a working-class revolt against both the traditional landowning leadership of the party and the conservative social policies of the party. It is doubtful, however, whether Unionist voters perceived such a difference between the three anti-Assembly parties in 1973. From his analysis of data on the 1973 and 1975 elections McAllister (1976 b) concludes that class differences accounted for no variation in party support.

Ideological Politics

The second major characteristic of the Northern Ireland political system can be described as its ideological nature.

The term ideology can be defined as a comprehensive, consistent set of beliefs revolving around a few pre-eminent values relating to a political system. An ideology is dogmatic rather than pragmatic and tends to be rigid and inflexible and resistant to new information or opposing views. It tends to distort or over-simplify reality and is prone to reductionism, i.e. complex issues are reduced to simple explanations. It can guide and influence thinking on all questions and issues, providing interpretations and solutions that can be easily grasped. An ideology also has what has been termed a high dynamic potential, i.e. it has a strong emotional appeal embracing ideas and principles that are capable of raising and inspiring men to action. Ideologies are orientated to conflict and are hostile and intolerant towards political opponents and tend to dichotomous 'black-and-white' thinking. An ideology is also personalised and ritualised: it has its heroes, leaders, martyrs, myths, documents, rituals and symbols. Some of the beliefs or principles of an ideology may not be held by its adherents to be as significant as others. Thus it is possible to break down an ideology into components.[12] A distinction may be drawn between fixed elements, which are rigid, dogmatic, impermeable to argument and evidence, passionately felt, and have a high dynamic potential, and flexible elements, which have a lower dynamic potential (as they are not so passionately held), are open to argument and compromise, and may be changed at some time.

It can be argued that in Northern Ireland there exists an ideological belief system. There are two opposed and actively conflicting ideologies, one of which has consistently been dominant in the province's political institutions. The basic principles or components of Ulster Unionism are the maintenance of a separate Northern Ireland polity, resistance to an autonomous United Ireland,

D*

rigid adherence to the tenets of the Protestant faith, determination to uphold British traditions and the British way of life, and loyalty to the British Crown. Ulster Unionism thus has many of the attributes of an ideology as outlined above. As Wallace (1971) has noted, there has always been a strong element of fear in Unionism—fear of Roman Catholicism as inimical to the political and religious values of Protestants, and fear of coming under an all-Ireland parliament dominated by Catholics.[13] Ulster Unionism has consequently a strong defensive element. It has been strongly opposed to compromise or bargaining on its basic principles and has been particularly hostile to the principles of Irish nationalism. Adherence to the Roman Catholic religion combined with a belief in a unified Irish nation-state and consequent attachment to Irish cultural values form the basic elements of the opposing Irish nationalist ideology. While expressions of the ideology are non-sectarian, in practice Irish nationalism has become very closely associated with Roman Catholicism.

A criticism of the use of the concept of ideology is that ideologies usually have only an elitist appeal. Thus a distinction is sometimes made between the beliefs of an elite and the dormant or latent ideological beliefs of the community at large. There is considerable evidence to support the view that in Northern Ireland ideological beliefs are widely held among the whole population. This is suggested by the high degree of political participation in elections, in political movements and in public demonstrations, and by attitude surveys and voting behaviour.

One reason for the strength of ideological feeling is the existence of supporting types of institutions. Minar (1961) has pointed out that wherever ideologies seem to be important in politics they have a firm organisational basis. Northern Ireland has extensive organisational underpinnings for its ideologies. In the case of Ulster Unionism, apart from the large, well-organised Ulster Unionist Party as the main exponent of the ideology, there is the underpinning of the Orange Order as a politico-religious movement advocating loyalty to the British Crown and the Protestant faith and interlocking with both the Unionist Party and the churches. The Orange Order has direct representation on the Ulster Unionist Council, the controlling body of the party, and traditionally was in a position to influence party and, therefore, government policy. Great importance is also attached to symbols, parades, demonstrations, commemorations, music and anthems. These are emotional mechanisms which have been an important factor in maintaining Unionism. Rival mechanisms and symbols were evident on a smaller scale among the nationalist opponents of Unionism.

Ulster Unionism presents a clearer example of an ideology than its Irish nationalist opponent, mainly because its principles have found their most unequivocal expression in the Unionist Party and have received mass support from the entire Protestant community. The Catholic/nationalist position was somewhat less clear, since there was a fundamental division within the Catholic community between an attitude of active hostility to the state and acceptance of it as a reality that had to be lived with. This ambivalence was reflected in the historical evolution of the principal political organ through which the nationalist ideology was articulated, the Nationalist Party. The party was always strongly opposed to the existence of the Northern Ireland state, but in the course of the 1920s it dropped its original absentionist parliamentary policy and eventually, in 1965, consented to accept the role of official parliamentary Opposition. Party principles were concerned almost solely with partition. By 1970 the Nationalist Party had been replaced by the SDLP, which accepted that Northern Ireland existed with the consent of the majority, although it remained firmly committed to the ultimate unification of Ireland. Adherents of the Catholic/nationalist ideology were not in a position to realise all its values and objectives, and many of its components or principles were in the flexible categories. Traditionally the basic principles of Ulster Unionism have been rigid and uncompromising. Lord Brookeborough in 1959 stated there is no element of change in Unionism: 'If it is called inflexible, then that shows our principles are not elastic.'

Some of the traditional dogmas have been placed under substantial pressure in recent years. The period of dislocation and disturbance began with the changes initiated by Captain O'Neill in the relationship with the Irish Republic and in community relations and with his attempt to meet the demands of the Civil Rights movement. This was followed by the suspension of the Stormont parliament in 1972 and by proposals for the sharing of political power in a new Executive and for a Council of Ireland. Whereas Captain O'Neill's reforms had concerned more flexible components, these later developments had profound implications for some of the fundamental principles of the Unionist ideology; and it is therefore not surprising that the section of the Unionist Party which urged acceptance of them was eventually isolated and rejected.

The Ulster Unionists have thus once again committed themselves to the fundamental beliefs of their ideology, although the constitutional crisis has forced some rethinking on a number of important principles. While it is difficult to categorise the component elements of Ulster Unionism, the following scheme delineates the principal features described above.

Fixed elements
{
  Rejection of a united Ireland
  Maintenance of the border
  Continuance of the Northern Ireland state and the Union with Great Britain
  Political ascendency of Unionists
}

Flexible elements
{
  Social and economic policy
  Housing
  Education
  Restoration of the old local government systems
  Economic relationship with Republic of Ireland
  Local control of security and police
  Maintenance of policies reflecting Protestant interests (e.g. Sunday observance)
}

Obviously it is possible for various principles to move from one category to another: thus some Unionists have even been discussing the possibility of negotiated independence for Ulster—a view totally at odds with the basic principle of the Union with Britain. Another way of classifying the Unionist ideology is to draw distinctions between liberal Unionist, traditional Unionist and Protestant Unionist, with the liberal wing being more flexible on most issues,[14] the traditional wing stressing the fixed and intractable elements, and Protestant Unionists placing more emphasis on the religious values.

Consequences of the Political System

It is possible to examine the major consequences of this political system which was characterised by a dominant party and ideological politics.

(1) *Conflict*

Northern Ireland's political system has always had a marked tendency towards conflict. When political parties and factions are based on religious, ethnic, racial, regional or language differences, compromise is more difficult than when parties represent a class or socio-economic interest. In the latter cases matters of dispute are more open to settlement by bargaining, and it is relatively easy for both sides to give way. But where political parties are divided on issues of national, religious or ethnic sentiment, party principles are more rigid and uncompromising, and consensus is therefore much more difficult. Furthermore, in Northern Ireland there was a fundamental division over the very existence of the state; this feature is in stark contrast to one of the underlying conventions of Western democracies—the consensus concerning the basic constitutional arrangements of the state. The interests and values of the main political parties in Northern Ireland were therefore inherently geared to the production of conflict rather than to the propagation of consensus and compromise.

(2) *An Ideological Style of Political Discourse*
The ideological nature of political thought has had a marked effect on the way in which policy problems are analysed. Political debate in Ulster has tended to be dominated by the sectarian issues implicit in the rigid division of society into two conflicting groups. The ideological style of political discourse reflects antagonistic relationships, partisan hostility, dogmatism and resistance to compromise rather than the give and take of pluralist politics. The style of debate is linked to ideological motivation and is based on hostility and intolerance towards political opposition. Ultimately the way politicians analyse issues of public policy affects both their own behaviour and the processes by which decisions on these issues are reached.

(3) *A Conflict Model of Policy-Making*
The way in which a large number of policies were determined was strongly influenced by ideological considerations, for example in the field of education. Different models of policy-making may operate in different systems, and in Northern Ireland policy-making has to a large extent involved what can be described as conflict and command processes. In the conflict model the preferences of various groups are largely incompatible, and if no group's view prevails automatically, the conflict process may be the means by which a decision is reached. Where group preferences are intensely held and divergent policy-making involves conflictual relationships, there may in some cases be recourse to violence. In the command process the views of one group of persons are clearly dominant over all others. There is no dispute or bargaining, and access to policy-making is simply denied to minority groups. These processes may be contrasted with bargaining processes, competitive processes or co-operative processes. In Northern Ireland there were many examples of command and conflict processes, although it is not possible to claim that all issues of policy were determined by one type of process.

(4) *Lack of Electoral Accountability*

Given the rigidity of political attitudes and voting habits, elections hardly served as a method of making politicians accountable to the electorate. This was most clearly illustrated by the large number of uncontested seats in Northern Ireland general elections. The largest number of uncontested seats was 33 in 1933, i.e. 64 per cent of the seats. At elections between 1929 and 1965 between twenty and twenty-five seats were uncontested. The majority were Unionist seats, but an average of six Nationalist seats were uncontested. In the 1958 election 25 out of a total of 37 Unionist candidates were returned unopposed. Some seats were almost permanently uncontested. Mid-Down was contested for the first time in 1964, and South Antrim in 1965. Given the predictability of voting and results, it is not surprising that candidates and parties saw no need to campaign or to devise electoral programmes; there were very few floating voters in Northern Ireland to be won over.

The two main parties concentrated on the border issue. Until 1964 the Nationalist Party had never issued any clear declaration of policy, and, as McAllister (1975 b) comments, 'Even if a set of policy objectives had been adopted, they would not have been able to press them, due to the second factor, the total lack of party organisation.'[15] The Nationalists were able to win nine or ten seats without any constituency or central organisation. The Unionist Party, on the other hand, had an efficient electoral organisation, though it was rarely needed. The party did not need to appeal to Catholics or have Catholic support to win elections, and both the Unionist and Nationalist Parties recognised that the chances of winning over a significant proportion of Catholics or Protestants was practically nil and therefore scarcely worth the effort. Between 1958 and 1962 the Northern Ireland Labour Party made a strong electoral challenge in Belfast, campaigning on the social and economic record of the government, but it was not able to win more than four seats. The Unionist Party had little tradition of issuing detailed policy programmes; its manifestoes concentrated merely on constitutional issues and safeguarding the Union. One commentator has noted that the party had members capable of producing policy documents on such matters as economic policy and penal reform, but their talents were never utilised.[16]

Appeals to the electorate on policies unrelated to fundamental constitutional issues were rare and largely unnecessary. With electoral support guaranteed, there was no political need to produce solutions to the unemployment or housing problems in order to attract voters. Government policy on social and economic questions had few electoral consequences.

(5) *A Frustrated Opposition*

Partition had left Nationalist politicians and their supporters with a legacy of bitterness and frustration which was reflected in their early abstentionist policy. It appeared impossible for the Opposition to gain access to power by winning a majority in parliament. When eventually they accepted the role of official Opposition and participated fully in parliament they were given little opportunity to influence policy. As has been described in Chapter 3, few of their policy ideas were ever accepted by the government, and they were given few posts of responsibility in parliament. The government had little need to pay attention to Opposition demands or protests, and the Opposition could be largely ignored. The Nationalists concentrated mainly on reiterating their traditional policies on partition and safeguarding the interests of the nationalist community through protests against government policy and actions. McAllister has concluded that the effect of the Nationalist style of opposition was to help further the endemic political parochialism in the province and give rise to apathy and a feeling of helplessness among the minority.[17] The small group of Republican Labour MPs tended to take a more active opposition role, but again the aim was mainly to fulfil a 'protest' function.

Clearly frustration with exclusion from power and influence can become a serious matter if it leads to militant groups advocating violence as the only method of ending this exclusion. Irish Republican groups willing to condone and use force to achieve the ideal of an Irish Republic embracing thirty-two counties have existed throughout Northern Ireland's history with varying degrees of activity and support. Republican candidates have won few seats at Stormont, although they were more successful in Westminster elections, where the Nationalist Party did not put up candidates.

By 1969 the political frustrations of the Catholic community were such that they led to the replacement of the Nationalist Party and its traditional outlook by the new Social Democratic and Labour Party as the main vehicle for the expression of Catholic/nationalist opinion. This reflected the failure of the Nationalist Party to articulate the changing demands of the minority community, particularly the demand for greater participation in public life. This change was influenced by the rise of a new articulate Catholic middle class, the rising aspirations of many Catholics, and their increasing awareness of their relative deprivation.[18] It has also been argued that there was a growing secularisation of politics in the Catholic community, with the Church less involved in politics and public policy, which made way for the emergence of a competent lay leadership in the community.[19] The SDLP thus came into being as a well-organised party determined that it should not be permanently excluded from political power.

(6) *The Distribution of Power within the Unionist Party*

The dominance of the Unionist Party has meant that the party's organisational and representative bodies have had a significant amount of power and influence. In a political landscape of un-contested seats and predictable results the real responsibility for producing a large number of MPs rested with the constituency organisations.

Table 14: Central Structure of the Ulster Unionist Party, 1970[20]

	Council	Standing committee	Executive committee
Constituency associations	306	102	30
Women's associations	234	78	–
Orange County Grand Lodges	122	16	2
Ulster Unionist Labour Association	20	5	2
Women's Unionist Council	20	5	2
Ulster Reform Club	12	2	–
Queen's University Unionist Voters' Association	12	2	–
Apprentice Boys of Derry	6	2	–
Willowfield Unionist Club	6	2	–
Association of Loyal Orangemen	10	2	–
Unionist Society	12	2	–
Northern Ireland peers	7	7	–
Stormont MPs	34	34	1
Westminster MPs	10	10	1
Senators	18	18	–
Wives of MPs, senators, peers	14	3 (max. 10)	–
Co-opted members	103 (max. 120)	20	–
Young Unionists	50	50	2 (+ 10 others)
Total	996	360	50

The details of the central structure of the party is shown in Table 14. There are some surprising features. Firstly, various Protestant organisations had a special position on the Ulster Unionist Council, the party's central controlling body. Representatives of the Orange Order and associated groups made up one-seventh of the council delegates. Secondly, there was a large proportion of women on the council. Apart from the large direct representation of women's associations, many of the delegates from the constituency associations were also women; in 1970, for example there were two female delegates to every male delegate from the Belfast constituencies. Thirdly, 120 places were reserved for the co-option of distinguished persons, who, having been once co-opted, have generally tended to become permanent members. Fourthly, there were a number of representatives from rather obscure bodies, such as the Willowfield Unionist Club, the Ulster Reform Club and the Queen's University Voters' Association. The main business of the council was delegated to its standing committee, a smaller body of 360 delegates which met quarterly. Politicians had a stronger voice on this committee. MPs and senators made up between 20 and 25 per cent of the membership, and the Orange Order had only a 5 per cent weighting compared with 12 per cent in the council. The standing committee had power to consider and comment on party policy. However, the real centre of power in the party was the executive committee of fifty members. This consisted of thirty constituency representatives elected from and by the standing committee, plus two delegates from the Ulster Unionist Labour Association, two from the Orange Order, two Young Unionists, the party leader, the chairman and vice-chairman of the standing committee, and seven council officers. This executive met once a month and operated through a house committee and other smaller committees dealing with finance and publicity. The executive really ran the party, and it appointed the party headquarters staff. It also had the power to reject, amend or oppose any resolutions submitted for the annual conference. The executive was in theory responsible to the larger standing committee, but in practice most of its decisions and recommendations were not questioned. The executive effectively controlled the party machine.

The power of the party's central organisation is demonstrated not so much by its influence on policy (since conflict on policy was rare) but by its influence on the position of the leader of the party. The standing committee was responsible for the selection of the leader of the party, and the leader of the party was, as a matter of course, also the Prime Minister. When Major Chichester-Clark was chosen as Prime Minister in May 1969 by the parliamentary party he had to go before a special meeting of the standing committee to seek its approval. The committee appointed him leader of the party and passed a vote of confidence in his policies. Earlier in 1969 a special meeting of the full Ulster Unionist Council had been called, and the narrow seventy-five-vote majority which Captain O'Neill received from an attendance of about 600 probably had a significant influence on his decision to resign. In 1970 there was a vote of no confidence in the law-and-order policies of Major Chichester-Clark at a meeting of the executive committee. In January 1974 Mr Faulkner resigned as party leader after his policy on the Sunningdale Agreement was defeated at a meeting of the council. Up until 1972 the party organisations could indulge in pressuring or replacing the leadership without endangering party unity or its election prospects. It is clear that, with the lack of any effective opposition from outside the party, the main threat to the Unionist leadership has always been an internal one.

Unionist constituency associations were also able to exert influence. Each local association was an autonomous body which largely made its own rules. Each constituency was responsible for the selection of candidates; there was no central list of prospective candidates. One of the more unusual features of the system was the practice of making sitting members reapply with other prospective candidates for adoption, a rare occurrence in British party politics. Constituency associations were particularly active in the period 1969–74 in making public objections to government policy. In 1970 five Unionist Party branches in the Prime Minister's own constituency of South Londonderry—including his own branch—passed motions of no confidence in the government.

Power within the Unionist Party has lain to a large extent in the hands of constituency associations and delegates to the central party organisations rather than with the parliamentary party or party headquarters. In these circumstances it was almost impossible to enforce a party line. Although for long periods the power of the extra-parliamentary groups was not used because of the lack of divisive issues, events between 1969 and 1974 showed the strength of the activists at grassroots level. The autonomy of constituency bodies and the local organisational structure of the party has allowed these local activists to play a frequently decisive role in controlling the Unionist Party and its policies.

(7) *Effect on the Civil Service*

The significant effect on continuous one-party rule on the Civil Service is discussed in detail in Chapter 7. Ideological politics have been a constraint preventing the Civil Service formulating more proposals for change and inhibiting progress in dealing with social problems.

Conclusion

The main characteristics of the Northern Ireland political system have been the close identification between party preference and religious affiliation, the dominance of the Unionist Party and the fragmentation of the opposition. It was only after 1969 that divisions within the Unionist Party led to the emergence of splinter parties able to contest elections with some degree of success. This development has been fostered by the introduction of proportional representation, but it may not be a permanent feature of the political system, as the splinter Unionist parties have evolved around particular personalities. Parties representing an interest outside the main religious/political divide (e.g. the Labour Party) did not make significant inroads into the traditional groups, so that the original alignments remained sharply defined. More recently the Alliance Party's advocacy of moderate policies has had a degree of success without making a dramatic breakthrough. The UPNI as a liberal Unionist party has had little support. The traditional parties, Unionist and Nationalist, took up dogmatic positions, largely resistant to change and compromise. Since the collapse of the power-sharing Executive in 1974 the Official Unionist Party has resumed its traditional inflexible policies. The SDLP has within it strains of both the traditional and more radical attitudes of nationalist thought. Its traditional wing has emphasised Irish unity and has tended to emerge as the dominant force within the party, as evidenced by the resignation from the party of Mr Paddy Devlin, and from the party executive of Mr Austin Currie, both prominent figures on the radical wing. Thus, following the upheavals of the early 1970s, both the Official Unionist Party and the SDLP have been reverting to more traditional positions. Unionist dominance and ideological politics seem likely to continue as major characteristics of the political system.

6

Pressure Groups

PRESSURE groups are organised groups outside party and parliamentary structures which at various times seek to influence government policy. Most groups or organisations from time to time seek to influence government on behalf of their members or in the promotion of specific interests, but some groups have more status and influence than others. Some groups seek to influence government occasionally, others on a fairly continuous basis. One of the main characteristics of pressure-group activity in Northern Ireland has been the influence of organisations representing religious interests in the community, especially the churches and the Orange Order.

The Churches

The churches in Northern Ireland have on occasions acted as powerful pressure groups. The Protestant churches had better channels of access to the government and have exerted a greater influence on government policy than the Roman Catholic Church, although in practice the government has also found it necessary to respond to demands from the Roman Catholic Church. Education was the main area in which the churches made a determined attempt to influence policy, and here they have been largely successful.

Given the proposals of Northern Ireland's first Education Act, 1923, the reaction of the churches was hardly unexpected. The act proposed the transfer of existing schools from mainly voluntary church control to local education authorities. It also proposed that education should be secular and that religious instruction should only be given after school hours. The school management committees were to include the former managers of transferred schools, but they would have no power to appoint teachers. Schools remaining outside the state system would receive a limited state subsidy. The Protestant churches objected strongly to these proposals and began a widespread pressure-group campaign to have the legislation changed.[1]

In 1924 the United Education Committee of the Protestant Churches was formed to co-ordinate the campaign in co-operation with the Grand Orange Lodge of Ireland. The committee had several meetings with the Prime Minister and the cabinet and threatened to ensure that voters at forthcoming elections should vote only for members pledged to amend the act.[2] After a series of negotiations in 1925 with the Minister of Education, Lord Londonderry, the United Education Committee was eventually successful in securing the deletion of the secularising clauses and their replacement by a provision permitting local education authorities to provide Bible tuition. The Minister of Education described this agreement as a concordat which had the approval of all parties to the dispute.[3]

In 1928 the United Education Committee demanded further amendment of the legislation and again threatened to ensure that candidates approved by Unionist associations for a forthcoming election would be pledged to support its case if returned to parliament. This led the Prime Minister to sanction further concessions in the 1930 Education Bill. The fact that in both 1925 and 1930 the government was forced to take an action (the endowment of religion) that was in direct contravention of the 1920 act illustrates the enormous political power wielded by the Protestant/Orange pressure group in the 1920s.

The United Education Committee was brought into action again in the 1940s when the Attorney-General ruled that a clause compelling teachers to give Bible instruction was unconstitutional and the 1947 Education Bill accordingly proposed changes in the light of this finding. Repeated meetings of representatives of the Protestant churches, the Orange Order, senior civil servants, the Prime Minister and the Minister of Education took place between 1943 and 1947. The Minister of Education, Colonel Samuel Hall-Thompson, with the backing of the Prime Minister, resisted the main demands of the churches. The minister did not hold a high opinion of the churches' representatives. As he reported to the cabinet in 1944 after a lengthy meeting with the representatives of the Protestant churches, 'The discussion was at times confused and once rather heated, and I had some trouble to persuade the deputation to discuss the draft clauses sensibly.'[4] In the end a compromise was worked out through a conscience clause, and agreement was also reached on the right of representation by Protestant churches on the management committees of new state schools.

The United Education Committee was clearly an example of a successful pressure group; Akenson (1973) writes that no band of

Catholic priests had engaged in politics with the energy and efficacy of the Protestant clergy who led the United Education Committee. Its campaign in the 1940s was less effective than earlier, as the Minister of Education was able to argue that it was not fully representative of the Protestant churches' views. In 1945 he informed the cabinet that the Methodist Church did not agree with the joint board and that there were splits in the Presbyterian Church and the Church of Ireland.[5]

The Protestant churches have maintained a close interest in education policy and are, of course, represented on the local education boards. The main Protestant denominations are represented on the Religious Education Council, which is responsible for the religious education syllabuses used in state schools. The main channel of communication with the government was through special committees in the central organisation of the churches, for example the Education Committee of the Presbyterian Church, which in 1970 submitted evidence to the Macrory Review Body on local government and later made representations to the Ministry of Education on the government's scheme for a new structure of educational administration. The same committee has also called for the abandonment of the 'eleven plus' selection procedure and for greater progress in the field of nursery education.

The Roman Catholic Church has also had a major influence on educational policy. The proposals in 1923 for a secular system of education and the transfer of schools to state control were even more unacceptable to the Roman Catholic Church than to the Protestant campaigners. It refused to transfer any of its schools and resolutely maintained its own separate system of Catholic schools outside state control. It did, however, negotiate with the government on the issue of grants to voluntary schools. In 1930 grants had been increased to cover 50 per cent of capital expenditure and running costs. A deputation consisting of church leaders, Nationalist MPs and a teachers' representative had met the Minister of Education in 1939 to press for 75 per cent grants, but the Prime Minister was later to reveal that 50 per cent was the maximum the Unionist Party could be persuaded to agree to.[6]

In the 1940s the Roman Catholic Church once again presented its demands for 75 per cent grants. In 1945 a deputation consisting of two bishops, ten senior clergy, fifteen MPs and a teachers' representative had discussions with the Minister of Education but rejected any demand of state control over the management of their schools in return for higher financial assistance.[7] In 1947 the grants for the construction and maintenance of voluntary schools were increased to 65 per cent.

In Britain grants to voluntary schools rose to 70 per cent in 1959 and to 80 per cent in 1967, and parity of treatment was demanded by the Roman Catholic Church in Northern Ireland. In 1968 a new government bill was introduced in Stormont to give 80 per cent grants in return for 'maintained' status, the school to be under a management committee of the 'four-and-two' type, i.e. containing four nominees of the school trustees and two nominees of the education authority. The Roman Catholic bishops were somewhat reluctant to accept this scheme. The Bishop of Down and Connor, Dr William Philbin, criticised the scheme on the grounds that increasing the grant to the English level had been made the occasion for an invasion of the established system of Catholic school management; however, the Roman Catholic Primate of All Ireland, Cardinal Conway, gave his approval to some of the proposals. In practice the bishops have found the system acceptable, and the majority of Catholic schools (87 out of 89 secondary schools) now have 'maintained' status. The Roman Catholic Church has been successful in retaining its separate system of schools and, although willing to compromise on the issue of state intervention in the management of schools, it has remained inflexible in its resistance to proposals for ending religiously segregated education. In 1970 Cardinal Conway published a pamphlet, *Catholic Schools*, which argued that segregation was not a divisive factor in society.

The Roman Catholic Church was also involved in a long running battle with the government over the status of the Mater Infirmorum Hospital. This Belfast hospital was owned and managed by the Roman Catholic Church, which wished to ensure that Roman Catholic medical ethics were taught and practised there. The government, however, was unwilling to follow the equivalent British legislation in providing grants for voluntary hospitals which wished to remain outside the state scheme. The hospital did treat National Health Service patients, and it was also a teaching hospital; it thus had a claim for a grant from public funds. There were prolonged negotiations between the Roman Catholic bishops and the ministry on ways of preserving the Mater's identity as a Roman Catholic hospital within the state scheme, and it was not until 1971 that a satisfactory formula was agreed upon.

It is not easy to find other examples of church influence on government policy. In 1964 the Churches' Industrial Council (representing all churches) took an active role in healing the dispute between the government and the Irish Congress of Trade Unions over the recognition of the Northern Ireland Committee of the latter body; and in 1956 the critical reception given by the General

Assembly of the Presbyterian Church to a bill then in parliament for the alteration of family allowances was a significant factor in the government's decision to withdraw the measure.

The Protestant churches have made many public statements on specific issues or passed resolutions at annual meetings, but it is not easy to determine to what extent such pronouncements influenced government policy. Some church resolutions have been fairly radical. In 1972 the Presbyterian General Assembly called for more government action on the lack of employment opportunities and inadequate housing and pledged the support of the Church for the voluntary housing movement.[8] The Methodist Conference also called for action on unemployment during the 1960s.

In the present period of political turmoil the Protestant churches have again sought to make their views known. The two largest churches have special committees for studying and commenting on political developments. In 1970 the Church of Ireland appointed a Role of the Church Committee to study the positive role of the Church in all aspects of political, social and economic life in Ireland. The Presbyterian Church has a Government Committee which has made known its views on political events and has been in frequent contact with members of both the Westminster and Stormont governments. Generally the Protestant churches supported the reform programmes of 1969–70. The social reforms, in particular, were welcomed by the Church of Ireland's Role of the Church Committee in 1970, and both the Presbyterian General Assembly and the Methodist Conference followed suit, the latter body urging the speedy implementation of the reform programme.

The Protestant churches were more cautious in their support for new political institutions. The Role of the Church Committee thought that the Sunningdale Communiqué could represent a major step towards a political solution. The Presbyterian Government Committee deplored the decision of the British government to prorogue the Stormont parliament in 1972, but the 1974 General Assembly affirmed that to provide a framework for order, stability and peaceful development it was essential that there should be a sharing of responsibility and power between different sections of the community.

The Roman Catholic Church has largely maintained its tradition of avoiding open comment on political questions and has thus tended to hold aloof from making public statements or participating in public debate on government policy. This is mainly a reflection of the structure of the church hierarchy. The bishops are individually responsible for their own public statements, and the prerogative of each bishop within his diocese is absolute. Thus although the Archbishop of Armagh is Primate of All Ireland, the office carries no extra jurisdiction and does not permit the Primate to interfere in the affairs of another diocese. The relative silence of the Church may be partly explained by the attitude of the bishops in the Province of Armagh. The present Bishop of Down and Connor, Dr Philbin, whose diocese includes Belfast, is widely recognised as being one of the more conservative members of the hierarchy and not prone to public statements.[9] Some Northern bishops have been criticised for not speaking out more on controversial public issues such as violence and internment. Some of the most articulate comments, including assessment of the government's constitutional proposals, have come from Dr Cahal B. Daly, an Ulsterman who is Bishop of Ardagh and Clonmacnoise in the Republic.[10] In the past some Northern bishops have spoken out strongly on issues, for example on religious discrimination.

From 1921 onwards the Catholic bishops developed a role as spokesmen for the Catholic community in the various dioceses and were recognised by their own community and by the government as having this status.[11] They also established the right to negotiate with government ministers and agencies, but confined their negotiations mainly to matters of education and health. Direct contact between the church leaders and the government was limited on the Roman Catholic side. The Roman Catholic Church while recognising Stormont's existence and while prepared to negotiate with the government was reluctant to give outright approval. There was provision at Stormont for a Roman Catholic priest to take part in prayers, but the Roman Catholic hierarchy never appointed a chaplain until representations were made on this issue by Mr Callaghan in 1969.[12]

The churches may also be described as exerting influence by means of the direct participation of clergymen in politics. There is little evidence of widespread political participation by the clergy in political parties. A survey conducted in 1971 among a sample of clergymen in Northern Ireland showed that only 12 per cent were members of a political party.[13] The Presbyterian Church had the greatest proportion: 20 per cent of its clergy belonged to a political party, compared with 14 per cent of Church of Ireland clergy, 9 per cent of Methodist clergy, and only 3 per cent of Roman Catholic clergy. However, those who did belong to political parties were strongly represented in the hierarchies of the party organisation. This low level of participation is contrary to the popular view of Ulster clergy, an impression unduly influenced by the activities of clergy from the Rev. Ian Paisley's Free Presbyterian Church, who in recent years have played an active role in politics through the Democratic Unionist Party. A few clergymen became cabinet ministers: the Rev. William Corkey, a Presbyterian, was Minister of Education in 1943–44, and the Rev. Robert Moore was Minister of Agriculture from 1947 to 1960.

While very few Roman Catholic clergy belonged to political parties, some local clergy took a leading role in the system by which Nationalist Party candidates were selected. There was a convention system through which prominent Catholics in a constituency were often invited by a local priest to come together to select a candidate. On other occasions priests acted as arbitrators between rival individuals or groups, who were disputing a candidature.[14] Clerical involvement in Nationalist politics was usually limited to the work undertaken at election times, but it did serve to further the identification of Catholicism with nationalism.

On a more general level, the churches have undoubtedly exercised a pervasive influence on the overall climate of public discussion and debate. The Protestant influence was apparent on the issue of Sunday observance, and also on policies concerning such social issues as abortion, divorce and homosexuality. The views of the Roman Catholic Church on these social issues was largely in accordance with the views of the Protestant churches, though the question of Sunday observance has remained a persistent bone of contention and has even on occasions become a source of conflict at local government level.

The Orange Order

The Orange Order was born out of agrarian conflict in the late eighteenth century but it did not attain its strong position in the life of Ulster until the later part of the nineteenth century.[15] Its basic objectives have been a mixture of religious and political aims: the defence of the Protestant faith, the protection of the Union with Great Britain, and the maintenance of the constitution of Northern Ireland. It has traditionally expounded civil and religious liberty, although critics would argue that this has been defined in terms of Protestant ascendancy and that the Order has been strongly anti-Catholic. The official view of the Order itself is that it is primarily a religious institution,[16] but it has never claimed that its political purposes are unimportant. Political rather than religious beliefs have been the main source of the Order's public resolutions.[17] In 1950 the head of the Order stated: 'While I agree that we are mainly a religious body, the Order has been in the front rank for generations in preserving our constitutional position.'[18]

The Orange Order performs an important function as an

umbrella Protestant organisation and a unifying force owing to
the fact that its membership is drawn from a large number of
different Protestant churches and sects. It also is a unifying influence
in the class sense in that it is open to all sections of the Protestant
community, although it tends to have few members from the professional and upper middle classes.[19] Despite its strong religious
connections, relatively few clergymen are members. A survey of 150
clergymen showed that only 23 (16 per cent) were Orangemen, and
that of these the majority (14) were Church of Ireland clergy.[20]
The Orange Order has closer historical links with the Church of
Ireland than with the other Protestant denominations. In its political
role the Order has helped to mould a unified Unionist Party and
ideology, and it has performed an integrative function in fusing
religious feelings with Ulster Unionism, British patriotism and anti-
Catholicism. It also occupies an important place in the social and
community life of the province, particularly in rural areas. Finally,
it acts as a friendly society and carries out a certain amount of
benevolent work.

The Orange Order has always had close formal links with the
Unionist Party and a large representation on the Ulster Unionist
Council and its standing committee. Many of the other delegates
from constituency associations are also members of the Order. The
number of members of the Unionist Parliamentary Party who have
not been Orangemen has been relatively small: in 1970 only seven
out of thirty-seven, and only three of the cabinet, did not belong to
the Order. Between 1921 and 1972 all Unionist senators, with only
one or two exceptions, were members of the Order. To a large
extent it appears that membership of the Order was necessary for
selection as a candidate. In the light of this, it is hardly surprising
that Unionist politicians should act and think as Orangemen, although not all would have taken Lord Craigavon's stance in 1934:
'I am an Orangeman first and a politician and member of parliament afterwards.'[21]

It is clear that the Orange Order has had a persuasive influence
on the Unionist Party through its formal representation and over-
lapping membership. Its main political manoeuvrings are alleged to
have been in the area of the selection of candidates. There are also
some examples of pressure on internal party matters. In 1959 the
chairman of the Ulster Unionist Council standing committee, Mr
Clarence Graham, suggested that Roman Catholics might be welcome to join the Unionist Party—a remark which led Sir George
Clark, Grand Master of the Grand Orange Lodge of Ireland, to
assert that under no circumstances would this suggestion be coun-
tenanced or accepted by the Orange Order. This veto was forcefully

reasserted in 1971. There have also been occasions when a conflict between the principles of the Order and the public duty of MPs has arisen. In 1968 Mr Phelim O'Neill, then a minister, was expelled from the Order for attending a Roman Catholic church ceremony.

The clearest instances of the Orange Order operating as a pressure group are provided by its activities in regard to education policy, particularly between 1923 and 1948. The Order threw its support behind the pressure group formed by the Protestant churches to force changes in government policy.[22] The most obvious single case of the Order's influence occurred in 1949. A bill proposing that the government pay the national insurance contributions of teachers in voluntary schools was introduced in parliament and aroused strenuous opposition in Unionist circles on the grounds that it was extending the principle of state aid to Roman Catholic schools. There is evidence that the Grand Orange Lodge of Ireland discussed the bill at a meeting attended by the Prime Minister in December 1949, when it was agreed that the Education Bill would be amended slightly and that the Minister of Education would resign. The Prime Minister announced his minister's resignation on the following day. The Orange Order's position was that the Education Act was fully discussed at the meeting and that, in view of the statement by the Prime Minister, it decided to postpone any decision. At the time Mr J. M. Andrews, the head of the Orange Order (and former Prime Minister), was quoted as saying that the Orange Order had a wonderful influence on the affairs of Ulster and that without the Order Ulster could not survive.[23]

It has been alleged that the Orange Order is the power behind the throne, that it is a secret society virtually controlling the Unionist government. There is relatively little documented evidence to suggest that the Order dictated policy to the party or the government. Apart from the educational issues, the Order has mainly expressed views on constitutional matters and on ecumenism. It has rarely made statements about social or economic policy. Sayers (1955) argued that as the Order embraces thousands of working men and is a democratic movement, it could have effectively balanced the upper- and middle-class elements that have traditionally constituted the prime ingredient of Ulster Unionism.[24] The Order's concentration on partition and cold-shouldering the Roman Catholic Church rather than on social reform is largely a reflection of the fact that it is an umbrella organisation covering a wide spectrum of opinion on many social and political issues.

In the 1960s, with support growing for the Northern Ireland Labour Party in Protestant working-class areas, the Order announced that its members were free to support the Labour Party. During the

1960s and 1970s the political ties between Orangeism and Unionism have become less obvious. There are no longer Orange-backed election manifestoes requesting Orangemen to support the official Unionist Party candidates. The growth of other Unionist parties has also helped to reduce the political influence of the Order.

The Orange Order has not played a major role in the political and constitutional upheavals of the 1970s. Apologists for the Order have described its influence on the government as being as proper as the influence of any other responsible organisation. They have claimed that there is no evidence of Orange pressurisation and that it is justifiable to expect that politicians who belong to the Order will think and act as Orangemen.[25] The head of the Orange Order, the Rev. Martin Smyth, said in 1976 that he saw nothing strange in the Orange Institution as a religious body wishing to be involved in politics and society.[26] The policies of the Order have generally been an expression of either sectarian interest or conservative demands in favour of the status quo and traditional values and practices.

It should be noted that there is a Catholic organisation, the Ancient Order of Hibernians, which has attempted to play a similar kind of role in the Catholic community. However, it is a much smaller organisation than the Orange Order and is mainly concentrated in the rural areas. It has a total membership of around 10,000, compared with the Orange Order's estimated membership of 100,000. It had, of course, little influence on the government, although it had some links with the old Nationalist Party, with whose principles it tended to be closely associated. It has at present no influence on the political groupings representing the Catholic community.

Trade Unions

Trade unions have not played as significant a role as a pressure group on the Northern Ireland government as trade unions in Britain have done on the government in Westminster. Trade unions in Northern Ireland have lacked the status to enable them to influence the province's government. This was due partly to the relatively small size of the trade union movement in a region with a large agricultural sector, and partly to the fact that Northern Ireland trade union law differed in many respects from the corresponding British legislation.

The major legislative difficulty was that whereas the Trade Disputes and Trade Unions Act of 1927 was repealed in Great Britain in 1946, it was not until 1958 that the equivalent act was amended in Northern Ireland. Under this act trade unions could not enter upon strikes without fear of them being declared illegal.

During the Second World War the sections of the act that gave the government power to imprison strike leaders were implemented when a number of members of the Amalgamated Engineering Union were given jail sentences. The measure was regarded as a challenge to the right of trade unionists to combine freely and was seen as a symbol of the state's unwillingness to grant unions their full status in society.[27] Even in more recent times the development of trade unionism was still restricted by law. The amendment of the Trade Disputes and Trade Unions Act in 1958 conferred far fewer rights on trade unions in Northern Ireland than had been gained by the total repeal of the original act in Britain.

However, the most important factor affecting the status and role of trade unions was the non-recognition by the government of the Northern Ireland Committee of the Irish Congress of Trade Unions until 1965. Some 80 per cent of trade unionists in Northern Ireland belonged to unions with headquarters in Great Britain, some of which operated through regional structures relating to Northern Ireland or the whole of Ireland. The remainder belonged to unions based solely in Northern Ireland or in the Irish Republic. Owing to local circumstances and the operation of different trade union legislation, the Northern Ireland branches of British unions tend to have much more autonomy than the branches in Britain. This has advantages in enabling unions to concentrate on problems in the Northern Ireland setting, but disadvantages in that the union branches tend to become isolated from their counterparts in Britain and are less able to make use of services provided by union headquarters, for example research and information facilities. The Northern Ireland unions tend to be less well organised and have fewer full-time officials than British unions.

Since 1894 both the Irish unions and the branches of British unions in Northern Ireland have belonged to an Irish Trade Union Congress, which continued to operate after partition. For a period after 1944 there was a split in the all-Ireland organisation, but in 1959 a unified Irish Congress of Trade Unions (ICTU) was formed, with membership open to unions with headquarters in any part of Ireland. Within the ICTU there was provision for a separate Northern Ireland Committee (NIC) composed of members belonging to unions with headquarters in Britain. Although the administrative headquarters of the ICTU was situated in Dublin, the Northern Ireland Committee was allowed a considerable degree of autonomy in dealing with Northern Ireland matters.

The position of successive Unionist governments was that they could not recognise the NIC because it was part of an all-Ireland organisation with its headquarters in Dublin and therefore subject to major rulings from the Republic. A further complication was caused by the fact that the ICTU constitution awarded a majority of seats on its executive council to unions based in the Republic.

The lack of direct communication between the government and the NIC clearly had harmful consequences. In a number of cases the Minister of Labour and government departments reiterated their refusal to recognise the NIC as a reason for rejecting requests for information or declining to receive deputations, although information was given and deputations received when union officials presented themselves as representatives of individual unions, which the government did recognise. On some occasions government departments and other public bodies did correspond with the NIC without raising the question of recognition. In 1952 the NIC reported that the Minister of Health and the Minister of Education had met its deputations and that the Ministry of Commerce had given it a degree of recognition, although the Minister of Labour persisted in his refusal to meet its delegates.[28] Other public bodies also varied in attitude. The National Assistance Advisory Committee refused to meet representatives of the NIC, but the Hospitals Authority in 1957 did ask for nominations to hospital management committees. Generally, however, there was little or no provision for the trade unions to nominate representatives to serve on government-appointed bodies.

In 1961 the Prime Minister, Lord Brookeborough, refused to see a permanent official of the NIC during a lobby on unemployment. In the following year the Prime Minister, together with the Ministers of Commerce and Labour, did meet a deputation from the NIC, but reiterated that the government's position was that the relationship between the NIC and the ICTU would have to be radically changed before there could be any question of a review by the government of its policy of non-recognition.[29]

As well as impairing its communication with the trade unions, the government's refusal to recognise the NIC was harmful to good industrial relations and caused concern to some employers. In 1958 it was not possible to form in Northern Ireland a branch of the British Productivity Council as the government would not allow officials of the NIC to be admitted as members. In 1963 the National Association of British Manufacturers stated that non-recognition was a bar to co-operation between employers and management.

A crisis arose in 1963 when the government proposed setting up an Economic Council to include in its membership both employers and trade union representatives. Six trade union representatives were nominated at a meeting under the auspices of the NIC. However, the government, while accepting five members as representatives of individual unions, refused to accept the sixth, who was a full-time official of the ICTU. The government reiterated its criticism of the lack of autonomy possessed by the NIC and of the constitution of the ICTU as being 'so drawn as to promote a continued movement towards Irish-based and Irish-controlled trade unions, at the expense of the traditional attachment of Northern Ireland's workers to British-based unions'.[30] The trade unions consequently refused to participate, and as a result of their decision the status and efficiency of the Economic Council were greatly reduced. The government did, however, begin informal discussion to overcome the problems. A leading role in these negotiations between the government, Unionist backbenchers and the NIC was played by the interdenominational Churches' Industrial Council.[31] A new climate had been created with the coming to power of Captain O'Neill, who was anxious to solve this problem, which he saw as a barrier to economic progress. In 1964 the Congress of the ICTU passed a resolution giving greater autonomy to the NIC in respect of Northern Ireland affairs, a move which paved the way towards healing the breach with the government.

Government recognition has hardly made a dramatic difference to the power and influence of trade unions, although it has improved their ability to look after their members' interests. The benefit of the new status was shown in 1971 when the government invited the NIC to join in a comprehensive review of industrial relations. Recognition also enabled trade unionists to participate fully in the Northern Ireland Economic Council, and union members played a major role in producing some fairly radical reports, e.g. on the feasibility of state industry.

A basic problem affecting the influence of trade unions was the absence of a large socialist party through which the unions could operate in parliament. Some unions were affiliated to the Northern Ireland Labour Party, but they represented less than ten per cent of total trade union membership.[32] The NIC had arrangements for regular consultations with the small group of NILP MPs, and it also held discussions with the Republican Labour Party, but generally trade unions were very much a pressure group outside the government and the political parties. The task of influencing government was made difficult by the fact that the social and economic policy of the government was largely conservative and the government itself largely unsympathetic to trade unions.

A major constraint on trade union influence has been the dominance of sectarian politics and the division of voters on political and religious lines. The sectarian violence of recent years has further reduced the possibility of a unified working-class movement based on the trade unions. The trade unions' role in the general political situation from 1969 onwards has been that of a pressure group advocating political and social reform, condemning the use of violence and sectarianism for political ends, and expressing concern at the economic effects of violence and political instability.

With the closer involvement of the British government in Northern Ireland since 1969 and direct rule since 1972, the trade union leadership has been granted higher status. The creation of a finance corporation to assist industry and trade was largely a response to trade union pressure. This increased status has also been reflected in the nomination of trade union officials to various public bodies, ranging from the Government Advisory Commission during the first period of direct rule to the Police Authority and the new area boards for running local services. Leading trade unionists have also been appointed to key positions in the new Labour Relations Agency and the Northern Ireland Development Authority.

At the same time the trade union movement and its official leadership has faced a threat to its status with the emergence of loyalist workers' organisations. The extent of their power was fully illustrated during the Ulster Workers' Council strike in 1974 which brought down the power-sharing Executive. An attempt by the NIC to organise a return to work, supported by the presence of Mr Len Murray of the British TUC, was totally unsuccessful and a severe blow to the standing of the NIC.[33] Nevertheless, the official trade union leadership has survived and has had little difficulty in defeating calls for a new loyalist trade union organisation.

These latest developments illustrate the anomalous position of the trade unions in Northern Ireland as part of an all-Ireland organisation with left-wing political views, yet with a membership mainly Unionist and loyalist in outlook. In this situation the trade unions have concentrated on detailed union matters, wages and conditions of work, and have carefully avoided taking a specific line on wider political issues, particularly partition. In this way they have preserved their non-sectarian image. But the price has been high: the trade unions have been forced to accept that they can have little influence on the political views of their members or on government policy regarding Northern Ireland's basic political problems.

Business and Farming Lobbies

Business groups in Northern Ireland tend to be regional organisations of United Kingdom groups. The Northern Ireland Committee of the Confederation of British Industry (CBI) has become the

E

recognised spokesman of employers in industry. The Northern Ireland CBI has been criticised on the grounds that its central office in Northern Ireland functions only as a regional branch of the British CBI, acting as an agency for ideas, policies and publications transmitted from headquarters. Consequently it has been argued that the CBI has not been in a position to provide critical or thorough comment on government policy in Northern Ireland, that CBI policies on local problems are characterised by a consistent lack of originality and freshness, and that many of the ideas are borrowed from Britain and are clearly unsuited to Northern Ireland.[34]

The chief officer of the CBI has quoted the Water Act, 1973, as the best example of how the CBI is able to influence government policy. On this occasion the CBI drew upon expert information available in Britain. On the other hand, it has been alleged that where expert knowledge of local conditions was required little or nothing was forthcoming.[35] Unlike the CBI's regional office in Scotland, the Northern Ireland office did not produce a document on the likely effects of EEC membership. The CBI submitted no written evidence to the government's committee of inquiry on the need to bring company law into line with Britain, nor did it present any submission on the government paper on regional planning strategy. The CBI did, however, present written submissions to the consultants responsible for framing the 1970–75 Development Programme, to the Royal Commission on the Constitution, and to the government body reviewing industrial strategy in 1976. The restricted role of the CBI was mainly due to a lack of resources, staff and funds.

The government accepts the CBI as the representative body of business and commercial interests. Its status as the recognised spokesman for the employers of industry was confirmed in 1971, when it was invited to sit, as the sole representative of the employers' side, alongside the trade unions on the government's review body on industrial relations.

The Unionist government was always strongly committed to private enterprise and depended on the attraction of new private concerns to provide industrial expansion. As well as giving generous grants and allowances to incoming industry, the government also emphasised its own accessibility. The CBI has stated that communications between industry and civil servants was much easier in Northern Ireland than in Britain and that local civil servants were geared to understand the problems of commerce.[36] This responsiveness to the needs and problems of private industry was not only a reaction to specific pressure from the companies; it was also a reflection of the views of the government and backbenchers.

Northern Ireland has always had a large number of small and family businesses, and this sector was strongly represented in the Unionist Party. In the past their concern for the welfare of the private firm has been responsible for their rejection of measures that might appear to challenge the interests of employers. In 1956 backbenchers forced the withdrawal and revision of a Statistics of Trade Bill on the grounds that such a measure was the forerunner of the nationalisation of production, distribution and exchange. Also in the 1950s the government did not follow Britain in increasing death duties on estates, the variation being justified by the high proportion of private companies and family business in Northern Ireland. The Northern Ireland Companies Act differs significantly from the British in that the companies are not obliged to disclose as much information; for example, they are not compelled to publish profit accounts.

Agriculture has always been an important sector of the Northern Ireland economy, and agricultural interests have also made their presence felt on government policy. In 1950 about one-sixth of the workforce, some 100,000 persons, were engaged in agriculture, compared with one-twentieth of the workforce in Britain. By 1972 the numbers had decreased to about 55,000, or about ten per cent of the workforce, and they continue to decline by about 2,000 per annum. The predominant form of agricultural organisation is the small farm worked mainly by the farmer and his family. In 1952 78 per cent of farms were under 50 acres, and only 2.4 per cent were over 150 acres. The government has been responsive to agricultural interests in the province through financial subsidies and advisory and marketing services. It has developed its own schemes for assisting the industry, for example through the payment of a remoteness grant and a subsidy on the transport of eggs. The Development Programme for 1970–75 noted that whereas in Great Britain subsidies are equivalent to half of farmers' incomes, in Northern Ireland they are equivalent to virtually the whole of farmers' incomes.

The farming community has also had its interests well represented at government level, as many MPs are themselves farmers or represent rural constituencies. It might also be concluded that the existence of large rural communities and a large number of small independent farmers has created a conservative influence in social and economic development.

Cause Groups

Cause groups are pressure groups which are formed to campaign on one specific issue or cause and are generally recognised as having less potential for successfully influencing policy. Northern Ireland does not provide many examples of cause groups, especially of successful ones. Most have operated with a small membership, typical examples being the Association for Comprehensive Education and the Northern Ireland Association for the Care and Resettlement of Offenders (an organisation campaigning for penal reform). Perhaps one of the best examples of a cause group is the Northern Ireland Civil Rights Association, founded in 1967 to campaign for such reforms as the recognition of minority rights, an end to discrimination in housing and employment, and the repeal of the Special Powers Act.

The Civil Rights Association was successful in attracting support throughout the province and eventually adopted an official policy of non-violent protest and agitation in order to gain publicity and pressurise the government. The association officially sponsored the march in Londonderry on 5 October 1968 (which produced the first disorders) but took no effective part in its actual organisation. The Civil Rights movement played an important part in the process leading to the adoption of many of the reforms it had demanded. More recently the 'Peace People' movement has emerged as a cause group, although its campaign is aimed at the whole population rather than the government.

Community Groups

Since 1969 there has been a rapid growth in a relatively new type of group, the community group. It was estimated in 1975 that some 500 community groups and associations were in existence. The groups are mainly concerned with improving amenities and facilities in their areas. Their development has been a response to a range of factors: the inadequate provision of public amenities; the breakdown in welfare services at times of acute disruption; and the widespread demand for new services, amenities and recreational facilities, etc., which the statutory authorities had failed to provide. The growth of community groups was also fostered by the official Northern Ireland Community Relations Commission, established in 1969. The Social Needs Act, 1970, made available substantial grants for community projects, including the building of community centres.

The origins of many of the groups lay in the violence of the 1970s, which produced the need for mutual aid and assistance at local level to cope with homelessness, damage to houses, absence of parents, etc., and to provide material aid and relief in cases of physical hardship. Other groups had their origins in street committees and similar local bodies set up to act as vigilante organisations during periods when the threat of attacks across the sectarian divide was particularly rife.

As groups became established they turned their attention to self-help schemes for providing new facilities or alternative forms of social services. They often worked in co-operation with statutory agencies and were dependent on public finance for major projects. Some groups were more successful than others in this kind of activity; among those whose achievements were particularly note-worthy was the Bogside Community Association in Londonderry, which, in addition to creating five community centres with statutory assistance, also set up a home for alcoholics and homeless men, a local advisory centre, and a 'Development Enterprise' project to generate employment.

At the same time nearly all the community groups act as local pressure groups, using lobbying, protest demonstrations, publicity campaigns and rent and rate strikes in order to influence government policies. This activity is largely aimed at forcing response from authorities on local matters such as house repairs and re-development. The Bogside Community Association was successful in persuading the Housing Executive to allow it to participate in drawing up plans for a new housing estate. The Finaghy Community Association in Belfast carried out a survey on an estate to estimate the need for day centres for old people; as a result of this work, the welfare authorities agreed to provide not only a centre but also a pre-school playgroup.

Much of the lobbying by community groups has been directed at redevelopment programmes. One of the most successful campaigns was by the Shankill Redevelopment Association, formed to in-fluence redevelopment policy and, in particular, to oppose plans for high-rise flats—an objective which it succeeded in attaining. Other groups have taken part in public inquiries or in negotiations with the Housing Executive. In 1974 a 'Save the Shankill' campaign won its fight to prevent the building of further flat complexes on the Shankill and to preserve the Lower Shankill as a shopping area. The 'Save the Shankill' lobby was able to threaten to block all demolition work, this threat being backed by the paramilitary groups.[37] Proposals for an inner Belfast ring road encountered strong resistance from an umbrella organisation, the Greater West Belfast Community Association, and this opposition was a factor in the eventual withdrawal of the scheme.

The Paramilitary Groups

While paramilitary groups may be viewed either as political groups or as terrorist groups, it is clear that they also fall within the category of pressure groups, using the most extreme forms of pressure that can be put on a government, namely violence, to force acceptance of their demands. The paramilitary groups, including both the Official and the Provisional IRA, the Ulster Defence Association (UDA) and the Ulster Volunteer Force (UVF), developed originally in 1969–71 as defence organisations for particular areas, but later espoused wider political goals and objectives and endorsed the use of widespread violence. The paramilitary organisations have demonstrated their ability to paralyse the whole of society and the political system. The Provisional IRA through its campaign can claim some responsibility for bringing the Stormont regime to an end and for weakening the political and constitutional links between Britain and Northern Ireland. Militant republican and IRA groups have existed since the establishment of Northern Ireland and have on occasions initiated campaigns of violence, but until the 1970s these had caused little disruption and had negligible effect on government policy. In recent years the paramilitary groups have had real political power and influence. In 1974 the UDA, along with other loyalist bodies under the umbrella of the Ulster Workers' Council, was responsible for bringing about the collapse of the power-sharing Executive through the organisation of a general strike.

Both the IRA movements are organised politically in that they are associated with political parties. The Republican Clubs, the political counterpart in Northern Ireland of the Official IRA, have contested elections, although not very successfully, whereas Provisional Sinn Féin has boycotted elections. The Provisional movement has clear political demands, the most important of which is the call for a British withdrawal, and has used violence to force the British government to make concessions. In this it has had a certain measure of success in that it has on occasions persuaded British government representatives to meet and negotiate with its leadership. A brief truce was negotiated in 1972, and the outcome of a meeting with civil servants in 1974 was the declaration of a truce by the Provisional IRA, accompanied by the introduction of 'incident centres'. These were offices manned by Provisional Sinn Féin and linked to the Northern Ireland Office by telephone to provide a means of dealing with incidents that might threaten the ceasefire. It was later claimed that there had been four other points of concession: the release of internees, troop withdrawals from certain areas, immunity from arrest for certain Provisional leaders, and some form of commitment to a future British withdrawal from Northern Ireland. Disagreement over the last point led to the eventual breakdown of the truce.

The loyalist paramilitary groups are not well organised politically. At one time as many as twenty different groups were identified,[38] although many were small and inactive and they all lacked coherent or agreed political demands. An Ulster Loyalist Central Co-ordinating Committee was created as an umbrella organisation, but the largest loyalist paramilitary body, the UDA, later withdrew from it. The bargaining status of loyalist groups has also been recognised by the government in its willingness to have meetings with representatives to discuss matters ranging from the campaign of violence to housing conditions.

The paramilitary groups have also been associated with community action.[39] They have operated welfare schemes, mainly for prisoners and their dependents. The UDA has put a great deal of effort into community projects, including the creation of the Ulster Community Action Group. The Official Republican movement has been involved in redevelopment and housing issues and has had meetings with civil servants and Housing Executive officials. Provisional Sinn Féin has established employment enterprises.

While it can be established that the militant organisations have strongly influenced government policy and that the violence and uncertainty they have created has affected all aspects of public policy in Northern Ireland in recent years, they have not been able to take over the politicians' role. Their representatives have polled a very low vote in elections on the few occasions when they have chosen to stand. They have failed to replace the political parties, and they remain in the policy process with the status of powerful pressure groups.

The Press and Mass Media

Northern Ireland's two morning newspapers reflect the interests of the two communities. Rose (1971) found that 87 per cent of the readership of the *News Letter* was Protestant, while 93 per cent of the readership of the *Irish News* was Catholic.[40] The sole evening paper, the *Belfast Telegraph* draws its readership from both communities.

The *Belfast News-Letter* has tended to express mainstream Unionist policy and ideas, although in recent times the editorial policy of the paper has altered and it has tended to support power-sharing rather than the official Unionist view. The *Irish News* has also expressed mainstream Catholic political views, largely in support of the Nationalist Party and its successor, the SDLP, and it has repeatedly condemned the use of violence. The *Belfast Telegraph* has tended to present a liberal image, including support for Captain O'Neill and his reform programme and the principle of power-sharing. It has also organised several opinion polls which have indicated widespread support for more liberal policies.

Newspaper readership is fairly disparate, as English newspapers enjoy a high sale and Dublin daily papers also circulate in Northern Ireland.[41] In addition, there are numerous local newspapers, many provincial towns possessing two—again reflecting the community division.

It is not clear whether the press has much influence in any direction. Rose shows that readership of a particular newspaper does not seem to be associated with the strength of political views. Furthermore, papers would appear to have little influence on Government policy, except in some cases where revelations or investigative journalism has prompted the government to take action. For example, it was only after publication in the press of accounts of ill-treatment of detainees that the government set up a committee of inquiry.

Television is probably the main information source for the community, but it can hardly be said to act as an agent for political pressure, although there has been some criticism by government members of the coverage given to the expression of extreme political views.

Conclusion

The activity of pressure groups in Northern Ireland has been dominated by sectarian and professional interests. The groups with most influence have been the churches, the Orange Order and private businesses—all of which tend to represent conservative interests. Trade unions, radical movements and 'cause' groups have had little influence. Apart from these groups, there has been a general lack of pressure-group input into the policy process. This has not been due to a lack of access to government departments and ministers. The available evidence suggests that there has always been relative ease of access for pressure groups to officials and ministers. Lord Windlesham (1973) in his account of his experience as a minister in 1972–73 notes a degree of accessibility and a frequency of contact for individuals and delegations representing political parties, local authorities, churches and special interest groups which was not generally found in national politics in Britain.[42] The existence of a devolved parliament and administration obviously encouraged easy and frequent contact between ministers, officials and pressure-group representatives.

Nevertheless, before 1970 the activity of interest groups on such matters as planning, housing and other social issues was minimal. The lack of a wide range of government committees reduced the choice of official channels open to pressure groups and precluded that element of official recognition which might have encouraged their more active involvement in seeking solutions to Northern Ireland's problems.

7

The Civil Service and Central Administration

The Development of the Central Administration

THE creation of a separate Northern Ireland parliament in 1921 made necessary the formation of a separate administrative structure to supervise the range of central government services that had been previously handled in Dublin. The legal transfer of powers and duties from a variety of authorities in Dublin to Belfast was carried out in June 1921. Six departments were established in Northern Ireland—Finance, Home Affairs, Labour, Education, Agriculture and Commerce, and the Department of the Prime Minister—to assume responsibility for all the functions previously administered for the whole of Ireland by some thirty boards and departments. The Ministry of Commerce had no previous counterpart in Dublin and was designed to meet the special needs of the Northern province's industry and commerce.[1] Each department had a ministerial head, and all the formal conventions associated with ministerial responsibility in London were applied to the Stormont departments.[2]

Officials in Dublin were given the choice of service with the Northern Ireland or Irish Free State governments or with the United Kingdom government. Senior officials were loaned or transferred by the British government to help man the new Civil Service, and Sir Ernest Clark, the former Assistant Permanent Under-Secretary for Ireland, became the first head of the Civil Service in Northern Ireland. Within a short time a Civil Service independent of that in Britain was built up.

Apart from minor transfers in functions, the structure of departments and allocation of duties remained unaltered until the Second World War. In 1940 a Ministry of Public Security was set up with responsibility for public order, civil defence and other related services. The first major reform in the structure occurred in 1944. In 1943 the government had asked a British civil servant, Sir Francis Flound, to carry out an internal investigation into the functional organisation of government departments. Flound reported that the Ministry of Home Affairs was seriously overburdened with its responsibilities for law and order, health and housing, roads, transport and local government.[3] The government accordingly decided to set up a new Ministry of Health and Local Government to take over the health services, housing, planning and local government. In Flound's opinion it was desirable that a Minister of Health should be responsible for the supervision of local government because of the close concern of local authorities in health matters. These changes were also a response to increasing concern about the low standard of the health services and about the need for a programme of post-war social reconstruction.

Although there was a substantial increase in the work of government departments after the Second World War, their structure remained unaltered for the next twenty years. Changes in the 1960s were again largely in response to advisory reports. In 1962 the Hall Report on the economy of Northern Ireland emphasised the need for promoting industrial development and led to the Ministry of Commerce being relieved of some of its responsibilities, roads and public transport being transferred to Home Affairs and fisheries to Agriculture. The purpose of these transfers was to allow the Ministry of Commerce to bring all its resources to bear on the all-important activity of industrial development. Shortly after this, in 1964, the most extensive overhauling of the departmental structure since 1921 took place. This involved the abolition of the Ministry of Health and Local Government and the Ministry of Labour. A new alignment of functions resulted in the creation of two new ministries, a Ministry of Health and Social Services to be responsible for health services, social security and employment services, and a Ministry of Development to take charge of local government, housing, planning and roads. These changes followed the Matthew Report and the accession to power of Captain O'Neill, who on taking office had spoken of the appalling difficulty of tackling the problems of the 1960s with an administrative machine designed for the 1920s.[4] The *Belfast Regional Survey and Plan,* 1963 (the Matthew Report), also recommended the creation of a Ministry of Planning and Development drawn from the existing government departments. The only other subsequent structural change until the major reorganisation following direct rule was the creation of a new Ministry of Community Relations in 1969.

The growth of the workload of the Civil Service is clearly illustrated by the increase in the number of non-industrial civil servants. It increased steadily from 2,000 in 1932 to 6,500 in 1947, 8,000 in 1959, and 12,000 in 1969; there was then a sudden and substantial rise to 22,500 in 1974 following the administrative changes of 1972–73.

Table 15: Changes in Departments, 1921–76

1921 Prime Minister's Department	1921 Finance	1921 Commerce	1921 Agriculture	1921 Home Affairs	1921 Labour	1921 Education
				1940 Public Security		
				1944 Health and Local Government		
				1964 Health and Social Services	1964 Development	
					Health and Social Services	
1972 NI Secretary of State: Central Secretariat						1969 Community Relations
Jan. 1974 Chief Executive's Office				Jan. 1974 NI Office: NI Civil Service Group	Jan. 1974 Manpower Services	Environment
May 1974 NI Secretary of State: Central Secretariat					Jan. 1974 Housing, Local Government and Planning	Jan.–May 1974 Law Reform Information Planning and Co-ordination } 3 departments
	1976 Civil Service Department				1976 (merged with Environment)	1975 (merged with Education)

The Imperial Civil Service

Under the Government of Ireland Act, 1920, responsibility for a number of services remained with Westminster, and this necessitated a number of British government departments having branches in Northern Ireland. The largest is the Department of Inland Revenue, which operates with local offices throughout Northern Ireland; another is the Department of Customs and Excise, which collects and administers its taxes in the province. Other British departments maintain a small number of civil servants in Northern Ireland for specific functions; for example, the Export Credit Guarantee Department has a regional office in Belfast, and the Home Office has some immigration staff. These officials, some 4,500 in number, are recruited by the United Kingdom Civil Service and are completely unconnected with the Northern Ireland Civil Service —hence their popular description as 'imperial' civil servants.

Conformity with the British Civil Service

Although independent of the United Kingdom Civil Service, the Northern Ireland Civil Service has tended to follow very closely the practices and procedures of its parent body. From the outset its internal structure and grading was based on the British system. The pattern of its future development was determined by government reports in 1926 and 1930.[5] In 1930 the question arose of whether, in a comparatively small organisation such as the Northern Ireland Civil Service, a clear separation of administrative and executive functions should be maintained in imitation of the British system. The system finally introduced was a kind of compromise. The British principle of a distinct administrative grade was adopted, and graduates were given training of a specifically administrative character. However, the post of deputy principal, which did not exist in Britain, was created, and staff officers (senior executive-grade officers) and assistant principals were both eligible for promotion to it. This helped to reduce the barrier between the administrative and executive grades and made the executive grades less self-contained than in Britain. This difference in structure gave Northern Ireland civil servants an advantage over their British counterparts, since it made it easier for them to rise from the lower ranks and the professional classes into the administrative grades. Some of the top posts were even filled by personnel who had originally entered the service as clerks—such progression being very rare in the British Civil Service.

Since 1923 Northern Ireland has had its own Civil Service Commission to perform functions in relation to the Northern Ireland Civil Service similar to those performed by the United Kingdom Civil Service Commission. It consisted originally of the Permanent Secretaries of the Ministries of Finance and Education and the Minister of Finance, the minister's membership being contrary to United Kingdom practice.

Table 16: Civil Service Grades before 1973

United Kingdom Civil Service	Northern Ireland Civil Service
Administrative Class	
Permanent Secretary	Permanent Secretary
Deputy Secretary	Deputy Secretary
Under-Secretary	Senior Assistant Secretary
Assistant Secretary	Assistant Secretary
Principal	Principal
Assistant Principal	Deputy Principal
	Assistant Principal
Executive Class	
Principal Executive Officer	
Chief Executive Officer	
Senior Executive Officer	Staff Officer
Higher Executive Officer	Junior Staff Officer
Executive Officer	Senior Clerk
Clerical Class	
Higher Clerical Officer	
Clerical Officer	Clerk
Clerical Assistant	Clerical Assistant

The Civil Service Commission is responsible for recruitment and for arranging examinations. It is independent of the British commission, although the procedures it follows are largely the same. The only appointments in Northern Ireland in which the United Kingdom Civil Service Commission was involved were those in the administrative class. Since 1929 candidates who were successful in the selection procedure in Britain for entry as assistant principals could indicate a preference to join the Northern Ireland Civil Service. Northern Ireland also had its own system of direct recruitment by interview. This arrangement was useful in that it enabled the Northern Ireland commissioners to appraise the standard of entry into the administrative ranks of both the British and the local Civil Services. Between 1929 and 1940 only one out of twenty assistant principals appointed was from Northern Ireland.[6] Since the war, recruitment to the assistant principal grade has consisted of about two-thirds Ulstermen and one-third cross-channel applicants, although those promoted from the lower grades to the administrative grade (i.e. to deputy principal) were without exception Ulstermen.[7] Otherwise each Civil Service was self-contained, and there was no process of promotion or regular movement between the two services, although occasionally there could be transfers.

Pay, conditions of service, promotion procedures, etc. tended to be similar to those obtaining in Britain, although parity of pay was introduced only in the late 1950s and early 1960s after constant pressure from staff representatives, particularly from the Northern Ireland Whitley Council. In 1928 a Civil Service Representative Council had been set up for the purpose of making representations to the ministry, but in 1946 the government set up a Whitley Council, some seventeen years after its introduction in the United Kingdom Civil Service. It consisted of twenty members, half appointed by the government and the other half by approved staff associations. The membership was increased to twenty-four in 1970. The council deals with all matters affecting conditions of service and works in close co-operation with the National Whitley Council. Increases in salaries in Britain are duplicated fairly automatically in Northern Ireland. The Northern Ireland Whitley Council has consistently upheld the principle of equal pay for equal work within grades corresponding to those in the United Kingdom Civil Service. This has presented difficulties at times, for example on whether junior staff officers could be treated as the equivalent of higher executive officers. But generally the Whitley Council has been an important factor in ensuring a great deal of uniformity between the two Civil Services.[8]

Sources of Specialist Advice

There were some areas where the Northern Ireland central administration did vary from its British counterpart. Northern Ireland had very few advisory committees attached to government departments. Such committees are useful for providing expert advice and opinions or serving as a forum for consulting a wide range of interests. The lack of advisory committees in the economic field drew adverse comment from the Hall Report on the economy in 1962. It noted that there was no central organisation to offer economic advice and suggested an Economic Council composed of persons outside the government, principally from both sides of industry.[9] This proposal was accepted, and the Economic Council was set up in 1964 with the role of advising the government on economic planning, with specific reference to the needs and potentialities of the regional economy. The council has also on its own initiative prepared a number of reports and made detailed recommendations to the government. Probably the council's most controversial action was in 1970 when a sub-committee produced a report on the feasibility of state industry.[10] This report proposed an Industrial Development Board which could itself set up new industry, but this recommendation was rejected by the government at the time. Another important expert committee in the economic field was the Advisory Committee on Industries Development, which considered applications for assistance and loans and had to be satisfied that developments were viable and likely to provide employment. The Wilson Report on economic development in 1965 recommended a permanent consultative Science and Industry Committee, but it never came into existence.

Probably the most influential expert committee has been the Advisory Council for Education, set up under the Education Act, 1947. Past reports by the council have dealt with rural education in 1952, school attendance in 1956, special educational treatment in 1957, and primary education in 1954. The object of its most frequent investigations has been the selection of pupils for secondary schools, concerning which it issued reports in 1952, 1954 and 1960, and in 1971 the Seventh Advisory Council recommended changes in the selection procedures which were largely implemented in the following year. In 1973 the final report of the Advisory Council on the reorganisation of secondary education was published (the Burges Report).[11] It made radical recommendations for a declaration of intent to eliminate selection by means of the 'eleven plus' examination and for the preparation of development schemes for non-selective secondary schools. The council took evidence from forty-six organisations and some twenty individuals, and its work was akin to that of a committee of inquiry. However, it was effectively abolished by the coming into force of new education legislation in 1972 which simply empowered the minister to appoint such advisory bodies as he thought necessary. Among other advisory committees on education were the Schools Curriculum Committee, the Council for Continuing Education, and the Higher Education Co-ordination Advisory Committee.

The other main areas where expert committees operate is in agriculture (e.g. the General Agricultural Advisory Committee, the Agricultural Training Advisory Committee, and the Horticultural Consultative Committee), the environment (e.g. the Water Council, the Nature Reserves Committee, and the Ulster Countryside Committee) and in health (e.g. the Health and Social Services Council, the Central Medical Advisory Committee, the Central Nursing and Midwifery Advisory Committee, and the Medical Manpower Advisory Committee). The increase in the number of committees investigating these subject areas has been due to the reorganisation of government departments in the 1960s.

Some advisory committees have a mainly administrative function. The Housing Council is an advisory body to the Housing Executive and the government department responsible for housing; it consists of representatives of the district councils and, as such, has also a consultative role. Other more obvious examples of consultative committees are the Northern Ireland Consumer Council, the Transport Users' Committee, the Northern Ireland Trade Statutory Consultative Committee, and the Local Government Consultative Committee of 1971–73. Examples of consultative committees which in practice also carry out administrative functions are the Advisory Committee on Postgraduate Awards, the Special Purchase of Evacuated Dwellings Advisory Committee, and the Hotel Grants Advisory Committee.

There were relatively few advisory committees in operation before the 1960s, and there are still certain areas in which there is a marked lack of them in comparison with Britain. This is most noticeable in the field of treatment of offenders and penal policy. The Home Office has several influential advisory committees in this area, but Northern Ireland has none. This may well be because they are politically controversial areas. Another area which is completely lacking in expert advisory committees is housing, whereas in Britain there was an important Central Housing Advisory Committee which operated through various sub-committees. Although advisory committees cannot force governments to adopt their recommendations, they can prompt policy changes and generate public debate, and the existence of a greater number of such committees in Northern Ireland might have proved valuable.

Committees of inquiry also were used infrequently. Among the most influential was a Planning Advisory Board which was set up towards the end of the Second World War to formulate plans for social reconstruction. Its membership consisted solely of representatives of government departments, local authorities and interested professional institutions. Sub-committees were appointed to deal with specific subjects such as water and sewerage, location of industry, housing and the tourist trade. The housing sub-committee was the most influential of these. It carried out the first comprehensive housing survey in Northern Ireland, and its report had a marked effect on the reshaping of housing policy and legislation. Among other committees which have made important recommendations subsequently accepted by the government have been the Gordon Committee in 1946, which proposed a Special Care Service for the mentally subnormal, and the Lockwood Committee on higher education in 1965, which proposed a second university. Other committees have had major recommendations rejected, for example the proposal to make the health services accountable to parliament put forward in the Tanner Report in 1955 and the suggestions outlined in 1957 in the Nugent Report on local government finance.

The use of specialist advisers and consultants has been largely restricted to the field of economic planning and development. In 1957 two university professors, K. S. Isles and Norman Cuthbert, carried out a detailed study of the economy. In 1962 Sir Robert Hall chaired a working party on the economy, and in 1965 Professor Thomas Wilson produced a five-year economic plan, the greater part of which was accepted by the government. In 1963 Sir Robert Matthew acted as consultant in producing a regional plan which led to the development of the growth-centre policy and the creation of the new city of Craigavon. The 1970–75 Development Programme was presented in 1970 as the report of a team of consultants, Professors Matthew, Wilson and Parkinson. This report consisted of an introductory survey by the consultants and a more detailed description of programmes prepared jointly by the consultants and an advisory steering group of senior civil servants and officials from government departments.[12] It was later alleged that the steering group's relationship with the consultants was an uneasy one.[13] In 1971 three new consultants were appointed to produce a review of economic and social development. It is clear that senior civil servants had a great deal of influence on consultants' reports and their eventual implementation.

There was no strong tradition of the employment of individuals as advisers by departments or ministers, and such advisers as were appointed in the 1950s and early 1960s were usually retired civil servants. The appointment of a retiring permanent secretary as industrial adviser to the Ministry of Labour in 1957 and a similar appointment to the position of economic adviser in 1961 drew criticism from the Opposition in parliament. In recent years economic advisers have usually been university economists on secondment to the Department of Commerce.

A weakness in the policy formulation process has been the lack of research carried out by government departments. This deficiency was criticised in the Hall Report in 1962, which noted that 'Until recently no central organisation existed to carry out economic research or to offer economic advice.'[14] Northern Ireland departments did not always have immediate access to the expertise and research facilities in Whitehall. As one civil servant put it, 'We have to go and ask specially, and we maybe do not hear about developments that would be of interest.'[15] Demands by Opposition MPs for a survey into poverty were repeatedly turned down. There was an Education Research Council which produced several research reports, for example in 1972 on the raising of the school-leaving age. Generally it was only after 1969 that there was an increase in departmental interest in research.

Co-ordination between Government Departments

Co-ordination of the administrative machinery was mainly the responsibility of the Department of Finance, operating through its Establishments Branch, which was concerned with recruitment, manning and training, through its Organisation and Methods Branch, and through a Treasury Division, which exercised general control over expenditure by departments. Co-ordination at the policy level was the responsibility of the Cabinet Office, which on occasions even arbitrated in interdepartmental disagreements. Sometimes disputes had to go to the cabinet for settlement, as, for example, in 1966 when the Ministries of Finance and Development were at loggerheads over the approval of a motorway contract.[16]

There are, however, grounds for believing that co-ordination between departments was inadequate. The Development Programme for 1970–75 condemned the lack of co-ordination between the Ministries of Development and Education and the Industrial Training Section of the Department of Health and Social Services over the siting of new schools and the expansion of existing ones; this failure was responsible for the imperfect implementation of growth-centre strategy. The report went on to criticise co-ordination within the Ministry of Development, stating that different parts of the ministry had not been drawn together and integrated as fully as was necessary.[17] This is perhaps surprising in the light of the compact nature of the administration, but the problem was partly inherent within the system, being to some extent due to Stormont's duplication of the Westminster model of administration. The practice of setting up separate departments with their ministries and permanent secretaries tended to reproduce on a lesser scale some of the same difficulties implicit in a very much larger administrative system. Departmental isolationism was encouraged in some departments by the policy of 'step-by-step' with Westminster. This meant that each department was often more concerned with what was being done by its opposite number in Whitehall, and there was thus a correspondingly lesser incentive for the different departments to get together to discuss their interests from a common provincial point of view. Another factor was that there was too little mobility at the administrative level. A substantial proportion of officials remained in the same department throughout the whole of their careers, and their experience was therefore correspondingly restricted. This practice also tended to raise and reinforce the psychological barriers between different departments and produce parochialism. The Department of Education, in particular, had a reputation for maintaining an isolated existence.

The Ministry of Finance might also have been expected to play a more important role in co-ordination, similar to that undertaken by the Treasury in Whitehall. The Development Programme argued that the Department of Finance would have to assume a stronger role in leadership and co-ordination, that its special responsibilities would have to be fully recognised by other departments, and that its priorities should be more fully adopted to that role. It proposed that the new techniques of five-year forecasting and output budgeting needed to be more fully extended, and stated that, if the ministry's status was to be enhanced and its functions increased, it would have to be strengthened at the administrative level.[18] For such a small regional administration co-operation and co-ordination appeared to present more difficulties than might have been expected. This raises the question of whether efficiency might have been improved by a smaller number of departments. Before 1970 *ad hoc* and informal consultation appeared to suffice, but since then the number of formal interdepartmental committees has grown rapidly.

The Political Role of the Civil Service

One of the major differences between the Northern Ireland and the United Kingdom Civil Services was that the Northern Ireland Civil Service always operated with the same political party in power. This meant that senior civil servants became accustomed to working within the same political guidelines. They were continually in contact with ministers who had broadly the same ideas and points of view, and they were not required to consider alternative policies or to adapt to different political perspectives on problems. With the same party continuously in office, radical new policy initiatives were rarely valued and the Civil Service was rarely asked to produce new policies. This tended to foster a conservative and cautious approach.

Brett (1970) has argued that at certain levels, including the higher level, the Civil Service

has been seriously perverted not by the party in power but by the hard fact of one-party government, and its impartiality is, to say the least, suspect. Many civil servants came in the end to pay little regard to the views of any but the party in power.

Hence the Civil Service has not been able to perform its proper functions as an element in the structure of government and society.

This criticism drew an unprecedented public statement from the head of the Northern Ireland Civil Service repudiating the view that its officials had been corrupted, unwittingly or otherwise, by the demands of the system of government under which they worked.[19]

Clearly, however, senior civil servants had to operate within ministerial and political constraints. There was also little pressure from parliament on policy formulation, as there were few select committees or policy committees; and Opposition MPs sometimes complained that it was not possible for them to go along to senior civil servants to discuss the thinking of their particular departments on aspects of policy.[20] There is some evidence that senior civil servants had closer contacts with their ministers than was the case in Britain, and that ministers were briefed more fully. This was partly due to the greater amount of time available at Stormont, where there was not the same multiplicity of subjects to deal with.[21] Furthermore, with smaller numbers involved, ministers and senior civil servants found it easier to get to know each other; most of the main departments were located in the same building as parliament and the ministers' offices. Ministers were fairly dependent on senior civil servants for policy advice and the preparation of statements for the cabinet and parliament. This was particularly true before the mid-1960s when ministerial office was largely a part-time occupation and few ministers would have had a full grasp of all policy issues and the necessary background information.

Civil servants were able to initiate changes in some areas in evolving new administrative structures to deal with problems (e.g. the Northern Ireland Housing Trust in 1945, the Tuberculosis Authority in 1946, and the Northern Ireland Special Care Service for the mentally handicapped in 1951). Other new departures were made in the fields of economic and regional planning, growth-centre policy, labour mobility and industrial training. It appears that civil servants were able to push through some policies that ran counter to the normal political thinking of ministers. The nationalisation of road transport in the 1930s is an outstanding example. Civil servants had to work hard to convince ministers and the cabinet of the need for particular policies that deviated from traditional Unionist Party thinking on such subjects as economic planning. The accession to power of Terence O'Neill in 1963 provided more scope for Civil Service initiatives. O'Neill worked closely with a small group of civil servants in the Cabinet Office in devising and negotiating new policies on North–South relations and the recognition of trade unions.[22] The Prime Minister and the cabinet had, of course, the final say on policy, and civil servants had to work within the political framework and terms of reference given to them. In areas of the greatest political sensitivity, such as education or home affairs, civil servants appear to have had less influence and less scope for initiating new policies.

Senior civil servants no doubt quickly learned what might be politically unacceptable to a minister or the cabinet. John Oliver, in discussing his own experience of civil servants' relationship with ministers, comments that

> Advocacy of officials of particular courses that were unwelcome to ministers under the Stormont parliament had ... to run the gauntlet twice over, once in the ordinary sense of being un-palatable to ministers as party politicians and again in the sense of appearing to put ministers in the impossible positions of encouraging the enemies of the constitution itself.[23]

Dr Oliver also reveals that during the 1950s senior civil servants tried to forewarn the government of the dangers being created by some local authorities who 'were playing unworthy games in the location of new housing estates in relation to electoral wards and in the allocation of tenancies'—issues that were later to become crucial as the basis for the Civil Rights campaign. But Dame Dehra Parker, the Minister of Health and Local Government from 1949 to 1957, would not be moved.[24] The civil servants could do little but adhere to the dictates of ministerial responsibility.

Discrimination in the Civil Service

One controversial issue which has been periodically aired is alleged religious or political discrimination in Civil Service appointments and promotions. Figures on the composition of the service in 1927 showed that 94 per cent of the 229 most senior officials were Protestants.[25] Barritt and Carter (1962) looked at the 740 officials holding similar posts in 1959 and found that this percentage was unchanged. Donnison (1973) quoted a study of the religious affiliation of 477 civil servants from the grades of deputy and assistant principal upwards which had been carried out in 1972 and which revealed that 95 per cent of the officials were Protestants.[26] Donnison's article evoked a response from the Ministry of Finance which stated that an informal exercise undertaken at the end of 1972 showed that some 15 per cent of officials in the grades mentioned were Catholics.[27] Even this percentage would represent little more than a third of the proportion of Catholics in the population. However, it must be remembered that these statistics reflect the results of recruitment which mainly took place twenty-five years before.

Another allegation has been that Catholics were excluded completely from certain key areas like the Cabinet Office, the Establishments Divisions, the Ministry of Home Affairs and the ministers' private offices.[28] Some ministers were clearly not happy to have Catholics in important positions, the Minister of Home Affairs actually stating at a cabinet meeting in 1926 that it was very undesirable that Roman Catholics should get into certain branches of the Civil Service until their loyalty had been absolutely established. Certain of the selection procedures may have mitigated against Catholics. Most appointments took place without specified qualifications being required; for example, the vast majority of male personnel in the clerical class were recruited from ex-servicemen, and the majority of women were employed as clerical assistants and had no specific qualifications. The position of the Minister of Finance as head of the Civil Service Commission led to allegations of bias and discrimination. Captain O'Neill relates that when he was Minister of Finance he had to face a campaign against him in the cabinet because it was believed that since he had taken up office Catholics were being encouraged to join the Civil Service.[29]

Looking at the matter from the point of view of the Northern Ireland Catholics themselves, many undoubtedly felt an antipathy towards the regime and may have been reluctant to enter the service of the state of whose existence they did not approve. Alternatively, they may have simply assumed that they would have been discriminated against in the Civil Service. These considerations created an atmosphere where it became rare for young Catholics to look to the Civil Service as a career. It was not until the late 1960s that the first Catholic entered as an assistant principal—through the competitive process in Britain. By this time the position of Catholics within the Civil Service had improved considerably, and further ameliorative measures were instigated after 1969.

Donnison concludes that it is difficult to know whether the figures in his article reflect discrimination, either conscious or unconscious, or are rather due to long-standing fears and expectations and a general tradition which has led Catholics into some occupations rather than the public service.

The British and Northern Ireland governments published a joint communiqué in 1969 stating the steps would be taken to reinforce the safeguards against discrimination in public employment. In 1969 the post of Parliamentary Commissioner (Ombudsman) for Administration was created in Northern Ireland for the purpose of investigating complaints against the actions of the central government; the commissioner also had the duty of scrutinising appointments and other personnel matters relating to the Civil Service. The British Parliamentary Commissioner was excluded from investigating such matters. An order was also made in 1969 reconstituting the Civil Service Commission: a five-man board was established, and the Minister of Finance ceased to be a member. The order laid down that in making appointments the order of merit of the applicants is to be fairly and impartially determined.

Civil Service personnel matters have constituted a major area of complaint to the Parliamentary Commissioner, comprising some 20 per cent of complaints received and 40 per cent of complaints fully investigated between 1969 and 1977.[30] About one-third of these complaints concerned allegations of religious discrimination. However, the commissioner found no element of discrimination in the actions of the departments concerned in any of these cases, although he did rule that maladministration had occurred in one or two of them. There was one case of apparent political discrimination when a civil servant was suspended for taking part in a rent strike during a civil disobedience campaign and his department had refused to reinstate him. It would be true to say, however, that the number of complaints alleging discrimination in promotion or recruitment has not been large and that discriminatory policies of this type appear to have been largely eradicated. The Civil Service has stated that it would welcome an increased flow of applicants at all levels from all sections of the Northern Ireland population.[31] At the clerical level the service is recruiting Catholics in about the same proportion as in the population, if not slightly above it. At the graduate level the proportion is rising, but is still below the population proportion. Given the rules concerning experience and seniority promotion, it may be a considerable time before the patterns at the higher levels are changed.

The Standard of Administration: The Parliamentary Commissioner for Administration

It is difficult to make an objective assessment of the standard of administration of the Northern Ireland Civil Service. Allegations of discrimination in administration by the Civil Service were made infrequently. The Cameron Report found that the only significant charges related to the areas chosen for major development, for example the siting of new industries, the new city of Craigavon and the New University of Ulster. At the level of the administration's contact with the individual, the work of the Parliamentary Commissioner for Administration indicates a high standard of efficiency in recent years.

The Parliamentary Commissioner (Ombudsman) took up his duties in Northern Ireland in 1969. In the period up to 1977 a total of some 300 complaints were received, almost half of which lay outside the Ombudsman's jurisdiction. Investigations were completed into 147 cases, and complaints were found to be justified in 24 cases. The commissioner tended in the majority of cases to avoid a finding of maladministration, preferring simply to note the complaint as justified, although in a few cases he did make a definite finding of an element of maladministration. There were no findings of religious discrimination. Taking into account the fact that about one-third of the completed investigations and one-half of the justified complaints concerned Civil Service personnel matters, this does not indicate any significant degree of defectiveness in central administration. The complications involved in making complaints through public representatives rather than directly to the commissioner may have discouraged the public from making full use of the system. As Table 17 indicates, complaints have been made mainly against three departments—Development and the Environment, Health and Social Services, and Agriculture—and the greatest proportion of justified complaints have also been those made against these departments.

Table 17: Complaints Made to the Parliamentary Commissioner for Administration, 1969–77

	Complaints received	Fully investigated	Complaints justified
Agriculture	36	24	6
Commerce	10	7	–
Education	19	5	–
Health and Social Services	58	8	6
Home Affairs	16	7	1
Finance	18	10	3
Development and the Environment	93	43	7
Civil Service Commission	22	17	1
Civil Service Department	2	2	–
Manpower Services	3	2	–
	277	125	24

The first Parliamentary Commissioner in Northern Ireland was

Sir Edmund Compton, who was at the same time the British Parliamentary Commissioner. He noted in his first annual report that the quality of administrative performance in the Northern Ireland ministries 'compares well with my experience of government departments in the United Kingdom'.[32] He went on to point out that the individual citizen frequently gets a better service from a Northern Ireland ministry than he would get from a United Kingdom department in similar circumstances owing to the smaller size. This would confirm that, generally speaking, the standard of administration has been regarded as high.

It is difficult to form an accurate assessment of the standard of policy-making in government departments, as the final outcome had always to be either determined or approved by ministers. The commitment to social reconstruction and the introduction of the welfare state in the immediate post-war period gave some civil servants scope for initiative and enterprise, resulting in the Housing Trust, the Northern Ireland Tuberculosis Authority and a new system of welfare authorities. This impetus was lost during the 1950s. Oliver (1978 a) comments that during this period 'appointments to senior positions in the Civil Service were timid; mediocre men were being encouraged; grey figures were beginning to predominate'.[33] The 1960s again saw more evidence of departmental initiatives in the field of industrial development, industrial training, regional planning and, most of all, in road-building. Less initiative was shown in housing and slum clearance, although this was a more politically sensitive area affording only limited opportunity for the direct involvement of civil servants in devising policies. Political factors also impeded modern developments affecting the police, prisons, courts and electoral law, although it has been suggested that a more vigorous Department of Home Affairs might have made a difference.[34]

The Civil Service, 1972–79

In recent years the Civil Service has gone through a period of unprecedented change. The imposition of direct rule from Westminster has been the most dramatic new departure, but this development coincided with other reforms introduced as a result of the reorganisation of local government in 1973 and in response to the Fulton Report on the British Civil Service in 1968.

The Process of Centralisation

The transfer of local government functions to a system of centralised boards, area boards and government departments (see Chapter 8) necessitated a large increase in the number of civil servants. The Civil Service as a whole has almost doubled in size since 1971 from

18,000 to 33,000, much of this increase being accounted for by the 8,000 local government employees who were transferred to the Ministry of Development. The reorganisation took place in a remarkably smooth manner during 1972–73 amidst all the violence and political turmoil. For many staff there was no change in the nature and location of their work, but the change in status from local government employee to civil servant did produce problems of assimilation.[35] Transferred staff were given guarantees of similar terms and conditions of employment but appeals to a special tribunal about breaches of this guarantee were still being held three years later. The other difficulty to which the transfer of staff contributed was a shortage in the middle management area of the Civil Service, particularly at deputy principal level.

Post-Fulton Reforms
The Fulton Committee on the reorganisation of the British Civil Service did not include Northern Ireland within its terms of reference, and its report, presented in 1968, made no mention of the Northern Ireland Civil Service. But given the practice of copying the structures and procedures of the United Kingdom Civil Service, it was clear that the Fulton recommendations would have important consequences for the Northern Ireland Civil Service. The most important recommendations of the Fulton Committee to be accepted in Britain were the replacement of the large number of classes by a single unified grading structure, an increase in specialist training (especially management training), the creation of a Civil Service Department to take over the Treasury's responsibilities for the Civil Service, and the establishment of a Civil Service College to provide training courses. Generally the Fulton criticisms of the inadequacy of the United Kingdom Civil Service were also applicable to Northern Ireland, and the staff side of the regional Whitley Council was anxious that any changes made in Britain should be followed in Northern Ireland.

In 1970 a Civil Service Management Division was established in Northern Ireland to take over the Ministry of Finance's functions for the management of the Civil Service, although the Civil Service Commission retained its separate identity. In 1976 a separate Civil Service Department was set up, but there was considerable doubt about the need for a residential Civil Service College. The proposals for the centralisation of many local government services opened up the possibility of establishing a Public Service College. However, in the Osmond Report in 1972 a working party concluded that a Public Service College operating as a full-time institution would not be justified.[36] It believed that at the lower levels the best results would be obtained by running courses within or close to the organisation concerned, while at senior level it was better to continue to partici- pate in courses at the Civil Service Colleges in Britain. The report, in rejecting a Public Service College, seemed to place a narrow emphasis on management training and was rather out of step with Fulton thinking, which had noted the value of wider training in economics and social administration. The report did, however, recommend the appointment of a co-ordinator of management training who would work in conjunction with a supervisory Public Service Training Committee in identifying and advising on common needs for management. The post of co-ordinator was eventually established in 1974. Since the Osmond Report there has been a rapid expansion in training directed particularly at middle manage- ment, and there has also been increasing attendance at courses in Britain.

The implementation of a unified grading structure in Britain in accordance with the Fulton proposal was followed in Northern Ireland. In 1972 it was decided that the organisation and nature of work in Northern Ireland should be in complete parity for all grades from clerical assistant to principal. With the subsequent introduction of the senior principal grade there was parity from clerical assistant to assistant secretary, except that Northern Ireland's special deputy principal grade was retained. In 1971 the United Kingdom intro- duced the new grade of administration trainee to replace the former assistant principal grade; candidates for this grade could be either graduates or officers from within the service. This system was intro- duced into Northern Ireland in 1973. Selection involves two days of tests and interviews in London and approval by a Final Selection Board in Belfast, and the standard of selection is rather lower than for the old assistant principal grade.

The Impact of Direct Rule

The Civil Service appeared to accept completely the utterly un- precedented occurrence in March 1972 when the Stormont minis- ters, cabinet and parliament under which it had worked disappeared. Civil servants had never before experienced even a change of government, and this fundamental constitutional change took place in very controversial and emotional circumstances; yet in fact the business of government departments continued to be transacted with the usual unvarying regularity. As one contemporary descrip- tion put it, 'The Civil Service took this extraordinary event in its stride and with scarcely a flutter continued to formulate and administer policies.'[37] One explanation given of the facility with which the Civil Service adapted itself to the new political leadership from outside referred to its common tradition with the United Kingdom Civil Service and to the fact that it has always seen itself essentially as a service of the Crown, concerned with the administration of a part of the United Kingdom.[38]

The only change in the departmental structure at this time was the creation of the Northern Ireland Office, directly responsible to the Secretary of State and with offices in Belfast as well as in London. A major upheaval for the Civil Service occurred during the interlude in direct rule from January to May 1974 when Northern Ireland politicians once again headed the government departments. The Ministry of Development was split into the Departments of the Environment and of Housing, Local Government and Planning, and the Ministry of Health and Social Services divided its functions between the Departments of Health and Social Services and of Manpower Services. A further realignment was implemented in January 1974 when the staff in the Ministry of Home Affairs were transferred as a separate unit, headed by a permanent secretary from the Northern Ireland Civil Service, to the Northern Ireland Office and became known as 'The Northern Ireland Office: Northern Ireland Civil Service Group'. While Northern Ireland senior civil servants may not have been happy with these structural changes and the additional work necessitated by them, they soon developed a good working relationship with the power-sharing Executive which included heads of departments from the SDLP.

Senior civil servants claimed to have an excellent relationship with SDLP ministers. After the collapse of the Executive following the Ulster Workers' Council strike it was alleged by Mr Paddy Devlin, a member of the Executive, that the permanent secretaries had indicated to Mr Faulkner, the Chief Executive, that they could conceive of a situation in which they could no longer support the Executive because of the effects of the situation on their department and their workings.[39] The head of the Civil Service was later to issue a statement declaring that the heads of departments had made no political comments and that there was no question of an ultimatum of any kind.[40] Mr Faulkner held a meeting with the permanent secretaries on 27 May 1974 and was informed of the terrible conditions which faced the province if the strike continued.[41] Their view was that they were presenting a realistic and impartial assessment; nevertheless, this meeting appeared to have a strong influence on Mr Faulkner's decision to resign the following day.

The main problem for the Civil Service has been the adjustment to the machinery of direct rule, most notably through the development of the relationship between the Northern Ireland government departments and the Northern Ireland Office. The total staff complement of the Northern Ireland Office is 1,200; 970 are Northern Ireland civil servants, and 230 United Kingdom civil servants, of whom 83 are currently in Belfast. There are also some Northern Ireland civil servants on secondment to the London office. The Northern Ireland Office serves as a direct link with the Whitehall administration, and its representatives sit on various Whitehall interdepartmental committees. It also constitutes the formal link with the Westminster cabinet and parliament. Its offices were located at Stormont Castle, away from the Northern Ireland departments. The influx of English civil servants to work in co-operation with the Northern Ireland departments created a number of problems which were eventually overcome when a new framework of co-ordination was devised in 1976.

The improvement in co-ordination was achieved by the creation of the separate post of head of the Northern Ireland Civil Service. He was made directly responsible to the Secretary of State for the co-ordination of the policies and programmes of all Northern Ireland departments, for the general management of the Civil Service, and for recommendations to top appointments. His liaison position between Northern Ireland departments and the Northern Ireland Office is emphasised by the fact that his office is supported by a central secretariat located partly at Stormont Castle, where the Northern Ireland Office is, and partly at Parliament Buildings, the main centre of Northern Ireland departments.

Direct rule has involved a major change for senior civil servants in that they are now responsible to the Westminster parliament and government. The Westminster parliament now deals with all legislation, with Estimates, accounts, parliamentary questions and debates. Civil servants have had to adjust to new procedures and timetables, increased documentation and consultation, more travel, and delays in decision-making. John Oliver, a senior civil servant, has written of the difficulties caused by differences in law and administration and has described their cramping effect on communication with the Westminster Public Accounts Committee: 'I did not know the members and they did not know me. I found it hard to assess how intimately they were acquainted with our administration. Altogether I found the occasion quite a strain.'[42] Civil servants have also found it hard to adjust to the new ministers from Westminster. Ministerial inaccessibility is a constant impediment: civil servants appear to have difficulty in simply getting ministers to sit down and sort out problems or take decisions. Each minister, of course, has to spend a good deal of time in England, both at Westminster and in his constituency, and he also has his duties to carry out at the Northern Ireland Office and as head of two or three Northern Ireland departments. It is often difficult for Northern Ireland departments to fit in with the minister in organising business, arranging meetings, seeing deputations, etc. This is all very different from the old system where the Stormont ministers and parliament were located in the same buildings as the Civil Service and close personal relationships developed.

Direct rule has also involved senior civil servants closely in policy-making and legislation. During the first period of direct rule, when Westminster ministers had almost no previous contact with Northern Ireland, the local departments were delegated more responsibility. Two important policy documents on regional planning and economic strategy were produced entirely by senior civil servants. Administrative changes such as the abolition of the Youth Employment Service and the Community Relations Commission have also reflected the authority and initiative of civil servants.[43] However, after the failure of the Convention in 1975 to agree on a new form of devolved government British ministers adopted a policy of bringing Northern Ireland legislation into line with Westminster legislation, and this has had the effect of reducing the dependence on Northern Ireland civil servants.

Since 1974 legislative proposals are put forward by the minister responsible for the Northern Ireland department concerned. The heavy workload of ministers has made it necessary for legislative proposals to be discussed and processed very thoroughly within and between departments before they go to the minister. In Oliver's view this process, as well as improving interdepartmental co-opera-tion, has given the Civil Service a cohesion which it has never previously possessed.[44]

Conclusion

The Northern Ireland Civil Service developed as an independent and autonomous body rather than as a regional organisation. Before the suspension of Stormont in 1972 contact with British government departments took the form of negotiations and co-operation between two separate administrations rather than between a central and a subordinate administration, and some Northern Ireland departments had little contact with their counterparts at Whitehall.

There is little evidence that Northern Ireland civil servants ever experienced any conflict of loyalties between Stormont and Westminster. Civil servants were accountable to Northern Ireland ministers and represented their views in communications and negotiations with Whitehall departments. The Civil Service built up a reputation as an efficient administrative machine. Northern Ireland experience illustrates some of the value of a devolved Civil Service: the accessibility of senior civil servants to pressure groups and individuals, their understanding of local needs, and the possibility of regional administrative structures. It also illustrates some of the problems. Administrative and geographical separateness led to the Civil Service lagging behind the United Kingdom Civil Service in training, management and research. The adoption of the West-minster–Whitehall model of relationships between the Civil Service and ministers, the cabinet, parliament and the Opposition was not entirely appropriate for the requirements of Northern Ireland. One-party dominance in a regional parliament leads to the Civil Service becoming identified with the policies of the governing party and increases the likelihood of a static style of government and admin-istration. The establishment of the principle of parity with Britain provided an argument for surmounting the traditional conservatism of Unionist governments, and the premiership of Captain O'Neill provided more opportunities for Civil Service involvement in policy-making. Northern Ireland civil servants were able to initiate major advances in environmental and industrial development and the social services in the late 1940s and mid-1960s.

Events since 1972 have led to closer integration of the Northern Ireland Civil Service with the British system of government. It is now responsible to the Westminster government and parliament. At the same time it has maintained its separate structure and identity and is the one major public institution that has survived the period of British government intervention relatively intact. While Northern Ireland has lost its legislative and executive devolution, it continues to have a system of administrative devolution through its separate Civil Service and structure of central administration. The reorgan-isation following the imposition of direct rule has increased its powers and responsibilities and has almost doubled it in size. In the absence of regional political institutions and amidst the violence of the 1970s it continues to administer public services and provide government.

8

Local Government and Local Administration

IN 1921 Northern Ireland had a similar structure of local government to Great Britain and the rest of Ireland. It had been set up under the Local Government (Ireland) Act, 1898, which had been based on the somewhat dubious assumption that the system devised for nineteenth-century England was also appropriate for Ireland. In 1921 Northern Ireland had a dual system of local government. There were two county boroughs, Belfast and Londonderry, whose corporations were all-purpose authorities. In the rest of Northern Ireland there was a two-tier system: a top tier of six county councils and a lower tier of urban and rural district councils. Four towns which were too small to be urban districts had elected town commissioners. This structure remained relatively unchanged until the mid-1960s. By then town commissioners had disappeared and ten larger urban districts had been granted borough status, although this did not alter their functions.

Table 18: The Structure of Local Government, 1965

Corporations	County Councils	
2	6	
Borough Councils	Urban District Councils	Rural District Councils
10	24	31

The functions of local government altered little between 1921 and 1948. A Departmental Commission on local government in 1927 had strongly recommended a more streamlined system of local government based on the counties and entailing the abolition of Boards of Guardians and the establishment of County Health Authorities and County Public Assistance Committees to administer the public health services and the Poor Law relief services and county homes.[1] A minority report signed by nine members proposed

F

the abolition of rural district councils, as had already been effected in the Irish Free State in 1925. The government rejected these proposals partly for financial reasons and partly because it thought that the increased workload would be too heavy for the county councils and that the reorganised bodies would be cumbersome and unwieldy.[2] Instead it decided to deal with local government matters by means of a series of separate measures on the Poor Law, public health and lunacy, and finally by a general local government bill.[3]

In fact major changes along the lines of the 1927 proposals did not take place until the post-war period. The Public Health and Local Government Act, 1946, established county and county borough councils as health and welfare authorities for their areas and provided for the transfer to them of relevant functions of the old Boards of Guardians as well as of borough, urban and rural councils. The statutory committees for health and welfare were composed not only of members of the county councils but also of representatives of district councils and other co-opted members. By this time the government had also accepted that there were too many regional education committees, eighteen in all. As the Minister of Education put it, these were more a hindrance than a help to education,[4] causing wide variations in scholarship schemes, etc., and with a membership often out of touch with modern educational developments. They were replaced by statutory education committees for the six counties and two county boroughs. These educational committees included representatives of the bodies (usually the churches) which had transferred their schools to the education authorities. Hayes (1967) has argued that 'These committees were so distinct in organisational structure as to be virtually self-contained bodies subventing annually to the county councils for their share of the rate fund.'[5]

Since 1921 local authorities have experienced a reduction in functions. Local authorities lost to central bodies responsibility for hospital and some health services, trunk roads, land drainage, the relief of poverty, electricity, and the fire services. At the same time local government responsibilities in the social services, education, social work and housing have expanded considerably.

The two county boroughs were all-purpose authorities, and the division of functions among the remaining authorities in 1965 is shown in Table 19.

The Use of Nominated Boards

The development of public services was marked by an increasing tendency to use nominated centralised boards to administer services even where these services were the responsibility of local govern-

Table 19: Division of Major Functions, 1965

County Councils			Borough Councils and UDCs	RDCs
Education			Housing	Housing
Health			Planning	Water
Welfare			Water supply	Sewerage
Libraries			Sewerage	Refuse collection
Roads	⎤		Refuse collection	Street lighting
Planning	⎟ in rural		Street lighting	Recreational
Public works	⎟ districts		Upkeep of roads	facilities
Tourism	⎦		Recreational facilities	Parks and cemeteries
			Parks and cemeteries	Entertainments
			Markets	licensing
			Entertainments licensing	
			Harbours ⎤ in some	
			Gas ⎦ areas	

ment in Britain.[6] During the nineteenth century the administration of many major services in Ireland had been centralised, and this arrangement persisted after 1921 in a number of areas, for example the police, courts and teacher-training. Government departments also took on some new functions (e.g. civil defence, weights and measures and the probation service) which in Britain were operated by local authorities. Other services were removed from local government and placed under the control of centralised boards.

Some of the most important centralised boards were those created in the health services, where two main nominated authorities were set up; firstly, a Northern Ireland Hospitals Authority, which was charged with the duty of administering hospital, specialist and ancillary services; and secondly, a general Health Service Board for the direct administration of the general medical, dental, ophthalmic and pharmaceutical services. Statutory boards also took over responsibility for fire services and electricity. In 1945 the Northern Ireland Housing Trust was set up as a public authority to build houses throughout the whole of the province. Its function was to supplement the building programmes of local authorities. It had become obvious that the housing need was far in excess of what the local authorities could be expected to meet from their resources, financial and otherwise. The Housing Trust consisted of five to seven members appointed by the relevant minister, and in practice it operated with a large degree of independence from ministerial interference. The Trust rapidly built up a reputation for efficiency and established itself as a major agency for the provision of public housing. Its success is often referred to as a proof of the advantages of *ad hoc* centralised administration.

Some centralised boards were also established to administer new services or look after new needs in preference to local authorities. The Youth Employment Board was an example. In 1946 a Northern Ireland Tuberculosis Authority was set up to secure the prevention and more effective treatment of tuberculosis, which was an especially severe problem in Northern Ireland. In effect the Tuberculosis Authority took over, with certain additions and extensions, the powers and duties of the county councils in regard to the institutional and domiciliary treatment of tuberculosis. A similar step was taken for the administration of services for the mentally handicapped. A report on the mental health services by the Gordon Committee in 1946 drew attention to the inadequacy of provision for the mentally subnormal. It examined the structure of services in England, where day and residential qualifications were provided by local health authorities; however, the committee's report advised against local authority involvement, partly because it was thought that this could lead to the neglect of the services, and partly because of the poor record of many local councils in providing other services. The Gordon Report therefore recommended that services for the mentally deficient should be provided by a specific authority. These proposals were implemented in 1951 when the Northern Ireland Special Care Service was set up under the auspices of the Hospitals Authority to operate administratively under three regional boards. The service provided residential, medical, educational, occupational and social work services for patients under a single administrative structure.

Several factors have influenced the growth of *ad hoc* centralised boards. The size of Northern Ireland in terms of both population and area make it suitable for regional administrative bodies. Boards have also provided a method of taking contentious areas of responsibility (such as the police and the building and allocation of houses) out of local political influence and control. The growth of administration by *ad hoc* statutory bodies was in part a reflection of the inadequacies in the machinery of local government. The trend towards the removal and centralisation of local government functions included the recognition that the existing local councils were unable to provide local services efficiently and carry out their statutory duties.

The Failures of Local Government

The failure to reform the basic local government structure since 1921 led to an accumulation of defects. The basic problems can be categorised as structural, functional, financial and political.

Structure

In 1967 there was a total of 73 separate local authorities. This figure revealed one obvious structural defect: there were far too many small authorities. There were 27 local authorities for areas where the population was less than 10,000, and 15 of the 24 urban districts had populations of less than 5,000. Keady Urban District had a population of only 1,500, and Tandragee Urban District only 1,300. Outside the counties and county boroughs only five authorities had a population of over 40,000, and these were all within the Greater Belfast Area. Furthermore, the local government structure took no account of changes in population, particularly the growth in the size of the Greater Belfast Area, where by 1970 almost half the population of Northern Ireland lived.

The structure was also based on a fairly rigid division between town and country, and the tightly drawn boundaries inhibited development. A small urban district in the middle of a county could not plan its development without impinging on the surrounding countryside. Some authorities had eventually to build new housing estates outside their boundaries. The large number of small councils was an obstacle to the proper functioning of local government. Many authorities were small in area, had inadequate financial resources, and were unable to employ adequate numbers of professional and technical staff. In addition, many areas had too small a population to justify the provision of comprehensive services.

The only change made in recognition of the problems caused by the structure of local government took place in 1967 when one borough council and three rural district councils in Co. Fermanagh amalgamated with the county council to form a single all-purpose authority.

Functions

The fragmented structure was also an obstacle to the efficient provision of services. Some councils in the south and west of the province were faced with a declining population and rate income and frequently found themselves hard pressed in fulfilling their statutory functions. Despite the wide disparity in size and resources between the various authorities, they all had similar statutory powers. The result was a proliferation of joint and *ad hoc* authorities dealing mainly with water and sewerage. There were thirty such bodies, and their existence caused numerous problems of co-ordination and confused lines of accountability and responsibility. Some of the smaller urban districts transferred their planning functions to the county council or used the county planning staff to deal with planning applications. The weaknesses of the local government structure was most clearly apparent in the scale and standards of the services provided. As Loughran (1965) has commented, 'Local government had thrust upon it some burdens in the field of social services which the existing structure was not designed to carry and which it has become increasingly incapable of carrying.'[7]

The clearest illustration of this problem lay in planning and housing provision. There was a total of thirty-seven planning authorities, an arrangement which was strongly criticised by the Matthew Report in 1963.[8] It stated that there were too many planning authorities, that there was a rigid divorce of town from country, and that it was a practical impossibility for thirty-seven authorities to attract, retain and finance planning teams of the required calibre. Consequently local planning offices in the present-day sense of the term scarcely existed; and it was clear that the concept of a balanced team of professional staff enjoying proper standing and influence within municipal government had not yet been grasped, let alone implemented. Finally, the task of co-ordinating the efforts of thirty-seven independent planning authorities added an unnecessary complication to the difficulties of planning.

Rural district councils were given the same range of housing responsibilities as the borough and urban district councils, and many local authorities had a very poor record of housing provision.[9] This was particularly true in the inter-war period, when local authorities in Northern Ireland provided 15 per cent of new housing, compared with 25 per cent provided in England and Wales. Local councillors were reluctant to increase the burden on ratepayers. In more recent times the rate of new buildings fluctuated greatly between local councils, with some of the larger authorities having particularly poor records; for example, Londonderry Corporation built only 3,887 houses between 1944 and 1968. Local authorities were also slow to initiate slum clearance schemes, and it was not until 1959 that they were placed under a statutory obligation to do so. Even using a fairly conservative standard for 1959, over 40 per cent of the housing stock in twenty local government areas was unfit. The establishment of the Northern Ireland Housing Trust to assist in house-building was an acknowledgement of the defects of local authorities. Memoranda submitted to the cabinet by the Minister of Health and Local Government in 1944 and 1946 noted the leisurely pace at which schemes handled by local authorities proceeded[10] and the very feeble efforts made by housing authorities in some districts.[11]

The inadequacy of housing provision and other local services can be partly explained by the structure of local government. The existence of a large number of local authorities employing separate staffs and carrying out unco-ordinated housing programmes had serious effects which were outlined in the government White Paper on local government reform in 1967. This document commented that

> Far from building up the experience and coherent expertise needed to mount efficient and economical construction programmes, the present local administration leads to fragmentation of technical skill. Some councils are even unable to avail themselves of modern mechanical appliances in an age of high-cost labour, and many are unable to reap the benefits of bulk buying or of long-run contracts.[12]

Evidence by the Ministry of Development to the Macrory Review Body in 1970 identified problems in other services. There were too many local road authorities, causing an overemphasis on local schemes at the expense of the regional road system and insufficient co-ordination between road planning and road management. The system of water supply and distribution was wasteful in its use of scarce professional staff, and the price of water varied widely in different areas.

Finance
The most significant financial factor in local government was the high proportion of its finance which was provided by central government grants. By 1970 some 75 per cent of expenditure was borne by Exchequer grants, a proportion which was much higher than in either Great Britain or the Republic of Ireland. In 1921–22 rates provided almost six times as much revenue as government grants; by 1945 the proportions were equal; but in the last twenty years the imbalance between rates and grants has grown.

Several factors accounted for the weak financial position of local authorities. Firstly, many rural areas were poor and sparsely populated, producing low receipts from the rates. Forty-six authorities were not financially viable, having a rateable valuation from which a 1d per pound rate levy produced less than £500. Another cause of low rate revenue was extensive derating. The Nugent Report on local government finances in 1957 stated that the government's derating policy had so reduced the number of directly rate-producing properties that the yield from the rates could not meet the cost of local services.[13] The conception of the rate as a tax on all real property has been continuously eroded. Northern Ireland had 100 per cent derating of agricultural land and buildings, 75 per cent derating of industrial buildings, and a special exemption from rating for hospitals, churches, schools, courts, welfare homes and other institutions whose buildings were used for charitable or public purposes. Industrial derating was abolished in England and Wales in 1963, but its retention in Northern Ireland was justified by the need for incentives to attract industry. The categories of properties eligible for exemption because of occupation for public or charitable purposes were more numerous than in England and Wales. The approximate loss of rate revenue through derating and exemption was calculated at £6.2 million for 1967–68.[14] The Nugent Report had recommended that industrial derating should be ended and that exemption from rating should be kept within strict limits, but the government did not implement these proposals. A third cause of low rate revenue was the failure to keep valuation up to date. No revaluation took place between 1957 and 1975. This failure meant that local authorities were deprived of a very substantial increase in their rate base. It has been estimated that the net annual value in 1969 on the basis of current rental values should have been some £65 million instead of £17 million.[15]

Local government finance was further complicated by the fact that local authorities contributed towards the cost of some services provided by central bodies (e.g. drainage, fire services and civil defence) and also to certain agricultural levies. The Education Act, 1947, introduced the principle whereby part of the cost of education throughout Northern Ireland was shared by the local authorities according to their relative shares in the total net annual value. The distribution of the levy was inequitable because of the out-of-date valuation. Boroughs and urban districts also had to make a contribution to the cost of county services in their areas; and it has been claimed that, faced with increasing levies and the county demand, district councils attempted to keep the rates down by cutting expenditure on their own local services and amenities.[16]

Ilersic (1969 a) argues that the allocation of revenue to local authorities from central sources was hardly over-generous and that even the poorest of the English authorities received considerably more than comparable bodies in Northern Ireland, both in absolute and relative terms.[17] There was a wide variety of grant-in-aid schemes from the central government. Some grants were fixed, some variable; percentage grants varied from 100 per cent down to 30 per cent; some grants took account of capacity to pay, while others did not. In addition to specific grants, there was a general Exchequer contribution based on a formula which took account of derating and included a needs element. Owing to increasing costs in the period from 1964 onwards, this had to be supplemented by extra statutory payments. Northern Ireland local authorities rarely attempted to raise or borrow money on their own, and most authorities obtained their entire capital needs from the Government Loans Fund. The growth of specific grants and the general financial dependence on the central government resulted in increasing day-to-day control by the central government. Ilersic argues that 'The gradual erosion of local authorities' independence and the contraction of their role in the community is directly related to their increasing dependence on the Exchequer.'[18] Little was done to improve the financing of local government. The opportunity of putting local government on a more secure financial footing was lost when the proposals of the Nugent Report were not adopted by the government.

Politics
Insufficient financial resources and structural and functional defects do not constitute a complete explanation for the failings of local government. Many councils were neither administratively nor financially viable, but it was the political issue that was to prove crucial. The close identification that exists between political preference and religious affiliation in Northern Ireland has had serious consequences for the local government system. Most local authorities were controlled by Unionists, including the two corporations and the six county councils. One of the first (and most controversial) actions of the Unionist government had been the abolition of proportional representation in local government elections in 1922. During the last years of the old local government system after the 1967 elections non-Unionists formed a majority in only ten councils (five urban district councils and five rural district councils). However, there was no provision in the election procedure for a declaration by candidates of party-political loyalties, and in some councils all the councillors were Independents, i.e., they did not stand as party representatives. The majority of Independent councils were largely Unionist in outlook.

Local government politics were largely dominated by sectarian considerations. This has had two general effects. Firstly, few councils changed hands at local elections and few seats ever passed from one party to another, so rigid were the political attitudes and loyalties. Limavady Rural District Council was the only council where control ever changed between Unionists and Nationalists. With so little prospect of altering the political composition of councils, very few seats were contested; at the elections in 1967, for example, there were contests in only 66 out of 496 seats in the rural

F*

district. A recent survey of local councillors who served in the pre-1973 system has shown that 25 per cent of councillors had never fought an election and that 50 per cent had fought only one or two elections; 50 per cent of rural district councillors had never fought an election.[19] In such circumstances it is difficult to speak of the accountability of councillors to the electorate.

Secondly, council debates and policy decisions were often dominated by ideological and dogmatic considerations. Local government discussions on education, housing, and by-laws, for example on Sunday observance, often involved matters on which Ulster's two communities held rigid, inflexible and conflicting attitudes, and considerations of social need and amenity were often overlooked.

The dominant position of the Unionist Party in the central government and in most local authorities had resulted in much controversy over allegations of discrimination in local government against the Catholic community. The allegations have concerned two main grievances. Firstly, it was claimed that there was a lack of equality of access to power within the local government structure. Until 1968 the local government franchise was restricted to house-holders, which was to the disadvantage of the generally less prosperous Catholic community. Also there were twelve local government areas which had a Catholic majority in the population but where there was a Protestant/Unionist majority on the council. These included Londonderry County Borough, which was 60 per cent Catholic. The Cameron Commission, which was set up in 1969 to inquire into the causes of the disturbances of that year, found

> well-documented cases of deliberate manipulation of local govern-
> ment electoral boundaries in order to achieve and maintain
> Unionist control of local authorities and so to deny to Catholics
> influence in local government proportionate to their numbers.[20]

The second grievance concerned the allegations of discrimination against Catholics by some councils in the distribution of goods and services, particularly housing and employment opportunities. Objective evidence on discrimination by local authorities is not available. Barritt and Carter (1962), with few statistics available, found it difficult to comment on the extent of religious discrimina-tion, although they concluded that discrimination was practised in local government employment, preference being given by whatever party was in power in the council to applicants who were assumed to be its adherents.[21] Busteed and Mason (1971) asserted that 'The outputs of the local government system, especially public housing and local authority employment, were widely regarded as a form of patronage, distributed by councillors to electors who shared their own religious and political outlook.'[22] The Cameron Report was satisfied that some Unionist-controlled councils have used their power to make appointments in a way which benefited Protestants, and presented an amount of statistical evidence relating to some authorities.[23] The report also noted that

Council housing policy was distorted for political ends in that houses were built and allocated in such a way that they will not disturb the political balance and that there were unfair methods of allocation.[24]

Few councils had a points system for determining priorities in making allocations. Basing his conclusions on his survey of the proportion of Catholics and Protestants in public authority housing, Rose (1971) has claimed that there is no evidence of systematic discrimination against Catholics in housing allocation. His sample consisted of 413 respondents living in public authority housing; 41 per cent of these were Catholics, and they occupied 45 per cent of the accommodation.[25] More accurate data on this question is now available from the 1971 census. This shows that in 45,436 (or 30.7 per cent) of a total of 147,854 publicly rented houses the head of the household was a Catholic. Census figures show that 25 per cent of all heads of households are Catholics and that 31.4 per cent of the total population are Catholic. It should be noted that this may be a slight underestimation of the proportion of Catholics occupying publicly rented accommodation, as there was an attempt at a census boycott in some Catholic areas. Previous census returns had a very low proportion of 'not stated' religious affiliation. The proportion of Catholics in the 1961 census was 34.9 per cent, and in the 1951 census it was 34.4 per cent.

It is difficult to assess the relevance of these statistics to the allegations of discrimination and to decide whether a proportionate distribution according to overall population is a fair distribution. It can be argued that as a higher proportion of Catholic families have low income, occupied poor housing and have larger families, they should comprise a larger proportion of those accommodated with new publicly rented housing if housing allocation is operated strictly on a needs basis. In the period 1969–71 there was indeed an increase in the number of Catholics moving into publicly rented accommodation. This was particularly true of Londonderry, where some 2,000 new houses were built during these years. The published census figures do not provide information about individual council areas. The Cameron Report pointed out:

In the light of a mass of evidence put before us, in the Unionist-controlled areas it was fairly frequent for housing policy to be operated so that houses allocated to Catholics tended to go to rehouse slum dwellers whereas Protestant allocations tended to go more frequently to new families. Thus the total numbers allocated were in rough correspondence to the proportions of Protestants and Catholics in the community.[26]

It is probably true that discrimination existed in a certain number of authorities, mainly in the west of the province. The Cameron Report confined its strictures to six housing authorities.

Barritt and Carter noted the widely held view among Protestants that Catholics were disloyal to the state but were ready to accept state assistance.[27] Research into Protestant attitudes on discrimination by Nelson (1975) has shown ambiguities in attitudes. A majority believed that the pre-1968 system did discriminate disproportionately against Catholics; others did not look upon certain practices as discrimination; but very few argued that discrimination was right or necessary.

While it is difficult to assess more precisely the degree of discrimination in local government, it is probably true that most Catholics believed there was discrimination in this area and had little confidence in the local government system. Harris (1972) summarised this attitude in her study of a Northern Ireland community:

His initial interpretation of the local level experience which provide his objective evidence for discrimination itself, rests on a prior assumption that actions relating to economic affairs are designed to benefit government supporters and are not decided on an objective basis.[28]

Such a situation does not arise necessarily because of overt or extensive maladministration or mismanagement, but through the conviction that such malpractice exists. Such a conviction need not be an accurate representation of objective evidence and may simply represent a loss of confidence in administrative agencies. Catholic grievances against local government were clearly an important factor in initiating the Civil Rights movement and in leading directly to the restructuring of local government.

One commentator has gone so far as to state that local government has not made a contribution to the development of Northern Ireland and that progress has only been made by superseding the local authorities in fields which they have traditionally administered.[29] It can at least be said that the local government system in Northern Ireland did not function as a very efficient method of administration for local services. There was no established tradition of policy initiatives by local authorities. The system also failed to fulfil the ideal of democratic self-government. Local politics have inevitably centered on questions of sectarian influence and control, and, as Lawrence (1965 b) suggests, the climate of opinion in Northern Ireland has not been conducive to local democracy.[30] No attempts were made to meet the special problems inherent in this situation, and the nineteenth-century structure of local government was preserved virtually intact. This was in marked contrast to the evolution of the system in the Irish Free State, where early steps had been taken to reduce the possible effects of political bias and conflicts in the council chamber through the introduction of a system of county management, a centralised Appointments Board, and the removal of potentially controversial services.

It might be argued that the central government should have intervened more directly wherever local authorities were not providing services or wherever there were allegations of discrimination, but the central government ministers and departments took the view that they could not intervene with the statutory powers of publicly elected councils. Again, given the comparatively small number of authorities, close relationships tended to develop between officials and ministers which were possibly detrimental to the exercise of more central control or to endeavours to change the system. But even those areas where supervisory and financial powers had been reserved to central government departments were not immune from contention. Dr Oliver, former Permanent Secretary of the ministry responsible for local government, has revealed that there were many points of political friction, especially with the more extreme Unionist councils.[31] In particular there was a more or less continual and sometimes bitter dispute between Stormont and the largest authority, Belfast Corporation, from the 1920s onwards over a number of issues. However, right up until the mid-1960s the government did not grasp the need for a radical reform of the system.

The political problems in local government were allowed to accumulate, and there was opposition to reform from vested political interests. As Busteed and Mason (1971) have noted, 'The normal reluctance of local representatives to support reform proposals was powerfully reinforced by a desire to retain control of a source of patronage and electoral advantage.'[32]

Proposals for Reorganisation

It was not until the mid-1960s that the Northern Ireland government began to move in the direction of local government re-organisation, prompted by the realisation that the existing system was not capable of coping with the contemporary problems of planned development. The Matthew Report in 1963 had stressed the importance of local government in providing the infrastructure for regional planning and economic development and had been critical of the existing structure. The Northern Ireland Economic Council had called it a completely outdated system which was a positive impediment to economic progress.[33]

The reform process got under way in 1966 with the initiation of a series of consultations between the government and local authority associations and the subsequent publication of a White Paper.[34] This document acknowledged the problem, stating that 'The present local government system stems from the nineteenth century, and it is now, by common consent, in need of overhaul.' It also set out the criteria for a successful system of local government: 'efficiency, economy and the effective representation of local aspirations, all in harmony with public policy as a whole'. The White Paper then made tentative proposals for a degree of reorganisation, suggesting that the boroughs and urban and rural districts should be abolished and replaced by twelve to eighteen new administrative areas based on towns and surrounding districts; county councils, however, would retain their existing functions. While this paper saw the main need in terms of restructuring, it also acknowledged some other problem areas, notably that created by the lack of expertise in local government. It referred to the possibility of delegating some of the work of councils to a general manager and held out the hope that a general stream-lining of local government would attract councillors of a better calibre and would provide more opportunities for greater professionalism and the application of specialist skills.

Following lengthy discussions with local government interests, the government brought out further proposals on local government reform in July 1969.[35] This paper proposed seventeen area councils and, unlike its predecessors, questioned the need for the continued existence of county councils. In initiating discussions on a new structure for health and personal social services and possible alternative forms of administration for education and library services, the White Paper suggested that the outcome might well indicate that there was no place for the county councils in the new system. At this time it was envisaged that housing, environmental services, planning and minor roads would be the responsibility of the new district councils. It was also recognised that the whole basis of local government finance would have to be altered.

It was the government's hope that the whole local government system could be effectively reorganised by 1971.

Government thinking on the restructuring of health and welfare services was made public soon afterwards in a consultative Green Paper in August 1969.[36] These proposals fitted in with the reforms outlined for local government, although most of them differed radically from current thinking in Britain on the subject. One recommendation which was, however, in line with those contained in the consultative paper on health services in Britain, which appeared at the same time, was the proposed integration of the three parts of the health service (hospitals, general health services and local authority health services) in a system of nominated area boards. The reasons given to justify this recommendation were largely similar to those put forward in Britain: firstly, that the present structure was tripartite, whereas the individual's needs for services should be seen as a continuum; secondly, that the separate branches of the health services were increasingly interdependent, whereas the administrative structure should be so designed as to secure fully co-ordinated planning; thirdly, that the three-tier management structure in the hospital service had led to duplication of effort and difficulties in communication, so that it was obvious that a single authority would make better use of resources. The Green Paper proposed a minimum of three and a maximum of five areas, each with its own board responsible directly to the government for the provision of services. Departing from the British scheme, the paper then went on to recommend that these boards should also be responsible for the personal social services. On the assumption that there would be no county councils in a future structure, several alternative possibilities for the administration of the personal social services were examined. The option of two separate boards was rejected on the grounds that it would not only separate health and welfare where there was a need for co-operation and joint planning, but also that it would add to the number of administrative authorities and would be uneconomical in the use of administrative and supporting staff. The option favoured by the Green Paper was for a single board in each area to administer health and personal social services. This principle of a unified health and personal social services structure under the control of a nominated board was directly contrary to the recommendations of the Seebohm Committee in England, which proposed autonomous social service departments under committees of local authorities.

Although there was considerable opposition to the reform proposals among local councillors, the situation was considerably altered by the outbreak of civil disturbances in 1968 and 1969 and by the declared intention of the British government to promote further social and administrative reforms. The reform programmes of 1968–69 were mainly concentrated in the local government sphere. In November 1968 the Northern Ireland government announced a series of new initiatives, including detailed guidelines for a housing allocation scheme, a local government ombudsman to investigate complaints, a Development Commission to replace Londonderry Corporation, and immediate action on a major housing programme. The government also announced its intention to carry out a comprehensive restructuring of the local government system and subsequently made a decision to reform the local authority franchise on a 'one man one vote' basis. In October 1969 further reforms were announced, including the provision of a centralised housing authority to take over all the housing functions of local authorities and other public agencies. This change was undoubtedly pushed through as a result of pressure from the British government. Mr Faulkner, then the Minister of Development, was later to admit that 'Until we had our discussions with the British government last October, we had no intention of producing any kind of centralised organisation for the building of houses.'[37] The original White Paper on local government reform in 1967 had stated that housing administration would remain a local government concern, but in 1969 it was recognised that the local authorities were not geared to handle the task of providing a large-scale building programme.

The creation of a central housing authority had important consequences for the local government structure and particularly for the future organisation of services ancillary to house-building. A government communiqué stated that a central housing authority would have to be able to rely upon 'the assured provision of water and sewerage and their organisation on a scale and in step with house-building, road programmes to suit, and, above all, the prompt release of land for housing estates, redevelopment and attendant social and recreational services'.[38] A new review body under the chairmanship of Mr Patrick Macrory was set up to study these and other aspects of the reorganisation of local government. The review body reported in June 1970 in a document that was brief and lacking in detailed discussion and analysis.[39] The terms of reference of the review body, unlike those of the Royal Commission on local government reform in England and Scotland, did not permit discussion of the principle of local democracy; nor did they confine the review body to the existing local government functions, but were extended to include functions performed by other public authorities. The review body noted what it referred to as three special circumstances of Northern Ireland: the size of the province, the dependence of local government on central government finance, and the existence of a regional tier of government at Stormont.

Given these circumstances and the need for co-ordination of housing with the other environmental services, the Macrory Review Body accepted the argument for centralisation of the major services. It also pointed to the need to eliminate the indecision, delay and duplication that had resulted from the existing division of responsibilities among a whole series of government departments, local councils and boards, and stressed the importance of bringing together people with expert knowledge of the various functions of local administration—the lack of which, the report noted, was related to the alleged failure of councils to attract sufficient numbers of elected representatives of the right calibre. The Macrory Report proposed that the existing functions of local government should be divided into two categories—regional functions (i.e. wide area functions which require large centralised units for administration) and local district functions—with services in the first category being administered by the Northern Ireland parliament, government and ministries. It rejected both the possibility of independent boards for each service, since this would again give rise to a plethora of *ad hoc* bodies with their attendant problems of co-ordination, and the idea of three to four large local authorities, since these would be too large to be close enough to the people in the small towns, villages and rural areas. It was also agreed that any two-tier system would be too elaborate. In the case of education, personal health and social services, delegation to a system of area boards was considered advisable. The creation of not more than twenty-six district councils to administer the range of district services was also recommended. These proposals were very different from those contained in the 1967 and 1969 White Papers. The 1967 White Paper expressly rejected centralised forms of administration as depriving services of valuable elements of local interests and initiative. However, given the decisions already taken on housing and health and personal social services, the main recommendations of 1970 were largely predictable, and it is not surprising that the Macrory Report was accepted as the basis for the reorganisation of the local administration.

The New Structure of Centralised Administration

In the new administrative structure the main public services have been removed from the local government sphere and are administered regionally as the responsibility of the central government. There are no longer all-purpose authorities for geographical areas but a distinct and separate administrative structure for each group of related services. Four different types of structure have been adapted for the different local services; each of these is described below.

(1) *Centralised* Ad Hoc *Boards*

This administrative structure had been adapted for the purpose of dealing with housing. The Northern Ireland Housing Executive was set up as a decision-making body responsible for housing policy and its implementation. It comprises a board of nine members, six of whom are appointed by the minister, while the remaining three are nominees from the Housing Council, which is a consultative and advisory body consisting of one representative from each of the district councils. For administrative purposes the province is divided into three regions, ten areas and thirty-nine districts. The Housing Executive took over the responsibilities of the Northern Ireland Housing Trust, the local authorities and the Development Commissions.

Some of the larger local authorities had formerly been responsible for services which in other areas were under the control of an existing regional body. Reorganisation involved the central body extending its functions. Thus the Northern Ireland Fire Authority has merged with the Belfast Fire Brigade to form a single service. The Electricity Board for Northern Ireland, the Belfast Corporation Electricity Department, the Londonderry Commission Electricity Department and the Joint Electricity Authority were merged into a single new authority responsible for the generation and distribution of electricity throughout Northern Ireland.

(2) *Area Boards*

Health and personal social services, education and libraries were placed under an area board structure. Four health and social services boards were established to undertake the area administration of services on behalf of the government department. Board members are appointed by the minister; approximately 30 per cent are nominated by the new local government district councils, a further 30 per cent represent professional interests, and the remainder business interests, trade unions, universities and voluntary bodies. The Eastern Health and Social Services Board has a membership of 34, the Northern board has 33, the Southern 24, and the Western 25. The area boards are co-terminous with a number of the new local government districts, and these districts, either singly or in groups, form units of management for the local provision of health and personal social services. There are three such districts for the Belfast/Castlereagh area and fourteen for the rest of the province, each comprising one or more of the areas of the new district councils. Within each of the districts there is a district committee, appointed by the appropriate area board and representing the interests of the local community in an advisory capacity.

There are also a number of activities which are organised on a regional basis. The Central Services Agency provides certain common services on behalf of the department and the boards, for example in making payments to contractors such as general practitioners, chemists and opticians and lawyers. The agency is composed of members nominated by area boards and the professional bodies involved. A Staff Council for the Health and Social Services undertakes functions relating to management training and appointments procedures. A Health and Social Services Council advises the department on matters of major policy, and specialist central advisory committees have also been established for certain professions and services.

There are five education and library boards managing the state schools and educational institutions and providing for the day-to-day maintenance of most voluntary schools; they are also responsible for the public library services. There is no tier of district administration. Approximately 40 per cent of the members of each board are nominated by district councils, and 25 per cent represent bodies who either transferred their schools to the state or are responsible for voluntary schools with maintained status. There are also three teachers, three persons with a special interest in libraries, and six or seven nominees of the minister. The total membership of each board ranges from 31 to 35.

(3) *Centralisation through Government Departments*

Planning, roads, water and sewerage have become the responsibility of the Department of the Environment and are administered through a chain of local offices. The department is the planning authority for the whole province, except for planning appeals, which are determined by an independent Planning Appeals Commission. The department operates through a headquarters unit, which formulates all legislation, policy, regional strategy and major development proposals, and six divisional offices responsible for the implementation and control of development planning. The powers and functions of the Development Commissions in new towns have also passed to the ministry. The Water Service Division of the Department of the Environment is responsible for water supply and sewerage and has four divisional executive organisations.

The Department of the Environment is also now the sole road authority, being responsible for all public roads, traffic management, public car parks, street lighting, functions relating to private streets, and road safety. These services are administered by the Roads Executive through six divisional offices.

Other matters which have also become the direct responsibility of central government departments include vehicle registration and licensing, electoral registration and criminal injuries compensation.

(4) *District Councils*

A range of responsibilities remained with the twenty-six new

Table 20: Reorganised Structure of Local Government, 1977

	Centralised boards	Area boards	Government departments	District councils
Health services		*		
Personal social services		*		
Education		*		
Housing	*			
Town and country planning			*	
Libraries		*		
Roads			*	
Water and sewerage			*	
Police	*			
Vehicle registration and licensing			*	
Fire services	*			
Registration of births, marriages and deaths				*
Electricity	*			
Gas				*
Recreational facilities				*
Car parks			*	
Cleaning and sanitation				*
Markets and abattoirs				*

district councils, although they mainly involved minor environmental and recreational activities. The new councils were elected under proportional representation on the basis of single transferable votes. Officially they are described as having three roles—a direct role, a representative role, and a consultative role. Their role in the direct provision of services is limited to environmental health, clean air, cleansing, litter, parks, cemeteries, sports, culture, entertainment, certain tourist development projects, enforcement of building regulations, licensing of certain premises for public safety, and the registration of births, marriages and deaths. Since their establishment some further powers have been granted, so that they are now responsible for some aspects of community development, for noise control, and for seeing that certain requirements as to the fitness and standards of privately rented houses are fulfilled. Some district councils also have responsibilities for gas, markets and abattoirs and local harbours. The councils' representative role is in nominating locally elected representatives to sit as members of the various statutory boards. Their consultative role is in acting as the medium for the expression of local opinion on the operation of the regional services in their areas. Central government departments have a statutory obligation to consult the district councils about proposals affecting their areas.

Finance

The centralisation of local government services has had important implications for the rating system. The government decided that there should be a division of rates into regional and district contributions, although both portions would be collected together by the Ministry of Finance. The regional rate is uniform for the whole of Northern Ireland, and it was estimated that for the year 1973–74 perhaps 85 per cent of the rate revenue would go towards expenditure on the regional (i.e. centralised) services. The regional rate for 1973–74 was determined by reference to estimates of expenditure on the services transferred and the grants which would have been payable. The procedure was not held to be practical in subsequent years, and it was decided to determine the rate by reference to parity with a comparable area in Great Britain, although allowance was to be made in this comparison for any relevant differences. Three reasons were given for adopting this method in preference to basing the regional rate on expenditure on local services in Northern Ireland. Firstly, it is very difficult to determine how much of what the central government is doing would have been done by local authorities. Secondly, by 1972, the last year before the new system was brought into operation,

80 per cent of local government revenue came from central government grants, and grants depended on local authorities' individual financial and rateability assessments. It would have been a complicated business deciding after 1973 what grants would have been given and how much local authorities would have paid; such calculations would have been largely mythical, as the grants system was to be discontinued as a result of the reorganisation. The third reason was that the new system would provide parity of services with Great Britain. The choice of Humberside for comparison was based on statistical information, e.g. family income surveys. The imposition of a uniform rate for all areas of Northern Ireland was felt to be justified by the view that there would be a fairly even spreading of expenditure and services when there was regional administration of services.

District councils were given the maximum possible control over their own finances. A system of general revenue grants assisted those councils with below average resources. Specific grants required on a particular service can also be provided. The changes in the rating system were also accompanied by a complete new revaluation—the first since 1957—which came into operation in 1976.

The Process of Reorganisation

There was a certain amount of opposition to the proposals, although the continuance of civil and political strife probably made the opposition more muted than it would otherwise have been. The decision to centralise housing was the most politically contentious item. In 1970 the Ulster Unionist Council passed a resolution opposing the government's plan for a central housing authority. The proposed removal of powers from local government brought opposition from the Association of Local Authorities, which deplored the idea that non-democratic boards, nominated by the minister, should administer the main local government services. However, the professional bodies concerned were generally in favour of the reorganisation proposals.

The reorganisation of the local administration of services was carried out comparatively quickly between 1971 and 1973. After a two-day debate in Stormont in January 1971 consultative documents on reorganisation were issued in March and April by the Ministers of Education, Health and Social Services and Development outlining the proposals for putting into effect the decisions taken in principle by the government. The actual process of reorganisation was carried out by government departments with the assistance of certain *ad hoc* advisers and boards.

In 1971 a Local Government Consultative Committee, representing the three main local authority associations, Belfast Corporation and the three Development Commissions, was established and became a major forum for discussion between central and local government on the reorganisation programme. The consultative committee was used to assist the ministry in working out the details of the functions of the district councils and in dealing with associated questions of staffing, finance, and links with other services. A Boundaries Commissioner was appointed in 1971 to make recommendations about the boundaries and wards of the twenty-six new districts. An interdepartmental working party on local government finance was established, and a team of management consultants was brought in to assist with the reorganisation of health and personal social services.

In all, the changes involved a large legislative programme. In practical terms it mainly involved setting up new administrative structures and increasing the functions of central government departments. The transfer of functions involved large-scale redistribution of staff and of office accommodation. The movement of staff was one of the major features of the reorganisation. Some 40,000 people had been employed by local government, and over 20,000 by the Hospitals Authority and the General Health Services Board. A Local Government Interim Staff Commission and a Staff Commission for Health and Personal Social Services were created to advise the ministries on general staff policy and specific appointments and also to liaise with staff associations. Those employees who were transferred were given guarantees that the new terms and conditions would be such that, so long as they were engaged in duties reasonably comparable to their duties immediately before transfer, their salaries would not be lower than before. Where someone suffered a loss of employment or reduction of salary he could claim compensation.

The reorganisation took place in a smooth fashion amidst all the political turmoil and violence. The legislation incorporating most of the changes was introduced early in 1972, although the suspension of Stormont meant that it eventually had to pass through the Westminster parliament. In October 1972 the first members of the new nominated boards were appointed, and in May 1973 the first elections for the new district councils took place. By October 1973 the new system of administration was in operation.

The Expected Advantages of Reorganisation

The advantages of reorganisation were viewed in terms of efficiency, expertise, specialisation and impartiality. The new structure would reduce the number of administrative bodies; and it was hoped, as the Macrory Report stated, that it would 'eliminate the indecision, delay and duplication that are said to result from the present division of responsibilities among a whole series of government departments, local councils, boards and other statutory bodies'.[40] It was also hoped that it would facilitate co-ordination between the services, co-operation in social planning, the concentration of resources in priority areas, the more economic use of resources, and a general improvement in services.

The advantages that the government foresaw from the establishment of the Northern Ireland Housing Executive were listed as

> a common public authority rent structure throughout Northern Ireland; improved mobility; an end to allegations about sectarian discrimination in housing allocations; the attraction of more high-quality professional and administrative staff to housing work and the opportunity to use modern efficient management techniques; economies of scales; the organisation of contracts to ensure a steady demand on housing contractors and thus more efficient building; the elimination of unnecessary variety, coupled with greater opportunities for research and experiment; the introduction of advanced estate management throughout the country, which will be in the hands of qualified housing managers; but, above all, a new opportunity to solve Northern Ireland's housing problems in the foreseeable future.[41]

The creation of a single planning authority was intended to smooth the way for comprehensive and co-ordinated development for the whole province and to ensure greater consistency in decision-making relating to development control.

The main advantages of the reorganisation and integration of health and personal social services, as seen by the Permanent Secretary of the ministry, were described as follows in 1971. Firstly, it would in future be possible to plan at each level—the central government and the four boards—in terms of the totality of medical and social care. Secondly, it should be possible, within this combined structure, to secure a much more rational grouping and disposition of professional resources and facilities than was formerly possible. Thirdly, the administrative structure would be greatly simplified. Instead of some forty-seven bodies outside the ministry, there would be only four, each planning and managing services in its area. For the first time it would be possible for one body in each area to *feel*—as well as to be—responsible for the medical and social care of the population it served. (This was regarded as an important psychological as well as an organisational gain.) Fourthly, while ultimate responsibility would rest with ministers and the central government, the system of indirect control through area boards would ensure public participation and would also protect professional freedom.[42]

It was also hoped that reorganisation would result in more uniform standards of social provision throughout Northern Ireland and reduce the existing gap in standards between the west of the province and the east, particularly in housing and personal social services. Official statements tended to emphasise technical efficiency as the major benefit expected from reorganisation rather than the more political benefits of expertise and impartiality.

One of the recurrent problems in local government has been its failure to attract elected representatives of sufficiently high calibre. Ilersic (1969 b) had noted that 'The main argument in favour of centralisation is that the quality of local government representatives falls far short of the requirements for a responsible authority.'[43] It was confidently expected that the new structure would enable the appointment to the controlling boards of people with the necessary expertise, experience and impartiality, and that 'many public-spirited citizens of all religious persuasions might be willing to serve on co-opted bodies, independent of the local party machines'.[44]

The final major benefit expected from the removal of the central or major services from local government was the ending of claims and disputes about religious discrimination and sectarian bias in housing allocations, house-building, planning, employment and other matters.

The Operation of the New System

Efficiency

It is difficult to assess whether reorganisation has produced a more efficient system of administration. The experience of the Housing Executive to date has been disappointing in terms of housing output. House-building slumped in the period 1972–75, and the number of houses built fell far below the targets set in the Development Programme for 1970–75, particularly in the public sector, where little more than half the target number was provided. In 1974 the Housing Executive built 5,412 houses and in 1975 5,143 houses compared with 7,692 built in 1970 and 9,102 built in 1971 in the public sector. The process of reorganisation and transfer of responsibilities caused major problems. Mr Harry Simpson, the first Director of the Housing Executive, has commented that 'Month after month we were accepting responsibility for more and more authorities whose affairs were not in order. Former housing authorities had let their programmes run down as soon as they knew they were about to be taken over rather than continue with the pre-planning of housing development.'[45] The centralisation of ancillary services to house-building, such as water, sewerage and roads, was an additional complication.

There have also been considerable difficulties in building up specialist staff. The recruitment programme has been hampered by the severe shortage of technical staff in the province and increasing competition from other public bodies which were also in the process of reorganisation. There were additional difficulties caused by the need to recruit, assimilate and train staff rapidly.

Recurring violence has contributed to considerable delays in the completion of Housing Executive dwellings. There have been difficulties in getting contractors to tender in troubled areas, and this has frequently caused delays in site starts. Further problems related to the violence include shortages of particular materials, vandalism and theft on new sites, manpower shortages, and the impact of sectarian antagonism on labour relations. Most of the province's builders' providers now carry smaller stocks, thus making it difficult to obtain regular supplies. Violence has inhibited labour mobility, since workmen are often reluctant to travel to different areas to work. There has also been a marked degree of emigration of skilled building tradesmen to other parts of the United Kingdom. In addition, an increasing proportion of the Housing Executive's work has been in the troubled redevelopment areas of Belfast, and this type of operation is often slow.

Criticism has also been directed at the internal structure of the Housing Executive, and in 1976 a Civil Service management team was invited to examine its regional and area administration. Their report criticised the existing structure for having a top-heavy bureaucratic organisation, poor communication and lack of co-ordination, all of which lengthened decision-making procedures and impaired efficiency. It also referred to the absence of delegation of authority to enable staff at the local level to decide day-to-day issues; the central directorate and board members, on the other hand, were too involved in detailed decision-making. This led to difficulties in ascertaining accountability, to confused responsibilities and to needless complications in planning and project control. The report's major recommendation to improve administrative efficiency was decentralisation to six regional executive units.[46] A second report in 1978 made a case for the complete overhaul of the senior management structure of the Housing Executive.

The new integrated system of health and personal social services has also run into administrative problems. The objective of the re-organisation of health and social services was given as the improvement of health and social services to the community by means of the establishment of an integrated approach to the delivery of hospital and specialist services, local health and welfare services, and general health services. The concept of corporate approach to management was introduced to establish a basis for the integrated planning, co-ordination and control of services. The area executive team consists of the Chief Administrative Medical Officer, the Chief Administrative Nursing Officer, the Director of Social Services, and the Chief Administrative Officer and the chairman of the area medical advisory committee. The district executive team consists of the equivalent district officials.

A research project into the functioning of the new structure and individual roles within the structure found that two-thirds of the officers interviewed felt that the two-tier system of area and district administration was not working effectively.[47] The main comments referred to a lack of clear definition of responsibility and functions and to a top-heavy administration with too many divisions, resulting in considerable delays in decision-making; they also pointed out that the area boards had too little autonomy and were continually obliged to refer matters to the Department of Health and Social Services. The district officers felt that their lines of communication with the area boards and the department were unnecessarily attenuated, again causing decision-making to be a very slow process.

On the question of the effectiveness of the new structure on the standard of services, about half felt that the patient had benefited or would benefit, a quarter thought that there was no evidence of any benefit, and a quarter believed that there had been no real benefit. Those who thought there had been benefits felt that reorganisation had achieved a more cohesive and co-ordinated service and also a more even distribution of finance across the province. Some felt that the new structure and the long lines of communication made the system impersonal and more remote from the public, so that contact between the authorities and the public was less satisfactory than before. There was general approval for the integration of health and personal social services. The majority of officials felt that it was providing better continuity of care between professions and between hospital and community, and that it had enabled hospitals to become more involved with social services and thereby to acquire practical experience of how community services fitted into the overall pattern of care. It was also observed that it had increased awareness of the total needs of the community and had given access to a greater fund of expertise and advice in decision-making.

Some doubts have arisen as to whether the three-tier structure is appropriate for the health service, and particularly as to whether the division of the province into seventeen administrative districts is necessary. There have been problems in that some senior medical staff in hospitals had had difficulty in accepting the status of members of the district executive teams. But any further reorganisation is unlikely at present.

The new structure has probably established more uniform standards of provision throughout the province, but it has produced problems because of the size and complexities of the bureaucracy. The number of administrative and clerical staff in health and personal social services, for example, rose by 36 per cent between March 1973 and June 1975.

The operation of the centralised planning service has also been criticised, particularly for the rigid implementation of a uniform policy to refuse planning permission for new single houses in rural areas. Criticism has been so widespread that a special committee was appointed in 1977 to review the department's rural planning policy. The report referred to evidence that the current policy was forcing the disintegration of rural communities and recommended that the policy be operated in a more flexible and sympathetic manner.[48]

Other services centralised under government departments have come in for less criticism, although difficulties have been caused by the attenuated system of communication from local level up to the central government which is now necessary for reaching day-to-day decisions formerly made by the local authority, e.g. on road maintenance. The new structure has incorporated a network of different administrative agencies, and the boundaries of the various boards also vary considerably at both regional and local level. Each district council has a post of District Development Officer, whose job it is to act as a link and a channel of communication and co-ordination between the local council and the other public bodies.

The Lack of Accountability and Participation

The injection of expertise and specialisation which was a key feature of the new structure was achieved at the expense of public accountability and participation. The majority of the boards' members are appointed by the minister and do not have to account to the public through an electoral mechanism for their policies. The lack of means of accountability has been accentuated by the absence of a regional government. The whole system of reorganisation had assumed the existence of a regional government as a top-tier authority in relation to services transferred from local government. Under direct rule the Northern Ireland Office ministers and the

Westminster parliament now provide the only level of account-ability.

It is also clear that many citizens have experienced difficulty in expressing their views and making meaningful contact with the boards. Although the boards do have local councillors as members, it can be argued that in general their membership is unrepresentative of the whole community. The members tend to come from a nar-rower socio-economic group and age group than would those belonging to a locally elected council. In most areas of Northern Ireland local councillors have traditionally been the main channels of communication for information and complaints about such matters as housing allocations and repairs. But nominated members of the various boards are not so readily accessible to members of the public, so that most people wishing to make a complaint or a request still bring the matter to the attention of their local district councillors, who, in turn, have to refer it to the appropriate board.

The lack of opportunity for public participation and involvement presents a particular problem for the planning and environmental services, which are completely centralised under the department. The Cockcroft Report in 1978 noted that the bureaucracy implicit in the department's assumption of overall planning responsibility has led to an increasing feeling of remoteness on the part of individuals and organisations involved in and affected by planning decisions.[49]

The only formal means of local participation in the new structure is through the district committees for health and personal social services administration. The government appeared to recognise a special need for the involvement of local communities in the welfare of patients and those with social problems. Membership of the district committees includes local members of the area board, district councillors, members from the former hospital management committees, and representatives of voluntary organisations; all members, however, must be nominated by the area board.

District committees can scrutinise and criticise services, and the area board has an obligation to consult the district committees on any significant changes it proposes. The committees can also make visits of observation to facilities within their district.[50] District com-mittees were expected to look upon the district executive team as its chief link and normal means of communicating with the board. Clearly this structure has limitations as a means of self-expression for local communities. Apart from their limited functions, the district committees have very little independence. They are nomin-ated by the area boards and are dependent on them for secretarial support and assistance.

Impartiality

The removal of services from local government was expected to produce more impartial administration. A further means of protection against discrimination and bias in the administration of local services has existed since 1969 in the form of the office of Commissioner for Complaints. The commissioner has the duty of investigating any written complaint made to him by a person claiming to have suffered injustice in consequence of maladministration on the part of local authorities or public bodies. The first Commissioner for Complaints adopted the following definition of maladministration:

> Maladministration may be taken to cover administrative action (or inaction) based on or influenced by improper considerations or conduct. Arbitrariness, malice or bias, including discrimination, are examples of improper considerations. Neglect, unjustifiable delay, failure to observe relevant rules or procedures, failure to take relevant consideration into account, and failure to establish or review procedures where there is a duty or obligation on a body to do so are examples of improper conduct.[51]

The Commissioner for Complaints' original jurisdiction was over local authority services and various regional bodies (e.g. the Housing Trust), whereas a Parliamentary Commissioner for Administration was established, also in 1969, to deal with complaints against central government departments. Following the reorganisation of local services, some subjects previously within the Commissioner for Complaints' jurisdiction have passed to the Parliamentary Commissioner, for example complaints concerning planning, water and roads.

The number of representations made to the Commissioner of Complaints was greatest in the first year following his appointment, but it has now levelled out at an average of 500 per year. About 30 per cent of complaints are rejected as outside the commissioner's jurisdiction. The commissioner is free to conduct his investigation as he sees fit, and he has the power to require the production of any relevant papers. If during the course of an investigation it appears that there are grounds for making a finding that may adversely affect any body or person, he must give them the opportunity to ask for a formal hearing with legal representation. There have been five such hearings.

The act setting up the Commissioner for Complaints gave him the dual function of investigating complaints and of effecting settlements. This broad directive has been so interpreted as to allow the commissioner to seek settlements of complaints in cases where he

Table 21: Findings of Maladministration, 1970–77[52]

Year	Complaints received	Investigations completed	Maladministration found	
			Number	(%)
1970	993	285	14	(5)
1971	499	594*	61	(10)
1972	368	257	28	(9)
1973	491	404	40	(10)
1974	316	252	15	(6)
1975	371	276	11	(4)
1976	374	299	16	(5)
1977	480	329	23	(7)
Total	3,892	2,697	208	(7.8)

* Includes investigations carried over from 1970.

Table 22: Classification of Complaints and Findings, 1970–77[52]

Classification	Complaints received	Maladministration found
Housing allocation	908	52
Housing repairs	747	12
Housing (other)	540	20
Employment	581	74
Public utility	146	5
Education	126	10
Public health	33	–
Roads	68	2
Planning	211	14
Miscellaneous	532	19
Total	3,892	208

did not actually make a finding of maladministration but where the complainant had clearly suffered some hardship. An average of about 35 per cent of all investigations resulted in settlements.

Housing and employment together account for over 60 per cent of the complaints investigated. The commissioner has noted that over half his work is taken up with an independent audit of the fairness and administrative standards of the Housing Executive.[53]

Maladministration was found in about 8 per cent of all the cases investigated. The commissioner's definition of maladministration (see above) is applicable to a wide range of matters, and he has pointed out that on some occasions the maladministration was not of a serious nature. In giving judgements he has also sometimes made a distinction between maladministration with injustice and maladministration without injustice.

The main problem that the office of Commissioner of Complaints was established to deal with was religious discrimination. The commissioner defined discrimination as the taking of a decision in favour of or against a person which is motivated by consideration of the person's religious belief or political opinions. Surprisingly in only about 6 per cent of complaints received were there allegations of religious discrimination, and in only three cases has there been a positive finding of religious discrimination. In some other cases the commissioner found a degree of maladministration but did not find the actions motivated by discrimination; and there have been some instances where he has admitted concluding less positively than in others that there was no evidence of discrimination. In reply to criticisms of his role in dealing with discrimination the commissioner has stressed that he can only deal with specific complaints by individuals and that he has no power to investigate allegations of a general nature or accusations of the type sometimes levelled against public bodies which happen to employ only persons of a particular religious affiliation. He has also commented that would-be complainants may be inhibited from bringing charges of discrimination, particularly in employment cases, by the fear of damaging prospects of future promotion or their relationship with fellow-workers.[54]

In cases where maladministration has been found the commissioner may make a recommendation, but such recommendations do not carry the force of law and no public body is obliged to accept them. There is, however, a provision under which a complainant who has obtained a finding of injustice in consequence of maladministration may make an application to the county court for redress. A complainant who was refused a resettlement grant by the Housing Executive applied successfully to the county court for an award of the amount. The county court may also make an assessment of compensation. A nurse who had suffered injustice as a result of maladministration by a county health committee in the making of an appointment was awarded £1,000 in the county court. This provision does give the Commissioner for Complaints more teeth than the Parliamentary Commissioner for Administration in either Northern Ireland or Britain, to whose findings the provision does not apply.

The Commissioner for Complaints has hardly made a dramatic impact upon the public. Mr John Benn, the first commissioner, saw the function of his office as twofold: to reassure the citizen that he is not defenceless or unsupported in his encounter with bureaucracy, and to encourage among officials better standards of administrative practice and a sensitivity to the needs and aspirations of ordinary people.[55] Mr Benn in his final report voiced the opinion that the existence of the office had helped to bring about a general improvement in the standard of local administration, although it appeared to have contributed little so far towards the establishment of peace and harmony in the community.[56] The work of the Commissioner for Complaints and the reorganisation of local administration would seem to ensure more impartial administration and provide safeguards against discrimination.

Public bodies in Northern Ireland are, along with private employers, within the scope of the Fair Employment Act, 1976. This legislation established a Fair Employment Agency which is empowered to investigate allegations of religious or political discrimination in employment matters; it may also issue directives, backed by the courts if necessary, to compel employers to act in certain ways. This means that the Commissioner for Complaints will no longer investigate allegations of discrimination in employment against public bodies. Some district councils with a United Ulster Unionist Coalition majority refused to sign a declaration of principle and intent 'to promote equality of opportunity in employment' circulated by the Fair Employment Agency. The Agency's first report noted that this attitude was not likely to inspire confidence about the equality of opportunity provided by these councils.[57]

The District Councils
The new district councils have few powers, but three aspects of their operations are of some significance: the politicisation of local government, the councils' performance in providing services, and their consultative role.

The first elections for the new local government structure took place in May 1973. The most remarkable difference between these elections and the previous local government elections in 1967 was the larger number of candidates and the intrusion of party politics. In 1973 there were 1,222 candidates for 526 seats, whereas in 1967 the majority of seats had been uncontested. In the 1977 elections only a few seats were uncontested. A major reason for this change was the introduction of proportional representation. The increased competition was also a result of the reduction of the number of

G

council seats from 1,300 to 526, although a study has shown that 57 per cent of councillors in the old system did not stand for election to the new system.[58] However, the principal reason for the large number of candidates was the decision of the main political parties to contest the elections. In 1973 only 142 candidates described themselves as independent or non-party, and only 52 of these were elected, together with 5 Independent Unionists. A recent survey has shown that 50 per cent of councillors in the old local government system were independent or non-party and that independent members were in a majority on a substantial number of councils.[59] In the 1977 elections only 39 independent or non-party councillors were elected, plus some 8 Independent Unionists. The main reason for the intrusion of party politics in the 1973 elections was the fact that they were the first elections of any kind since the introduction of direct rule. The election campaign was dominated by wider issues, and many of the party manifestoes covered issues far beyond the competence of local government, particularly the British government White Paper, *Northern Ireland: Constitutional Proposals,* published in March 1973.[60] Similarly in 1977 the local elections were the only elections that had been held since the Convention election in 1975, and once again a wide range of political issues dominated the campaign. The turnout in 1973 was 68 per cent, reaching over 80 per cent in some places, and in 1977 it was 55 per cent.

The political composition of the new councils reflects the PR electoral system in that there are relatively few councils where one

Table 23: Political Composition of Councils

	1973	1977
One-party majority	10	3
Unionist/loyalist majority	7	14
SDLP/Nationalist/Independent majority	3	4
Multi-party (no majority)	6	5
	26	26

party has an overall majority. In 1973 the Unionist Party had a working majority in ten councils. The 1977 election saw a decline in the number of Official Unionist councillors, and the party retained an overall majority in only two, Antrim and Banbridge, with the Democratic Unionist Party gaining control of Ballymena. Fourteen councils now have a Unionist/loyalist majority of councillors, but in some eight councils this assumes harmony between Official Unionists and Democratic Unionists—which is frequently not the case. Although all varieties of Unionists between them occupied only 54.7 per cent of council seats, they won control of 70 per cent of the councils. The SDLP has not had an overall majority in any council after either of the elections, but in a number of councils it has formed a majority in association with Independents. In some councils no group appears to have a majority; instead there is either a larger number of Independents (as in Moyle) or a dead heat between Unionist and SDLP/Independent groups (as in Fermanagh in 1973) or the balance of power is held by Alliance councillors (as in Down). While the new councils have few powers, two issues have proved controversial: the election of council chairmen or mayors and the chairmen of committees, and the appointment of council representatives to the various nominated boards. The majority of councils controlled by Unionist groupings have refused to appoint non-Unionist councillors as chairmen or vice-chairmen. In Londonderry, where there is an SDLP/Independent majority, the top positions are rotated among the various parties. An examination of council representation on the major nominated boards shows that the SDLP has only 15.4 per cent of places on the boards, while in sixteen out of the twenty-six councils the party has no representation at all. In a few councils there has also been controversy on questions of the opening of council amenities on Sundays and discrimination in employment.

The power of the new district councils to initiate activity is so limited that it is difficult to assess their efficiency in this regard. In 1976 the councils got a small boost when they were given certain responsibilities for community work and development, for which special funds were also made available. Some councils were rather suspicious of the political involvement of community groups, but fifteen councils now employ community service officers and some councils have spent considerable sums in this area. Others, such as Banbridge and Magherafelt, have spent nothing on community services.[61]

Given the district councils' lack of powers, a large part of their work consists of putting pressure on other bodies which do have the power. The fact that councils have to be consulted on planning applications and housing issues but that their views may not affect the eventual outcome has led to a great deal of frustration. Councils in rural areas have been particularly annoyed by the number of planning applications for building in the countryside which have been turned down by the Department of the Environment and the Planning Appeals Commission. The Cockcroft Report noted that the merely token consultation with councillors produced a feeling of alienation among them.[62]

Conclusion

Northern Ireland inherited a local government system which had originally been devised to suit the conditions of nineteenth-century England and was modified to meet the requirements of the highly centralised British administration in Ireland. Little consideration was given to the reform of the local government structure that existed in 1921 until the mid-1960s. The structural, financial and political problems of local government were allowed to accumulate. The Nugent Report recommendations on financial changes in 1957 were ignored by the government. No action was taken to deal with grievances about the restricted franchise or discrimination. Defects in the provision of services were ameliorated by *ad hoc* measures, by the creation of joint boards, by the transfer of the service to a centralised body or by partial transfer (as in the case of the Northern Ireland Housing Trust). It was not until the succession of Captain O'Neill that a new emphasis on the need for regional and economic planning raised the possibility of local government reform. The events of 1969, the findings of the Cameron Report and pressure from the British government led to an even more radical overhaul of the system than had been intended.

Northern Ireland had a three-tier system of government—the local councils, Stormont and Westminster—and the existence of the regional tier had implications for the local government system. Firstly, the regional government took direct responsibility for a number of services which otherwise might have been the responsibility of local government. Secondly, the regional government and its departments took a close interest in the supervision of local authorities and there was an ease and frequency of contact between central departments and local councils. Thirdly, the existence of a regional government reduced the status and powers of the local authorities, precluding their development as strong innovative bodies or as a focus for local community aspirations.

This state of affairs raises questions about the need for a developed local government system alongside a regional government, and about the appropriateness of a regional government relating to local authorities as a central government.

Social Policies (1):
Planning, Housing and Social Security

THIS and the following chapter are concerned with the development and operation of social policies in Northern Ireland. It is in the area of social policy that the legislative, administrative and executive powers of the Northern Ireland government have been greatest, where expenditure is greatest, and where the financial relationship between Stormont and Westminster was most important. One way in which the effects of devolution can be assessed is by considering how powers in the area of social policy have been used and with what effects. There are two other important dimensions to this discussion. Firstly, the action of the government in implementing its social policy involves the redistribution of resources between groups and households and affects the relative opportunities of different groups. Policy operates in the context of ideological, political and constitutional conflicts and, in turn, can exacerbate or modify those conflicts. Secondly, Northern Ireland has its own particular social and economic problems. One of the central arguments in the debate about devolution is the claim that a locally accountable administration is better able to respond to the particular circumstances in a country or region than a more distant central bureaucracy. In order to consider this aspect, these two chapters present a summary of certain aspects of social problems in Northern Ireland, a review of policy in certain key social services, and some general conclusions.

Social Problems in Northern Ireland

In relation to other parts of the United Kingdom, or indeed the regions of the European Economic Community, Northern Ireland is an economically deprived region exhibiting all the features of a backward, peripheral economy with serious problems in its economic structure.

The population of the six-county area has been increasing since 1891, but in 1971 it remained (at 1,536,065) some 110,000 fewer than in 1841. Any discussion of population structure and distribution would emphasise a number of points.[1] Some 50 per cent of the population of Northern Ireland lives within fifteen miles of Belfast city centre, and the density of population in this zone averages over 350 persons per square kilometre compared with a density of 49 p.p.s.k. in the west. This dominance of Belfast has increased since 1841, when more than 50 per cent of the population lived in Counties Fermanagh, Armagh, Tyrone and Londonderry. The growth of population since 1841 in Belfast and Co. Antrim is associated with rural depopulation elsewhere. Since 1951 the population of Greater Belfast has grown dramatically at the expense of the area within the city boundary (Belfast County Borough's population in 1951 was 443,671 compared with 362,082 in 1971) as well as the rest of the province. Northern Ireland has the highest rate of natural population increase in the United Kingdom, a higher crude birth rate, and (associated with the younger age structure) a lower crude death rate. In 1971 Northern Ireland had proportionately more persons aged under 25 and fewer aged over 25 than the United Kingdom. The dependent population (children and the retired) was proportionately higher in Northern Ireland. Although the birth rate has broadly followed United Kingdom trends, the decline has been less steep than in Great Britain.

The rate of natural population increase (excess of births over deaths per 1,000 population) has fallen in Northern Ireland from 11.1 in 1961 and 11.4 in 1966 to 10.1 in 1971 and 6.3 in 1975, but it remains above comparable rates in England and Scotland, which in 1975 were 0.5 and 0.9 respectively, and in Wales, where in 1975 deaths exceeded births. Although Northern Ireland has had the fastest rate of natural increase of population of any part of the United Kingdom, some 40 per cent of the increase between 1961 and 1971 has been offset by emigration; and it has been estimated that since 1971 the rate of emigration has increased. In spite of this, the net result is still a rate of population growth faster than elsewhere in the British Isles. But it is important to bear in mind that persons leaving Northern Ireland are more likely to be younger working-age persons. This factor contributes to the dependency structure previously referred to.

Compton and Boal (1970), commenting on the age and sex selectiveness of the migration process in the period 1961–66 and introducing a 'religious differential', comment:

For both communities, the rate of male population loss from the 25–29 years, and all younger, age groups is significantly higher than the rate of outflow from the corresponding female population. The reverse holds for the population older than 29. Secondly, for cohorts losing population, the net emigration rate amongst Catholics is at least twice as high as the non-Catholic rate, among both males and females. Thirdly, a fairly strong net immigration rate is suggested amongst males of the 60–64 and older age groups in 1966, the rate of inflow being greater amongst the non-Catholic population.[2]

These flows of population are linked with different social and economic opportunity, especially in areas with different population characteristics.

Two trends are evident: the loss of population within the administrative boundaries of the county boroughs to their broader hinterland, and the movement of population towards the east of the province. As it is the younger, more highly skilled sections of the population who are more likely to move, these trends are associated with the differences in age and occupational characteristics of households in different areas.

In 1972–73 average household size in Northern Ireland was 3.2 persons. This compared with 2.8 in England, 2.9 in Wales, and 3.0 in Scotland. Households in Northern Ireland had, on average, more males, more females, more children under 18 and more adults aged under 65, but the average number of wage-earners was less in Northern Ireland households than in England, Wales and Scotland. These demographic features have important implications for incomes.

In 1974–75 67 per cent of personal income in Northern Ireland was derived from wages and salaries, 9 per cent from self-employment, 16 per cent from social security benefits, and 8 per cent from other sources including rent, interest and dividends. Comparative figures for the whole United Kingdom were, respectively, 74 per cent, 6 per cent, 10 per cent and 10 per cent. The higher proportion of incomes derived from grants from public authorities in Northern Ireland particularly reflects the higher rates of sickness and unemployment. This more than offsets the relatively smaller elderly population.

Average earnings in Northern Ireland are significantly lower than in Great Britain, both for males and females. In April 1977 the average gross weekly earnings figure for male manual workers in Northern Ireland was £64.60 while it was £71.50 in Great Britain. The comparable figures for female manual workers were £41.80 for Northern Ireland and £43.70 for Great Britain as a whole.[3]

The simple explanation for this feature lies in the structure of industry and employment. Low-wage employment is more prominent in Northern Ireland, and professional and non-manual occupations are underrepresented. In addition, hourly earnings appear to be lower in Northern Ireland, and other evidence supports this view of lower earnings.[4] Although statistics are deficient in a number of ways, the weight of evidence suggests that weekly earnings and weekly household incomes are considerably lower in Northern Ireland. This applies to different categories of workers, but is most marked among male manual workers—an important factor in view of the importance of manual employment in Northern Ireland.

With the exception of Wales and south-west England, Northern Ireland has a lower proportion of its male population aged over 15 involved in economic activity. Among females aged over 15 only Wales has a lower activity rate. These comparisons are of considerable importance in explaining differences in household and *per capita* incomes. In so far as they indicate a low demand for labour in Northern Ireland, they may also serve to illustrate the under-use of labour resources, the low productivity in the province, and the low hourly and weekly earnings. One normal measure of economic and social circumstances shows Northern Ireland to have a higher rate of unemployment than the other regions of the United Kingdom. This situation has existed for a considerable time. In April 1977 10.6 per cent of all employees (employed and unemployed) in Northern Ireland were unemployed; the rate for male employees was 12.4 per cent. These figures compare with 5.9 per cent and 7.3 per cent respectively for the United Kingdom as a whole. The unemployment rate in Northern Ireland was higher than that in the 'disadvantaged' areas of Great Britain—the development areas (8.4 per cent in April 1977), the special development areas (9.4 per cent), and the intermediate areas (5.5 per cent).[5]

Clearly the smaller the area chosen for analysis the greater the variation in unemployment rates between areas. Thus the area statistics of unemployment show areas in Britain with local unemployment above that for the whole of Northern Ireland. However, Northern Ireland's disadvantageous situation is still clear at the local level. None of the United Kingdom local areas for which statistics are regularly reproduced have unemployment rates as high as those for Cookstown, Dungannon, Londonderry, Newry and Strabane. Unemployment rates of over 20 per cent exist in Strabane, Newry and Dungannon, and while the rates in Belfast, Craigavon and Ballymena are below the Northern Ireland average, these areas account for some 50 per cent of the unemployed and include pockets of high unemployment.[6] Local surveys in Belfast in 1972 and 1973 have indicated rates of unemployment among heads of households in working-class areas of West Belfast of over 30 per cent. Total unemployment rates were as high as 50 per cent in West Belfast.[7]

As would be expected from data on average earnings, household incomes in Northern Ireland tend to be lower than in the United Kingdom as a whole. Recent evidence suggests that the gap is widening.[8] This reflects the fact that households in Northern Ireland not deriving their income from employment tend to have low incomes. Both the self-employed and unemployed tend to have low incomes, and the gap in household income between Britain and Northern Ireland is even more marked than the earnings gap. In addition, fewer households in Northern Ireland have two incomes. Whereas 46 per cent of married women in the United Kingdom as a whole are at work, only 38 per cent are at work in Northern Ireland.

As household size in Northern Ireland tends to be larger than in Britain and as a smaller proportion of the total population are at work, the gap between personal income per head in Northern Ireland and in Britain is wider than for household income. In 1974 personal income per head is estimated to have been 78.5 per cent of that in the United Kingdom, but the tendency for this gap to narrow had not been sustained after 1973. In 1966 the figure was 69 per cent. Not only does the gap remain very wide, but it is probable that difficulties in recording income have caused it to be underestimated and that fewer households have access to fringe benefits of various kinds; this is to be expected because of the dominance of manual employment, and it is confirmed by the limited evidence available.[9]

The disadvantageous position of households in Northern Ireland can be demonstrated in other ways. In 1976 the infant mortality rate (number of deaths of infants under one year of age per 1,000 live births) in Northern Ireland was 18.3 compared with 14.5 for the United Kingdom. The rate of certified incapacity and qualification for sickness benefit (per man at risk) in 1974–75 was 26.9 in Northern Ireland, 15.2 in England, 31.8 in Wales, and 19.8 in Scotland. Rates of sickness have been consistently higher in Northern Ireland, and the rate of sickness and disablement is an important aspect of need, low household income and interrupted earnings, especially among elderly households and large families.

Evidence of this type provides a partial picture of the underlying social and economic circumstances of Northern Ireland. Most of the evidence emphasises household circumstances and is based on government information reflecting administrative definitions of problems. It is important that such emphasis should not lead to the assumption that the origins of problems lie *within* the household—in apathy, personal inadequacy, transferred deprivation, and so on; this kind of interpretation is not considered appropriate. But information of this type does indicate the scale and nature of social problems which have emerged in the process of economic development. The statistics refer to a particular point in time, but the process through which households and groups came to be in disadvantaged circumstances is not explicit. Clearly the central feature relevant to incomes and unemployment is economic structure and change.

Although this is not the place to attempt a review of the nature and determinants of economic change, some reference to economic development in Northern Ireland is called for. Since 1961 the population in civil employment has changed little, but there have been major changes in the structure of employment.[10] A number of elements of this change can be stressed and serve to emphasise the crucial role of government and public policy.

The traditional industries of Northern Ireland—agriculture, textiles and shipbuilding—are declining and have declined considerably in recent years. But Northern Ireland remains dependent on these declining industries. Compared with Great Britain it is three times as dependent on agriculture and textiles and clothing (including man-made fibres) and twice as dependent on shipbuilding. Geographical remoteness, lack of raw materials, transport costs and the smallness of the local market can all be identified as factors which made Northern Ireland relatively unattractive to the small pool of 'footloose' expanding private enterprises seeking new locations. None the less, considerable new industry has been established with government assistance.[11] Unfortunately much of this is in larger capital-intensive units and is established as branches of companies controlled outside Northern Ireland (this is a disadvantage when decisions on redundancy and closure are taken).

Government-sponsored jobs have been increasingly concentrated in planned growth centres, and these are not the areas which have been experiencing the major job losses. The importance of these government-sponsored jobs has grown from 22 per cent of employment in manufacturing industry in 1961 to 48 per cent in 1973.

Although Gross Domestic Product per head rose more rapidly in Northern Ireland than in the other parts of the United Kingdom between 1966 and 1970 (this is no longer the case), output per head in 1972 remained only 73 per cent of the United Kingdom average. In addition, the rate of new job creation is insufficient to offset job losses elsewhere.[12]

Evidence of relative income, and especially of *per capita* income, suggests that the incidence of poverty in Northern Ireland will be higher than Great Britain. A variety of data supports this assumption. Coates and Rawstron (1971), analysing Inland Revenue quinquennial data, conclude that the lowest mean incomes in the United Kingdom are found in Northern Ireland.[13] They also quote evidence of children receiving free school meals (16.5 per cent of children in Northern Ireland compared with 7.7 per cent in Scotland and 4.8 per cent in England and Wales) as confirming the impression. Furthermore, they estimate the *per capita* tax yield in Northern Ireland in 1964–65 at £24 compared with a United Kingdom average of £50 and a figure of £32 for the lowest Economic Planning Region in England.

The significance of low wages is indicated by the proportion of wage-earners making use of Family Income Supplement: Northern Ireland, representing only 2.8 per cent of the United Kingdom population, accounted for 13.9 per cent of all United Kingdom cases in payment of FIS in 1975, and there is evidence of even wider eligibility.[14] Evidence of the uptake of other social benefits supports the view of a higher incidence of poverty in Northern Ireland.[15] A recent household survey based on a large sample indicates that some 35 per cent of households in Northern Ireland fall below a poverty line which, if applied to the United Kingdom as a whole, shows 21 per cent of households in poverty.[16] Although academics may argue over these proportions, the picture of low relative living standards is not open to serious doubt. Although older small households are numerically the largest group of households in poverty, they account for only 96,000 persons, whereas some 241,000 people in large families are living below the poverty line. At least 190,000 children aged under 16 (39 per cent of the age group) are in poverty.

The close links between poverty and the pattern of regional economic development were emphasised by this household survey. The declining urban area of Belfast exhibits the classical features of a nineteenth-century industrial revolution city in decline. The declining economic base, particularly its manufacturing sector, is associated with differential migration, leaving an imbalanced population in which the elderly, the low-paid and the unskilled are left behind. Lack of investment in the social infrastructure is reflected in an obsolescent nineteenth-century housing stock which has not been sufficiently maintained. In contrast, there is a circle of relative affluence in the Greater Belfast Area. New investments in housing, industry and the infrastructure have been concentrated in this area, and its population is consequently younger, more mobile, more highly skilled, better paid and better housed. The remainder of the province includes large areas, especially in the west, in which rural depression and underemployment are the dominant features. The decline of staple industries, including agriculture, has not been offset by newly created employment. Although out migration has been significant, many younger families remain in low-paid employment, and problems of family poverty are considerable.

The situation of households with low incomes relative to needs is further indicated by evidence about expenditure.[17] In Northern Ireland, compared with the United Kingdom as a whole, a higher proportion of total household expenditure is on food, fuel, light and power, clothing and footwear, tobacco, and transport and vehicles. Lower proportions are spent on housing, alcoholic drink, durable household goods, services and other goods. With the exception of housing, this is compatible with a view that more is spent on essentials and that less income is available for extras and luxuries. In this context it is also important to note evidence that the costs of many important items of household consumption, in particular fuel, are higher in Northern Ireland. A smaller proportion of households in Northern Ireland in 1973 had use of six identified durable goods (car, central heating, washing machine, refrigerator, television, telephone) than in the United Kingdom as a whole or in Wales or Scotland. The only exception is that in Northern Ireland cars were more widely owned than in Scotland.

One significant element in the social geography of Northern Ireland is a religious and social segregation. The Roman Catholic community is proportionately most heavily represented in the west and south of the province and in West Belfast. Statistics of social malaise indicate that while these areas have no monopoly of hardship, households in the west of the province have lower incomes, more unemployment, worse housing provision and larger families. In West Belfast the same features have been exacerbated in recent years by violence, intimidation and population movement, which has in fact increased segregation and stress in an area with few job opportunities and inadequate housing. Variations in, for example, fertility or unemployment are linked to both religious denomination and social class. Unemployment, for example, is higher among those in areas more remote from Belfast, among unskilled labourers and among Roman Catholics.[18]

The nature of social and economic problems in the region is important in considering the operation of government. The discussion of devolved institutions involves not only an analysis of formal institutional and legislative mechanisms but also an assessment of the value of these institutions in dealing with a region's social and economic problems and other issues affecting individuals and families. Evidence of the type given above shows that the environment within which government has been carried out is one of relative social and economic deprivation. In comparison with the rest of the United Kingdom, Northern Ireland is an under-developed area; and the problems of government are directly related to this basic fact. Because of the gap in standards, questions of parity and regional policy have become important elements in devolution. A key issue during the entire period of devolution in Northern Ireland was not simply one of the formal relationships between parliaments and governments but one of the practical operation of government to ensure equity for all citizens living in the different parts of the state.

The pattern of economic and social deprivation in Northern Ireland is not random. It represents highly structured divisions expressing themselves in cumulative differences in command over resources through time. These differences reflect the pattern of economic change and, through this, result in spatial concentration of problems. Thus within Northern Ireland there are groups who experience greater and lesser degrees of deprivation, depending on the nature of economic development. Relative deprivation within Northern Ireland is in this way an important factor in the development of politics and government.

Considerable evidence can be put forward to show significant social and economic progress in Northern Ireland in recent years. Northern Ireland had in the late 1960s experienced a decline in net migration, as well as greater growth in Gross Domestic Product per head, industrial production, employment, labour productivity and personal income than in the United Kingdom.[19] However, this progress did not fundamentally alter the unfavourable comparative position of Northern Ireland. Moreover, the tensions created by such progress, and the different extent to which groups with different skills and in different areas have been able to benefit, may increase rather than reduce the problems of government. Such economic and demographic changes exacerbate and complicate the situation. Governmental responses to these changes, to the differences between standards in Northern Ireland and Great Britain and to differences within Northern Ireland itself, become crucial tests of the nature and operation of government.

Throughout any such discussion it is important to bear in mind the degree of integration of the Northern Ireland economy with that of Great Britain. The history of economic and industrial development of Northern Ireland is inextricably bound up with the British economy, the decisions of controllers of capital in Britain, and the determinants of the economic and financial policies of the British government. In this way the social and economic conditions that exist in Northern Ireland are not the product of some natural or independent process of development.

Social Policies in Northern Ireland

The role of government and of public policy in the economic and social development of the six-county area has been important since before 1921. However, the nature and extent of public intervention has changed and especially since the early 1960s has been of primary importance in explaining the pattern of development. The role of government may be broadly defined as the development of a welfare state, of welfare state capitalism or of a corporate state. However, such labels are not clear or precise enough to express adequately the nature of state intervention. Thus the concept of a welfare state may imply alternatively a mechanism for redistribution of resources between different groups in the community and through time, or minimum arrangements to prevent the breakdown of society and maintain the political status quo by meeting the needs of a residual population who would not be catered for otherwise. The consideration of the role of government and the use of devolution requires more detailed consideration of the economic and political processes and the philosophies and values embraced by those in positions of power.

The term 'social policy' is used more widely in this and the following chapter than convention dictates. The reason for this is that the wide range of policies for which the Northern Ireland government had responsibility have no common origin or 'social' aim but do have important social and distributional effects. As areas of policy they all represent elements in conflicting interests within society. It must also be recognised that the assessment of the distributional impact of individual policies is complex, and it is arguably impossible to isolate the impact of specific policies. All that we can hope to do is to raise relevant pointers to possible impacts. Even this is a lengthy exercise. The British literature on the distribution of income and redistribution of resources is extensive and inconclusive, and we cannot hope to make any comprehensive or definitive assessment of such matters. What we can consider is evidence on spatial and social effects specifically related to Northern Ireland. Such evidence should be considered within the context of the broader debate on the distribution and redistribution of resources through fiscal, occupational and welfare arrangements. The major part of these two chapters is a description of the origins, current levels of provision and recent developments in a series of policy areas: regional policy and planning, employment, housing, social security, income maintenance, medical care, education, and personal social services.

One of the continuing themes is inevitably the question of how far in these services has Northern Ireland made use of its devolved powers, and on what basis, and with what effects. How far has it gone for parity of provision with Britain, and how far for an independent policy?

The initial policy areas under consideration include those most directly concerned with economic policy—with the control of industrial and residential development, land use, investment in the built environment, the creation of jobs, and the maintenance of wage levels and an adequate household income. In view of the nature of the Northern Ireland problem depicted above, these policy areas are particularly important. In the more recent debate about devolution in the United Kingdom the arguments for devolution in Scotland and Wales have focused strongly on differences in social and economic circumstances and the need for regional agencies to operate to achieve progress in these areas. In this context it is particularly relevant to consider what response the Northern Ireland government adopted, and also to consider why these responses took the form they did rather than that of any other—in most cases more interventionist—policy.

Regional Policy, Planning and Employment
Government interventions to influence patterns of settlement and economic development in Ireland have not a very long tradition.[20] It was not until 1931 that there was any legislation providing for statutory land-use planning in Northern Ireland. The legislation left action to the discretion of local authorities, and there was little or no conscious planning other than control of development through bye-laws. Some attempts to influence the pattern of economic development were made between the wars, and some success in ensuring the survival of some existing enterprises has been claimed.[21] In spite of a series of technical reports prepared between 1945 and 1951, recommendations to draw up comprehensive planning schemes were not productive. The major legislative development (the Planning (Interim Development) Act, 1944) resulted only in the production of outline advisory plans which did little more than extend existing land-use zoning. No detailed strategy was worked out, and the main method of controlling development was through density restrictions and planning decisions exercised by thirty-seven authorities differing greatly in size, resources and political composition. Thus in 1961 one county provided £20,000

for planning, another £50, and a third nothing at all. One municipal borough estimated £3,725, and another, of similar size, £150. One urban district estimated £2,000, while eleven others estimated less than £100 each. In this way Northern Ireland had neither the administrative structure, the legislative powers, the staff or the resources to deal with overspill, new towns, control of development, national parks, green belts, the countryside or urban redevelopment.

The reasons for this absence of planning machinery include two major political factors. Firstly, local government and local politics were not policy- or product-orientated. There is no apparent tradition of local government enterprise comparable to that in Britain. Rather, local government remains an aspect of regional political organisation and patronage. Aspirations are associated with basic constitutional questions; there are few separate local political issues, and none of these figure significantly in local electoral postures. Factors which do influence local elections in Britain—the popularity of the party in power at Westminster, or local issues such as rates—are not significant in Northern Ireland. Thus there has been no local pressure to develop active local planning policies.

With the focus of political initiative so firmly at the regional rather than local level, the second major political factor limiting the development of planning in Northern Ireland was the attitude of the Stormont government. As an example of this, Captain O'Neill in his autobiography refers to Lord Brookeborough's two pet aversions: 'First, he was determined never to recognise the trade unions, and second, he condemned planning, which he regarded as a socialist menace.'[22] These two aversions were complementary and prevented any development in planning comparable to that in Britain. It has been argued that there were other barriers to planning; for example, the Government of Ireland Act, 1920, was interpreted as limiting the powers of the Northern Ireland government to restrict the right of an owner to compensation if the value of his land was reduced by the decision of a planning authority. This fear was not removed until a House of Lords judgement in 1959.[23] However, the failure to clarify or remedy the legal situation before 1959 can be explained by the lack of any wish to do so. In other policy areas (notably education) the Government of Ireland Act was not treated with unquestioning respect. Thus the fact that the constitutional position was clarified in 1959 was not accidental and did not lead to increased development planning. Rather, changes in the economic situation and the Stormont government produced a new enthusiasm for planning which necessitated some constitutional clarification.

Public planning policies had therefore changed significantly by the early 1960s. From a consistent *laissez-faire* situation and an aversion to planning the Stormont government moved to a position in which it became increasingly identified with a regional development strategy. A series of consultants' reports were accepted and legislation introduced to implement a strategy for regional economic growth based on the increasing consolidation of economic development in key centres, in which investments in housing and infrastructure were concentrated and industrialists encouraged to invest.[24] There can be no doubt that the status of the Northern Ireland government enabled it to develop and implement more generous and more flexible incentives to industrialists and to introduce special legislation to support its regional strategy.[25] Moreover, the lack of experience, interest and capacity of local authorities in planning enabled Stormont's planners to develop a strategy without coming to serious conflict with local authorities.

This latter feature is of importance because of the distributional consequences of increased public intervention. The close involvement of government in decisions which could influence local employment, income, prosperity and migration would in itself have had political implications since it conferred differential advantages. However, because the government (perhaps for reasons which at the time appeared to be technically correct) opted for a strategy of concentration of development, the relative advantage and disadvantage conferred was more apparent. If, as Rose (1971) states, 'no economic plan could be without implications for Protestant–Catholic relations',[26] then it is even more true to say that the nature of the regional planning strategy adopted made the implications all too apparent.

One notable feature of planning in Northern Ireland until very recently has been lack of legislative parity with Great Britain and the lack of pressure from Westminster. Economic and regional policies in Britain, and especially controls on development in Britain through Industrial Development Certificates, have benefited Northern Ireland in the same way as other regions. However, the Northern Ireland government was not consulted on these matters. Equally the development of planning in Northern Ireland in the 1960s, although consistent with trends in Britain, does not appear to have been 'sponsored' by Westminster. Only with direct rule is it apparent that Westminster became aware of the importance of planning policy. Thus the regional strategy adopted in 1975 was generated from within the Civil Service and broke the continuity of recourse to academic consultants and the type of strategy these consultants had favoured, and of the concentrated growth-centre strategy the government had adopted.[27] The adoption of a less concentrated strategy reflected some concern for the political realities of concentration (the Cameron Commission on the disturbances of 1969 had referred to regional development strategy as a source of grievance),[28] for the economic realities under which labour and fixed capital resources could not be fully used in a growth-centre situation, and for the importance of concepts of equity and territorial justice in a regional strategy which takes into account the immobility of families and capital.

The Planning (Northern Ireland) Order, 1972 brought planning in Northern Ireland broadly into line with the system in England and Wales.[29] A series of area plans would detail local land-use proposals and be related to an overall regional strategy. It instituted 'additional planning control' features to cover buildings of architectural and historical interest, and also introduced the concept of conservation areas. However, under local government reorganisation none of these planning activities fall on local authorities. It is the Department of the Environment in Belfast which is responsible both for the regional and area plans—the twenty-six district councils are only consulted, and decisions are the responsibility of professionals. In 1975 a discussion paper heralded changes in the regional strategy.[30]

The preferred option (subsequently endorsed) for a regional physical development strategy is a 'district towns strategy' which identifies four classes of settlement related to local government districts. It has been argued that to base a physical strategy on such an administrative pattern rather than vice versa is illogical.[31] Nevertheless, the preferred option represents an important (but unexplained) move away from the strategy adopted following the Matthew Report and towards a more scattered pattern of development related to the needs of the whole community rather than based on the economics of concentration. Subsequent reports have, for example, emphasised the need for positive rural planning and the development of appropriate industry in rural areas.[32]

Although the new strategy in 1975 is in this way based on a greater variety of considerations, it remains a strategy geared towards regional economic growth and using the same basic policy instruments. The principal activities of the Northern Ireland government in relation to the level of employment are determined by its regional development strategy. The broader monetary and fiscal policies which are likely to affect levels of employment, as well as social security arrangements to compensate the unemployed, are determined at Westminster. However, there are schemes to remedy defects in the supply of labour which have been developed in Northern Ireland to a greater extent than elsewhere. In particular, the provision of retraining facilities has been considerably higher than in Britain. The capacity of government training centres has increased considerably and was in 1974 (on a *pro rata* basis) about ten times greater than in the rest of the United Kingdom. In addition, counter-redundancy training grants are available to keep workforces together in periods of recession.

Other schemes to affect unemployment merit some brief reference.[33] The Northern Ireland Finance Corporation (NIFC) was established in 1972 to support Northern Ireland firms in financial difficulties where closure would have adverse economic effects and to assist firms to undertake new investment. This innovation in policy marked a willingness to intervene on a large scale in private industry. This marked the full adoption by Unionist governments of an approach to industrial policy which is normally associated with the Labour Party. Indeed, while the Conservative Party was dismantling the Industrial Reorganisation Corporation in Britain, Unionists were putting £50 million backing to a body based on a similar philosophy in Northern Ireland.

In 1976 the NIFC was replaced by the Northern Ireland Development Authority (NIDA) and continuity of senior staff has not been maintained. By the end of March 1974 the NIFC had saved or promoted some 5,500 jobs at a cost of £10 million. A scheme for integrated workforce units was established in 1972 to provide training and work experience in units which could have a continuing production activity. By 1975 fifteen units had been established, four of which had been taken over for production. The Local Enterprise Development Unit (LEDU) was set up in 1971 to promote employment in existing small firms (with less than fifty employees) and to foster craft skills. In the five years to March 1976 LEDU promoted 5,359 new jobs in 398 companies. LEDU has a wider range of services to offer than its British counterparts —the Council for Small Industries in Rural Areas, and the Small Industries Council for the Rural Areas of Scotland. It offers loans, grants, training and advisory services. It has remained independent of NIDA. The less ambitious Urban and Rural Improvement Campaign, inaugurated in 1970, provides jobs for the unskilled in ways which improve social amenities and the quality of the environment. Along with Enterprise Ulster, which was set up in 1973 to combine direct employment for the unskilled with training, it was providing more than 5,000 jobs by 1973–74. These recent schemes and the longer-established emphasis on training and retraining are examples of response to unemployment well in advance of the somewhat similar Job Creation Programme in Britain.

In this way it is clear that devolution has in no way inhibited the development of a variety of policy responses to tackle unemployment. Once Stormont entered its 'interventionist' phase, it has experimented and developed major projects. Once the basic ideological objections were overcome, the questions of how and when to intervene have not been the subject of party-political debate; as has been stressed previously, the debate is dominated by more basic ideological and symbolic issues. Thus proposals which in Britain have aroused considerable political, academic and 'expert' controversy have in Northern Ireland aroused little public debate and have emerged in advisory reports to be accepted as apparently uncontroversial and logical steps. This is both the strength and weakness of Northern Ireland's position.

Once commitment is made, there are few problems in policy-making. But whether or not there is commitment, this lack of scrutiny and political dispute of the hows, whys and whens of policy may lead responses to be less well considered than would otherwise be the case.

The actual success of all these schemes has been disappointing. They have unfortunately been exposed too early to the economic depression of the mid-1970s. Such an economic climate is not the buoyant one needed to encourage new initiatives; it involves too drastic and complete collapses of demand to 'save' existing firms; and it results in a considerable failure rate of supported projects. Thus, for example, the failure rate among LEDU projects after five years was almost 10 per cent. In addition, it is doubtful if these projects could ever compensate for the general economic difficulties of Northern Ireland. The annual rate of job loss is well in excess of what could generally be expected to be met by these schemes.

Indeed, the demand for labour and the general economic backwardness of Northern Ireland are such that successful job creation does not necessarily reduce unemployment before it reduces levels of underemployment. Public policy may increase female activity rates, reduce self-employment, speed the decline of low-paid employment and reduce migration. In this way the effects of policy are mediated by a wide range of decisions which are outside the control of policies. Also it is evident that policies to create jobs and rationalise the industrial structure have repercussions which can further reduce the potential for employment of certain groups. Thus it has been argued that the growth-centre strategy pursued in the 1960s, relying as it did on the mobility of labour, may have had the effect of increasing the migration of the younger and better skilled away from areas of high unemployment. In doing so it reduced the likelihood that employers would invest in those areas and so provide opportunities for the older and less skilled, who tend to be less mobile for a number of reasons.[34]

As a result of these factors, it is exceedingly difficult to estimate the number of jobs which must be created in order to reduce unemployment. It is easier to recommend policies which could move in the right direction than to identify policies sufficient for the need. Thus, for example, the Quigley Report in 1976 proposed a wide range of policy initiatives but was unable to indicate how far these initiatives would meet the need for new jobs.[35] The pattern remains under which government does not have the basic economic planning powers and resources necessary to tackle unemployment in a systematic manner.

In discussing the effectiveness of regional planning and the various policy initiatives designed to create growth and reduce unemployment, one additional matter merits reference. Some commentators place considerable emphasis on the effects of the 'troubles'. Certain estimates suggest a loss of 15,000–20,000 manufacturing jobs between 1969 and 1976.[36] But the problems of assessing the impact of violence are considerable. For example, it has been pointed out that between 1970 and 1975 only sixteen firms in the manufacturing sector of the economy had closed as a direct result of terrorist activity—with the loss of 824 jobs.[37] The effects may have been more marked in other sectors. Between 1968 and 1974 employment in the distributive trades fell by 7.4 per cent, and employment in the hotel and catering industry fell by 27 per cent compared with an increase in Great Britain of 28 per cent. These changes may have been considerably affected by terrorist activity—as is indicated by the government's efforts to counter them through provision of rent and rate rebates and grants for security staff. But the problems of assessing the economic effects of the troubles only draw attention to the difficulties of assessing the impact of regional policies and planning. While the actual direct loss of jobs may have been less than 1,000, what was the loss in terms of jobs that would otherwise have been established? In 1966 some 4,900 jobs were promoted in new enterprises by the Northern Ireland Department of Commerce. In 1975 only 473 were promoted. The number of jobs provided declined steadily from 1968 to 1972.

But these changes cannot be attributed wholly to the political troubles and civil disturbances. The economic climate of the late 1960s and early 1970s was not likely to encourage new promotion. Regional policies will not persuade industrialists to embark on new investment. The availability of sites, labour, government grants, etc., will only be relevant to firms seeking to change location (almost certainly expanding firms in expanding industries), to firms which are 'footloose' or not severely locationally constrained, and to firms which evaluate or assess alternative sites and costs. Thus the effects of regional strategies are limited and initially determined by the overall economic situation, by the number of firms which are expanding, and by the nature of their activities. In the late 1960s and 1970s it is likely that the potential pool of industry interested in regional incentives had declined. In a period when Western Europe suffered widespread unemployment and the amount of expanding mobile industry is limited it may be that the troubles had little impact. Perhaps greater significance should be attached to the fact that there was simply no scope for growth anyway.

In the 1970s industrial costs in Northern Ireland rose considerably faster than the sale prices of finished goods.[38] Cost comparisons have moved in a way which is unfavourable in attracting new industry. Arguably a major improvement in cost effectiveness in industry lies outside government control. Finally, there are sufficient examples of large companies maintaining or increasing investment in Northern Ireland to suggest that the civil disturbances are not such a major factor. Northern Ireland's economy is influenced by and vulnerable to changes in the international economic situation, the peripheral location of the province, problems of ownership and control, and issues of cost and productivity. No doubt the disturbances have contributed to this, but changes directly attributable to them are likely to be well below some estimates.

The impact of Northern Ireland's regional policy is not simply measurable in terms of new jobs created each year. It may be argued that the impact is most likely to be on where industrialists locate activities and in what techniques they use, and not on whether or not they embark on new investment. Of the (declining) employment in manufacturing industry, an increasing proportion is in firms which have received grants from the Northern Ireland government. Thus in 1961 22.3 per cent of total employment in manufacturing industry was in 'government-sponsored jobs', and in 1973 this had risen to 48.0 per cent. The majority of these firms originate outside Northern Ireland and have their head offices outside the province. Their plants in Northern Ireland tend to be larger than average and to use more capital-intensive techniques. An increasing proportion of government-sponsored new jobs are in growth and key centres; in consequence the majority of these are located in the relatively affluent eastern portion of the province.

It is these features—external control, large scale, spatial concentration—which are referred to as evidence of the deficiencies of regional planning. While it is unlikely that regional planning has counteracted these trends, it is probable that the real determinants of the pattern of economic change lie in economic and financial tendencies at a national and international level. Indeed, there is some recognition of this in the attempts made by the government to encourage 'native' industries through special assistance schemes.

One feature of the economic crisis of the 1970s is relevant in this context. It has often been argued that regional policies in Northern Ireland encourage the promotion of 'unstable' jobs in branch factories which would be the first to close in a period of recession. Thus Northern Ireland's faster rate of growth in a boom period would be matched by a faster rate of job loss in recession. But while before 1966 Northern Ireland appeared to be the most cyclically sensitive region in the United Kingdom, this sensitivity has declined since then.[39] For example, between May 1974 and December 1975, whereas unemployment rose by 116 per cent in the United Kingdom as a whole, it rose by 84 per cent in Northern Ireland. This is not as adverse a result as had operated previously. However, before this can be accepted as evidence that the worst fears of the effects of industrial promotion have not been realised, account must be taken of the increase in emigration and reduction in return immigration (together accounting for some 3,000 additional emigrants) and the enormous growth of public expenditure and creation of employment in the public services (42 per cent between 1968 and 1974) which have counteracted rising unemployment.

One final point is relevant in this context. Throughout the period in which jobs promoted in new enterprises have declined, existing enterprises—including some established with the encouragement of regional policy—have been persuaded to expand through various aids and incentives. Department of Commerce job promotions in existing industry have not declined as steadily as those in new industry; they rose between 1969 and 1971, recovered from a 1972 low to relatively good figures in 1973 and 1974, and fell back in 1975.

Housing
Whereas the full commitment to planning arrived only with the economic policies of the 1960s, legislation affecting housing dates back much further. The Irish Public Health Act, 1878, established cities and towns as urban sanitary authorities, and Poor Law unions in rural areas became rural sanitary authorities. In 1898 elected urban and rural district councils were to maintain the responsibility for minimum standards of sanitation. As Lawrence (1965 a) has noted, this change did not reduce the close link with the Poor Law

authority, especially in rural areas.[40] Councillors and Poor Law Guardians in urban districts were separately elected, but rural district councillors joined the urban Guardians to form the Board of Guardians for Poor Law union areas. The responsibility for maintaining sanitary standards and eliminating nuisances involved inspection and control of private housing. From 1883 rural district councils could qualify for government grants to build cottages for farm labourers; however, between 1890 and 1919 local authorities had built only 634 dwellings, including one lodging house.

In addition to this, the northern province was, of course, included within the scope of all legislation designed to remedy Irish grievances.[41] This had consistently included a major element aimed at tenant farmers. Legislation in 1870 in effect reduced rather than enlarged the rights established through customary practice in Ulster. The Land Act of 1881, which granted fair rent, free sale and fixity of tenure to the tenants, was not satisfactory in practice, but this legislation and extensions in 1887 were specifically designed to divide the land question from that of Home Rule. Subsequent legislation for Ireland not only accepted that tenants should be enabled to purchase, but also made available both cash and coercive power for this purpose. Such measures were essential if tenant farmers' housing was to be improved.

It is not intended here to elaborate on these matters. Rather, it is sufficient to say that in 1915 Ireland had a tradition of intervention in property matters much more extensive than elsewhere in the United Kingdom. It was not perceived as a housing policy in the modern sense, but economists and politicians were none the less aware of the principles involved in adopting such approaches.[42] It might be expected that, with legislative devolution, these principles would have been built on. Land and housing policy could have been governed by a set of premises about the particular economic and social traditions and needs of the province. However, by the time such matters were set before the Northern Ireland government there had been important developments in policy in Britain.

In 1915 the threat of social unrest in wartime led directly to the introduction of rent-control legislation in both Britain and Ireland.[43] Perhaps equally significant was the importance attached to housing in the plans for reconstruction following the 1914–18 war. In 1919 a new Ministry of Health was established at Westminster with responsibilties for housing policy. New legislation followed, placing an increased responsibility for the direct provision of housing on local authorities. Ireland was not excluded from these developments; but neither was it fully incorporated. Housing remained the responsibility of the Local Government Board; and the board's attitudes and personnel, as well as the Poor Law tradition which it represented, continued to exert a primary influence upon housing policy.

After the establishment of Northern Ireland the Ministry of Home Affairs became ultimately responsible for housing. As the ministry was also responsible for public order and justice, debates relating to the department and its Estimates tended to neglect housing. The Housing (Ireland) Act, 1919, had differed from its British counterpart in failing to lay down the respective contributions of local authorities and the Treasury to any loss incurred through the provision of housing. Northern Ireland followed the British example in providing a subsidy to stimulate private building and in the increasing emphasis on private building up to 1923. But it did not follow the shift in emphasis back to local authority provision in 1924. Thus by 1924 the basis for housing policy was considerably different in Northern Ireland. Centrally it was the responsibility of a different department which lacked any coherent picture of need. Legislation, by 1924, did not incorporate the same incentives for local authorities; the principle of subsidising private building still constituted a major element in policy, and the whole subsidy system itself was different.[44]

The markedly different record of local authorities (which in Northern Ireland provided some 15 per cent of new housing between the wars, compared with 25 per cent in England and Wales) can be partly explained by the lack of any urgency at Stormont. Exchequer assistance to encourage local authorities required rate contributions which local authorities were unwilling to make. Perhaps some local authorities, particularly the smaller and poorer rural district councils, did not have the capacity to raise rates for this or any service. Thus some rural councils were only prepared to build if there was no rate contribution—thereby pushing rents beyond the means of those in most need.

It is not intended here to argue that the financial arrangements were ungenerous. The reluctance of rural authorities to take advantage of them was also related to other factors: a restricted view of need, and a preoccupation with the geography of votes.[45] But Stormont did little to overcome these barriers or to create an environment within which policy requirements would have become more apparent. In effect this suggests that Stormont did not wish to pursue an active housing policy. This is even more apparent when subsidy arrangements for urban areas are examined. From 1923 the subsidy took the form of a lump sum (initially £60 a house). Large permanent subsidies were not offered. By comparison, the 1924 Housing Act in England and Wales paid a subsidy of £9 for each house, each year, for forty years. In 1934 the Northern

Ireland government made its subsidy dependent on the payment of an equivalent subsidy or ten years' rate exemption by the local authority. In theory this aimed to make local authorities 'responsible' in their decisions; in practice it meant discouraging building. This discouragement is perfectly consistent with Stormont's preference for private enterprise building and the view that the housing problem was small and temporary. In 1924 the housing shortage was estimated between 10,000 and 25,000 dwellings. By contrast, the report of the Planning Advisory Board in 1943 (in spite of adopting the minimum justifiable standards) estimated that 229,500 of the stock of 323,000 dwellings required repair and that a minimum target of 200,000 dwellings was needed to eliminate overcrowding and slums. And this took no account of requirements arising from demographic changes or continuing obsolescence. This contrast stands as a measure of the lack of concern with housing policy between the wars. If the financial arrangements explain the low general rate of building, they certainly do not explain variations through time and between areas. Low rateable values and lack of trained and experienced local administrators may have had some effect, but the failure to accept responsibility, to recognise the scale of the housing problem, to investigate or to plan, was evident at every level of government.

This failure is also reflected in the poor quality of many dwellings built in the period. In addition, neither the private sector (which preferred to build to the maximum size—and therefore price—within subsidy) nor local authorities channelled resources to the poorest sections of the community. Thus the Ministry of Home Affairs in 1938 commented:

> While the subsidy given under the Housing Acts had been successful in getting houses built for people able to pay an economic rent, the problem of providing accommodation for the poorer classes, mostly residing in houses more or less unfit for habitation, remained, and representations were received by the ministry from a number of local authorities in favour of some government assistance being given for the purpose of enabling them to re-house people belonging to these classes.[46]

The Stormont government applied its general dislike of interventionist policies to housing as to other areas. It provided the minimum residual housing service itself, sought to encourage the private sector, and attempted to relieve the position of the private landlord. In all these matters it is important to recognise the dominance of the rural, agricultural, landed element in the Unionist Party.

Housing was also a natural victim of the financial arrangements in devolution. Equivalent standard services were not as easily measured—especially when statistics of housing conditions and occupancy were not available. Given the low levels of income in Northern Ireland, any extensive state provision of housing would have involved a commitment to a continuing level of rent subsidy, and this would have been difficult to finance even if it had been desired. In addition, it could always be argued that the state's best contribution was by encouraging the private market. Nevertheless, the record of public housing authorities in Northern Ireland between the wars is in striking contrast with that of their counterparts in Britain. Rates of new building and slum clearance remained low throughout the entire period and were not compensated for by private building. These low rates cannot be explained solely by economic factors or legislative differences but would rather seem to reflect political stances referred to earlier. At the same time it is not possible to imply that policy was exclusively *laissez-faire*. Rent control has continued to operate in Northern Ireland (although persistent efforts to relax it had been made), and a further proof is provided by the continued maintenance of a subsidy to certain private building.

The effect of this period of neglect was that by 1945 the divergence from British standards had increased. The Planning Advisory Board's housing survey of 1943, adopting minimum standards, estimated that 229,500 of the stock of 323,000 dwellings required repair.[47] Immediate needs merited a doubling of the inter-war housing programme. A total of 200,000 dwellings were required to eliminate overcrowding and slums, and additional building would be needed to meet the demands from population growth and further obsolescence. The report went on to comment on deficiencies in respect of materials, standards of accommodation, fittings and services in new dwellings. A memorandum from the Minister of Health and Local Government in July 1944 commented: 'As a result of the housing survey in 1943, it is essential to the prestige of the government that something more must be done and done as quickly as possible.' Three main problems were identified: the leisurely pace at which schemes were handled by local government; finding suitable sites; and obtaining materials in a time of wartime controls. A further memorandum stated: 'We must establish some sort of machinery to act in parallel with local authorities, a housing trust similar to the Scottish Special Housing Association.'[48]

A proposal of this type had been put forward before the war,[49] but its adoption in 1945 with the establishment of the Northern Ireland Housing Trust was a mark of increased urgency and lack of confidence in the capacity of local authorities. The Trust was set up to complement (and compensate for the lack of) local authority housing activity. In 1946 a ministerial memorandum stated: 'It is time to give the assistance of the Trust to some backward rural districts. Some of the housing authorities are making very feeble efforts in these backward districts. Some of them have built no houses for over twenty years.'[50] It was suggested that the Trust should build to meet half of the immediate needs of each area, receiving the same annual rate contribution from local authorities as would be paid by them in respect of houses they built themselves. In this way the Housing Trust was explicitly a challenge to the administrative and political traditions which had hitherto governed policy and to the inertia which these had created.

The Second World War had also seen a strengthening of rent control and of the financial basis for public housing. Given the particular economic and social circumstances of Northern Ireland, these developments offered some prospect for the backlog of housing stress and the gap in housing standards to be diminished. But this trend in the immediate post-war period represented only a temporary shift in approach, and subsequent years saw a reversion away from it. Rent-control relaxation was still popular, and major legislation was passed in 1956. At the same time legislation continued to lag behind that in Great Britain. Not until 1956 was a statutory duty to deal with problems of unfit housing imposed on local authorities and improvement grant procedures brought into line. And the Housing Act, 1971, introduced area-based improvement measures similar to the British Housing Act of 1969.

More impressive is the continuing lack of support received by the Northern Ireland Housing Trust both from local government, which on occasion actively frustrated Trust activities, and from Stormont, which failed to provide the financial backing required for effective activity. The failure of the Trust to make a more effective contribution to new building can be partly attributed to the Ministry of Finance's hostility to it, and it seems that many battles were necessary to stop the Trust's being wound up.[51] Thus in housing the *laissez-faire* approach was dented by the post-war awareness of lack of social provision, but this was in no way consolidated by later events, and indeed it was a major problem to maintain this limited divergence.

A more serious modification to the view that in Northern Ireland public policy until the 1960s was based on a *laissez-faire* philosophy is revealed by the evidence that local authorities used their housing powers for political and electoral purposes. Discrimination cannot be shown to have existed in a persistent and systematic fashion, but there are sufficient examples of building decisions being based on electoral calculation and of individuals receiving preferential treatment because of their politico-religious affiliations for the discriminatory element in policy to be undeniable.[52] And this discriminatory element carried over into the period of expanded housing activity arising from the new conversion to economic and regional planning in the 1960s (see pp. 203–9).

Although, under this impetus, new building, improvement and slum-clearance activities increased in the 1960s and 1970s, they were not consistently at a higher relative level to Britain. Thus, even with the impetus of the economic plans, policies have rarely been sufficient to begin to eat into the backlog of housing inactivity. Part of the explanation for this was that while Stormont was convinced of the need to boost house-building and found a willing ally in the Housing Trust, local authorities remained the powerful but inactive initiating authorities. Many local authorities were ill-equipped for their role and many were unwilling to modify their traditional political interpretation of their housing powers. In this way the administrative structure which had served Stormont in providing both a residual housing service and local political management could not adapt to a housing policy role which conflicted with the political management role.

The increasing distance between the Stormont government's view of what Unionism was (at its clearest a mainstream British Conservatism with a task of economic and social reconstruction) and local politicians' views (to maintain the Unionist hegemony for the Union) became clear in policies other than housing. However, housing is perhaps the best example of social policy being used to maintain and sustain political power and the lack of effect of welfare/redistribution aims. For housing policy to serve social or economic goals more effectively some rationalisation of administration was necessary. In 1971 sixty-six local authorities had housing powers. Although some authorities had pooled their powers, proposals for major reorganisations of local government structure and responsibilities had not been welcomed by local authority representatives and had not been pursued by Stormont (see Chapter 8). Although there were notorious examples of gerrymandering and misuse of powers, the political dependence of Stormont on local government and local political management left it in a stalemate situation—unwilling to rock the political boat further but unable to secure its desired administrative rationalisation without doing so. This stalemate was only broken by the prominence which housing issues played in the disturbances of 1969 and the subsequent importance attached by the Westminster government to housing reform.

The Northern Ireland Housing Executive was established as a

'single-purpose, efficient, and streamlined central housing authority' to take over responsibility for the building, management and allocation of all public housing from the local authorities, the Housing Trust and the Development Commissions. By July 1973 it had taken over responsibility for some 155,000 dwellings. The nominated board of the Housing Executive is responsible for central decisions, and the Housing Council, representing district councils, acts as an advisory body.

In 1974 nearly one in five dwellings in Northern Ireland was unfit (compared with 7 per cent in England and Wales in 1971). These dwellings and the substantial additional number requiring repair and improvement were disproportionately used by the poor.[53] Problems of poor housing conditions were exacerbated by sharing and overcrowding. However, the Housing Executive has been unable to respond by increasing, or even maintaining, its new building programme. In 1971 there were 9,102 public sector completions, and in 1975 4,885. Clearly this decline has been affected by the civil disturbances—contractors unwilling to tender in certain areas, shortages of materials and labour shortages arising from sectarian problems and emigration, problems of decanting to enable redevelopment progress. It has also been affected by the disruptive initial effects of the reorganisation of local government, roads, water and sewerage administration and by the decision to raise new building standards to the British level.[54]

None the less, the targets for new building remain well below those recommended in a series of reports.[55] Equally important as these failings has been the inability of the Housing Executive to maintain a coherent lettings policy in parts of Belfast. This failure is more immediately explicable in terms of the effects of violence, intimidation and the control exercised by paramilitary organisations. The effects of violence on problems of tendering, vandalism, shortages of materials, squatting, sectarianism, empty housing, and public sector new building have been documented.[56] The responses of public agencies in accepting unpalatable but unavoidable realities, modifying existing policies and adopting new policies have also been described. The consistency of responses is uncertain. Faced with a rent strike, Stormont adopted a policy of deducting from social security payments to meet arrears. The enabling legislation, the Payments for Debt (Emergency Provisions) Act, 1971, remains in force, and its powers continue to be used.

However, the Housing Executive has no adequate powers to deal with squatting, and tenants accommodated through the official processes would rarely seek the threats and intimidation which would arise if squatters supported by sectarian groups were ousted

in their favour. The problems are not merely ones of legal procedures and enforcement; they result directly from the realities of
social and sectarian segregation in Belfast.

To this extent the Housing Executive has been overwhelmed by
the politico-religious influences on it. Both the Housing Executive
and the Department of Environment have had to come to terms
with this situation, even to the extent of supporting new building
programmes which would extend religious segregation (for example
the Department of the Environment's proposed Poleglass development scheme of May 1976).

The Northern Ireland Housing Executive has been able to introduce a common structure of policy and policy review throughout
Northern Ireland and to give some central consideration to questions
of equity-sharing, tenant participation and improvement policy. It
has participated in and made public the results of major surveys.
None the less, the continuity in policy is surprising.

One of the problems of an appointed and professional body with
little competition in the provision of new building for rent is its
accountability. Early in its career the Housing Executive's independence from ministerial influence was at issue.[57] Currently it is
reasonable to regard the Housing Executive as an agent of the
Department of the Environment with no independent view of the
housing problem. In this its role differs fundamentally from that of
the local authorities in Britain. Thus while there is an apparent
rationality in the organisation of housing provision, some of the
principal features of planning, policy-making and implementation
are not operated on such an inoffensive, non-political basis as is
often represented. The sale of dwellings built in rural areas or the
approach to the privately rented sector would arouse strong political
opposition in local authorities in Britain with less serious housing
problems. In this way the centralised structure of housing administration and policy-making offers little scope for debate at a local
level. Although the past record of the government does not recommend itself, it is not clear that a centralised structure is necessarily
better equipped to formulate policy or to effect innovations. The
immediate innovations in policy—for example, a common lettings
policy—are unrepeatable, and the continuing scope for a different
style of management may be limited.

The closeness of the Housing Executive and the central department does, however, have advantages. There is a major opportunity
to influence policy and legislation. Arguably the arrangement makes
it more possible for regional government to operate in a co-ordinated
fashion. The two most important areas of policy development since
1973 provide some evidence of this co-ordination. The Housing

(Northern Ireland) Order, 1976, strengthened the voluntary housing movement and offered a more flexible procedure for dealing with older housing. But the costs and difficulties of implementing policies in this area have been less fully dealt with.[58] The development of new policies towards the privately rented sector, culminating in the Rent Order, 1978, were also designed to deal with older housing. But the practical implications of the order were not clearly appreciated, and the process of its development and revision exposed structural divisions between the Housing Executive and Department of the Environment and revealed areas of dissension between them. (This view is particularly supported by the revisions made to the draft Rent Order, 1978.)

In spite of the lack of public investment in housing in the inter-war years, by 1971 37 per cent of Northern Ireland households were living in dwellings owned by public authorities.[59] The privately rented sector had declined to 14 per cent—a level comparable to England (16 per cent), Wales (14 per cent) and Scotland (13 per cent). But with owner occupation at 49 per cent in Northern Ireland, 55 per cent in England, 58 per cent in Wales and 33 per cent in Scotland, Northern Ireland's tenure structure indicates a greater public sector role than in England and Wales. Between 1961 and 1971 the public sector nearly doubled in size, and the increase in owner occupation in that period was only three-quarters of the increase in the public sector. In this same period there has been a substantial reduction in crowding—although this may have been exaggerated by census definitions. But the benefits of policy and investment have not been evenly spread. Compton (1978) indicates that the gap between the best (Antrim) and the worst (Fermanagh) in terms of provision of amenities widened between 1961 and 1971, and a similar picture emerged with overcrowding. But this investment in housing and the increased adoption of a step-by-step policy, as evidenced in the treatment of the older housing stock or the adoption of ideas about equity-sharing or sale of dwellings, has not remedied the situation. The Northern Ireland housing situation is still marked by much greater levels of crowding, physical obsolescence and shortage than exist elsewhere in the United Kingdom. Recent rates of new building in Northern Ireland have been inadequate to meet the demand from natural population growth, let alone meet the backlog of need. And it is those with least opportunity and choice to move house or increase their expenditure who are worst housed. But this does not mean that public intervention has not succeeded in channelling resources to lower income groups and larger families.

One of the interesting features of public policy in Northern

Ireland is the apparent acceptability of public housing. Perhaps because of the high proportions of inadequate dwellings in the owner-occupied and privately rented sectors, there is a surprisingly high rate of movement of households from those tenures to the public sector.[60] In this way it is clear that although public policy has not succeeded in maintaining any parity of housing provision between Northern Ireland and Britain, it has provided an important element of high-quality housing and affected the trend in the private sector. It is also evident that those who have benefited included many who would have been unable to obtain comparable housing on the private market.

Recent survey evidence shows that the high-quality modern dwellings in the public sector significantly break Northern Ireland's cycle of deprivation. The Housing Executive houses large sections of the poorest, especially families with children. Groups who could not obtain high-standard housing on the grounds of income and employment are able to qualify on grounds of need. It is also apparent that new building in the public sector is a more effective way of channelling housing resources to the worst-off than new building in the private sector.[61] But the benefits of public intervention are not distributed in a way that breaks sectarian barriers.

Perhaps the most prominent and best-documented aspect of Northern Ireland is the nature and extent of residential segregation in Belfast. Jones (1960) has clearly described the demographic, class and religious dimensions of residential division.[62] More recent work by Boal (1970, 1971) has established the continuity of this pattern and the lack both of contact between social classes and religious groups. The historical origins of this division are described by Jones, who also hints at the process through which segregation is reinforced. Studies of displacement and residential movement arising because of intimidation or destruction during civil conflict show how the lines of segregation are strengthened and made more rigid as a result of such conflict.[63] What these studies do not analyse is how the activities of government have affected this pattern. A number of factors can be referred to. Initially it can be argued that the lack of public activity both in new building and slum clearance left competition for housing subject to the arbitration of agencies whose operations were made easier by maintaining sectarian division. Thus the discriminatory processes of the market added a religious test to tests of income, credit and status. The physical geography of Belfast contributed to the situation where new public building on the outskirts of the city was only accessible through districts which were identified with a particular politico-religious label. Thus the Andersonstown and Ballymurphy estates were

H

adjacent to traditionally Catholic areas and became in turn largely Catholic estates—a process affected by choice, intimidation and the inevitable compliance of housing authorities. The conflicts of the early 1970s have created circumstances in which the Housing Executive must consciously take the existence of the sectarian divide into account in the operation of building policy (as, for example, in the proposed development at Poleglass): it must provide and locate houses and must determine their quantity according to the requirements of the different sectarian divisions of the community. In these ways it can be argued that housing authorities are unable to oppose or counter divisions within society, and that in responding to these they may reinforce those same divisions. At this level the discriminatory process is one which the state in no way creates or even intentionally sustains, but it is nevertheless one which begins to affect its activity. However, at the same time it is clear that in the 1960s the concern of the Northern Ireland government with economic development and modernisation led it to facilitate slum clearance and redevelopment programmes which seriously disrupted the life of long-established Protestant and Catholic communities.[64]

While it is difficult to regard these policies as conspiracies by the state designed to manipulate and divide opposition, it is apparent that policies of modernisation and public expenditure carried out in an environment of ideological and political polarisation do arouse sectarian responses. They are interpreted in the light of those responses and in practice can sustain sectarian divisions.

Social Security

The Northern Ireland government inherited a mixed system of social security provision. Under the National Insurance Act, 1911, a section of the working population were entitled to insurance benefits based on contribution record. Such benefits were available for a fixed period, after which recipients had to rely on the Poor Law. Some 20 per cent of the labour force (in particular agricultural workers) were outside the scheme, and extensions in 1916 and 1920 had not made it comprehensive. Outside this scheme provision for the unemployed was made through the Poor Law and unemployment relief schemes. There were some 1,937 unemployment relief schemes sanctioned by the Northern Ireland Ministry of Labour between 1922 and 1935. These were operated by local authorities and financed by a grant (£500,000, later reduced to £300,000) from the United Kingdom government and by funds voted by Stormont.[65] By far the most important element, however, was the provision made under the Poor Law.

It is argued that the Irish Poor Law seriously diverged from the English model since its inception in 1838.[66] Before 1838 there was no Poor Law operating in Ireland, and treatment of the poor was repressive and concerned with control and punishment of vagrants and beggars rather than with relief. This picture must be modified to take account of philanthropic effort, specific local acts and measures for particular groups. Although Ireland was 'miserably poor', no national response was developed before 1838. The Poor Law Commissioners established in Britain in 1834 were to administer a Poor Law based on the principles of less eligibility and the workhouse test. Applicants would be offered relief only within the workhouse, where conditions were to be less desirable than those experienced by the lowest-paid independent labourer. This basic approach was extended to Ireland in spite of reports in 1835 and 1836 which had claimed that Irish circumstances required a different response.

Not only was the 1838 act based on principles which were of dubious merit in both Britain and Ireland, but it also seems probable that the act was more rigidly enforced in Ireland than in Britain, where it aroused public opposition and where enforcement of the workhouse test and the refusal of outdoor relief was left to the discretion of the Boards of Guardians, was not uniform, and in some areas was never carried out. Although it is equally apparent that enforcement was not uniform in Ireland, the act of 1838 gave no discretion to the Irish Poor Law Commission or the Boards of Guardians. If circumstances suggested a modified approach to the poor, new legislation was required. The general view that the Poor Law in Ireland was more penal and inflexible has not been seriously challenged. The demand that Irish property should pay for Irish poverty was unrealistic in areas where there was insufficient wealth to levy a Poor Law rate. Although outdoor relief was available, it was limited to the provision of food and restricted to the destitute: no person occupying more than one-quarter of an acre of land was eligible.

In 1898 the Local Government (Ireland) Act established a structure of county, county borough, rural and urban district councils. County councils and urban district councils were responsible for levying and collecting the poor rate. Rural district councillors became the Poor Law Guardians for their own areas, while Guardians were directly elected in other areas. The act also empowered Boards of Guardians to provide outdoor relief for up to two months, to renew this decision and to vary the terms for granting relief. Thus while there was a harsh tradition in administering the Poor Law after 1898, the flexibility to modify this tradition was available. In addition, the Workmen's Compensation Act, 1897, the Old Age Pensions Act, 1908, and the Labour Exchanges Act, 1909, were extended to Ireland. Although Ireland was included under the National Insurance Act, 1911, contributors did not receive medical benefit. In 1916 and 1919 legislation for the provision of school meals and medical inspection and treatment for schoolchildren in Ireland was enacted (later than in England and Wales).

Thus by 1921 there was a considerable structure of social security provision. But it was not the system operating in Britain, where Boards of Guardians had wider discretion and outdoor relief was more widely accepted and available. It also depended on the use Boards of Guardians made of these powers. It was this structure which was called upon to deal with the mass unemployment of the 1920s and 1930s. The rising unemployment of the 1920s, especially in Belfast, aroused considerable discontent which increasingly focused on the operation of outdoor relief and led to combined Catholic–Protestant agitation and growing support for the Labour Party.

The inadequacies of the unemployment insurance system left a major role for the Poor Law. Not only did insurance not extend to all workers, but contribution conditions and an availability for work 'test' (which in Northern Ireland could mean that those who refused jobs in England were struck off) and the fixed duration of benefit placed increasing numbers in the hands of the Poor Law as high unemployment continued. Although Northern Ireland provisions relating to unemployment insurance differed from those in Britain, both the scheme and its failures were fundamentally similar. But public reaction to the administration of the residual Poor Law was a factor that had to be taken into account. The most striking example of this is in the effects of the dispute between the Belfast Board of Guardians and Stormont over outdoor relief.[67] The Belfast Guardians maintained that the introduction of unemployment insurance had transferred responsibility for the able-bodied poor to the state. Consequently in the early 1920s they refused to exercise their discretion to provide outdoor relief under the act of 1898. They sought to maintain the principle of the workhouse test and limit outdoor relief to the aged, disabled and widows. The 1898 act enabled extension of outdoor relief to the unemployed, as exceptional cases, by the Boards of Guardians obtaining a (renewable) two-monthly order. But the Boards of Guardians refused to do this until 1924. Outside Belfast the reluctance was even greater (only two orders were made between the wars), although it seems that boards did act illegally to give outdoor relief. In Belfast the order of 1924 was renewed until October 1927, when, in conflict with the Ministry of Home Affairs over responsibility for long-term unemployment (as opposed to 'emergency' situations), the Boards of Guardians decided not to apply for a renewal. After discussion, however, the order was renewed, though it was coupled with a labour test under which applicants were set to work.[68] In May 1928 the boards again refused to apply for the order. This dispute was only resolved with the Poor Relief (Exceptional Distress) Act (Northern Ireland), 1928. Under this act the Ministry of Home Affairs could require the Boards of Guardians of any union to administer outdoor relief. This power was immediately used in April 1929 in Belfast.

In spite of this, the problem of benefits for the unemployed remained. In Britain Public Assistance Committees, appointed by local authorities, were paying higher benefits than the Belfast Boards of Guardians. It was these circumstances that led to the most extensive and violent disturbances.[69] Strikes and demonstrations were supported by all sections of the working classes and led to serious clashes with the police. Demonstrations in 1925 and 1926 had failed to secure changes in the treatment of the unemployed, while in the next few years improved employment opportunities led to a corresponding abatement of agitation. But in the early 1930s protests were better organised and were supported by high unemployment which affected Protestant and Catholic workers alike. In September 1932 demonstrations led the Boards of Guardians to increase relief rates by 50 per cent and make all payments in cash. Demonstrations continued although barred under the Special Powers Act. The RUC attacked and fired on demonstrators, two fatalities resulting. By October additional revision in relief rates satisfied the men on outdoor relief. Relief rates had been doubled, and the conditions of receipt were considerably modified. Although the success of this campaign did not carry over and was not reflected in elections, the evidence from this and the 1933 railwaymen's strike emphasised the potential for non-sectarian working-class action and the importance of wage and income issues in this. The Unionist government's fears of socialism, communism and an active and united labour movement are related to the priority it gave to parity in this area of social policy. Although it succeeded in exploiting sectarian divisions (aided by the IRA's intervention, the Roman Catholic hierarchy's fear of communism, and the growth of the Ulster Protestant League as a militant sectarian group), the lessons of these strikes undoubtedly exercised a permanent influence on the social policy of the Northern Ireland government.

The Poor Law, marked by differences from the British pattern, remained important throughout the inter-war years. However, the Northern Ireland government adopted British measures which reduced the role of the Poor Law. The Old Age Contributory Pension Act (Northern Ireland), 1925, followed the British model, as did extensions to the scope of pensions in 1929 and 1931 in spite of increased costs. Along with changes in unemployment insurance and the National Health Insurance Act (Northern Ireland), 1930, which extended medical benefit to insured persons in the province, the 1925 measure was the basis of the step-by-step policy adopted by the Northern Ireland government in its social security legislation. In 1938 responsibility for means-tested cash benefits for the unemployed was transferred to the Unemployment Assistance Board of Northern Ireland, and this body's role was extended in the war years. Nevertheless, in 1938 nearly 5,000 persons were in workhouses, and over 14,000 were in receipt of outdoor relief from the Boards of Guardians. These boards (abolished in Britain in 1929) had a larger 'caseload' in 1938 than they had had at any time between 1922 and 1932.[70]

The original expectation of arrangements made under the Government of Ireland Act, 1920, was that Northern Ireland would be able to finance its own services out of the revenues due to it. However, it was not long before expenditure began to outstrip revenue. The principal reason for this was the insistence on maintaining cash social benefits at the British level. In view of the higher demands made on services (because of relative social and economic disadvantages) in Northern Ireland, this was inevitable. In other areas of social service the problem was largely avoided, as standards were not maintained and, as Lawrence (1965 a) states, they were allowed to stagnate or even to grow worse. This, however, was not the case with cash benefits. As early as 1922 the desirability of maintaining unemployment insurance on lines parallel with Great Britain was stressed, and this position was consistently reiterated by Stormont ministers.[71] The implications of this insistence became clear as early as 1925, by which time the Unemployment Insurance Fund of Northern Ireland had a large deficit.

This problem was resolved by the first of many *ad hoc* measures to keep benefits at the British level while avoiding a deficit. Britain agreed to pay three-quarters of the excess over the proportionate rate per head in Britain. As the province's financial difficulties increased it became clear that more financial support from the British Exchequer would be necessary to maintain cash benefit at the British level. In 1938 there was a formal declaration by the Chancellor of the Exchequer, Sir John Simon, that Northern Ireland should be in a financial position to enjoy the same social services and have the same standards as Great Britain. The period of social reconstruction after the war saw measures taken to ensure that the full range of Britain's post-war social security schemes were extended to Northern Ireland, with special assistance to lift the underdeveloped services to Britain's level.

Legislation between 1945 and 1948 completely remodelled the system founded in 1911 for the whole of Ireland. The basic characteristics of the old scheme no longer operate, and insurance is both comprehensive and universal. Specific occupational groups are not excluded, although (until the Social Security Pensions Act, 1975) coverage was optional for married women, the self-employed, and employed persons whose income is very low. The flat-rate insurance benefit in Northern Ireland has since 1966 been supplemented in sickness, unemployment and widowhood by an earnings-related supplement. As well as making the small graduated addition to the pension paid to the retired person, the taxation system and pensions legislation actively encourage employers to provide occupational welfare. Finally, these measures are complemented by non-contributory, non-means-tested benefit (child benefits, pensions for the over-eighties, attendance allowances), the residual assistance scheme (since 1966, supplementary benefits) and locally administered means-tested rebates and allowances. The new pensions scheme was also extended fully to Northern Ireland by the Social Security Pensions Order, 1975.

In Northern Ireland flat-rate insurance benefits represent a higher proportion of average earnings than in regions of Great Britain which have higher average incomes. In spite of this, a very considerable proportion of beneficiaries do not have sufficient income to lift them above the level of income defined by supplementary benefit scale rates. If we add to these rates allowances for rent, income from resources which are disregarded in calculating entitlement, and certain discretionary additions, final income can be very considerably above the basic scale rates. The payment in the majority of cases of rents in full is of very great importance in this, especially in a period when rents can be expected to rise considerably.

In Northern Ireland, as a consequence of the low level of insurance benefit compared with non-contributory benefit, a very considerable proportion of insurance recipients make use of supplementary benefits. This is in addition to those who are not entitled to or have exhausted insurance benefit. For example, in 1973–74 some 31 per cent of those receiving retirement pensions and some 20 per cent of those receiving unemployment benefit were also receiving supplementary benefits.[72]

A higher proportion of the population of Northern Ireland are dependent on state benefits than in Britain. The proportion of households receiving benefit is considerably higher; so also is the proportion of children in those households. The importance of child benefit in Northern Ireland has already been referred to. It is evident that because supplementary benefits and Family Income Supplement take the age and number of children into account, these schemes are of considerable benefit to Northern Ireland. However, it is not clear that dependants' additions are adequate, especially when households are dependent for long periods of time. In so far as these payments do not cover the real costs involved, the deficiencies are more serious in Northern Ireland. In exactly the same way the operation of a wage stop in supplementary benefits—to prevent the unemployed in receipt of benefit receiving more than an employed man in the type of job the recipient normally does—had more serious deficiencies in Northern Ireland, where low earnings, larger families and long-term dependence on benefit made the reduction in respect of the wage stop more serious. The Supplementary Benefits Commission in Northern Ireland followed the British lead and abolished the wage stop in July 1975. But the impact of the wage stop had been serious for some time before that (in 1973 13 per cent of claimants were wage-stopped—proportionately four times as many as in Britain), and this element is indicative of the problems of pursuing a step-by-step approach.

The limited evidence relating to Northern Ireland suggests that many entitled to means-tested benefits do not receive them. The inquiry *Financial and Other Circumstances of Retirement Pensioners in Northern Ireland* found that the proportion of retirement pensioners entitled to supplementary pensions but not receiving them was as high as in Britain.[73] The report concluded that

> It was clear that there was a residue who really needed assistance: among these some had not applied because they were ignorant of the provision made or mistakenly thought there was some bar to their application, while pride or prejudice still stopped some others from asking for help, even after their interviews in connection with the survey.

Although some surveys have indicated a wide awareness of available benefits and although it has been assumed that uptake of Family Income Supplement was higher in Northern Ireland than in Britain, the overall impression is that the means-tested components of the social security system are not effective.

Uptake of FIS varies considerably between areas but shows no 'rational' pattern.[74] Furthermore, recent evidence suggests that the use of Family Expenditure Survey as a basis for calculating uptake of this benefit is inadequate. Calculations based on the largest, most recent and most comprehensive household survey information indicate that a substantial number of households eligible for FIS and rent rebates are not receiving them.[75]

One final piece of information is relevant in this context: Northern Ireland followed British practice in replacing the national assistance scheme with supplementary benefits. As in Britain, the transition coincided with a considerable increase in claims (59 per cent in Northern Ireland). This could be taken to indicate an increase in acceptability or uptake. However, such an increase is not consistent with the evidence referred to above and more probably was the result of the increased benefit rates which accompanied the change. It would also seem likely that the administration of discretion in supplementary benefits in Northern Ireland operates in a similar way to that in Britain.[76]

The most debated area of comparison has been the relative use of discretionary additions in Northern Ireland and Britain. Under the 1966 act discretionary additions to basic weekly benefits can be made. But in exceptional circumstances additions (weekly amounts for heating, diet, laundry and certain other items) were less likely to be paid in Northern Ireland. In 1974 28 per cent of supplementary benefit recipients in Northern Ireland received them (compared with 34 per cent in Britain), and average amounts paid were lower (56 pence compared with 67 pence). Similarly, exceptional needs payments (lump sum grants) were twice as likely to be paid in Britain than in Northern Ireland (although the average amount paid in Northern Ireland was higher). The official explanations for these discrepancies (removal costs were met by agencies other than the commission; job changing was less in Northern Ireland; there were fewer immigrants and more self-employed farmers with disregarded resources) are not regarded by some as sufficient to explain the scale of variations. However, it is most surprising that the focus of debate should be on discretion, which deals with very small sums. The problems are more fundamental ones. As it consciously avoids independent modifications, it would be surprising if the operation of assistance in Northern Ireland did not exhibit shortcomings comparable with those recorded in Britain. Arguably the consequences of such shortcomings are likely to prove more damaging in Northern Ireland than in Britain because of different circumstances.

In view of this, it might be expected that devolved powers would have been used to adopt different procedures. But the limited sums concerned in discretion and the inherent limitations of discretionary

H*

procedures do not suggest that this would be a fruitful area for deviation. And the more dramatic variations implied in deviation from basic scale rates would have major financial implications. Northern Ireland has nevertheless chosen to deviate in two significant ways. The first of these is the operation of the Payments for Debt (Emergency Provisions) Act (Northern Ireland), 1971. This provides that where a person is in debt, any money due to him by any government department or local or public authority may be allocated in whole or in part towards the recovery of that debt. Furthermore, where a person becomes subject to the provisions of that act, he is not entitled to an exceptional needs grant unless there is a special determination by the Supplementary Benefits Commission, against which there is no appeal. The ministry is prepared to consider any representations made on grounds of hardship.

It appears that under this act families have had their benefits reduced by some 10 per cent (in practice possibly by as much as 16 per cent, and for owner occupiers owing rates even more). In addition, it appears that the act affects appeal rights. Although there has been some easing from this position, the act has remained in use long after the bulk of the debt resulting from the 1971 rent and rate strike has been recovered. It has become part of the normal machinery for recovering rent arrears and has been extended to cover fuel debts.[77]

The origin of this act does not rest with the Supplementary Benefits Commission; it was in fact introduced to counter the withholding of rent and rates payments in 1971. The act can be criticised both in principle and on the grounds that rates of deduction from benefits are unreasonably high. There can be little doubt that the act not only undermines the concept of welfare rights, but is also most damaging to those in the greatest need. Nevertheless, it should be noted that the British supplementary benefit scheme enables payment of part of an allowance to a third party and, together with 'arm-twisting' over voluntary deductions, can operate with the same effect.

A second specific feature of social security in Northern Ireland raises complex problems. This is the provision under the Supplementary Benefits, Etc. Act (Northern Ireland), 1966, that a person who has not been resident in the United Kingdom for five years preceding the date of his claim is excluded from receiving supplementary benefit. In certain circumstances, which are covered by regulation, periods when a person was not so resident may be treated as residence. This is in sharp contrast to the British position, confounds the principle of uniformity, and calls into question whether this is the most appropriate area for separate regulations if such variations are to exist.

This residence condition operates in conjunction with the Safeguarding of Employment Act (Northern Ireland), 1947, which continued to operate for a transitional period following entry into the EEC, although it conflicts with the EEC's provisions for the free movement of labour between member states. The act is designed to protect the interests of Northern Ireland workers by making it illegal for other persons to engage in ordinary employment in Northern Ireland without the permission of the Ministry of Health and Social Services. All persons who are not 'Northern Ireland workers' must obtain a work permit.

Applications for a work permit can be made after a definite offer of employment has been received. It will then only be granted if circumstances are considered to be appropriate. Such circumstances take local employment conditions into account. The permit must be renewed regularly and may be revoked whenever the ministry considers that the circumstances that justified its grant or renewal have changed. If the permit is not renewed or is revoked, the person becoming unemployed as a result may be excluded from receipt of supplementary benefit because of the residence condition. It is evident that a regulation of this type is difficult to administer equitably and is a potential source of hardship.

In an area experiencing high unemployment it is understandable that attempts to reserve employment arise. However, the consequences for those whose labour is periodically or temporarily required are hardly consistent with the welfare state model. It is doubtful if the effects of such a regulation on job security, dismissal procedures, labour organisations and wage levels are negligible. It may be argued with some justification that it erodes the rights of the whole population by maintaining an explicitly discriminatory system under which residents have different social rights.

With these exceptions, social security provision in Northern Ireland has remained identical with that in Britain. It is important to recognise that the decision to retain parity was a conscious decision throughout the existence of Stormont. Thus, for example, there was serious debate on the merits of increasing family allowances in 1956, as well as the debate on the Payments for Debt Act, 1971, and its continuation. In both cases the debates were linked with politico-religious questions. In the former it did not lead to deviation from parity but, as has already been stated, the latter example is different. With the exception of these examples, there is no evidence of the use of devolved powers in recent years. What becomes curious is the absence of comment and pressure to modify the United Kingdom system in order to benefit Northern Ireland. The introduction of FIS and the abolition of the wage stop have benefited Northern Ireland households. But the initiative for these came from Westminster. The step-by-step approach has not embodied pressure to urge Westminster to take steps which Northern Ireland could follow with advantage. In this sense the devolved government has not acted to formulate proposals and represent Northern Ireland in national policy reviews.

It is instructive to note that the Northern Ireland government has been remarkably backward even in identifying problems. Except on the subject of the elderly, no official reports or research have looked at groups at or near the poverty line. The Northern Ireland government has been much less well informed about the nature and extent of poverty than has its British equivalent. Even the 1975 household survey, which included the first extensive attempt to measure poverty, was not commissioned for that purpose and represented a 'backdoor' means of establishing the situation.

There are other services closely linked with income maintenance. Legal Aid and Advice was only introduced to Northern Ireland in 1965—sixteen years after England. There is no equivalent of the English Legal Advice and Assistance Act, 1972, which provided for legal advice centres in areas of need staffed by solicitors and paid by government. In addition, the system of personal compensation for damage or injury incurred in the civil disturbances has been an important source of funds in spite of considerable delays and legal costs.

There is no adequate procedure to assess the effectiveness and performance of devolution in Northern Ireland in respect of income maintenance. The gains Northern Ireland has received—resources to support relatively high benefits—are not positive results of devolution. The British model has been of great advantage; and devolution cannot be said to have failed or been unused, since Northern Ireland administrations chose not to develop variation. It is noticeable, however, that the advantage afforded by parity has not been accompanied by a significant positive role in the assessment of problems of poverty or the operation of social security. Various explanations for this have been referred to and have operated at different times. Essentially they have led to an assumption that parity is desirable and that the positive contribution of devolved government lies elsewhere.

Lawrence (1965 a) regards the question of 'why Ulster kept in step . . . when she was legally free to go her own way' as one of the more interesting questions for the student of parliamentary devolution.[78] He argues that part of the answer lies in the financial arrangements between Stormont and Westminster. In this context the insistence that non-contributory pensions could not be financed from the imperial contribution unless there was parallel expenditure in Britain effectively limited any deviations from British practice. Whereas the pensions provided under the 1908 act had been non-contributory, in 1925 Northern Ireland had to follow suit and switch to a contributory scheme. Furthermore, the Unemployment Insurance Agreement and less formal arrangements with the Treasury prevented modifications to the financial basis of insurance and assistance. Northern Ireland legislation could only respond to the problems of the province by utilising locally financed services; failing this, Stormont simply waited for the British government to take action.

Lawrence argues that finance was essentially a limiting factor and that, as Northern Ireland was relatively poor, pressure for faster progress than in Britain was unrealistic. Whether or not this view is accepted, it seems clear that the major aim of the Northern Ireland government was to avoid any 'less favourable' provision. Lawrence lists a number of reasons for this insistence. Some of these—for example the fact that cash social services had been the same as in Britain since their inception—are of dubious quality and do not appear to have been consistently applied in other policy areas. More convincing is the simple fact that comparisons of cash services are easily made. Whereas in other social services the quality and quantity of services is not easily measured, any individual can make a comparison between benefit levels. Parity with British levels of cash benefit had important practical political elements and also could be seen as symbolising the political and economic integration of Northern Ireland in the United Kingdom. Thus it can be argued that the political principles underlying parity first emerged in this sphere of social policy. Their extension to other spheres of social policy has never been complete. Lawrence describes the choice available to the province's leaders in the following way:

> On the one hand, they could allow insurance schemes to deteriorate sharply, provoke resentment about the finance of Home Rule, precipitate conflict with Britain, and create administrative difficulties. Or they could conclude financial agreements and sacrifice part of the local autonomy that Ulstermen had never greatly valued. Their resolution to reject the first course made the second inescapable, and the decision became more irreversible with time because financial benefits created and strengthened expectations among the electorate.[79]

Because of the close link between social security schemes, employment and the economies of Britain and Northern Ireland, it could be argued (especially by Westminster) that any serious discrepancy in benefit was incompatible with the equality of taxation and the integration of the two economies and would affect patterns of migration and labour mobility. It seems convincing to argue that there were economic imperatives which affected this area of policy but were absent from other areas. However, some of these imperatives were present in the rest of Ireland, whose economy was equally integrated with Britain and where movement of labour was equally open. Benefit levels and legislation in the rest of Ireland did not follow Britain as closely. Indeed, the benefit gap between the two parts of Ireland became marked. It could even be argued that the very existence of this gap increasingly justified the North's parity with Britain and its maintaining a 'superior' system of benefits.

In view of all these considerations, it may be more logical to ask why income maintenance was transferred to the Stormont government. Why, in view of all the constraints on pursuing an independent policy, was the scope for independence maintained? It does appear that there was some dispute over the merits of transferring this responsibility. Perhaps business interests hoped that it could be used to keep wages and benefits lower than in Britain and so assist in providing a competitive edge. Some politicians at least were not attracted by this and regretted that Northern Ireland was not included in British legislation.[80]

Although there were serious financial constraints, economic imperatives, and particular facets of income-maintenance services which have been important factors, Lawrence's explanation, complemented by wider economic considerations, still ignores vital elements. The most testing period for income-maintenance services was the inter-war years; and in this period, as has been described, deviations from parity were limited by serious political pressures. More recent research carried out by Buckland (1979) emphasises some different elements and shows that while financial constraints were of primary importance, they did not eliminate debate and dispute. Ministers favouring a step-by-step policy stressed the need to maintain equal social standards, believing that failure to do so would have economic and political disadvantages. Buckland states that 'Some ministers certainly believed that unemployment insurance helped to retain in Northern Ireland reservoirs of labour essential to enable its industries to take advantage of any upswing in the economy' and refers to Sir James Craig's conviction that the inclusion of agricultural labourers in the unemployment insurance scheme would help stem the drift from the countryside. Failure to maintain equal social standards would alienate the working classes: as the Minister of Labour put it in 1925, 'We cannot carry on as a government here unless our working classes enjoy the same social standards as their brother trade unionists in Great Britain.' Finally, however, if the Northern Ireland government denied the need for equity in social security benefits, it would stand little chance of securing finance to achieve equity in any other area.[81]

Other ministers, and the Ministry of Finance in particular, always tried to limit social expenditure. They shared the view favoured by many industrial and agricultural employers and thus emphasised the burden of taxation and contributions and their unproductiveness and impact on costs and competitiveness. Such arguments often incorporated a suspicion that the working classes were being unduly pampered at the expense of other sections of the community. Buckland also refers to the opinion prevalent in the Ministry of Finance that 'a substantial reduction in income tax and in the level of state activity was infinitely preferable to handing out doles, increasing state responsibility and imposing additional burdens on industry'. In some circumstances an additional argument was that Northern Ireland was too small and too poor to keep pace with Britain and that lower wages and living costs should be reflected in lower contributions and benefits. One final argument involved local authorities and the lower proportion of rate-borne public expenditure in Northern Ireland. Insistence on equal benefit could lead to equal taxation. Local authorities' determination to keep rates down underlay the conflict with the government over outdoor relief. (Buckland cites Belfast Corporation as a body particularly prone to disputes of this type.) Although complicated by prejudiced and sometimes sectarian attitudes to idleness and waste, the views of some local authorities indicated a conflict over who was responsible for services. The interest of the ratepayers was to limit relief and costs. Principles of equity and step-by-step did not enter into it.

Conclusion

Some of the broader implications of the developments in policy have been considered in this chapter. However, initially it is clear that in housing and planning, and even with respect to certain detailed aspects of social security policy, Northern Ireland has made use of its devolved status to develop separate policies. But these differences do not imply that devolution has given a capacity to control the province's future. The problems of the inter-war period have remained and have proved intractable. Where progress has been made in absolute terms in such areas as housing or economic development, the rest of the United Kingdom has progressed at least as fast, and relative differentials remain. The most obvious implication of this is that planning, regional policies and the range of policies available are not the principal determinants of what happens in Northern Ireland. The economy is dependent on the decisions of private individuals and investors and on the broader international economic situation. The stubborness of problems and the ineffectiveness of policy responses fundamentally indicate that Northern Ireland's economy is not independent or insulated. The peripheral position of Northern Ireland may even impart a greater dependence than is usual for regions of the United Kingdom. The capacity for a devolved government in achieving change is fundamentally restricted by its position in an international economic environment.

Within these limits, however, it is clear that there are also financial constraints on policy. The financial relationship between Stormont and Westminster has been far more significant than other aspects of the constitutional arrangements. These financial constraints can, however, be exaggerated. For example, Buckland's presentation of disputes over unemployment insurance and relief emphasises the conflict between the Belfast Board of Guardians and the government and the controversy over a question of interpretation of the law which had implications as to whether expenditure should fall on local rates or on Stormont. Buckland also stresses the Ministry of Finance's consistent opposition to increased expenditure—hardly a stance compatible with a view that financial constraints left no alternatives. The view that there were no real policy alternatives was a political view held by a majority in the government. It cannot be claimed to be an objective or incontestable view. The final evidence that neither economic, financial nor constitutional factors reduce the capacity for independent policy development is that of internal political pressures. Social security, housing and planning policies have been the subject of conflicts within government and parliament, between central and local government, between groups within the Unionist Party, and between Unionists and their political opponents. Choices have been made between alternative policies—policies which were feasible even allowing for the wide constraints on action—and the choices made have been of great importance in the politics and conflicts in Northern Ireland.

10

Social Policies (2):
Education, Health and Social Services

THE principal policy areas for the exercise of devolved powers include education, health and, of increasing importance in recent years, the personal social services. In this chapter the discussion of policy in these areas is presented in a similar fashion to that of planning, housing and income maintenance in the previous chapter.

Education

The progress of legislation in the sphere of education in Northern Ireland has been fully documented elsewhere.[1] Akenson (1973) describes the lack of overall guidance and co-ordination in a tripartite schools system largely under clerical control in 1920. At that stage there was neither local civic financial support through the rates nor statutory provision for local lay participation in controlling the schools. The initial objective of the new unified Ministry of Education in Northern Ireland was to organise a new scheme of educational provision. In education more than any other service the partition of Ireland in 1920 made innovation essential. Much of the financial and administrative work of the Catholic elementary school system was handled in Dublin, which was also the centre for intermediate examinations. Such a situation was not compatible with the administrative responsibilities of Stormont; this was especially so in the case of examinations, as the view was held that in Dublin after partition 'the Provisional Government wished to give undue prominence to the Irish language in the intermediate examinations'.[2] The initial steps of the new Northern Ireland ministry were therefore directed to establishing authority and control. The non-co-operation policy of Catholic schools was ineffective and further weakened their bargaining position.

Having gained control, the ministry began to think of reforms. Two principal influences lay behind the Education Act, 1923: the British model of social policy and financial support, and the report of the Lynn Committee. The Roman Catholic authorities had been invited to send representatives to sit on this committee but had refused. The Catholic view was 'that the only satisfactory system of education for Catholics is one wherein Catholic children are taught in Catholic schools by Catholic teachers under Catholic auspices'.[3] Cardinal Logue, in rejecting the invitation to sit on the Lynn Committee, stated: 'I have little doubt that an attack is being organised against our Catholic schools. I fear the Lynn Committee will be a foundation and pretext for that attack.'[4] Akenson states that

> In all probability the refusal of the Roman Catholic authorities to join the Lynn Committee was the single most important determinant of the educational history of Northern Ireland from 1920 to the present day. By refusing to sit they surrendered their last shred of influence at the very time when the basic character of Ulster's educational development was being determined. From the recommendations made by the Lynn Committee emerged the principles of the 1923 Londonderry act and that act was the foundation of all later development.[5]

Nevertheless, it was not this abstention which was crucial in the development of a sectarian school system. The genuine attempt to place the educational system on a non-sectarian basis was abandoned in the mid-1920s as a result of other political pressures. Two distinct classes of schools emerged with similar religious rights but different relationships to local education authorities and therefore different degrees of financial support. The attempt to introduce a purely secular system of education was alien to Protestant and Catholic alike.[6] The successes of Protestant-led campaigns backed by the Orange Order led to the introduction of partisan stipulations, unacceptable to the Catholic Church, into the educational code.

Protestant opposition to the government was led by a clerical lobby which combined great organising ability with a passionate emotionalism and a zealous concern for religious education. The opposition were willing to take strong action, to appeal to the laity and to use electoral threats. In the face of an alliance between this group and the Orange Order, a government which initially underestimated the movement and which received no support from either Roman Catholic or moderate Protestant teachers gave way and introduced an amendment act in 1925. This made provision for religious instruction and allowed the religions of candidates for teaching posts to be taken into account. Lawrence's view that these were 'minor changes' does not reflect the real situation.[7] Akenson comments:

> As far as the result of the Protestant agitation is concerned,

there can be no doubt that Lord Londonderry [the Minister of Education] surrendered and permitted the introduction of a pernicious double standard in Ulster education. The concordats permitting regional education committees to require that teachers give Bible instruction actually meant that teachers could be required to give Protestant religious instruction. (That this instruction was not to be distinctive of any specific Protestant denomination does not obviate the fact that simple Bible reading was distinctly Protestant, being acceptable to all the Protestant denominations but not to the Roman Catholics.)

Recalling that the entire salary of the primary school teachers was paid by the Ministry of Education and, further, that all educational expenses of transferred and provided schools* were paid for by local and central government authorities, it is quite clear that the new arrangement involved an endowment of the Protestant faith.[8]

Despite the fact that state endowment of religion was in direct contravention of the Government of Ireland Act, 1920, the Attorney-General of Northern Ireland certified the legality of the 1925 act, and the Home Office in London contented itself with expressing private reservations.[9] The Westminster government's policy of limiting involvement in Northern Ireland affairs was a precondition for the increasingly sectarian bent of the Stormont government as indicated by developments in education.

Agitation for further amendment of the Education Act commenced in 1928. Evidence presented by Buckland (1979) from the cabinet papers shows that the government, faced again with an alliance of the clergy and the Orange Order, capitulated completely in spite of the opposition of the Ulster Teachers' Union.[10] As in 1925, the Westminster government chose not to formalise its reservations by taking action. It chose to await any representations it might receive from 'responsible parties' after the bill became law.[11]

An amending act in 1930 required that any transferred or provided school had to provide Bible instruction at the request of the parents of not less than ten pupils. This made it impossible for Catholic schools to become transferred or provided schools and thus to benefit from preferential financial aid given to such schools.

The attempted neutral stance of Stormont which had been replaced by a sectarian stance in the late 1920s re-emerged in the 1940s. In 1945 the Attorney-General stated that the Education

---

* 'Transferred' schools were schools transferred to state management by their former managers; 'provided' schools were schools built by the local education authorities.

Act, 1930, had been *ultra vires* of the parliament of Northern Ireland. At the same time the experience of wartime conditions and the consequent changed expectations of government and people about the proper role of government created a new environment. In 1944 the Minister of Education, Colonel Hall-Thompson, stated that the question of building grants to Catholic schools should be dealt with on the basis of according just treatment to the minority, and this view was approved by the cabinet. It is also notable that the Westminster government was concerned in this re-emergence of neutrality. A letter from the Home Secretary in January 1945 stated that there would be great objection to any attempt to evade the constitutional problem associated with compulsory religious education: 'It would be seen as impairing safeguards for the principle of toleration and the protection of minorities.'[12]

The Education Act, 1947, raised the school-leaving age and introduced a split between primary and post-primary education at the age of eleven. In addition, public financial support for voluntary (i.e. Catholic) primary schools was raised. The most controversial provision in the act was the repeal of the rules for Bible instruction framed under the 1930 act and now declared *ultra vires*. Strong Protestant objections were made over a 'conscience clause' excusing teachers from religious teaching and collective worship and repealing previous statutes on religious instruction. Roman Catholic authorities were concerned at the costs involved in reorganisation and raising the school-leaving age and had a general objection to state involvement. However, the 1947 act did not reflect responses to these views, and 'for the first time since 1925 the government of Northern Ireland had not altered its course in the face of an agitation by the more volatile Protestant elements'.[13] This does not mean that controversy over these educational themes did not continue. Indeed, in 1949 a bill concerned with minor financial changes resurrected controversies and produced opposition under lay leadership which eventually brought about the resignation of the Minister of Education, Colonel Hall-Thompson.[14]

After 1947 most Protestant schools had transferred to civic management. The separateness of the two school systems remained almost complete. Whereas over 95 per cent of primary school pupils in Protestant denominations in 1964 were in state schools, 98 per cent of Roman Catholics were in voluntary schools. Akenson remarks: 'The most important theme running through Northern Ireland's educational history has been the seemingly irresistible demand for segregated schooling.'[15] Religious segregation was embodied in an educational system which separated Catholics and Protestants and treated them unequally. The basis of segregation lay in a conflict between church and state in which the state system was increasingly bent towards a Protestant system and hence increasingly became identified with the Protestant churches.

The political weakness of the Catholic minority was partly a product of early clerical non-co-operation in educational rationalisation and political abstentionism before 1925. The Roman Catholic clergy's unwillingness to enter into partnership with the Catholic laity in controlling schools was based, in Akenson's words, on a 'medieval determination to control the schools singlehandedly' and on unreasonable fears which the arrangements for management control of transferred schools could have prevented from materialising. The real barrier to participation and financial equity was an 'unnecessary insistence on maintaining their sole clerical prerogatives in the management of primary schools'.[16] The consequence of this insistence was to reduce the extent to which Roman Catholic children in Northern Ireland benefited from public support for education. Nevertheless, the Catholic education system has received increasing public financial support. The provisions for Catholic schools were less generous than those available in the Irish Free State but more favourable than those obtained by voluntary, particularly Catholic, schools elsewhere in the United Kingdom (until 1936) and in the world.[17] By 1968 the capital contribution grant to voluntary schools had risen to 80 per cent.

Although the educational debate has consistently and directly involved religious matters and because of this fully indicates features and tensions in the role of government, it would be wrong to imply that the only developments in education were those which aroused religious controversy. Improved school attendance, a higher school-leaving age, improvement in school facilities, amalgamation of schools, the discontinuance of grants to schools operated for profit, and the abolition of payment by results all marked important advances. These changes demonstrated a continuing concern to improve the quality of schools and teaching and reflected the peculiar problems of a school system which had previously been supported only by voluntary funds and was dominated by small schools in rural areas. Such developments highlighted areas in which the step-by-step principle might have been more fully applied to keep Northern Ireland education more fully in line with changing British educational policy. Thus, for example, when the British government in 1929 raised the school-leaving age to fifteen this was not followed in Northern Ireland because of costs and the problems in rural areas.

In addition, it should be noted that some sectional arrangements were not financially inequitable. Thus facilities for teacher-training were separate for Catholics and Protestants, but the financial support was the same. All these elements, however, show that the government of Northern Ireland has used its devolved powers to pursue an independent policy in education. The system of finance and the detail of educational control and legislation have been developed separately from Great Britain. The predominant debates and conflicts have been internal to the province, and the devolved government has taken these conflicts into account in its development of policy. Differences in policy and practice in education between Northern Ireland and Great Britain cannot be adequately quantified, and the qualitative differences are not easily reconciled with ideas of parity. The importance of differences in school organisation and selection procedures are difficult to assess.

Some general comments can, however, be made to illustrate three themes: the progress made in education standards, the general standard of education compared with that in Britain, and the inequalities in education within Northern Ireland.

The Education Act, 1923, heralded considerable changes.[18] The introduction of a compulsory-attendance regulation may be seen as responsible for the increase in elementary school attendance from 77 per cent of enrolment in 1924 to 86 per cent in 1938. Between 1923 and 1947 195 new public elementary schools had been built and 50 per cent of children attended state elementary schools. Not only were there two systems of elementary schools—state schools and voluntary schools—but before the 1947 reorganisation of secondary education the majority of school-leavers (the minimum school-leaving age was fourteen) had received all their full-time education at elementary schools. Only nine of the recognised secondary schools had been transferred to the local authorities, and secondary schools charged fees—in 1942 only 213 free scholarships were awarded. This level of provision was considerably behind that in Great Britain, even when increased provision for technical education is allowed for.

With voluntary fee-charging schools so dominant in secondary education by the early 1940s, the process of educational reform was constrained. The 1944 government White Paper proposed legislation to establish a system that should not be inferior to any in the United Kingdom and providing equality of opportunity for every child 'to develop his abilities to the full'. The system was to be 'acceptable to all the different interests which have given service to the cause of education in the past'. A tripartite system of primary, secondary and further education was proposed. Debate did not concentrate on selection but on proposals for religious instruction— the 'conscience clause' to enable teachers to refuse to give religious teaching without prejudice to their careers and grants to voluntary schools. Nevertheless, the Education Act, 1947, placed a statutory duty on local education authorities to provide efficient education in primary schools, secondary schools (grammar, technical and inter- mediate as selected) and further education. Clearly it was the measures for secondary education that were important. Donaghy (1970) has argued that the 1947 act in Northern Ireland was less child-centred and idealistic and placed less emphasis on parity between the different types of secondary school. It did not abolish fee-paying and built on the traditions and distinctions (even in staff salaries and holidays) between grammar schools and others. If the act was less egalitarian in these ways, it nevertheless supplied the basis for reducing the gap in secondary education between Britain and Northern Ireland. It provided for welfare services (transport, milk, meals and medical services), free books and materials, more school-building (there were 184 intermediate schools in 1975–76 compared with 8 in 1948–49), more free scholarships, and 65 per cent building grants for voluntary schools (compared with 50 per cent since 1950). Under this act the statutory school-leaving age was raised to fifteen in 1957–58 and to sixteen in 1972–73.

The period since 1947 has seen increasing expenditure on scholar- ships to grammar schools and increased grants to voluntary schools. Secondary intermediate schools (incorporating technical intermedi- ate schools, which were phased out after 1964) have increasingly provided education beyond the compulsory leaving age and have contributed to reducing the importance of the 'eleven plus' selection. In 1976 there were seven amalgamated or intermediate schools which catered for the entire range of secondary education need in their areas.[19]

In recent years the most regular topic for debate on educational reform has been the comprehensive reorganisation of secondary education. The comprehensive experiments pursued in England and Wales since the 1940s had very few parallels in Northern Ireland, and the more extensive developments in the 1960s and 1970s have no counterpart.

In 1977 secondary education in Northern Ireland was provided in 183 secondary schools (92 of which are voluntary schools) and 79 grammar schools (57 of which are voluntary schools).

Selection for grammar schools has been revised in the period since the 1947 Education Act. Since 1964 a system based on a combina- tion of verbal reasoning quotients and teachers' estimates has replaced the previous external examination in English and arithmetic. Following the remarks of the Sixth Advisory Council for Education in 1968, the topics of selection for secondary education and age of transfer from primary to secondary education were referred to the Seventh Advisory Council under Dr Alan Burges in 1969. The council reported in 1971 and 1973.[20] In the first of these reports a general conclusion that the existing procedure was the best available for selection was coupled with a view that the principle of selection was suspect, since even this method was so susceptible to distortion that it could not be accepted as valid. The second report (1973) expressed the view that the objections raised were not to transfer from primary to secondary education at the age of eleven but to *selection* at that age. The majority of signatories of the report favoured elimination of the 'eleven plus' selection procedure as soon as possible through a restructuring of the educational system. The main reservations expressed were associated with preserving the voluntary grammar schools.

Under the system of direct rule the Labour government became directly responsible for educational policy in Northern Ireland from 1974, and they were largely in sympathy with the recommendations of the Burges Report. A consultative document, *Reorganisation of Secondary Education in Northern Ireland*,[21] containing a full report on the feasibility of reorganisation, was published in July 1976; but this paper was not well received, and the government decided that it was not an acceptable basis on which to reorganise secondary education. However, in June 1977 the government announced its intention to eliminate selection at the age of eleven through a restructuring of the educational system.[22] The 'eleven plus' examination was replaced by an 'alternative transfer' arrangement based on teacher's assessment of pupils and parental choice of school. The area education boards were invited to undertake the planning of the restructuring of secondary education. The decision to move towards a comprehensive system met with strong opposition from the existing grammar schools, a pressure-group campaign and some of the area boards. The defeat of the Labour government in 1979 left the whole question open, with the grammar schools likely to remain in existence but the 'eleven plus' examination unlikely to return.

The Burges Report in 1973 had also considered the question of religious integration in the proposed restructuring of schools, but had decided that it would be unrealistic to expect the introduction of integrated schools in the near future. In 1974 the Northern Ireland Executive's Minister of Education, Mr Basil McIvor, proposed to change the law 'in order to facilitate another class of school, which we might think of as the shared school and in which the two groups of churches would be equally involved in management',[23] but the fall of the Executive set progress back. The basic problem remains the differing reactions of the religious authorities. While the Protestant churches have expressed some support for reorganisation, the Roman Catholic hierarchy has consistently opposed it.

The size of the child population, the steady improvement of educational facilities and the increased tendency to remain at school beyond the statutory leaving age have led to increasing expenditure in education. It has been calculated that this expenditure was more than proportionate to levels in Great Britain. However, it remains very difficult to compare standards of provision in the two areas. Thus, for example, while the provision of nursery schools and classes is lower in Northern Ireland, there are more infants aged between two and four in primary schools; although there are pro- portionately more old small rural schools in Northern Ireland, considerable amalgamation and new building has occurred—over- size classes (over forty pupils) have declined to the 1972–73 level, the same as for England and Wales (1.9 per cent) and below that for Scotland (4.4 per cent), yet pupil/teacher ratios remained higher in Northern Ireland, partly because of the continuing higher birth rate and the practice of admitting rising fives. Similarly, in secondary education the gap in staffing ratios has been reduced, although it remains unfavourable to Northern Ireland; the growth of inter- mediate schools has been a response to, and has accelerated, the breakdown in the lack of parity of esteem between schools; in spite of the comparatively late reorganisation of secondary schooling and the late increase in the leaving age to fifteen, it appears that the proportion of pupils staying on at school beyond the minimum leaving age is higher in Northern Ireland than in England and Wales or in Scotland.[24] However, in the context of the urban/rural division and fee-charging grammar schools, this advantageous com- parison may obscure profound divisions in social class, sex and religious use of educational resources.

Similar problems exist over any attempt to compare educational provision within Northern Ireland. Although Belfast has generally superior services, the basis of comparison even to arrive at this view is controversial.[25] But while important differences undoubtedly exist within Northern Ireland and between Britain and Northern Ireland, there has been consistent and measurable progress ever since 1925. Although this progress is more evident than a consistent pattern of disadvantage, the doubts surrounding the institutional arrangement and sectarian basis for education are also evident.

The stipulation in the Education Act, 1947, that local authorities should submit plans for the development of further education requires some comment. Further education provision in Northern

Ireland appears to have lagged behind the rest of Great Britain until the early 1960s,[26] when the emphasis on economic development led to a more systematic approach. Technical college resources were rationalised and pooled with advanced courses, which were increasingly concentrated, especially in the Ulster Polytechnic. The increased interest in further education is easily indicated. In 1962–63 4 per cent of school-leavers went on to educational institutions other than university and training colleges. In 1972–73 25 per cent did so (including 2.5 per cent at the Ulster Polytechnic).[27] The numbers of students attending full-time and day-release courses at advanced and non-advanced levels has grown. Over the same period university attendance has also expanded. The New University of Ulster first admitted students in October 1968; it and Queen's University now provide for some two-thirds of Northern Ireland students. But numbers attending universities in Britain have risen sharply (from 17 per cent in 1970–71 to 27 per cent in 1973–74). Attendance at universities in the Republic of Ireland has fallen from 14 per cent to 8 per cent over the same period.

Consideration of higher education draws attention back once again to the extent to which social policy in Northern Ireland is intertwined with more fundamental political issues. Following the Lockwood Committee's recommendation in 1965 that a new university should be established in Northern Ireland, a site in Coleraine was selected.[28] The siting of such a large income- and employment-creating institution was clearly a matter of interest to the province as a whole—and especially to Londonderry, Northern Ireland's second-largest city, where Magee University College, which was affiliated to Trinity College, Dublin, was already a long-established institution. The decision to locate the new university in Coleraine is often quoted as an example of a provocative decision which certainly contributed to the grievances associated with the Civil Rights campaign in 1969.[29] It further illustrates the extent to which the allocation of goods and services through social policy is sensitive to and interpreted in terms of politico-religious positions.

Health Services

Whereas Northern Ireland lagged behind Britain in housing, education and income-maintenance services in 1921, the development of health services was, in some ways, more advanced.[30] Voluntary hospitals and hospitals assisted by public grants were complemented after 1838 by fever wards attached to workhouses and by other Poor Law provision. In particular, the Medical Charities Act, 1851, provided for the division of Poor Law unions into dispensary districts for the provision of buildings and such medicines and appliances as might be required for the medical relief of the poor. Dispensary services and hospital provision under the Poor Relief (Ireland) Act, 1838, were available not just to the destitute, to those entering the workhouse or to those unable to contribute to the cost of treatment. As a result, and in the absence of a strong voluntary sector, at the end of the nineteenth century the structure of medical services was more planned and more comprehensive in Ireland than in England and Wales. Provision was dominated by the Irish Poor Law, which provided dispensary doctors and midwives and controlled the majority of hospitals.

The very comprehensiveness of this provision itself reduced the pressure for new facilities outside the Poor Law. Thus, most importantly, the National Insurance Act, 1911, did not apply fully in Ireland, where insured persons received sickness benefit through approved societies but were not entitled to the services of a general practitioner or to drugs and appliances. Nevertheless, Ireland did begin to develop services outside the Poor Law. The Tuberculosis Prevention (Ireland) Act, 1908, the Notification of Births (Extension) Act, 1915, the Education (Provision of Meals) (Ireland) Act, 1914, and the Health (Medical Treatment of Children) (Ireland) Act, 1919, placed responsibilities on local government for the treatment of tuberculosis and for medical inspection and provision for children and nursing mothers. But this did not ensure that responsibilities were carried out, and it did not extend to the provision of medical benefit. Medical treatment had to be obtained outside the national insurance scheme, either privately or through the Poor Law. Statistics of mortality and morbidity indicated that health was worse in Ireland than elsewhere in the United Kingdom. This was largely a consequence of the fragmented structure of health provision and, in particular, of the inadequacy of the local authority administrative structure. If some parts of health service provision were advanced, other parts were seriously deficient. But the years after 1919 did not remedy this deficiency or build on the advantages of the system developed under the Poor Law. Indeed, it appears that in the inter-war period the gap between death rates in Northern Ireland and Britain closed only slowly, while the gap in infant mortality and maternal mortality actually increased.[31] Even the extension of medical benefit to Northern Ireland (but only to wage-earners) after 1930 cannot, in the light of these figures, be held to have had any real impact on the health of the region.

In 1919, when a Ministry of Health and Local Government was set up in Britain, no equivalent body was established in Ireland. In the years following partition no central co-ordinating department was set up at Stormont, and the Poor Law Guardians continued to be the most important provider. In this situation, Evason *et al.* (1976) argue, local health authorities were reluctant to exercise powers and duties.[32] Advice to the Stormont government on the need for a drastic reorganisation of the health services was not lacking. Lawrence (1965 a) refers to the recommendations of the Irish Public Health Council in 1920: the creation of an Irish Ministry of Health, the unification in each county and county borough of hospital, medical and public health services, and the removal of health matters from the Poor Law.[33] Similar recommendations were made in 1927. Although early ministerial statements indicated a desire for reform, nothing happened, and in 1932 the government finally announced that no major changes would be made. The reasons for this failure are principally those which also applied to other services. Financial problems were particularly important and were complicated by the problems of rate-aiding, given the structure and wealth of local authorities. After 1930 rural derating altered this last problem, but the burden on the Exchequer would have been considerable if any substantial reform had been implemented. It does not appear that there was any significant ideological objection to state intervention in health. But any reform would have focused attention on the control of hospitals (see below).

The way in which the government of Northern Ireland has used its powers to provide medical services has varied from its responses in other fields of social policy. Policies in the health services have conformed to neither the income-maintenance 'parity' model nor the education 'discrimination' model. However, they contain elements of both of these models, as well as the important addition of professional pressure.

The organisation of the health services in Northern Ireland in 1921 differed in important ways from that in Britain. Lawrence has described the four layers of the service: the Poor Law offshoots of dispensary districts, dispensary medical officers and midwives, and former workhouse infirmaries; the public health services, medical officers of health and sanitary officers; the extension of the National Insurance Act, 1911, to Ireland; and the special services which local authorities could provide after 1898 for various preventive and treatment services. The real character of the services, however, is best illustrated by the dominance of workhouse infirmaries rather than charitable or private foundations among public general hospitals, by the continued operation of part-time and unqualified sanitary officers in many areas, and by the lack of development of special services. Lawrence comments:

When Northern Ireland was established, 25 of the 64 county

borough and district councils had taken no measures to prevent tuberculosis, 38 did nothing about maternity and child welfare, only one authority had begun to feed needy schoolchildren, and only one had arrangements (which were not fully operative) for their medical inspection. Secondly, the administrative structure lacked coherence. Since the part-time medical officers of health depended mainly on fees from private patients, their private interest could easily conflict with the public interest. Neither they nor sanitary sub-officers were required to possess special qualifications in public health. The very ubiquity of the Poor Law dispensaries did not encourage local councils to develop their own services—why duplicate the work of dispensary doctors and midwives?—and, there being no single health authority in the counties nor any ministry of health for Ireland as a whole, responsibility was diffused and weak.[34]

One further major difference in services is partly related to this. Only parts of the National Insurance Act, 1911, were extended to Ireland. Thus insured persons who were certified as being too ill to work were given sickness benefit but no medical treatment. Such treatment had either to be paid for or obtained from the Poor Law dispensary service. It may be argued that this arrangement was only arrived at because the dispensary service developed under the Poor Law was so comprehensive. Nevertheless, the legislative and administrative arrangements for health provision had diverged from the British model.

The lack of administrative reform in these arrangements is explained initially in terms of the uncertainties created by constitutional developments and, after 1921, in terms of finance and economic circumstances. Thus although it was recognised that 'reforms are urgently needed',[35] no counterpart to the 1919 Ministry of Health in England was created, and the poor levels of service provision are illustrated by the high mortality and morbidity rates.[36]

Responsibility for health (and for housing policy) rested with the Minister of Home Affairs, and the Poor Law tradition was strongly maintained through administrative continuity. Although ministers aspired to reform until 1932, no major administrative changes were forthcoming. Outside Belfast and Londonderry medical officers of health combined their duties with private medical practices and various other responsibilities. Sanitary officers were unqualified and also had other responsibilities. Such a part-time system was cheap, but it was not conducive to the best standards of service; and in small administrative districts where, for example, condemning property could raise conflicts of interest and of personal relationships it constituted a positive barrier to an active pursuit of high standards.

Lawrence notes the lack of any public service for collecting or disposing of refuse, the pollution of rivers and tidal waters, the inadequate arrangements for water supply, and the neglect of supervision of dairies and food.[37] Concern about the incidence of tuberculosis and typhoid fever did not lead to closer inspection or higher standards. Indeed, it appears to have been the need to guarantee the standards of exported food that led to a tighter supervision. Even in the 1930s 'inspection of meat for sale remained patchy in urban districts and virtually non-existent in rural areas'.[38] In the same way, although a number of new district hospitals were created, financial considerations prevented the complete replacement of Poor Law infirmaries, and in some areas these remained the only source of general hospital treatment. Services for the prevention of tuberculosis, maternity services and school medical services were also neglected. Lawrence sums up as follows:

> By and large, Ulster's health services were mediocre by British standards. Mortality was high and no doubt would have been higher had not almost half the population been scattered in rural areas. British administration before 1920 and financial stringency thereafter were mainly to blame. There can be no doubt that the Minister of Home Affairs was speaking from bitter experience when in 1942 he said: 'On every conceivable opportunity [*sic*] I have had friendly fights with the Ministry of Finance. I received any amount of sympathy but the whole difficulty was finance.' Health was a Cinderella. And public opinion—such as it was— was indifferent to her plight because the administration was designed neither to focus attention on the health services as a whole nor to stimulate debate about piecemeal change. For one thing, responsibility was divided among the Ministries of Home Affairs, Labour (national health insurance and health in factories) Education (the school medical service) and Agriculture (the milk scheme and the Diseases of Animals Acts). For another, the functions of the Ministry of Home Affairs were ill-assorted. Political debate rarely rose far above the level at which the foundations of the state were assailed and defended, yet the minister was responsible both for health and for public order and justice. Nationalists too often ignored the first subject and seized on the others when Estimates were debated. Common needs and interests were submerged in the most bitter party warfare.[39]

But Lawrence does not explain, except by inference, why health was neglected when income-maintenance schemes (subject to the same financial constraints but without costs falling on the rates) were sustained at a high level. Political and economic factors relating to this have been referred to earlier. In the failure of the health services to receive administrative reform or greater financial support (in spite of the minister's promptings), health, like housing, was victim of the general reluctance to expand government activity and of the *laissez-faire* approach of the Northern Ireland government before 1939. However, there were two additional pressures which were felt (as with income maintenance) at national/regional level rather than at local level.

Firstly, although the British government was generally indifferent to the position of the health services in Northern Ireland, in 1930 it pressed Northern Ireland to offer medical benefit under the National Insurance Act, 1911. Westminster wished to ratify international health conventions for the whole of the United Kingdom and pressed Northern Ireland to come into line rather than continue to rely on the Poor Law. Secondly, the approved societies who administered health insurance in Northern Ireland found the costs of sickness and disablement unacceptably high. They felt that the lack of medical services increased the incidence of sickness. They also suspected a high incidence of fraudulent claims. Thus the system under which patients could receive cash benefit without receiving treatment (a system which could not be avoided where medical benefit was unavailable) enticed the patient to try to obtain a certificate from as many doctors as he chose and enabled the doctor to receive payment solely for issuing certificates. In response to this drawback a medical referee service was introduced in 1927 and discovered a high incidence of abuse. A more drastic solution which was canvassed was to value Northern Ireland members separately until a system of medical benefit was introduced.[40] The decision to put health insurance in Northern Ireland on the same basis as in Great Britain in 1930 was a significant development. The threat of separate valuation introduced a direct clash with any aspiration to apply parity in this area. Some change in the status quo was inevitable, and the medical referee system was clearly insufficient. Trade unions, the labour movement and some Unionist MPs had long advocated the introduction of medical benefit, and the government chose to follow this path in spite of opposition from farmers and rural local authorities and in spite of the Ministry of Finance's delays.[41] The combination of arguments on this occasion were similar to those affecting income-maintenance policies—real financial concern mingled with a range of political, economic and social calculations—and the outcome of the debate was the same in the adoption of a step-by-step approach.

One additional feature of health insurance in Northern Ireland merits attention. The medical referee system was supported by a system of sick visiting to supervise claims. In 1932 the approved societies were urged to establish joint arrangements for this, and central health insurance funds supported initial steps.[42] However, when in 1937 it was suggested that this scheme should be extended to the whole of Northern Ireland an objection was noted:

> The first objection was taken by some of the societies whose general practice it is to accept as members only persons who belong to certain religious denominations. They expressed the view that the success of any co-operative scheme in Belfast would be prejudiced if their members were visited by visitors who belonged to a different religious denomination.[43]

The departmental committee, reporting on this, stated:

> In our opinion this is a difficulty which ought to be met; and we recommend that it should be overcome by arranging that any of these societies should have the right to require that, when it asked for a visit to one of its members, the visit should be made by a visitor of the same denomination as the member.[44]

Perhaps this is more understandable when it is noted that in 1937 there were nineteen approved societies with headquarters in Northern Ireland. These catered for about one-third of all insured persons. Of these about 30 per cent were in the Orange and Protestant, a similar number in the Presbyterian Health Insurance Society, and 11 per cent in the Ancient Order of Hibernians Society.[45]

Perhaps this tells us more about the operation of private insurance in general and national health insurance in particular. However, it confirms the extent to which sectarian division pervades institutions in Northern Ireland. This is further illustrated by the Northern Ireland National Health Service Act, 1948. Although the equivalent 1946 act in Britain included the 'Stokes clause', which was designed to enable hospitals with religious links to maintain their character within the National Health Service, this clause was excluded from all legislation in Northern Ireland. In consequence the largest casualty hospital in North Belfast, the Mater Infirmorum Hospital, which is managed by a Catholic board and staffed largely by nuns, remained outside the national scheme. The hospital has always catered for non-Catholics, but it also makes specific provision for the spiritual as well as the physical needs of Catholics, and it is this freedom which the board of management felt it must uphold, in spite of the fact that the hospital had benefited from public funds in the past and was a teaching hospital associated with Queen's

University. Since 1948 the patient entering the Mater has not been embraced within the National Health Service. This problem has simply been one of finding a proper relationship between the state service and a voluntary hospital. This has, however, been reduced on the one side to a question of subsidising a hostile tradition and assisting the doctrines of a conflicting ideology, and on the other to a question of losing the special relationship with the Roman Catholic Church. Negotiations to remedy this situation have consistently enabled the exercise of traditional accusations and counter-accusations. Only in 1967 was legislation passed which made possible the inclusion of the Mater in the health service without loss of its particular character and associations. Although it was still evidently not welcomed by some, an agreement in 1971 did provide a formula under which the hospital could enter the National Health Service, receiving financial support and being managed by a committee acceptable to both the Roman Catholic diocesan bishop and the Stormont government.

The extension towards a comprehensive health service after 1945 has been largely ascribed to the impact of war and the development of agreements with the British government to support parity of service. The spur to reform was not the 'discovery' of deficiences in services but the political will and financial capacity to make changes. Thus in 1944 a new Ministry of Health and Local Government split these services off from the Poor Law tradition and the political conflicts which had bedevilled their incorporation under the Ministry of Home Affairs. Between 1946 and 1948 new legislation established the administrative basis of the new service. At the same time that local government lost its responsibilities for hospital, specialist, ambulance, laboratory and blood transfusion services to the new Northern Ireland Hospitals Authority, it also lost its preventive and treatment role in tuberculosis to a Tuberculosis Authority. Local government was left with personal health services (maternal and child health, home nursing, health visiting, school health, vaccination and immunisation) and environmental services; these county and county borough functions were organised under a medical officer of health. Borough and district councils remained responsible for refuse collection, housing, water supply and sewerage. The Northern Ireland General Health Services Board organised provision of contractor services (doctors, dentists, opticians and pharmacists).

Although the Northern Ireland government had largely followed the British lead, the inclusion of ambulance services under the Hospitals Authority and the creation of a separate Tuberculosis Authority were innovations. Lawrence points to the narrowing of the gap in both general and tuberculosis death rates and both

I

maternal and infant mortality as evidence of the success of the health service reorganisation.[46] Although not all of this improvement can be attributed to the health services, it is reasonable to draw some such conclusion. Even more important, however, than the administrative reform may be the professional and financial basis which has enabled the *per capita* cost of drugs and sickness benefit to be consistently higher than in Britain. These factors are less easily attributable to devolution and the Northern Ireland government than to the agreement reached in Britain between the doctors and government as a basis for the National Health Service, the actions of general practitioners and the nature of the Social Services Agreement of 1949.

The National Health Service Act, 1948, set up a comprehensive health service covering both physical and mental health, including diagnosis, treatment and aftercare. The service is available to all according to need (this being assessed solely by the medical practitioner without reference to any insurance or income status). The service is free at the point of consumption save for certain notional charges. Payment is made through general taxation and a small insurance contribution (which does not influence entitlement). A structure of this nature is based on different assumptions than those indicated in the Republic of Ireland in 1966, where 'the government did not accept the proposition that the state had a duty to provide unconditionally all medical, dental and other health services free of cost for everyone, without regard to individual need or circumstances'.[47] While general medical services and hospital services in Northern Ireland are provided free by doctors and hospitals, there are some charges for ancillary services. A charge is made for drugs and appliances prescribed by doctors, but certain categories of persons are excluded—children and old persons, expectant and nursing mothers, and persons suffering from certain medical conditions. Dental treatment and ophthalmic services are also subject to charges, although again there are exempted categories. Any person who cannot afford to pay these charges without hardship can apply to the ministry for assistance.

Remuneration of the medical practitioner and the financing of hospitals and local authority services is made through the ministry and committees established for that purpose. In this way there is no financial relationship between doctor and patient, and there are no institutional factors which would lead to unequal treatment of patients. Similarly, the rate contribution to services is restricted to those services which are provided by local authorities and amounts to some £1 million a year. This is considerably lower than in the Republic.

In addition, there is a private sector used by a minority section of the community, and this may enable non-essential additions or conveniences to be obtained. In essence, however, the health services represent an attempt to offer an equal and comprehensive service to all sections of the community. It represents the translation of the concept of citizens' rights into the field of health.

The Ministry of Health and Social Services is responsible for the co-ordination of all the health services in the province and for the provision of hospital and specialist services. The administrative structure, previously based on a tripartite division for general practitioner, hospital and local authority services, has been altered in parallel with the reorganisation of local government. In 1969 a consultative Green Paper suggested that the Hospitals Authority, the hospital management committees, the General Health Services Board and the local authority health committees should be replaced by nominated area boards, which would be responsible for the planning and provision of a single co-ordinated health service for their areas.[48] These proposals also suggested setting up a unified health and welfare service by making the area boards responsible for local authority welfare services. The legislation setting up such a system was introduced in 1973 under the Health and Personal Social Services (Northern Ireland) Order, 1972.

The new system is intended to provide for better co-ordination and planning of medical treatment and community care and to enable better use to be made of financial and manpower resources. Four Health and Social Services Boards are responsible to the department for planning, management and delivery of health and personal social services in their areas. Two central agencies provide common services, and district committees, area and central advisory committees and the Northern Ireland Health and Social Services Council complete the system.

This process of integration has already been seen in the growth of health centres in Northern Ireland.[49] In health centres the general medical and health authority services are fully integrated, and provision may be made for general dental and ophthalmic services, and for the attendance of social workers. The rapid growth of health centres is easily illustrated. In 1966–67 there were two health centres in Northern Ireland involving six doctors and 11,000 patients. In 1970–71 there were twenty-two health centres involving 118 doctors and 200,000 patients. By 1975 35 per cent of doctors operated from health centres. There has also been a marked trend away from single-handed practices towards partnership practices. These figures are more remarkable when it is noted that there were some 750 general practitioners in Northern Ireland in this period, catering for some one and a half million patients and with an average list size slightly over 2,000. Measured in terms of list size, Northern Ireland is better 'doctored' than England and Wales. However, two factors must be acknowledged. Firstly, the consumer demand for medical treatment, as indicated by sickness and incapacity for work, is higher in Northern Ireland. Secondly, the provision of medical services in rural areas is more costly of manpower than is the case in pre-dominantly urban areas. This element must also be considered when variations in the numbers of patients on doctors' lists in Northern Ireland is considered—the longest lists are in the cities of Londonderry and Belfast, and the shortest in Co. Fermanagh.[50]

Any attempt to consider the quality of the health service in Northern Ireland is bound to draw attention to the importance of the medical practitioner. Whereas in education, housing or social security the government has direct control over expenditure and standards of service, this is less true in medical care. General practitioners in Northern Ireland are members of the same pro-fessional bodies as their counterparts in England and are subject to the same conditions of service. The freedom to prescribe remains an essential feature of the service and distinguishes it from the pre-war circumstances of lay control through local government or approved societies. One consequence of the freedom to prescribe is (in spite of the extent of self-medication) the high cost of prescribing and the lack of strict control over this. The cost of the pharmaceutical services in Northern Ireland has risen from £1.3 million in 1950 to £7.2 million in 1970 and £25.0 million in 1978.[51] Between 1950 and 1970 there was a threefold increase in the *per capita* cost of prescrib-ing. The number of prescriptions written annually has remained fairly steady in spite of changes in prescription charges (although there was a rise following the abolition of charges in 1965). In 1966 the *per capita* cost of prescribing was 40 per cent higher in Northern Ireland than in England and Wales. Commenting on this difference, Hood (1971) states that 'It is either due to the doctors' "prescribing habits" which were formed under the influence of their training and subsequent practice, or due to genuine differences in the types, distribution and duration of illnesses, or practice characteristics, and patient attitudes in an area.' In either case these are not costs which can be controlled by the government under the present professional arrangements. The evidence that prescribing of certain drugs is higher, for example in the belt of affluence in the east of the province, cannot be used to suggest that different standards of service apply. Without relating prescribing to the needs of patients, it is impossible to draw such conclusions.[52]

In concluding a discussion of health service provision, it is apparent that the way in which devolved powers have been used includes many elements previously evident. The influence of political will; the financial arrangements with Britain; the marked effect of politico-religious conflicts upon institutions—the importance of all these factors is clearly discernible. However, there is an additional institutional factor which is extremely significant in determining the nature of the service. In other fields of social service provision in a welfare state the basic decisions on rationing and distributing scarce resources are made by politicians or by direct government employees. In Northern Ireland these politicians and employees tend to reduce issues in social policy to basic elements in an ideological dispute concerned with recognition and legitimacy of the state. Thus in housing and in education the debate about policy objectives, implementation and administration has been wholly a political debate. In social security the debate has been largely pre-empted by the nature of legislation and the financial basis of devolution. In the health services, however, the political debate has been circumscribed by the power and professional position of the medical practitioners and by the way in which legislation has sustained that position. Thus in health the distribution of benefits is less open to examination in politico-religious terms than in other services.

Personal Social Services

The unification of the personal social services under the Health and Personal Social Services (Northern Ireland) Order, 1972, followed a history of the separate development of services for the elderly, handicapped and disabled and for children and young persons.

The Elderly and Handicapped

Personal services for the elderly, the physically and mentally handi-capped and the disabled are a relatively recent development.[53] Before the Welfare Services Act, 1949, the provision for the welfare of handicapped and elderly persons had come through voluntary bodies or, under the Poor Law, through workhouse accommodation or relief. Only after 1949 was provision in this area separated from income-maintenance policy. The 1949 act required the Ministry of Health and Local Government to promote and co-ordinate welfare services, including the provision of residential accommodation, which was to be so administered as to take account of the different needs of different groups.

As with other policy areas, the legislation of the immediate post-war period was very similar to that in Great Britain. Welfare authorities had similar powers to promote the welfare of the blind, deaf, dumb, handicapped and disabled. They were also authorised to provide home helps for the handicapped (the provision of this service for other groups was the duty of the local health authorities) and to assist voluntary bodies. From a very early stage, however, the organisation of welfare services in Northern Ireland adopted a more unified structure than was general in Great Britain. The Welfare Services Act (Northern Ireland), 1954, placed a responsibility for the whole range of domestic help (including the ill, blind, deaf, dumb and handicapped) on the welfare authorities. As Evason *et al.* (1976) state, 'The integration of this [domestic help] service into the department carrying responsibility for residential and other services for the elderly, handicapped and children meant that the problem of fragmented responsibility for meeting need was less acute in Northern Ireland than in Britain virtually from the inception of the services.'[54]

In 1961 the Welfare Services (Amendment) Act and the Mental Health Act extended the powers of the welfare authorities. The former added powers for the provision of meals for the handicapped and the elderly and recreational facilities for the elderly. The latter extended the powers to provide residential and other services to those suffering from mental disorders.

In the period since 1949 Northern Ireland's legislation for welfare services has followed British practice very closely. After 1968 some parts of the service which had become mandatory in England and Wales remained permissive in Northern Ireland. More particularly, the Welfare Services (Northern Ireland) Act, 1971, was not as extensive as the Chronically Sick and Disabled Persons Act, 1970, in England and Wales. Northern Ireland was beginning to fall behind in this area, and the 1971 act did not, for example, impose duties in respect of adaptations to the homes of disabled persons, holidays, access to public buildings, and assistance in obtaining a telephone or in taking advantage of educational facilities. The extent of the resulting gap has been obscured by the Health and Personal Services (Northern Ireland) Order, 1972. This simply imposed a duty on the central department to provide or secure the provision of personal social services. Some commentators regard this inexplicit duty as a backward step which does not enable rights to services to be identified.[55] One effect of the order is to place the onus in assessing the comparability of services squarely on evidence of provision; in view of problems in the limited implementation of the Chronically Sick and Disabled Persons Act in England and Wales and the limited rights it therefore establishes, this may not be a backward step.

But it is not appropriate to limit consideration of the use of devolved powers in this area of policy without emphasising the more unified administrative structure operating since 1954. Problems of co-ordination, fragmentation and co-operation seriously undermined the quality of service in England and Wales before the Social Services Act, 1970—one of the main aims of which was to improve these aspects of the service. Consequently it could be argued that the more unified Northern Ireland service would be more cost-effective, and it appears that for the elderly (in 1966) Northern Ireland (on a *pro rata* population basis) had double the provision of home helps, almost identical provision of health visitors and social workers, and only slightly fewer home nurses.[56] As with doctors, Northern Ireland appears to have had a high standard of service measured in terms of manpower. While it may be argued that a largely rural area would require higher levels of staffing to provide a given level of service, the reduction in duplicated effort arising from the unified administrative structure must also be taken into account. But a real gap in service provision begins to emerge, as would be expected from the foregoing discussion, once newer, less basic services are considered (e.g. clubs, social centres, meals, chiropody). In addition, in the provision of residential accommodation Northern Ireland's record appeared poor in comparison. But before accepting this view account must be taken of two factors: Northern Ireland's success in ceasing to rely on former workhouses for such accommodation,[57] and the extent to which better patterns of community care reduce the need for residential accommodation.

Children and Young Persons

The structure of policy towards children and young persons remained largely unchanged in the first twenty-five years of Northern Ireland's existence.[58] The Children's Act, 1908, had consolidated legislation to protect children's lives and to inspect and control premises and persons caring for children. The emphasis of the act was on the offences of the parent or guardian of a child or young person, and amendments made in 1931 concerned the powers and duties of local authorities in relation to full-time care and daily child-minders rather than the basic approach to the care and protection of children. Provision for orphaned and deserted children remained the responsibility of the Poor Law, which arranged accommodation in workhouses as well as through boarding out.

This structure of policy remained in operation largely unchanged until 1950. The one significant development in this period was the new provision made for the adoption of children after 1929. The

Adoption of Children Act (Northern Ireland), 1929, followed three years after its equivalent in England and Wales and allowed for transfer of parental rights and responsibilities.

The period 1945–50 saw major changes which closely followed developments in England and Wales. The Children and Young Persons Act (Northern Ireland), 1950, ended Poor Law provision and placed responsibility for the care and protection of children upon welfare authorities. Whereas in England and Wales local authorities had to set up separate children's services, Northern Ireland's administrative structure was unified with other personal social services. Having come into line with British legislation in 1950, Northern Ireland legislation has not fully kept pace. The main changes introduced in England and Wales in 1963 were only matched in Northern Ireland in 1968 in the Children and Young Persons Act (Northern Ireland). Until the Health and Personal Social Services Order, 1972, was introduced it would appear that Northern Ireland was lagging behind in the development of preventive work and in reducing distinctions between those defined as in need of care, protection or control and children coming before the courts as offenders. The emphasis on the needs of the child, irrespective of the reason for coming before the courts, was not apparent in Northern Ireland's provision. These comments must not be taken as implying that the notion of prevention was not included in legislation before 1972. The 1968 act in Northern Ireland required welfare authorities to give advice, guidance and assistance (including assistance in kind or, exceptionally, in cash) to promote the welfare of children.

In 1976 a review group under the chairmanship of Sir Harold Black was set up to examine legislation and services relating to the care and treatment of children and young persons under the Children and Young Persons Act (Northern Ireland), 1968, the Adoption Act (Northern Ireland), 1967, and the Probation Act (Northern Ireland), 1950. A consultative document dealing with children and young persons and probation was published in 1977.[59] If this promises a new step to bring Northern Ireland into line with England and Wales, it must also be noted that it appeared at a time when concern with the control of young offenders was high. There was a fear, for example, among social workers that legislation would be geared to the civil disturbances rather than to the problems of social disadvantage and poverty. The situation in Northern Ireland in the 1970s highlights elements affecting policy on these services.

A similar picture of Northern Ireland following, but lagging behind, England and Wales is apparent in legislation on adoption. The Adoption Act, 1950, which brought legislation more into line, was followed by the Adoption Act, 1967, which brought Northern Ireland fully into line. Although this revision had been informed by inquiries into the operation of law and procedure in Northern Ireland, there is no evidence that policy in relation to children's services developed in response to political, professional or other pressures. The pressures for change were legal and administrative or derived from the desire for parity. In 1969 legislation to enable courts to recognise certain overseas adoption orders and make orders under the Hague Convention was passed to enable Westminster to confirm this international agreement. This change is often seen as an example of Westminster's direct intervention to influence policy.

Health and Personal Social Services: A Unified Structure

The development of personal social services in Northern Ireland has, in comparison with Great Britain, been more unified. This was further consolidated by the Health and Personal Social Services (Northern Ireland) Order, 1972.

Both before and after this reorganisation problems of assessing the operation of devolution in the personal social services were at least as great as with other services. Where so many legislative provisions are permissive ones any real comparison of social provision is even more dependent on some measure of output or performance.

One aspect which can be considered in this way is the role of social workers in making cash payments. The Children and Young Persons Act (Northern Ireland), 1968, gave a similar power to that which came into operation in England and Wales under the Children and Young Persons Act, 1963, to make cash payments in order to diminish the need to take children into care, keep them in care, or bring them before a court. The Northern Ireland order of 1972 provided a wider and more flexible power than this by permitting such payments 'in exceptional circumstances constituting an emergency'. There is no comprehensive evidence available on how the power to make money payments has been used. But it is clear that many of the districts under the Health and Social Services Boards gave field workers only limited discretion over the use of such funds.[60] In many cases money is only given as a loan. There has been little pressure from social workers for their powers to be increased,[61] and they were often reluctant to extend their activities in making cash payments. The wider discretion under the 1972 order is rarely used.[62] Some social workers were unaware of its existence, and some senior staff regard it as so wide as to render it useless. In view of this evidence, it seems unlikely that the extended

I*

formal powers have much significance in determining the nature of the provision which results.

Some reference has been made to staffing levels. This can be elaborated. For example, in Northern Ireland in 1971 34 per cent of social workers were professionally qualified, compared with 41 per cent in Great Britain.[63] Between 1968 and 1973 the number of field social workers increased by more than half, and the number who had qualified doubled. But evidence of this type does not enable any reasonably reliable conclusion to be drawn about relative standards of service. In particular, there is an absence of sufficiently detailed information about need. What is demonstrated is the great difficulty in attempting to assess the impact of devolution by comparing formal and legal developments which may obscure significant features of professional and informal practice.

As has been mentioned above, the new structure of administration of health services introduced in 1973 made the administration of both health and personal social services the responsibility of four area Health and Social Services Boards which are accountable to the Northern Ireland Department of Health and Social Services. The new structure for health services followed the contemporary British reorganisation. It created a unified system of health boards responsible for the whole range of health services and replaced the previous tripartite system. However, Northern Ireland took the logic of unification, co-ordination and rationalisation further by relieving local authorities of their responsibilities for personal services as well as for health services.

The official explanation of the divergence from the British model was that

> The pattern of local government shortly to be introduced in Northern Ireland, with its twenty-six district councils, would be an inadequate base for major social services. . . . There is a need for very close links between health services and personal services.[64]

Although other statutory personal social services remain outside this structure (for example probation and various social service aspects in education and housing), the unification of health and social service functions has proceeded further than in England and Wales. The role of the central department in co-ordinating an integrated service offers a facility for planning as well as more efficient, cost-effective and comprehensive provision. The new structure could only achieve policy aims with increased resources, but the potential it afforded for collaboration in meeting needs was an important starting-point. It was hoped that it would bring about improved co-operation between the different parts of the health and social services and the voluntary sector and that it would enable the practical substantiation of the concept of a comprehensive, family-centred service based in and deriving authority from the community.[65]

The hopes that the new structure of 1973 would be administratively superior have not yet been fully realised (see Chapter 8).

Conclusion

Some of the broader implications of the developments discussed in this chapter will be referred to in the next chapter. However, some particular conclusions can be drawn. As in the areas of social policy referred to in the foregoing chapter, it is evident that devolved status has been used to produce distinct policies in education, health and the social services. But in these services economic and financial constraints are less dominant in explaining what policies were adopted. Sectarian concerns are of great importance, particularly in education. The constraints and influences on policy vary significantly between policy areas; financial constraints and parity have not been, even in medical care, as important as in social security provision. There is considerable evidence of the impact of Westminster in the period 1945–50, but the resulting changes proved difficult to sustain and subsequent developments often lagged behind Britain. Problems of local resources and local authority provision are evident, as in housing and social security and, most noticeably, in the personal social services, where the tendency to maintain permissive rather than introduce mandatory legislation can be partly attributed to such difficulties.

Many of these features have been affected by direct rule and by Orders in Council introduced since 1972. These developments suggest that the devolved government either was unable or did not wish to make certain changes. What they do not indicate, and what is more difficult to assess, is how far these features of the devolved system led to a satisfactory service provision. Differences in legislation in health and social services may be less important than evidence about the levels of staffing in these services. More significant still may be the continued adverse picture in respect of, say, infant mortality. Any discussion of devolution should not latch too quickly onto apparently significant differences. Just as differences in formal policy arrangements do not necessarily imply poorer services, so evidence of greater outstanding need does not necessarily imply a failure in the policy areas providing particular services or in devolution itself. It certainly indicates that at the minimum the nature and causes of problems and needs have impeded the capacity of social policies to provide dramatic solutions. It should not be taken as a criticism of these policies that they have failed to achieve what is beyond their scope and, sometimes, their intention. Similarly, continuing high levels of need cannot be taken as evidence of the failure of social policies or of devolution, unless it is assumed that such policies and powers could have dealt with the underlying causes of need.

11

Social Policy and Devolution

THE previous two chapters have presented examples of social problems and social policies in Northern Ireland. The aim has not been to attempt a comprehensive or definitive assessment of issues but rather to raise questions about legislative devolution and social policy in Northern Ireland. Discussions of constitutional arrangements are too often restricted to describing legal and institutional structures. Too often they lack consideration of the operation of government in practice or of the dynamics and processes underlying the development of policy and practice. Yet without some consideration of these aspects the 'verdict' on systems of government is based on a narrow range of considerations.

The analysis of social policy also tends to be restricted. Many standard texts are criticised for assuming some natural, logical, rational or functional imperative underlying the 'growth' or 'evolution' of policies. Policies are assumed to reflect or respond to changing needs, and consequently the process of policy development is unproblematic. All that is required is description, and the explanation can be taken for granted. In more recent years this approach to social policy has been more rigorously criticised.[1] The analysis of the state has focused increasingly on its activities in social and economic policy. The state itself is not regarded as being neutral or having some existence separate from the social formation. Rather, it is seen as representing and serving particular (dominant?) sections of that social formation. Particular views of the state are concerned to stress whose interests it promotes and to imply consistency in this promotion. Although these particular views are open to dispute, the general proposition that it is unwise to treat the state's role in social policy as unproblematic is indisputable. The very attempt to distinguish social and economic policies is unwise. 'Social' policies for health, education, housing or income maintenance have economic objectives and implications. Similarly, 'economic' policies concerned with demand management, with influencing patterns of investment or with taxation or money supply have social welfare implications and involve the identification of social priorities.

The role of the state, the operation of devolution and the nature of social policy in Northern Ireland are interrelated topics. Although the local or regional government in Northern Ireland has always been dependent on Westminster, it has exercised considerable discretion. The way in which its power has been exercised indicates political and economic realities rather than natural or neutral processes of allocation and distribution. Thus, allowing for political and economic constraints, the regional government has used its powers to affect significantly the distribution of opportunity and access to resources within Northern Ireland. In this chapter the use made of devolution is discussed and assessed in the light of economic, political and financial dependency. Within this context it is argued that the exercise of power at regional level has been subject to certain consistent internal pressures which have had different consequences in different policy areas, and that the position adopted by the government has changed through time both in response to and with effects on political life in Northern Ireland.

Views on Devolution

Some commentators have taken the view that the Northern Ireland government made little use of its powers to develop separate social policies. Thus Nevil Johnson (1974), commenting on the report of the Royal Commission on the Constitution, stated: 'The experience in Northern Ireland demonstrated conclusively that a small autonomous political unit within the United Kingdom could not afford politically to diverge substantially in respect of the services it provided from the standards set by the central government and parliament in London.' This view is linked with a more general assertion: 'Whatever freedom to legislate might exist in theory, financial constraints would compel substantial compliance with policies determined at the centre.' Johnson therefore concludes that 'A scheme for legislative devolution appears to allow for independent action and different policies, but in fact this becomes impossible for political and financial reasons. . . . Legislative devolution cannot mean much in terms of real and substantial policy variations.'[2] These conclusions are compatible with those reached by Buckland (1979) in his study of the inter-war period: while it 'provides a cogent argument in favour of administrative devolution . . . Northern Ireland's experience in the inter-war years is a poor advertisement for parliamentary devolution.'[3] Buckland's view is partly based on a belief that parliamentary devolution encouraged parochialism and bigotry and that greater powers of economic management and more appropriate political institutions would have been necessary if legislative devolution was to have succeeded. Buckland concludes: 'Parliamentary devolution cannot be a permanent settlement of the political and constitutional problems of the United Kingdom. There is really no half-way house between union and complete separation.'⁴

While it is not intended to condemn these conclusions as unreasonable, it is necessary to stress that they do not follow inevitably from examination of the evidence; indeed, it may be argued that they tend to rely upon myths about the nature of government. Without going into great detail, it is possible to refer to certain considerations which any assessment of devolution might include and take account of. Essentially these are considerations which might influence the kind of criteria against which the operation of devolution could be assessed.

(1) Any government is constrained by the international economic environment, resources, taxable capacity and concerns about the impact of policy on economic development. To imply that governments in an international competitive, trading economy (in which assets are privately owned, multi-national companies operate, and flows of funds, rates of exchange and plans for investment, acquisition and disposal of assets are determined by the market and by private agencies) are not constrained in their policy choices is to perpetuate a myth of control. In this sense it is spurious to argue that because devolved government is constrained by a financial or economic factor it is a sham. The questions involved are ones of degree.

(2) Similarly, to view government activity at any level as being characterised by planned, rational, neutral or disinterested decisions is to turn a blind eye to historical evidence. Devolution cannot be held to have failed because the *particular* political pressures which it has facilitated are unpalatable.

(3) All systems of government are characterised by change; and, furthermore, it is the operation of policy rather than the formal arrangements that are significant in considering how government works and changes. Again, to argue that arrangements are or can be permanent is to set up unachievable standards—not merely for devolved government.

But any debate at this level must remain unsatisfactory. Any attempt to pass a verdict on devolution is, at worst, so subjective as to be no more than interesting, and, at best, so bound up with qualifications, reservations and exceptions as to cease to be of any relevance when separated from these. Consequently it is not inappropriate to limit discussion to questions which can be subjected to empirical investigation.

The evidence considered in this study supports the view that, in spite of very real constraints, Northern Ireland and its government could and did diverge substantially from the standards and legislation operating in Great Britain and at Westminster. Independent action, different policies and substantially different legislation did emerge. Nor can this be simply explained as a freedom to do less. Many of the differences were qualitative and the positive expression of different political priorities and ideology. Even where identical policies were adopted in Northern Ireland it is demonstrably not true that they were adopted in a compliant or compulsory environment. There were real political decisions and choices made at every stage, and the steps taken were not always those which involved least conflict with Westminster or 'rocked the boat' to the smallest extent. Even between the wars, when the financial environment was most restrictive, the Northern Ireland government often rejected the cautious and compliant advice of the Ministry of Finance and pursued policies which that ministry felt went beyond what was possible. The insistence on equality of benefit would, the Ministry of Finance feared, enable Westminster to insist on equality of taxation, especially in respect of local rates. But when this constraint or limit on what was possible was tested it proved flexible. The whole history of devolution since the Second War World is one of pushing back the constraints and creating room to exercise choice. It may be that this was not done vigorously enough. However, to imply that there was a fixed and permanent Stormont–Westminster relationship and that what could be done was predetermined by Westminster ignores the evidence about the process of government and policy-making.

Of course, the actions of successive administrations in Stormont have been constrained by the nature of the link with the rest of the United Kingdom. But the constitutional link was not designed, and has not been used, to introduce detailed supervision of policy. The financial and political constraints at this level leave wide scope for variation, and this scope has been taken advantage of. The degree of divergence from United Kingdom services and standards is limited by the political and economic constraints of the region. An autonomous political unit, and especially one established in the climate of modern Irish politics, is primarily constrained by the need to maintain a basis of power and control in order to maintain that autonomy. The compulsion to sustain the origins and justification for a Unionist position has always been stronger than the abstract constraints of finance and London's standards. Emphasis on the formal relationships between levels of government can obscure the real political determinants of a wide range of activities.

This is most apparent when particular policies are examined; but even at the grander level the argument holds. Administrations faced with pressures at Westminster have had to look at the reaction of their supporters. Where they have gone too far in recent years in surrendering on issues held to be ones of principle, they have been subjected to pressures, have lost support and have resigned.

The real world of Ulster politics before the introduction of direct rule in 1972 was not one of functional relationships with Westminster but one of steering a political course through a variety of obstacles of which Westminster was only one and was not clearly dominant. Maintaining and balancing other elements of political support and opposition was in theory as important and in practice proved the major concern.

Indeed, the whole proposition concerning legislative devolution can be turned the other way. The real constraints in a situation of devolution are those faced by the 'senior' partner. How did this partner control, cajole or persuade a reluctant administration? Could Westminster easily override a Stormont government which had electoral backing for its actions? Where Stormont dug in its heels, the consequences of such an exercise of power might well have been more undesirable than the results achieved. Thus the constraints on Westminster were considerable. They were represented in political judgements about likely responses and in the long-term consequences of action and inaction. The relationship between Westminster and Stormont could not be boiled down to financial and constitutional forms. The politics of devolution involved political judgements about political situations and the willingness or otherwise to upset or revoke constitutional arrangements. In practice these were severe constraints on the exercise of 'control' where that control had elements incompatible with the local administration's view of its legitimacy and social role and where the local administration had electoral support for that view. The implication of legislative devolution was, in effect, a willingness by the senior partner to accept that the local administration was the best judge of local needs and to reserve its control for exceptional and serious matters. Whereas this implication could be acceptable when devolution was a considered act of government, it was unpalatable in the context of Northern Ireland's dominant party situation and sectarian politics.

Although it is not intended to pursue here a fruitless search for a 'balanced' view of these issues, the version presented by the Kilbrandon Commission is worthy of attention. This stated:

The fact that devolved government did not provide a lasting

solution to a political and community problem which has persisted for several centuries, and is peculiar to Ireland, in no way
implies a defect in the concept of devolution which was there
applied. While 'home rule', to use the popular term, failed to
resolve this problem, the existence of which gave rise to its
establishment, it had . . . considerable success as an experiment
in devolved government, which was presumably not uppermost in
the minds of its authors. That Northern Ireland's economic
difficulties have persisted is also no adverse reflection on home
rule; they are a product of the province's history, economic
structure and geographical position, accentuated by the disorders
arising out of the community problem.[5]

The detailed analysis offered in the Kilbrandon Report illustrated
the problem of evaluating Northern Ireland's experience of government. For example, the report accepted the generally held view that
finance is the key factor in the working of devolution; it suggested:

Greater use of the power to adopt independent policies was made
in those matters which did not involve substantial expenditure
than in those which did. Northern Ireland was not financially
independent, and the application at the choice of the Northern
Ireland government of the parity principle on which the financial
relationship with the United Kingdom was based had the inevitable consequence that much of the legislation passed by the
Northern Ireland parliament differed only in minor respects, if
at all, from the comparable legislation at Westminster. Where
policies did differ and there were financial implications, they
differed only with the agreement of the United Kingdom
government.[6]

But if this is taken as implying detailed and restrictive Westminster
control, it is in conflict with the view expressed elsewhere in the
Kilbrandon Report that the Treasury tended to look at Northern
Ireland's proposals on broad lines and without detailed scrutiny.[7]

Before returning to the question of finance, there are other
elements in the Kilbrandon Report which merit attention. The report argued that finance was not the only factor operating to restrict
the use made of devolved powers in developing different policies.
Public opinion and the political disposition of the Unionist Party
were both inclined to parity in social policy. In some services—
notably trade and industry—international agreements and obliga-
tions were significant. (Some of these issues have been referred to
earlier.) There are also two particular conclusions which can be
drawn from the kinds of discussion presented by the Kilbrandon

Commission and other commentators. Firstly, their tendency to seek to generalise about devolution throughout a changing and developing period of over fifty years is unwise. The problems of evaluation and assessment derive very strongly from this reluctance to admit that economic, political and financial circumstances have changed, and from the static approach that has been correspondingly adopted. Secondly, too many reviews of the Northern Ireland experience have been made with too little reference to actual development in Northern Ireland. They are too reliant on evidence of formal arrangements, including those concerned with finance, and too limited in their consideration of practice. Thus the breakdown of the financial arrangements in the 1920 act and the continuing economic crisis have undoubtedly affected the operation of government. But without considering the unwillingness of Westminster to intervene or scrutinise in detail, and without considering the political and ideological issues affecting various aspects of policy in varying ways, the picture which emerges is unsatisfactory.

Economic Crisis and Control

More than financial or constitutional relationships, the dominating element in Northern Ireland's experience of devolution has been the environment of economic crisis and social and economic disadvantage. In comparison with Great Britain as a whole and with other regions of the United Kingdom, Northern Ireland is an underdeveloped area. The problems of government are directly related to this. Because of the gap in standards, questions of parity and regional policy have become important elements in devolution.

The environment of economic crisis is fundamental in two ways. Firstly, it has meant that financial dependence has been of great importance. Secondly, it has meant that the difficulties the devolved government was confronted with were products of underlying economic problems. The severity and continuation of problems of low income, poverty and unemployment, with their demographic complications, spring directly from the pattern of regional economic development. The only solutions to these problems lie in economic development.

One response to this situation is to argue that the absence of significant powers in respect of economic, fiscal and monetary policies exposed a crucial lacuna in devolved powers. Devolution, it was argued, was a sham unless the devolved government had some control over its economic situation. In answer to this, it might have been argued that the costs and extent of economic intervention necessary to achieve economic control would have been enormous, and perhaps impossible to achieve in such a small economic unit as

Northern Ireland. Thus it might have been claimed that to expect Northern Ireland's economy to develop along lines and under policies fundamentally out of step with its neighbours, and certainly without enormous subsidy, was unrealistic.

This debate centres around different views of the nature of the economic crisis. Different emphases reflect different assessments of the problems resulting from Northern Ireland's economic crisis. For example, it is argued that Northern Ireland has unavoidable disadvantages deriving from its peripheral location and relative isolation from the major European markets and sources of raw materials. Transport costs are high, and there are direct economic consequences in reluctance to invest. Without major natural resources there is no natural base for economic growth.

But these features are not necessarily barriers to economic growth; indeed, it can be argued that there are economic advantages in the availability of land, water and labour, the lack of congestion, and other factors vital to economic development. If Northern Ireland's economic backwardness is not the inevitable result of natural causes, it might be reasonably supposed that its problems were due to malfunctioning of the market. Emphasis could be placed on outdated industrial capital, overdependence on declining industry and agriculture, and slowness to modernise. Concern about the level of investment has been a major element in the development of regional policy. For example, evidence that investment in Northern Ireland was considerably less than investment from Northern Ireland elsewhere has been influential in developing policies to encourage both domestic and external investment in Northern Ireland. While there has been considerable success in this attempt, it has not solved the regional problem and has created a new kind of dependency.

Industrial investment is too often controlled either by multinational or British-based companies or by family-owned Northern Ireland companies. Companies in the former group do not produce a sound basis for industrial development—branch factories are more vulnerable in periods of recession. On the other hand, the traditional family firm is not always the best basis for effective management and expanding industry. The policies and incentives available to the government do not enable it to control the pattern of development. The success of regional policy has left an overdependence on textiles, clothing, food, drink and tobacco. The thirty-four largest companies operating in Northern Ireland accounted for 48 per cent of all manufacturing employment, according to a 1977 estimate. Of this total 87 per cent of employment was controlled outside Northern Ireland.[8] Arguments that greater economic and fiscal powers could enable regions to gain more control over their economic future often neglect to deal with this problem. The solution is not easily identified. Increased devolved powers to enable the provision of more encouragements to private investment are not a panacea for regional problems; and the level of increase in public ownership, investment and expenditure necessary to expand job creation to a significant extent by this means would be extremely costly. The emphasis does not only rest on taxation and ability to determine levels of investment. There remain problems of how to achieve regional economic development through public intervention, and questions of the degree and nature of involvement in the economy, and the effects of that involvement. It is not always clear that those who stress the need for devolved governments to have greater economic and taxation powers have a clear view of how these problems would be resolved without increasing dependency in some way. Perhaps mainly as a consequence of the structure of control, it can be argued that the Northern Ireland economy has suffered from underinvestment and a lack of substantial exploitation of economic opportunities. Alternatively it can be argued that the nature of economic investment has led to an excessive exploitation of cheap labour and natural resources without the major benefits of that exploitation being channelled back into the Northern Ireland economy and community. Whichever interpretation is correct, the difficulty is not easily resolved.

If the origins of economic crisis lie in the structure of control over capital and investment, it may be argued that economic powers which fall short of direction or acquisition would not yield significant economic responses. The economic problem will not respond to minor tinkerings and interventions. Such a consideration is important in the debate about devolution and should be borne in mind in considering economic and taxation powers. The regional problems may be more resistant than is implied by pleas for more powers which do not take account of the limited impact which those same powers may have, regardless of whether they are exercised by Westminster or by a devolved government. The central issue may be not so much that of *who* is to have the powers than that of *what* those powers are to be—what the broader implications will be for ownership and control in the economy.

Bearing this general view in mind, there are aspects of the operation of devolution in Northern Ireland which could be taken as indicating that devolution has not been irrelevant to the economic condition of Northern Ireland. Firstly, Northern Ireland has exercised more extensive powers in relation to regional policy. Legislative devolution was used to increase powers in this field.

Secondly, it is important to bear in mind the merits of more local control. Aids to industry and industrial training are often quoted as examples of the advantages derived from having government departments in Belfast with authority to take decisions concerning a wide range of executive matters.[9] Thirdly, considerable evidence can be put forward to show significant social and economic progress in Northern Ireland in recent years. For example, in the late 1960s, in comparison with the United Kingdom as a whole, Northern Ireland experienced greater growth in Gross Domestic Product per head, industrial production, employment, labour productivity and personal income. However, this progress did not fundamentally alter the unfavourable comparative position of Northern Ireland. Moreover, the tensions created by such progress, and the different extent to which different sections of the population benefited, may have increased rather than reduced problems for the government.

It seems possible, however, that by the period 1966–72 the sensitivity of the Northern Ireland economy to changes occurring in Great Britain declined, and there is some tenuous evidence that the Northern Ireland economy has strengthened relative to that of the rest of the United Kingdom. But more evidence is needed before such a view can be properly substantiated.

These brief comments on the economic situation in Northern Ireland do not adequately deal with the issues concerned. What is indicated is the difficulty of assessing what the impact of devolution has been on the economy and, in turn, what the impact of continuing economic disadvantage has been on devolution. It is too easy to assume that the financial, constitutional and political aspects of devolution can be considered in the absence of this context. The attention given to industrial investment, energy and other national resources does not merely provide an interesting sidelight on devolution or evidence of its operation; instead these factors are seen as crucial to the scale, nature and intransigence of the problem which governments are expected, however unrealistically, to deal with.

Political Dependency

Some reviews of the Northern Ireland experience of devolution place great emphasis on the formal constitutional relationship between Stormont and Westminster and on the legislative supremacy of Westminster. Buckland (1979), for example, complains that Stormont's freedom of action and power of development 'was more apparent than real' because of the need to share responsibility with unco-operative local authorities, because of constitutional prohibitions, and because sovereign power rested at Westminster.[10] But in practice successive British governments chose not to exercise that power. This held true until 1972. The political (as distinct from financial) dependency of Northern Ireland has not been a major element in the operation of devolution. Constitutional prohibitions have been referred to, for example in relation to planning and education (both cases in which it could be argued that the constitution has been mobilised to support or enable whatever was the predilection of the Stormont government). Westminster has in practice not challenged the Stormont government by reference to the constitution or its sovereign status.

Nor has subordinate status prevented legislative innovation. Information provided for the Kilbrandon Commission (see p. 10 above) showed that a substantial part of Stormont's legislation did not follow that previously enacted at Westminster. The commission commented:

> In terms of parliamentary time the significance of the remaining legislation was further reduced by the readiness of the Northern Ireland parliament to pass it without giving it such close scrutiny as was given to measures which did not to so great an extent rest on Westminster statutes. It was estimated that the proportion of parliamentary time spent on re-enactment of Westminster statutes was something less than a third of the total time spent on legislation, and a much smaller part of the total parliamentary time, a good deal of which was taken up with debates, questions and other non-legislative business of special Northern Ireland concern.[11]

Examples of the use of legislative devolution have been given throughout this book. Largely on this basis it has been argued that the effects of legislative devolution cannot be dismissed. Not all legislative differences were trivial or represented less advanced or less costly reactions to problems. Furthermore, it has been argued that where a step-by-step approach operated this was as a result of a conscious choice debated in cabinet and parliament in a way not open to regions without devolved parliaments.

Administrative devolution has been more generally regarded as a success. This view must be subject to reservations, especially relating to possible loss of objectivity and impartiality because of the close and continuing relationship between ministers and officials. On the other hand, the Kilbrandon Commission noted:

> Many witnesses commented on the close and intimate relationship which existed between ministers and their officials on the one hand and members and officials of local authorities, businessmen and the general public on the other. Because the former were more accessible and more aware of local needs and of local

difficulties, and perhaps less heavily pressed, than their counterparts in London, and were in a position to take decisions on matters arising day by day, business could be dealt with more promptly and smoothly and grievances could be redressed more readily. We were interested to note that this view was shared by Sir Edmund Compton, who was for some time Parliamentary Commissioner for Administration in both the United Kingdom and Northern Ireland. In his report on Northern Ireland for 1970 he wrote that 'The individual citizen frequently gets a better service from a Northern Ireland ministry than he would get from a United Kingdom department in similar circumstances, owing to the easier access to central government that is both feasible and customary in a territory the size of Northern Ireland.'[12]

Discussion of constitutional and political dependency does not end with consideration of legislative or administrative devolution or with a conclusion such as the Kilbrandon Commission's:

We have no doubt at all that home rule was of considerable advantage to Northern Ireland. Particularly in the large areas of government which were unaffected, or at least were not dominated, by the community problem, conspicuous progress was made under it. Perhaps the most impressive of these was in the field of health, where Northern Ireland, which used to be well below the standards of Great Britain, caught up with and in some respects surpassed them. The other social services were steadily built up. Education was greatly improved, and, though it still continues, below university level, in two almost entirely different systems, both are supported by the state. Economic policy was flexible and imaginative, and, though the level of unemployment continued to be higher than the average for Great Britain, the gap had been significantly narrowed at the time of the outbreak of the disturbances. Considerable progress was made in attracting new industry and in diversifying the economy of the province. It must be questioned whether so much would have been accomplished in all these fields without a separate administration to watch over the affairs of Northern Ireland.[13]

Discussion of political dependency must also involve consideration of the essential nature of the political status of Northern Ireland and of how far this status is a colonial one. Such a status is wholly compatible with differences in policy and practice and financial support to sustain political dependency. It is not intended to pursue this line of thought further here. The central theme in such a debate is the question of how far the problems of Northern Ireland are internal and how far they arise from the British link. It can be argued that a crude colonial analogy is inappropriate in Northern Ireland. Because the clear majority in Northern Ireland insist on their emotional and political ties with Britain, the British are not colonialists. Although it can be claimed that the dependency of Northern Ireland is the principal feature of political status, the realities of economic dependence are equally strong when the Republic of Ireland is referred to, and in both cases it is an economic rather than a political/colonial relationship which is most important.[14]

Financial Dependency

The primacy of economic factors in the experience of devolution has given financial relationships a key role. In a different economic climate the financial arrangements contained in the Government of Ireland Act, 1920, would not have proved so problematic. From the outset, however, economic depression both reduced revenue and increased expenditure attributable to Northern Ireland. Throughout the inter-war years the problems this raised were dealt with in an *ad hoc* manner. In the post-war period a series of more robust agreements at least gave the Northern Ireland government more security and certainty in financial planning. The revenue basis for financial support has been increasingly replaced by a 'need' or expenditure basis.

This financial environment has played a significant part in the operation of devolved government. It has, however, been argued that it did not dictate decisions. The principle of parity was not accepted in all policy areas, and where it was accepted it is misleading to regard it as an inevitable product of the financial relationship. In the inter-war years discussion of policy, especially in the field of social security, was carried out in an atmosphere of financial crisis and uncertainty marked by fears that increased demands for funds could lead to closer scrutiny, especially over local taxation. In the post-war period the increasing emphasis on expenditure rather than revenue has relaxed these pressures. Financial dependency has increased.

In view of the adverse social and economic circumstances of Northern Ireland, one test of the operation of devolution is the level of public expenditure per head. Perhaps the most surprising feature of this is that identifiable public expenditure* per head has only

---

* Identifiable public expenditure is expenditure which can be identified as having been incurred in the country concerned but excluding expenditures incurred for the benefit of the United Kingdom as a whole, e.g. defence, overseas service and debt interest.

risen above that for Scotland since 1973–74 and for Wales since 1969–70.[15] It could be argued that regions without legislative devolution and with cabinet-level ministers at Westminster have succeeded in obtaining a larger share of public resources in spite of less pressing problems. Northern Ireland has fared better in this sense *since* direct rule. Current debates about devolution emphasise the importance of financial arrangements and of powers to tax and assist trade and industry. The Northern Ireland example does not disprove this concern; indeed, it confirms the importance of finance. But it does suggest that the parent government is able to sustain an arrangement which is financially advantageous to the devolved government without involving detailed 'niggling' supervision.

Three considerations remain. Firstly, was this arrangement acceptable for Northern Ireland simply because of the remoteness of the province both politically and economically? The fact that Northern Ireland could compete with and outbid other regions in attracting industry did not arouse the problems which have been experienced as a result of similar suggestions for Scotland. Secondly, Northern Ireland's financial benefits have not in fact been as marked as is often imagined. Until contributions in respect of civil disorder changed the picture in the 1970s Northern Ireland did not fare particularly well. Some calculations suggest that the extent of subvention from Westminster was limited. Thus after deducting the cost of civil disorder and compensation payments, the total subvention may have been less than £200 million in 1973–74. Arguably some £50 million of this is really only channelled through Westminster and originates as EEC grants. In addition, if all Northern Ireland's capital needs were financed by borrowing (allowing a *pro rata* level of borrowing and allowing for interest charges), a further £50 million or more could be deducted. Even the remaining £100 million as a source of financial support takes no account of particular features of Northern Ireland manufacturing and excise duties associated with them.[16]

Thirdly, it is only following the imposition of direct rule that the nature of problems in Northern Ireland has been accepted at Westminster. Mr Callaghan has referred to the convention that enabled Westminster to treat financial negotiations and issues of parity at an administrative level rather than as an aspect of policy. Before 1967 Northern Ireland, unlike Scotland or Wales, rarely, if ever, came before the cabinet, and its concerns had fallen into a settled routine at the Home Office. In contrast, the Westminster government in the 1970s was heavily involved politically and administratively. This was reflected in references to social policy. In the White Paper, *The Northern Ireland Constitution*, published in 1974, it is stated that 'There are still gaps in standards of living, employment, housing and social conditions between Northern Ireland and Great Britain.'[17] This disparity has been referred to in relation both to the EEC and to British regions (for example, 'The general housing situation in Northern Ireland is worse than in any other United Kingdom region.').[18] It is possible that this recognition has only developed *because* of the breakdown of devolved government. Given the lack of involvement with Northern Ireland affairs of parliaments and governments at Westminster, devolution may have encouraged an avoidance of the issue of comparable standards. The problem of developing regional strategies could be more easily avoided because responsibility for policy in Northern Ireland was devolved. The Northern Ireland constitutional arrangements could be regarded as fundamentally responsible for a state of affairs which enabled successive British governments to sidestep on the issue of developing policies. The whole Home Rule arrangement was not initially desired by Ulster Unionism; however, as a means of maintaining the Union and political initiative it was acceptable. But the extent to which the *laissez-faire* policy suited both Stormont and Westminster has undergone transformation in accordance with changes in the economic and political situation.

Social and Political Divisions

The basis and dominance of politico-religious division have been referred to earlier. This division has permeated every aspect of the operation of government. The social geography of Northern Ireland draws attention to social and religious segregation. The Catholic community is proportionately most heavily represented in the west and south of the province and in West Belfast. Statistics of social malaise indicate that while these areas have no monopoly of hardship, there are significant correlations.[19] Thus households in the west of the province have lower incomes, more unemployment and worse housing provision.

Once established, patterns of residential and social segregation are not easily broken down. They come to be supported by expressed preferences. Residential segregation maintains and reinforces institutional segregation through schools, jobs, clubs and other social and recreational facilities.[20] It is possible to explain the development and continuation of this pattern. In Belfast, for example, its origins lie in the early development of the city and patterns of migration, and it has been maintained and reinforced by periodic outbreaks of communal violence. The pattern of segregated settlement has in consequence never been broken down. The population is ranked and polarised. Factors which appear to prevent assimilation are evident: a large minority whose 'alien' behaviour poses a threat to values; a situation of low income; deviation from the dominant culture; traditional institutionalised rejection; a highly conservative society. Conservatism and persistent segregation sustain and are sustained by antagonistic ideologies and by the status, social standing, prestige and identity attached to place of residence. Segregation is created by, and at the same time creates, ideological politics.

The most recent example of this process has been the civil disturbances since 1969.[21] Population movement occurring as a result of these disturbances has reinforced segregation. In areas such as West Belfast residential segregation has complicated employment patterns and journey to work. An urban geography of 'safe' home neighbourhoods surrounded by 'hostile' areas has contracted labour mobility and obstructed journey to work and has left high rates of unemployment in localities next to those with considerable job vacancies. These problems affect both private and public policy. In both cases the pattern of need and demand reflects the facts of political and religious division. But the most likely means of meeting needs may, in the long term, reinforce segregation. Thus the lack of housing opportunity in West Belfast can only be remedied by extending 'safe' areas (for example, by building on the western edge of the city). The crucial factor of siting has been prominent in the debate on major housing development schemes, such as that proposed at Poleglass. Policies to meet need are constrained by the facts of preference and segregation; in turn, these constraints are sufficient to ensure that policies are powerless to alter the environment that creates such problems.

The nature of social and political division can be explained by referring to Northern Ireland as a bi-national or multi-national state, a religiously divided (bi-confessional) society, a plural society, a bi-racial society, or a fragmented society.[22] Perhaps none of these elements is useful unless considered in connection with ideas of political dominance. Alternatively an underlying theme linking political and economic forms is concerned with class conflict. In this thesis emphasis may be placed on the effect of traditional and religious disputes to prevent class divisions becoming the basis for political division.[23]

It is also relevant in relation to these divisions to consider the effects of social and economic changes. Thus emphasis can be placed on changes in the relative social and economic circumstances of groups, changes in expectations and aspirations, changes in the educational and occupational composition of groups, and changes in the political organisation or views of groups.[24] It is not intended to attempt to assess or discuss these views of the social development of Northern Ireland here. However, two points are important. Firstly, it is likely that the most accurate explanation will be one which embodies a number of the individual elements alluded to above. Secondly, themes of modernisation and change, particularly economic change, underlie most of the theories. From the point of view of a study seeking to focus attention on development and use of administrative structures, it is helpful to emphasise certain elements. The development of social policy is principally determined by the powers of the state and by its use of these powers. This draws attention to questions of party dominance and the economic and social orgins of that dominance. Thus, in crude terms, devolution in Northern Ireland has provided an opportunity, through politico-religious divisions and a dominant party system, for established economic and political interests to maintain and use a considerable range of powers. These powers have been principally used by the dominant group to further what it considered to be its own interests, and until recently little pressure was placed on it to modify this type of activity. The most significant factor straining this position has been tension within the controlling political group between those who saw the role of the state as best serving their interests by maintaining the basic status quo and those who saw their interests as requiring state intervention to modernise and reform. Boserup (1972) has identified the basis of this division as an essentially industrial/economic division between land-holders and family-controlled, non-expanding industry and the new economic interest represented by modern capitalist joint-stock enterprises and investors in them.[25]

We are not concerned here to argue that this is a wholly adequate analysis of social change in Northern Ireland, but rather to indicate that any explanation of the pattern of social reform or the operation of devolution requires some analysis of the basis of political power and the nature and role of the state. The fact that Northern Ireland is not a sovereign state does not remove this requirement. Indeed, Northern Ireland's status as 'essentially a self-governing province with some of the trappings of sovereignty'[26] make it all the more applicable.

Thus it can be argued that evidence about the use of devolved powers is fully consistent with a view of social reform sustaining economic and political power and at the same time highlighting conflicts within the dominant political group and between that group and other sections of the community. It is not appropriate to expect to analyse devolution solely by looking at the formal legal position. Nor, however, is it adequate to explain the use and practice of devolved government in terms of the ostensible problems it is dealing with. It is essential also to relate practice to evidence of political, social and economic development. It is misleading to seek logical and rational explanations for why powers have been used in particular ways by examining, say, social needs and changing needs in a vacuum. They must be complemented by some broader consideration of economic and political power.

Policy Responses

The Government of Ireland Act, 1920, gave the Northern Ireland government responsibility for the provision of social services and the freedom to determine its own social policy. The importance of this area of policy has grown out of all recognition since then. The responses of the Northern Ireland government have been constrained not only by constitutional and financial factors but also by continuing economic crisis and internal political division. The pattern of policy emerging from this situation has been described in the preceding two chapters. But certain themes merit fuller attention.

The Principle of Parity

Some commentaries represent the development of social policy as dominated by a common principle of parity.[27] In practice, however, the picture is more complicated. An official definition of the principle of parity was not developed until the Joint Exchequer Board in 1955 chose to emphasise four elements. Firstly, it held that there should be parity of social services in Great Britain and Northern Ireland; secondly, that there should be a general parity of standards as between Northern Ireland and comparable areas of Great Britain; thirdly, it recognised the necessity to incur special expenditure in Northern Ireland to make up the substantial leeway on various services such as housing, schools, hospitals, and so on; and fourthly, there was a need for special expenditure in Northern Ireland to offset the economic disadvantage from which it suffered in comparison with Great Britain as a whole by reason of its geographical separation from the rest of the United Kingdom. It has often been assumed that this commitment to parity has produced a situation in which social services are identical with those in Britain. The social services have been described as an area where the step-by-step policy prevails. Barritt and Carter (1962) have written that 'The social services are for the most part copied from those in Great Britain.'[28] Rose (1971) has similarly stated that a 'policy of step-by-step legislation in welfare matters meant the Northern Ireland regime adopted British welfare programmes shortly after the Westminster parliament approved such measures for Great Britain'.[29] However, a close examination of social policy shows that in certain services there were quite considerable divergences from policy in Britain. It is apparent that parity is a general principle and, as such, open to differing interpretations. Three main interpretations of parity can be illustrated by examining policy and legislation in various social services.

(1) Parity as absolute uniformity

This interpretation applies to social security perhaps because of its close connection with taxation. Northern Ireland has usually enacted similar legislation to Great Britain, and in 1972 a Social Services Parity Act stipulated that, when legislation is introduced at Westminster effecting changes in the rates of social security benefit and similar matters, a resolution that corresponding changes are to be made in the law of Northern Ireland can be passed by Order in Council and put into immediate effect. This means that cash social benefits operate as a single system throughout the United Kingdom, and it reduces any Northern Ireland role to little more than a rubber stamp for Westminster legislation. In the past there have been occasional attempts to diverge from the absolute uniformity principle. In 1956 Stormont proposed altering the rates of family allowance so as to give more money to small families and less to large ones. Not only was this a breach of parity, but it also seemed an instance of religious discrimination against the many large Catholic families, and the proposal was eventually abandoned amid much controversy. Other minor divergence from the principle of parity has been referred to previously.

The Social Services Parity Act also requires Northern Ireland to keep the scale and standard of comprehensive health services in general conformity with the scale and standard of such services in Britain. This has not prevented quite a number of differences developing in the administrative structure of the services and the allocation of functions.

(2) Parity as similarity in most respects

In this category legislation is basically the same but there are quite significant differences which may arise from special arrangements to meet local needs or for other reasons. One example of this is found in the personal social services, where Northern Ireland has had a policy of integrated welfare departments since the war. County welfare authorities have been responsible for child care, care of the old and handicapped, home helps, community psychiatric social work, residential care, occupational therapy and supervision of day nurseries. This has meant that social work has developed on a generic basis. Since 1973 the personal social services have been removed from local authority control and placed in a unified structure with the health service under the control of nominated boards. There are also many differences with Britain in policy on children and young offenders.

(3) Parity as similarity only in the broadest sense

Parity also appears to be interpreted in some policy areas as applicable only to general principles, while allowing very large differences to exist. This seems particularly true of housing policy. Although there is an acceptance of the general principle of the state's role in the provision of housing, most of the legislation differs from that in Britain; this affects a wide range of matters, including subsidies, rent policy, rent rebates, housing allocation schemes and housing administration. Housing legislation has never followed a step-by-step policy with Britain.

Education policy exhibits a rather similar pattern, although there are substantial areas of similarity with Britain. But Northern Ireland differs in its system of providing comprehensive secondary schools, its retention of 'eleven plus' selection, and its special arrangements for the financing and management of voluntary schools.

It is difficult to place each social service completely into one of these categories, but the problems of arriving at a precise definition of parity are evident. The parity principle has been enforced loosely, if at all, in regard to many social services. An analysis of social legislation enacted between 1965 and 1970 illustrates the extent of differences in legislation.[30] All but two items of parity legislation concern social security.

Table 24: Social Policy Legislation, 1965–70

	Number of acts	%
Parity legislation	20	32
Legislation peculiar to Northern Ireland	19	30
Legislation falling between the two categories	24	38
	63	100

Some of the differences are responses to local needs or stem from administrative practices or experiments suitable to a regional government, but many of the differences appear to reflect the nature of the political and social system.

Ideology and Social Policy

In considering variations in policy adopted in different services reference to political ideology is helpful.[31] Ideological conflict has limited the degree of consensus over basic constitutional arrangements in Northern Ireland. It is also important to consider how these ideological factors affect social policy. In countries where there is a large degree of consensus on social policy it may be assumed that specific policies do not have rigid or dogmatic contents, are not strongly held, and are open to change by evidence or argument. However, examples from Northern Ireland cast doubts on the degree of consensus over the principles and aims of social policy, and many issues have become matters of ideological debate. Northern Ireland provides many instances of social policies which are strongly influenced by ideological considerations. In some cases social policy is directly determined by the dictates of the ideology. In other instances social policies are used as an instrument for realising the ends or values of the ideology. The extent to which policies reflect these processes differs between services. There are a number of factors which determine how susceptible services and policies are to ideological influences.

(1) The 'sensitivity' of the service

Some services are much more sensitive to ideological values and demands than others. Education is a good example, as it relates closely to the rigid and dogmatic elements of the ideologies pervasive in Northern Ireland. The educational system has always been examined according to the degree of 'protection' it affords to different religious denominations. The Catholic minority has supported a Catholic school system which puts a strong emphasis upon religious instruction, the teaching of the Irish language, and Irish culture and history. Catholic schools have remained outside the state sector, while the state schools have been developed in such a way as to make them 'safe for Protestant children'. Pupils at state schools are almost exclusively Protestant, and the influence of the Protestant clergy is seen on the management committees and in religious instruction courses, while the schools are orientated towards British cultural values. Some modification of intransigent positions has emerged, but there is little evidence of a desire to adopt a different basis for educational organisation. The government negotiated a position under which it could claim that it carried out its responsibility to maintain educational standards. However, this accommodation acknowledged the existing division of control and the principle of segregated education. It is often argued that this segregated system perpetuates community divisions. There is

K

little evidence of any movement towards non-denominational education.

A further illustration of the relationship between ideology and social services is provided by the National Health Service Act, 1948, and the exclusion of any clause to enable hospitals with religious links to maintain their character within the National Health Service (see p. 250 above). The problem has subsequently been one of finding a proper relationship between the state service and a voluntary hospital. This has been reduced on the one side to a question of subsidising a hostile tradition and assisting the doctrines of a conflicting ideology, and on the other to a question of losing the special relationship with the Roman Catholic Church.

It is difficult to explain the intractability of issues in education and health service provision save in the context of ideological division. It may be argued that the conflicting outlooks demonstrate how social policies reflect and reinforce features of the communities in which they operate—that they represent a realistic view of the problems of a segregated society. None the less, they serve to institutionalise and rationalise divisions and to establish and perpetuate discriminatory administrative practices. In addition, they provide evidence of the tendency to reduce arguments to their ideological elements.

(2) The role of the service in maintaining the political structure

The ideological influence on policies relating to the political structure is most clearly seen in areas directly connected with the maintenance of the political system, e.g. security, police and judicial/legal matters—areas on the margin of social policy. However, social policies connected with the distribution of services and rights and the allocation of resources may also serve to maintain the political and social system. Many local authorities have been accused of discrimination in housing and employment against Catholics. The Cameron Commission, investigating the causes of civil disturbances in 1969, found many such accusations justified.[32] The commission reported that council housing policy had been distorted for political ends in some Unionist-controlled areas and that some Unionist-controlled councils had used their power to make appointments in a way which benefited Protestants. Two main reasons may be suggested for this type of discrimination. Firstly, it may be due to a mixture of political and religious prejudice. Barritt and Carter (1962) found several examples of this type of thinking among Unionists who 'did not see why Protestants should be expected to find capital to build houses for such families [i.e. large Catholic families] and to subsidise their rents. The Protestants were being asked to subsidise an increase of population which would vote them out of control of their own money.'[33] Given competing claims by majority and minority groups for social benefits and goods, the process of allocation by members of both groups is likely to be coloured by social perceptions and by politico-religious attitudes. Secondly, the creation of new housing estates causes population movements which may alter the political composition of electoral wards within local authority areas. This was an important factor in the dozen or so local authority areas where there was a Unionist majority on the council but a majority of Catholics in the population. As the Cameron Report noted, the principal criterion of allocation in such cases was not actual need but the maintenance of the current political preponderance in the local government area.

Aspects of housing, planning and education policy have not been amenable to reform, and there have been few attempts to make radical changes to meet local grievances, reduce complaints or bring policy and legislation into line with the British equivalents. Demands for reform have not always been acknowledged as legitimate, and proposals to modernise or rationalise procedures can be interpreted as attempts to reduce the privileges or powers of the coalition of interests held together by ideology. The extent to which this occurs and the penalties, in loss of popular support, of weakening the basis of ideology are obstacles to reform. Certain problems of reforming social services in Northern Ireland are more intelligible if they are regarded in this way as central to political interest and the precepts of the ideology and not as peripheral or bargainable factors.

(3) The distribution of responsibility for administering services

Responsibility for the implementation of social services which appear prone to ideological influences has rested in many cases with local authorities. This may reflect the perceived function of local government. There is no tradition of strong, innovative municipal or local government action in Ireland. The local authorities in Northern Ireland have not apparently regarded the provision of services as a major function. This activity was essentially incidental to their central role as local political managers. In this situation services provided at local level can be seen as supportive to the political task. Busteed and Mason (1971) argue that 'The outputs of the local government system, especially public housing and local authority employment, were widely regarded as a form of patronage, distributed by councillors to electors who shared their own religious and political outlook.'[34] Clearly this was not universally true, and there is also evidence that such practices were operated by authorities of different political complexions and may reflect an expected manipulation. In certain cases it may be offset or openly recognised through 'gentlemen's agreements' between opponents. In these cases social policies are still considered within the ideological context and without any considerations of their 'social' objectives or any calculation of need.

This situation partly reflected the lack of manpower and financial and administrative resources, as well as the long-standing municipal tradition. Centrally administered services were less likely to be discriminatory as a consequence of a lack of resources or inefficient procedures. There have, of course, been alleged examples of discriminatory policies by the central government, for example the operation of a scheme of regional development which has not been successful in developing the province's economic resources in a balanced fashion. However, local government was responsible for the clearest examples of discriminatory practices.

(4) The absence of pressure from Britain for parity

It could be expected that the policies least subject to strong ideological influences would be in areas covered by parity legislation where British standards and practices have applied. In so far as policies in Britain are based on the shifting resolution of conflicts (between different interests which broadly accept a bargaining process to resolve these conflicts), we would expect policies which in Northern Ireland have been subject to British influence to reflect this process rather than to be determined by ideological pressures. But even in social security services the principle of parity is not an absolute one. There have been variations from accepted British practices in social security for reasons associated with ideological considerations. One example was an attempt by the Stormont government to abandon parity in family allowances in 1956. A more recent example was the introduction in 1971 of the Payments for Debt (Emergency Provisions) Act, which authorised the government to make deductions from social security benefits to meet debts to public authorities arising mainly from the withholding of rents. This legislation was designed to combat the civil disobedience campaign which followed the introduction of internment. Leaving aside the significance of the rate of deduction or the validity of making deductions from benefits which included a specific rent allowance, it is clear that the decision to authorise deductions from insurance benefits directly contradicted two principles enshrined in the British model: entitlement on meeting the qualifications of need for special benefits, and payment by right of contribution. Such entitlements were clearly still considered to be conditional upon other tests of loyalty and community allegiance. In general there have been few deviations from British practice in social security and health services. In the other major social services (education, housing, welfare and child care), as we have noted, Northern Ireland has legislation and policies markedly different from those operating in Britain. There are also wide divergencies from British legislation on other important social issues such as divorce, abortion, homosexuality, gambling and various aspects of citizens' rights.

There is little evidence that pressure from either Westminster or the Treasury has been directly exerted to influence social policies in Northern Ireland. In some areas Northern Ireland did adopt British legislation as a 'selective imitator'. In other areas innovations in social policy have probably been more radical and progressive than in Britain, for example in regional planning and possibly in the administration of personal social services in integrated departments and the operation of a comprehensive unified Special Care Service for the mentally subnormal. The more ambitious and radical policies appear to have been restricted to less sensitive areas and have not threatened the political system. The nature and operation of social policies are likely to be most strongly subject to ideological influence in areas where they are locally determined and where British involvement is minimal. The experience of British intervention in the period 1969–73 indicates that British authorities were more impressed by political necessities than social need.[35] Policies conceived in these terms may bear no relation to the needs or demands of the community involved. Furthermore, they may not be welcomed, may be considered irrelevant, or may not be implemented with an urgency or conviction which bears relation to social needs. The extent to which this is likely to be true will be increased by a lack of knowledge of the Irish situation prior to the imposition of 'social' policies. Until recently Northern Ireland was the divided responsibility of the Home Office, the Ministry of Defence, the Foreign Office and, sporadically, the Cabinet Office. The Home Office had no officials specialising in Northern Ireland affairs. Policies originating in Britain to alleviate problems have often been excellent in conception; but introduced in the midst of crisis, without adequate preparation or discussion, and without favourable interpretation or vigorous implementation, they are unlikely to succeed. It may be argued that it is not the failure of governments to recognise problems or middle-class values which make success uncertain, but rather the insufficient attention given to the timing, methods and processes of policies, both at introduction and during implementation. Where policies do not relate to public recognition of need and merit they are unlikely to be successful. It is factors such as these which have limited the impact of more recent reforms in such areas as housing and community relations.

(5) The absence of non-sectarian pressures

The absence of pressure-group activity as an influence on social policy may be regarded as an important factor at both local and regional levels. The Northern Ireland CBI has not been an effective lobby, and the trade union movement was not recognised by Unionist governments until the late 1960s and has never had much influence on government policy. Sectarian policies have eliminated the possibility of the formation of a united front by a labour and trade union movement from which radical social policies and criticism might have been expected to emerge. The most influential pressure groups have been those drawing on the same support as the dominant party based on a sectarian interest. It can only be asserted that the continual dominance of one party in power and the long association of ministers and civil servants with particular policies and departments have created serious problems. Pressure groups do not operate effectively as countervailing forces in such a situation. Civil Service departments have been accustomed to working within the same political and policy context. There is an absence of pressures from any source to question assumptions or to initiate changes in policy. In a situation where all proposals are likely to be subjected to ideological examination it is not surprising that little research has been carried out or sponsored. There were few statutory advisory committees attached to government departments.

Phases in the Development of Social Policy

While it is reasonable to seek to generalise about the development of social policy and to highlight key issues, there is a danger that change is neglected. The important influences on policy have not operated in the same way throughout the period of devolved government. There have been significant shifts in the Unionist Party's approach to social policy. Similarly, there have been important economic changes which have had implications for the operation of devolution. In this section six stages in the development of social policy are identified in order to illustrate changes in the way the government has approached social policy. Clearly these stages blend into each other and could themselves be subdivided.

(1) *The Establishment of Northern Ireland, 1920–21*

The initial stage in the development of social policy in Northern Ireland derives from the political circumstances in which the Northern Ireland parliament was established. Aggressive loyalism, and the threat of civil war if Ulster was incorporated in an all-

Ireland Home Rule settlement, led to a political compromise based on partition. But such a settlement was not universally acceptable, and its permanence was questionable. Consequently the initial concerns of government were those of establishing control and recognition, if only as the *de facto* government in Northern Ireland. In social policy this phase of government is clearest in the field of education. Akenson (1973) has fully described the primary task of setting up new administrative machinery in order to establish control.[36] Although this could be seen as an initial task, in effect the continued challenge to the authority of the Northern Ireland government has lent some permanence to it. It may be argued that asserting the nature of devolved government in Northern Ireland has remained a consistent underlying theme in the development of policy.

(2) *Non-Interventionist Government, 1921–43*

The whole of the inter-war period is marked by the *laissez-faire* approach of the Stormont government. The government maintained established functions but was reluctant to develop these or take on new tasks. In fields such as housing a gap in comparable levels of provision in Britain and Northern Ireland developed because of this reluctance to extend government. The proper role of government was seen in terms of maintaining the Union and sustaining the supporters of the state rather than seeking to achieve social or economic objectives. Only where services were seen as essential to the Union—in rates of insurance benefits—were comparable standards maintained.

The Northern Ireland Prime Minister stated in 1922: 'We will most carefully and most jealously look into steps that are taken across the water. . . . It will never be said that the workers in our midst worked under conditions worse than those across the water.'[37] He emphasised the intention to see that, where unemployment and benefits were concerned, treatment in Northern Ireland would be as good as in Britain. But living up to this step-by-step approach proved difficult. In the income-maintenance area there were significant disputes within the government concerning a desire to make local government bear costs and the tactics to be adopted in negotiations with Westminster. There was also an underlying concern with the 'proper role' of the state in welfare and the economy— a concern not to pamper the working classes and damage private enterprise in industry. While this concern did not prevent continuing expansion of social security provision, it was an essential component in all debates on this topic. Similarly, while the decisions to keep benefit levels in line with those in Britain no doubt reduced the room to manoeuvre on other services, it is not evident that the political disposition of the government was inclined towards ambitious, interventionist approaches. Had there been more room to manoeuvre, it is unlikely that it would have been used. Financial constraints and the uncertainty engendered by an annual renegotiation made a planned interventionist approach difficult. But the attitude of the government to intervention and, for example, its concern that local government should make a full contribution to education and housing cannot be regarded as simple reaction to these pressures. Stormont was itself naturally inclined to restrict expenditure, limit the role of the state and limit appeals for funding from Westminster where these were not justified by the established financial arrangements. The role of the Ministry of Finance in this is important, and it is interesting to note a reference made by Oliver (1978 a) to the problem of getting money into Northern Ireland in the 1930s:

> I remember that it was popular at the time to blame the British Treasury. But that is always easy to do—from a distance. Some of the blame may well have lain on the Ulster side. Both of the top officials in the Ministry of Finance (Ernest Clark and G. C. Duggan) had come from the London Civil Service, and it is possible that they may have been over-zealous in showing their new independence of London.[38]

Not until wartime did Northern Ireland become 'flush with money', and Oliver has indicated that departmental and administrative factors may have reinforced the tendency of Unionist ministers to look warily at new plans. Summing up the operation of the Civil Service in the 1930s Oliver stated:

> But it was a complacent service. There was little urge to press on and break new ground. Above all there was little urge to bring about social change. Social attitudes and structures changed much less in those decades than in the decades that were to come.[39]

Neither politicians nor administrators had seen devolution as an opportunity to pursue social goals in Northern Ireland. Devolution was simply a political expedient which had to be worked. The atmosphere was very different from that affecting debates on devolution in the 1970s.

This period of non-intervention is not wholly attributable to economic pressures and the lack of financial independence. The dominant Unionist view equated intervention with socialism and planning and was opposed to interference with free market forces. The influence of particular clerical and other pressure groups was evident in this as well as in the debate on education. The political dominance not only of Protestant Unionism but of a leadership of landed gentry hailing from the largely rural western areas of the province is an important factor. Although high unemployment and severe distress dominated Belfast and manufacturing industry, the maintenance of the Union remained the only real political issue and served to prevent serious challenges to the leadership at Stormont and to the policies being pursued there.

This political environment may explain why the Northern Ireland government in this period did not act as an aggressive advocate of Northern Ireland's needs. Stormont did not always see its role as that of securing whatever it could for Northern Ireland. The picture drawn by Buckland (1979) of financial negotiations between Stormont and Westminster is one of disagreement and uncertainty in the Unionist government rather than one of conflict, claim and counter-claim, and hard-fought negotiations between the two governments. The Ministry of Finance, indeed, appears to have been concerned to secure local authority support or to restrict expenditure more for their own sake than because of pressures from Westminster. The financial needs of Northern Ireland in this period were never a real source of crisis. Threats of resignation concerned the electoral system rather than social need.

While Westminster might have been more reluctant to increase financial subvention in this period than it did subsequently, it seems likely that more could have been achieved had the Northern Ireland government wished to push a more interventionist policy. Indeed, by 1938 the financial arrangement between Stormont and Westminster had been placed on a sounder footing under which a deficit on the Northern Ireland budget (provided it was not the result of a lower standard of taxation or a higher standard of social expenditure than those obtaining in Great Britain) would be met to enable the same standards of services to be adopted. But the barriers to parity provision were as much concerned with attitudes to welfare, with inertia and with the role of local government as with Westminster. The devolved government did not press to improve standards of provision until the post-war years.

(3) *Institutional Review and the Idea of Parity, 1943–48*
Although the impact of war on Northern Ireland was not the same as in Britain, the major reviews of policy in this period were influenced by war and developments in Britain.[40] Indeed, the absence of conscription and the appearance that Northern Ireland was not a full partner in the war effort were in themselves sufficient to create a demand for the reassertion of the Union and the duplication of

K*

developments in Britain. The shortages and disruptions of war affected Northern Ireland, forced and encouraged some modifications (e.g. in health), altered economic circumstances and led to some breakdown in socio-religious barriers (the common threat especially of air attack and the inevitable co-operation in opposing this threat).

The wartime situation itself caused some services to be re-organised on an emergency basis. And this change, as in Britain, could never be wholly reversed. The staff of wartime departments and services were in the post-war period integrated into pre-existing departmental spheres. The traditions, inertia and practice of those departments were bound to be challenged by new blood and by the impetus for change already created. Oliver has described the formation of the new Ministry of Health and Local Government in 1944 out of the wartime Ministry of Public Security and the local government side of the Ministry of Home Affairs:

> It was a matter of amalgamating a go-ahead group of miscellaneous staff who had carried out the wartime emergency services and who, in doing so, had developed unorthodox methods as well as a sense of camaraderie, with on the other hand a cadre of severely orthodox officials from one of the oldest traditional offices that derived from Dublin Castle and the Local Government Board for Ireland.[41]

If these factors created the environment for policy change, they do not explain why the review of policy extended so far. The immediate post-war years saw a batch of reports leading to major legislative developments affecting planning, housing, health services and education. In most cases some significant variations from contemporary British development were adopted. Thus although comparison with Britain was an underlying theme, it is also evident that local factors and individuals were important. Similarly, although the agreement on parity may have motivated a review of social policy, it does not explain particular details. Some importance must be attached to changes in the leadership of the Unionist Party. The administration of Mr J. M. Andrews is closely linked with this period. One element explaining the cessation of policy innovations was the reversion to old-style leadership in 1948.

(4) *Return to* Laissez-Faire, *1948–63*

Rather than building on the reforms of the previous five years, the period 1948–63 was one of retreat and return to *laissez-faire*. Some innovations came under threat and only survived in an environment which restricted their operation and effectiveness. Thus the Northern

Ireland Housing Trust—now regarded as a successful experiment and the model for the Housing Executive—was under threat of closure and was not given the financial and political support necessary if it was to reach its potential as an agency remedying deficiencies in the housing market.[42] In the personal social services permissive measures continued in areas where provision had become a statutory obligation in Great Britain. Leeway developed rather than declined, and reliance on the voluntary sector continued.

Perhaps the most remarkable reversions to type are in the failure to use planning powers or to set up consultative machinery with trade unions or the Republic of Ireland. The consolidation of Unionism under leadership of the landed upper classes involved a reassertion of opposition to planning and 'socialism' as well as reassertion of separate politico-religious standpoints. O'Neill provides a general comment on the premiership of Lord Brookeborough which is relevant here: 'As I see it the tragedy of his premiership was that he did not use his tremendous charm and his deep Orange roots to try and persuade his devoted followers to accept some reforms.' As a result of the backbench reaction to reform, the English-inspired Education Act, 1947, 'was his last act of political courage, and that had been in 1946, seventeen years before [his retirement]. The following year he had sacked his Minister of Education under extremist pressure and ever since then had played safe.'[43]

By 1954 the Joint Exchequer Board had accepted that in determining the imperial contribution it was relevant to consider current standards and the need to incur special expenditure to make up a substantial leeway on services and offset economic disadvantage. The lack of expansion of social provision cannot be attributed principally to financial constraints. While these constraints certainly existed, they were not tested by ambitious demands, and it is doubtful whether the demands made could be regarded as other than unambitious, reflecting a *laissez-faire* view of the role of government. Some flavour of the change from the immediate post-war situation is provided by Oliver:

The atmosphere in the country was being soured by the long-drawn-out campaign of terrorism. The attitude of many people in positions of authority or influence across the country was becoming negative and defensive. Appointments to senior positions in the Civil Service were timid; mediocre men were being encouraged; grey figures were beginning to predominate. I recall the head of the Civil Service advising me: 'Your main job is to keep your minister out of trouble.' . . . Local authorities—of both political complexions—were losing their wartime and post-war sense of purpose and willingness to collaborate; and a few were playing unworthy games in the location of new housing estates in relation to electoral wards and in the allocation of tenancies.[44]

Faced with and aware of such practices and the dangers they involved, the minister responsible was placed in a difficult position; in Oliver's words,

> She could grasp, every bit as well as we officials could and perhaps a lot better, the arguments in favour of changes in electoral affairs or in housing allocations or (more aptly) in the relationship between the two; but she could grasp even more clearly the political case for leaving such sensitive matters as they were.[45]

(5) *Economic Intervention and Rationalisation, 1963–72*

The change in premiership in 1963 coincided with an increased pace of change in the role of the state and its relationship with industry. Since 1959 certain developments had occurred which marked an increasing concern by the Northern Ireland government to intervene in the economy. Basic supposed barriers to planning were tested in the courts in 1959. Economic advisers had been appointed to produce a series of economic plans. The resources and powers of the state were increasingly used to aid economic rationalisation. This often involved encouragement of large-scale multi-national enterprise and therefore tended to damage smaller firms. At the same time the social objectives of the policy were always less clear than the economic objectives. The major inputs of resources were devoted to promoting industry, a motorway programme and the development of new towns and growth centres. All sections of the community did not benefit equally; indeed, there is little evidence that this was an intention in policy. The changing role of the state is more explicable as the development of a corporate approach in which the state identified with and responded to the particular demands of modern large-scale business enterprise. Some tension intruded into the long-established identity of interest with small firms, with family businesses, with local enterprises and with the agricultural/landed interest. The pattern of economic development was still strongly influenced by party considerations, and the government accordingly continued to adopt policies which would benefit its supporters most. Nevertheless, the tension which was created by this change from traditional stances was a factor in the loss of support experienced in turn by Prime Ministers O'Neill, Chichester-Clark and Faulkner. It contributed to the change in the nature of the Unionist 'coalition' and to the change in the balance of power within that coalition—the declining influence of the landed gentry and the growth of 'popular' leadership.

The increasing government intervention in this period is most simply illustrated by the growth of public expenditure per head. But, as has already been indicated, even in this period the dramatic growth is largely attributable to law-and-order expenditure. In the early years of this period of intervention public expenditure rose (between 1966–67 and 1968–69) from a lower *per capita* level than Wales or Scotland and at a slower rate than Scotland and at the same rate as Wales. The years between 1968–69 and 1971–72 saw Northern Ireland *per capita* expenditure catch up with and pass that for Wales. But in 1972–73, if the high expenditure on law and order is discounted, public expenditure per head in Northern Ireland was only fractionally above that of Scotland.

Table 25: Percentage Increase in Public Expenditure Per Head[46]

	England	Wales	Scotland	Northern Ireland
1966/7–1971/2	59	57	74	80
1966/7–1968/9	20	24	36	24
1968/9–1971/2	33	26	28	45

The picture is even more remarkable if public expenditure per head is looked at according to programme. In 1974–75 *per capita* expenditure in Northern Ireland was below that for Scotland in health and personal social services; education, libraries, science and arts; housing; environmental services; roads and transport. It was above that for Scotland in social security; law and order and protective services; trade, industry and employment; agriculture, fisheries, food and forestry; and other expenditure. With the exception of social security (where, perhaps, the benefits of parity are evident), expenditure comparisons with Scotland present a simple image of Northern Ireland concentrating on aids to industry, enterprise and the economy and to law and order, and neglecting the traditional social service areas of health, education, housing, the environment and the personal social services. Of course, the Scottish comparison exaggerates this picture; of course, many qualifications need to be made about such statistics; and, of course, some consideration of relative needs is necessary before these figures can be assessed. But in view of all the previous discussion presented in this book and, in particular, the evidence about social and economic circumstances in Northern Ireland, such a picture is hard to reconcile with an image of vigorous use of devolved powers to remedy social disadvantage.

A number of conclusions can be drawn from this. Firstly, the greater intervention of the 1960s involved programmes with a considerable time-lag in implementing and spending. Some programmes, such as housing, suffered substantial fluctuations during the period. Perhaps associated with this, the process of carrying through more ambitious plans relied on agencies (and particularly local government) which were not well staffed and equipped for such a role and sometimes did not wish to respond to pressures for more activity. At the same time the barriers to administrative reform were substantial and politically important to a Unionist government. Even the increased intervention of the 1960s hardly bears comparison with contemporary levels of activity in Scotland, given notions of parity and leeway. The style of the Northern Ireland government, while no longer *laissez-faire*, was a determined corporatism which still retained a conservatism in relation to large areas of social policy. In housing and the personal social services, for example, differences in legislation and policy indicated a continuing reluctance to intervene rather than an aggressive desire to make up leeway or achieve comparable standards.

(6) *Direct Rule, 1972–*

Although direct rule has brought Northern Ireland into the mainstream of British politics, there has not been a resulting end to variations in social and economic policy. The British government, in spite of some reluctance to legislate from afar, has introduced a series of orders which bring Northern Ireland legislation closer to that of Britain. But it has also tended to maintain 'continuity', for example in its approach to rent control and regulation. In spite of some exceptions in planning policy, as well as a proposed experiment with car seat belts and promised divorce law reform, there are few examples of innovation or attempts to devise policies in the light of local circumstances.

This division into stages of policy development indicates that while there are certain continuities in policy—the effects of political ideology, a dominant party and administrative (Civil Service) views—there are important sources of variation. In addition to those elements (referred to in the foregoing chapter) which led to differances between individual functional areas within social policy, there are important differences deriving from the changing role of government and its adoption of different economic strategies. The starkest contrast is the change from an essentially non-interventionist stance before the late 1950s to a modernisation/rationalisation interventionist approach subsequently. This change is reflected in the priority given to social policies and, more importantly, in the particular priorities within social policy—industrial training and retraining, the provision of infrastructure and direct aids to industry (indirectly to create employment), concentration of social expenditures in growth centres rather than in areas experiencing decline—an emphasis on programmes which could be seen as contributing to economic growth rather than on redistributive policies. Social policy development occurred essentially as an arm of economic strategy. The ideas of rationalisation and reorganisation were themselves introduced into local government and social service provision. Increasing professionalism has been evident in planning and social work. Pressures for a modernised management structure existed before 1969 and indicated a concern in the government for administrative efficiency rather than effective service delivery or public participation in decision-making.

Thus the business-management philosophy filtered through a wide range of activities. The government itself moved closer to business interests and developed stronger contacts with both sides of industry, holding more meetings with them and receiving more reports from them. The emphasis in policy shifted considerably, and it can be argued that this shift contributed to the loss of support for Stormont. Many of the theories explaining recent events in terms of relative deprivation, rising aspirations and unrealised expectations derive from the profound economic changes of the 1960s and the role of the state in facilitating change. Thus the effects of state intervention are apparent in the number of jobs created in state-aided industrial developments. The dominant role of these enterprises is apparent in their share of all new jobs. Associated problems are indicated by the high cost of each job created, by the prevalence of companies with head offices outside Northern Ireland, by the lack of responsiveness of unemployment rates to these developments, and by the increasing contrast between areas and households benefiting from changes and those unaffected, standing still, declining or appearing to decline through comparison.

Conclusion

The Government of Ireland Act, 1920, was not a plan for devolution. It was intended to be a temporary expedient pending a permanent solution to the Irish crisis. Not only was the act never revised as part of such a solution, but it was not revised to take account of the changing role of the state, economic crisis or social and political conflicts. Not until the 1970s did Westminster make demands which amounted to a revision of the 1920 act and prompted constitutional change. The coalition which had formed the Ulster Unionist Party found itself in 1920 with a legislative and administrative responsibility which it had not sought. The party and government had no programme or policy to implement. This situation has had no parallel in modern times. Today devolution, if not the aim of regionally based parties, has a place in political programmes. All political parties have policies and plans for how to use devolved power. In Scotland and Wales those plans are fundamentally connected with demands for greater control and better use of resources. The likelihood is that any devolved government would see its principal role as negotiating for a greater share of resources. It is probable that by 1979 this would also be the expected role in Northern Ireland—but it was not in 1920.

Nor were the political circumstances in Northern Ireland after 1920 ones which were favourable to the development of a political programme related to devolution. The establishment of authority, the politics of abstention, the political power of sectarian organisations, the Unionist–nationalist divide, the economic, social, political and ideological basis for political parties, all stultified and narrowed political debate. The Unionist government had a permanent majority and was largely able to ignore other parties and pressure groups. At the same time it could be influenced by pressures from within its own coalition to adopt discriminatory policies and was restricted in what policies it could adopt (for example in the reform of local government) by the nature and source of its political support. It adopted a stance which was anti-planning and anti-interventionist. No substantial opposition emerged on the basis of a social or economic programme to challenge this.

Although notions of parity with Britain and a step-by-step approach to policy were adopted, substantial differences in policy emerged. In some areas leeway between services has been apparent and at times has even increased. In others ideological divisions are apparent and a discriminatory model[47] of social policy is appropriate. Even in the 1960s, when substantial changes in the economic assumptions of the government were available, the impact of sectarianism on policy remained. At the same time economic changes have focused attention more explicitly on conflicts of interest and the distributional effects of public intervention.

All these comments tend to emphasise the extent to which factors internal to Northern Ireland are important in the analysis of devolution. Although it is undoubtedly false to imply that external constraints, and especially economic constraints, were not significant, it is equally false to present the experience of devolution as the inevitable outcome of external constraints. It may be possible to argue that devolved power has not always been used to best advantage or that the devolved government might have adopted better policies. But this cannot be attributed to external factors—to the constitutional position, to Westminster, or to parsimonious local authorities.

Without the benefit of access to cabinet papers, it would appear that in the post-war period the major determinants of policy were internal affairs rather than external political constraints. Continuing economic crisis was a dominant factor, and there were overriding financial and political constraints, but these did not impede basic political choices in Northern Ireland. Stormont was not in constant conflict with Westminster, and Westminster did not apply rigorous or detailed controls. Three alternative views could be related to this. Firstly, that Buckland's view of the inter-war period does not hold subsequently and there must be some doubt in general about his emphasis on external, financial and constitutional factors and on the role of local government. Secondly, that Buckland's view, while it holds for the inter-war years, does not hold for the post-war period, when internal factors are more significant, and is therefore not an adequate 'post-mortem' on the way devolution has worked. Thirdly, it may be that Stormont in both the inter-war and post-war periods adopted an avoidance strategy in relation to Westminster. There is ample evidence in the approach of the Ministry of Finance between the wars of a desire to assert independence and avoid a clash with Westminster. It is possible that such an approach was continued throughout and that the lack of conflict with Westminster and the apparent importance of internal factors is a product of the way the devolved government used its power.

Perhaps the most satisfactory view of devolution would incorporate elements of all three of these hypotheses. The operation of devolution in the inter-war period was marked by concern with the Union, a step-by-step approach in certain fundamental services, a concern to avoid conflicts with Westminster except on key political issues, a continuing economic and financial crisis and *ad hoc* responses to it, and a determined conservatism in economic affairs. In the post-war period financial arrangements were on a firmer footing, with the notions of parity and leeway well established. This change gave the Northern Ireland government more scope to adopt longer-term plans involving expenditure and left the way open for innovation in policy-making. Nevertheless, problems of political unity and ideology, including the role of local government, persisted and perhaps became more important as the opportunity to innovate increased and attitudes to the government's role in the economy changed. In spite of these changes, the most costly and difficult policies (given financial constraints) were established on a parity basis with the enactment of pensions legislation in 1925 and a health insurance scheme in 1930. Other policy areas have never been established in such a clear fashion, and some have lost ground since 1948. The image of pre-war financial contraints and post-war policy innovation and emphasis on parity is clearly not sufficient to explain how devolution has been used.

In conclusion, there are some other points about devolution that merit brief attention. Although it is clear that measures of the effects of devolution will form the most important part of any analysis, unfortunately they are also the most difficult to assess. While powers and formal constitutional arrangements are significant in determining what the effects of devolution will be, they are not the sole determinants. The debate about devolution to any area has to involve assessment of the nature of local politics and of political programmes and has to concern issues of legislative and administrative practice and the processes of policy-making and implementation. In the Northern Ireland context three factors stand out: the ideological basis of politics and continuing one-party control; the Westminster government's acceptance of a policy of non-involvement; and the resistance of problems to policy changes.

It may be argued that the first two of these factors are problems peculiar to Northern Ireland. While continuing one-party control could emerge in other regions of the United Kingdom, political divisions are less likely to be along sectarian lines, and debates about the substance of policy are likely to operate within and between parties. It is unlikely that the governing party would be so antipathetic to the trade union movement and to political debate. Nor would the government be faced with the political and social complications arising from the dominance of a single city and single local authority, as has been the case with Belfast. It may also be unlikely that Westminster would remain so detached from affairs in other regions. Finally, it is improbable that other devolved governments would be so passive or unwilling to clash with Westminster. Indeed, there is a greater likelihood that the politics of a devolved region would involve a regular, perhaps ritual, clash with Westminster designed to demonstrate political intent and assert autonomy. Such a clash would serve various political purposes and would yield greater results, for example in public expenditure terms, than have been achieved in Northern Ireland. But it would hardly achieve more than has been achieved by a minister with a cabinet seat at Westminster. Indeed, it is tempting to argue that Northern Ireland would have fared better had it had stronger representation at Westminster, including a Secretary of State with a seat in the cabinet. This would seem particularly likely if such a system could have operated alongside, and with the benefits of, administrative devolution. Logically it could be argued that the threat of secession or devolution and the strength of an organised regional lobby in parliament are likely to serve a region (including Scotland) better than devolution itself. The proposed increase in Northern Ireland's parliamentary representation from twelve to seventeen seats will provide in the future some indication of the validity of this point of view.

But the clearest impression of devolution arising from the Northern Ireland situation is the lack of impact it has made on the regional problem. There has been considerable progress made in certain fields; for example, the gaps in health and incomes have narrowed. But the gap remains in most of the standard measures of social and economic malaise. At the same time intra-regional differences and social class inequalities remain. Devolution has made remarkably little impact on social and economic differences. It may be that this situation arises because of the lack of ambition and energy of the devolved government or because of the absence of economic and taxation powers—though the latter explanation is unconvincing unless a totally different economic structure is envisaged. Without developing a fully controlled, planned economy, greater powers to offer incentives and advice does not amount to greater control. The kinds of policies operating to encourage private investment do not enable the government to exercise control over the regional economy. Without this control, the devolved government will fail to remedy underlying issues of the regional problem, and, conversely, any change in relative circumstances is likely to reflect the lack of control which governments have. Resistance to change does not only derive from lack of control over the economy, it also derives from the resilience of institutions, attitudes and traditional conventions to governments. It is easier to legislate than to ensure that legislation is implemented, especially if it is to be implemented in a way that is not easily adaptable to the status quo. This predicament is most clearly evidenced in the measures which, introduced in a sectarian society, serve to sustain divisions or are interpreted and used differently by different sections of the community. Deeply held social and economic and sectarian prejudices are not so easily challenged by formal government actions.

One of the principal lessons of devolution in Northern Ireland is that the adoption of a devolved system itself solves nothing. It is how devolution operates and how other institutions develop alongside it that determines the nature of remaining problems. This, in turn, involves other considerations: how the economy as a whole develops, how Westminster responds, how social policies and social institutions sustain or challenge inequalities and discriminatory practices, and, in relation to these, how far the institutions of government themselves reinforce divisions, redraw divisions or fulfil an integrative role. If it is too much to expect devolution to solve the regional problem in terms of economic and social provision, perhaps more attention should be given to the style of government, the quality of administration, the rights of citizens, and participation in decisions. Devolution in Northern Ireland too often failed in these respects, and it would clearly be unwise to ignore them in any overall assessment, just as it would be inadequate to respond by arguing that only administrative devolution is desirable or by discounting the great variety of ways in which the experience of Northern Ireland offers positive as well as negative elements to debates on devolution elsewhere.

12

Postscript:
Future Forms of Government

ALL the major political parties in Northern Ireland are agreed on the desirability of a devolved legislature. Its desirability is justified by reference to the tradition of a devolved government and parliament responsible for internal matters, distinctive laws and patterns of administration, access to local decision-makers, and the geographical separateness of Northern Ireland. Since the reorganisation of local government there has also been a reiteration of the argument, originally propounded by the Macrory Review Body, 'that the centralisation of services assumed the existence of Stormont as a top-tier authority'. The British political parties have also strongly supported devolved institutions. The political debate on future devolved institutions has so far concentrated on the question of power-sharing, but there are three main problem areas: the powers of an Assembly, the supervision and control of an Assembly and Executive, and the nature of the Executive. In the Northern Ireland Constitutional Convention of 1975–76 the parties failed to explore the various constitutional possibilities in the first two areas.

The Powers of an Assembly

The political parties in Northern Ireland more or less agree that a devolved administration should have as comprehensive a range of functions as was laid down in the Government of Ireland Act, 1920. Control of political power is at the heart of the dispute over new institutions, and neither of the two main groups trusts each other with regard to the exercise of certain powers. Thus there is a case for the removal of controversial powers from a devolved Assembly, either temporarily or permanently. The British government has already made clear its intention to retain legislative and executive responsibility for elections and the courts on a permanent basis and to exercise responsibility over the police, prisons and emergency powers for some considerable time to come. A reduction in the powers of a devolved government would also help to emphasise the regional and local nature of the administration and perhaps concentrate its work on social and environmental policies. The drawbacks of this development are the increased workload which it will place upon Westminster and the likelihood that, once established, an Assembly would push strongly for an extension of its powers. An Assembly with fewer powers than the Stormont parliament is not an attractive prospect for Northern Ireland's political parties, but it might be worth considering as an interim measure. Another consideration is that an administration with a majority (i.e. a Unionist) Executive might be more acceptable to the SDLP and other minority groups if its functions and powers were drastically reduced.

An alternative is a system of executive devolution which would establish an Assembly with no legislative powers but with control over the administration of services and the allocation of resources between services. In 1978–79 a system of executive devolution was proposed for Wales which would have involved Westminster laying down legislative guidelines and a Welsh Assembly filling in the details through delegated legislation.[1] Executive devolution could operate with a committee responsible for each subject area and need not require an Executive or cabinet, although some type of central co-ordinating committee may be necessary.

A scheme along these lines was recommended in 1977 by Mr James Molyneaux, leader of the Ulster Unionists at Westminster, although it has been rather misleadingly referred to as a proposal for administrative devolution (Northern Ireland continues to have administrative devolution through the Stormont departments). This proposal envisages an elected Assembly with a committee system responsible for a range of executive and administrative decisions at present carried out by ministers and Stormont departments and relating largely to the old local government services, housing, education, planning and roads. Proposals along these lines tend to be associated with closing the gap between district councils and the Westminster parliament and have often become mixed up with proposals for local government reform. It is not clear that there is room for a regional tier of local administration assuming supervisory functions over area boards, the Housing Executive and district councils operating below the level of Stormont departments.

A clearer alternative is for one regional council or three to five large local authorities with responsibility for direct provision of services. As local authorities they would naturally work through a committee system, and this would involve the transfer of some major services back to local government.

Under all the schemes for executive devolution or local government reform, the Secretary of State and his ministerial team would remain in office and Westminster would remain the source of all legislation. The Conservative Party and the Unionist Party have shown interest in these proposals, but the SDLP is not very enthusiastic and is particularly opposed to the return of substantial powers to local councils. There is little in the past history of local government to suggest that it would perform a useful role in producing a political solution.

Control and Supervision

An important topic that was not discussed in the Constitutional Convention was the usefulness or desirability of veto mechanisms. There are two possible types of veto: an external veto by the British government and parliament over legislative and executive power, and an internal veto over legislative power and possibly executive power. It is quite clear that in any future Northern Ireland Constitution Bill, unlike the 1920 act, the supervisory powers of the Westminster government and parliament will be clearly spelled out. A strict legislative veto could allow the Secretary of State to send a bill back to the devolved Assembly if it was unacceptable on policy grounds and ultimately to set it aside. The Secretary of State could also have the power to issue directives prohibiting executive action or requiring a particular course of action.

Alternatively, legislation from the Assembly or 'divisive' legislation could require an affirmative resolution from the Westminster parliament. Despite the desire in 1975–76 of the United Ulster Unionist Coalition majority in the Convention to limit the role of the Secretary of State and Westminster's right of intervention,[2] it is likely that Westminster will have strong veto powers over any new Assembly and Executive, however constituted. Whether a very strict veto mechanism and a declaration of intent on its use would prove a sufficient guarantee to the SDLP to make a majority or coalition cabinet acceptable is a question so far not discussed.

The second type of veto is by internal devices, sometimes called blocking mechanisms. The most simple form would require that legislation had the support of 75 per cent of the members of the Assembly. This would help protect minority interests and promote compromise policies. This device would probably reduce the amount of legislation, but that may be seen as part of the value of the system. In practice it would mean that Opposition members representing the Catholic community would have to support a measure if it was to become law. The provision could apply either to all legislation or only to specified important issues.[3]

A more customary institutional method of giving weighted representation to various interests is through a second chamber or Upper House. A second chamber could be weighted to give greater representation to members of the minority community. It would be following the example of many other countries if the Upper House were given the power to reject and amend legislation passed by the Lower House. This could involve either a veto for a lengthy period of time or a permanent veto on legislation on divisive matters.

It is perhaps surprising that the SDLP has remained largely unconcerned that a Unionist majority would always be assured of having legislation passed in an Assembly. The SDLP may be assuming that participation in an Executive would be based on collective responsibility and that there would have to be agreement on all legislative proposals. On the other hand, Unionists have not regarded their majority in the legislature as making participation by the SDLP in an Executive acceptable.

Discussion on an Executive has emphasised the need for the principle of collective responsibility rather than the possibility of any form of internal veto; this latter alternative would be a cumbersome device, liable to produce conflict and frustrate decision-making. Some consideration has been given, however, to a system of checks and balances through the creation of a Council of State, either nominated or elected on proportionate lines, with either executive powers or veto powers on controversial subjects.[4]

The Nature of the Executive

The nature of the Executive has proved a crucial question for British governments interested in replacing the old Stormont system of cabinet-making with an alternative which would provide a way for the minority to participate. In the Northern Ireland Constitution Act, 1973, the British government rejected statutory formulae such as a proportional representation cabinet or the reservation of a number of seats for majority and minority representatives. Instead the Secretary of State held negotiations with the parties to reach agreement on a broadly based Executive. The Secretary of State had to be satisfied that the Executive would be widely accepted throughout the community and that it constituted a basis for government by consent. In practice this meant that the Executive had to contain members from parties representing both sections of the community; it also meant that the Executive as a whole had to have majority support in the Assembly. This system maintains an

Opposition but does not necessarily solve the major difficulty of power-sharing schemes, i.e. procedure for resolving disputes. Does the Chief Executive (i.e. the Northern Ireland premier) have the final say? Is there a majority vote, or does each party have a vote? Can the doctrine of collective responsibility be enforced?

A power-sharing Executive is only viable if regular agreement is possible, if there is a significant degree of consensus, and if it has support among the population. The Convention of 1975–76 demonstrated that these requirements were lacking. In the final Convention Report the UUUC majority rejected any system of compulsory coalition in executive government and called power-sharing an unnatural system of government. They also objected to SDLP participation because of that party's aspiration to an all-Ireland Republic.[5] At the reconvened Convention in February and March 1976 the UUUC refused to negotiate on three important issues: partnership in cabinet between UUUC and SDLP; participation of any group in government as of right; and an institutionalised Irish dimension.[6] They offered the SDLP equal opposition participation on parliamentary committees. Since the Convention the Official Unionist Party and the Democratic Unionist Party have maintained this position. The idea of temporary voluntary coalition put forward by Mr Craig at the Convention attracted little support then or since.

The British government can be criticised for not taking a more active role in directing the activities of the Convention. The Convention was a scene for political confrontation rather than a forum for constitutional discussion, and scarcely any attention was paid to alternative forms of government, blocking devices, etc.[7] However, since the failure of the Convention informal political discussions have come no nearer to breaking the deadlock over power-sharing.

Northern Ireland is not unique in having deep political cleavages based on religious, ethnic and cultural differences; and several societies, including some in Western Europe, have evolved power-sharing systems or forms of what is usually referred to as 'consociational democracy' in order to provide stable government as the appropriate response to internal conflict. This involves rejecting the competitive practices of the British system, recognising that political groups cater above all for their own particular ideological clienteles, and accepting that elections result in little change. Commentators on consociational democracy have identified factors which are conducive to this form of government. Elites must have the ability to transcend divisions and join in common efforts with elites of rival sub-cultures; this, in turn, depends on their commitment to the maintenance of the system and to the improvement of its cohesion and stability; and the successful operation of the system is based on the assumption that the elites understand the perils of political fragmentation.[8] The prospects for realising these preconditions in Northern Ireland are not high. In a sense the basic assumption is not obvious in Northern Ireland because the politicians can remain at loggerheads, knowing that the alternative is not chaos but a continuation of rule by Westminster and an efficient Civil Service.

Alternatives to Devolution

The political deadlock over new devolved institutions has led to much discussion of more radical political solutions. These can be classified under four headings: an autonomous united Ireland, repartition, an independent Ulster, and integration with Great Britain.[9] A united Ireland is the immediate aim of republican groups and is the long-term aspiration of the SDLP. The main obstacle to this solution is not so much the views of the British government as the views of the Protestant population of Northern Ireland, who are totally opposed to any such development. While a united Ireland may be long-term aspiration of Catholics, in the border poll of 1973 only 6,463 people (0.6 per cent of the electorate) voted for Northern Ireland joining with the Republic of Ireland outside the United Kingdom. The anti-partition parties boycotted the poll, arguing that the issue should be determined by the people of Ireland as a whole.[10] The Government of the Republic of Ireland, although maintaining lip-service to the ideal of a united Ireland, is probably not too anxious to absorb Northern Ireland's population and problems in the immediate future. It has been estimated that the takeover by the Republic of the United Kingdom financial support for Northern Ireland would absorb 15 per cent of the Gross National Product.[11]

There have been suggestions for unification based on a federal system: either a federation of two areas, Northern and Southern Ireland, or an establishment based on parliaments for the four historical provinces, Ulster becoming a nine-county province with roughly equal numbers of Protestants and Catholics. This latter scheme is advocated by Provisional Sinn Féin. However, a federal Ireland is hardly a more attractive proposition to Ulster Protestants than a centralised state.

Repartition would involve redrawing the border to transfer part of Northern Ireland's territory to the Republic of Ireland. The major problem with the mechanics of repartition is the fact that the Protestants and Catholics are dispersed together throughout Northern Ireland. The transfer of areas with Catholic majorities adjacent to the border, i.e. South Down, South Armagh and the western parts of Counties Tyrone and Londonderry, would enable 161,000 Catholics to live in the Republic but would also include 89,000 Protestants.[12] This arrangement would still leave some 300,000 Catholics in a truncated Northern Ireland. Any scheme for repartition would necessarily involve some voluntary transfer of populations, with large-scale upheavals and disruption of employment and commercial and agricultural activity. Repartition would not mean the end of partition nor the end of a divided community in Northern Ireland and might only encourage militant republican groups to make a final push to end partition. It is only if there was civil war and/or death and destruction on a massive scale that serious thought might be given to population transfers or repartition.

The arguments for an independent Ulster stress the value of producing a common allegiance to the new state transcending the present loyalties of the majority and minority. Negotiated independence, to be viable, would have to have a wide degree of support from the political parties. The question of power-sharing in government would have to be faced; but, with the SDLP giving full support to the new state, the loyalist slogan of 'No power-sharing with Republicans' would no longer be valid, and loyalists might be willing to share power. It is also likely that any such scheme for independence would have to have safeguards against any change, perhaps with guarantees provided externally by Britain, the Republic of Ireland or the EEC.

One of the major obstacles that has been raised against negotiated independence has been its financial viability. Those advocating independence usually assume that external financial aid would be available from Britain and the EEC.

There must be serious doubts as to whether an independent Ulster would be a stable state. Would both national traditions identify with the new state? It is perhaps unlikely that a majority of Catholics would drop their aspiration for a united Ireland. Apart from some interest shown by certain loyalist groups,[13] there has been as yet little support for independence among Unionists, who tend to see it as a step towards a united Ireland and a threat to their standard of living. Similarly, the SDLP is somewhat lukewarm, although prepared to explore the matter further.

It can also be noted that Northern Ireland could be forced into an independence solution if there was a unilateral withdrawal by Britain. A Westminster announcement of an intention to withdraw might put the onus on Northern Ireland politicians to come to some form of agreement on independence.

The complete integration of Northern Ireland into the Westminster system would mean either that British legislation would apply to Northern Ireland or that separate legislation would be enacted through the normal Westminster processes. The system of administrative devolution through existing Northern Ireland central departments would probably remain, with the departments operating as divisions of a Northern Ireland Office. However, complete integration is unacceptable to the British government and also to the Dublin government. The British government's view is that integration would be offensive to the minority community in Northern Ireland and is unlikely to produce a decrease in IRA activity. In addition, many English MPs have no wish to bring the troublesome politics of Northern Ireland more fully into the Westminster system. Finally, the main political parties in Northern Ireland would prefer some form of devolution.

In practice the present form of direct rule is little different from complete integration except for the legislative process, and in the present circumstances direct rule is likely to continue as the only workable form of government which offends neither community too much and has tacit acceptance.

There is little prospect of any dramatic political advance in Northern Ireland, and the only possible future developments appear to be in two directions: firstly, a modification of direct rule machinery to allow the Northern Ireland Committee at Westminster to take the committee stage of Northern Ireland legislation, or the possible appointment of one or two Northern Ireland MPs as junior ministers in the Northern Ireland Office; or secondly, the creation of a regional administrative council or a reorganisation of local government. The new Conservative government may attempt some form of local government reorganisation, but any attempt to give increased powers to local authorities would produce strong opposition from the SDLP. There is little sign of any compromise emerging between Northern Ireland's main political parties. The prospects of more liberal Official Unionist policies or leadership is unlikely when the party is confronted with a strong challenge from the Democratic Unionists. The SDLP also has little room for manoeuvre now that it is facing policy divisions within the party and increasing disillusionment among its supporters with the lack of political advance.

The form of government that Northern Ireland will have in the future is still open to question. The experience of Northern Ireland's political past tells us more about the intransigence of political attitudes than the appropriateness of particular political institutions. It is difficult for the analyst to isolate the effects of a particular set of political institutions or constitutional arrangements; they are too closely interlinked with other factors. The major influence on government, administration and policy-making have probably been the political intransigence of both politicians and electors and the long-term economic problems that have beset the province. These fundamental elements of the political life of Northern Ireland imposed a severe restriction on the possible success of the system of legislative devolution. Devolution as practised in Northern Ireland did little to mitigate dogmatic and ideological views or reduce conflict, although it may be judged to have been more successful in the economic and administrative fields. Irrespective of what form of government might be introduced in the future, the fundamental problems of ideological division and the economy are likely to remain. It is at least possible to say that these problems are internal to Northern Ireland and are unlikely to be resolved by any particular form of relationship with Great Britain or with the Republic of Ireland. It seems clear that they must also place a limitation on what can be expected from any new form of devolution or constitutional arrangement as a permanent political solution.

Appendix

Ministerial Responsibilities, 1979

Following the Conservative victory in the general election of May 1979, Mr Humphrey Atkins was appointed Secretary of State for Northern Ireland and a new team of ministers took office. The division of their ministerial responsibilities is as follows.

Minister	*Responsibilities*
Michael Allison (Minister of State)	Northern Ireland Office matters; prisons; police; compensation for criminal injuries; Department of Health and Social Services
Hugh Rossi (Minister of State)	Department of Finance; Department of Manpower Services; Civil Service
Philip Goodhart (Parliamentary Under-Secretary)	Department of the Environment; House of Commons spokesman for Department of Education
Giles Shaw (Parliamentary Under-Secretary)	Department of Commerce; Department of Agriculture
Lord Elton (Parliamentary Under-Secretary)	Department of Education; House of Lords spokesman on all Northern Ireland matters

Notes

Chapter 1
THE STORMONT–WESTMINSTER RELATIONSHIP
(pp. 5–29)

Principal sources
Birch (1956); Birrell (1973); Brett (1970); Callaghan (1973); Calvert (1968); Cook (1953); Donaldson (1955, 1959); Furness (1975); Gibson (1972); Lawrence (1956, 1965 a); McBirney (1967); Mansergh (1936); Narain (1973); Neill (1953 a, b); Newark (1940, 1948, 1953, 1955); O'Neill (1972); Robson (1955); Rose (1971); Simpson (1977); Wallace (1967, 1971); Whale (1970); Wilson (1955 a, b, c)

'The Finances of Northern Ireland' in *Ulster Year Book*, HMSO Belfast, xix–xxxvi
The Constitution of Northern Ireland, HMSO, Belfast 1969
'The Links between the National Insurance Funds of Great Britain and Northern Ireland' in *Commission on the Constitution: Minutes of Evidence, III: Northern Ireland*, HMSO, London 1971, Appendix III
Northern Ireland: Financial Arrangements and Legislation, HMSO, London 1973 (Cmnd 4998)
[Kilbrandon Report] *Royal Commission on the Constitution, 1969–73*, Vol. I, HMSO, London 1973 (Cmnd 5460) (Chapter 29 deals with finance)
Northern Ireland Office, *Northern Ireland: Discussion Paper: Finance and the Economy*, HMSO, London 1974

1. *The Constitution of Northern Ireland*, HMSO, Belfast 1969.
2. McBirney (1967), 10.
3. Newark (1953), 11.
4. Donaldson (1955), 41.
5. Rose (1971), 119.
6. Lawrence (1956), 15.
7. Jennings (1959), 157.
8. Oliver (1978 a), 41, cites the example of a revaluation measure in 1932.
9. For details of this process see *Commission on the Constitution: Written Evidence, 3: Government Departments of Northern*

Ireland, HMSO, London 1969 [hereafter cited as *Comm. Constitution: Govt Depts NI* (1969)].

10. Barritt and Carter (1962), 109.
11. Rose (1971), 97.
12. Callaghan (1973), 2.
13. *Ibid.*, 1.
14. Letter from Home Secretary, 16 Jan. 1945, CAB 4/611/5.
15. For a full discussion of this convention see Calvert (1968), 94–103.
16. Mansergh (1936), 173.
17. Rose (1971), 117.
18. O'Neill (1972), 47.
19. Callaghan (1973), 2.
20. Memorandum by Prime Minister, 7 Nov. 1947, CAB 4/735/5.
21. Rose (1971), 117.
22. *Hansard*, dli, 1686 (25 Oct. 1967).
23. Wilson (1971), 695.
24. *Northern Ireland: Text of a Communiqué and Declaration issued after a Meeting held at 10 Downing Street on August 19th, 1969*, HMSO, London 1969 (Cmnd 4154), 3.
25. Callaghan (1973), 62.
26. [Hunt Report] *Report of the Advisory Committee on Police in Northern Ireland*, HMSO, Belfast 1969 (Cmd 535).
27. Callaghan (1973), 66.
28. For a description of the financial relationship see 'The Finances of Northern Ireland' in *Ulster Year Book*, HMSO, Belfast 1950, xix–xxxvi, and [Kilbrandon Report] *Royal Commission on the Constitution, 1969–73*, Vol. I, HMSO, London 1973 (Cmnd 5460), Chapter 29. For further discussion of the period 1921–64 see Lawrence (1965 a).
29. 'Finances of Northern Ireland', xxviii.
30. 'The Links between the National Insurance Funds of Great Britain and Northern Ireland' in *Commission on the Constitution: Minutes of Evidence, III: Northern Ireland*, HMSO, London 1971, Appendix III, 186–7 [hereafter cited as *Comm. Constitution: NI* (1971)].
31. *Ibid.*, 17.
32. Source: Northern Ireland Office, *Northern Ireland: Discussion Paper: Finance and the Economy*, HMSO, London 1974, 31.
33. Wallace (1967), 161.
34. *Comm. Constitution: NI* (1971), 17–18.
35. *Northern Ireland Development Programme, 1970–75*, HMSO, Belfast 1970, 156–9.
36. O'Neill (1972), 39.
37. See Robson (1955).
38. For fuller discussion see Isles and Cuthbert (1957), 301–7, 412–29.
39. Simpson (1971), 526.
40. For full details of the work of the Cabinet Office see *Comm. Constitution: Govt Depts NI* (1969), 15–17.

41. *Comm. Constitution: NI* (1971), 17.
42. CAB 4/557/15, 5 Oct. 1943.
43. Kilbrandon Report, I (1973), 392.
44. For details of cases see Calvert (1968), Chapter 15.
45. CAB 4/611/5, 8, Jan. 1945. These cabinet papers include a memorandum giving a full summary of the debate on religious instruction from 1923 to 1945.
46. Donaldson (1959), 199.
47. *Ibid.*, 198.
48. Palley (1972), 390.

Chapter 2
CABINET GOVERNMENT AT STORMONT
(pp. 30–49)
Principal sources
Bleakley (1974); Faulkner (1978); Harbinson (1973); O'Neill (1972)

1. *Constitution of NI* (1969), section 8.5.
2. Calvert (1968), 350.
3. Brookeborough Memoirs, *Sunday News,* 4 Feb. 1968.
4. Faulkner (1978), 84–5.
5. For a detailed account see Corkey, 106.
6. *Parliamentary Debates (Northern Ireland House of Commons),* xxvii, 259–94 (22 Feb. 1944) [hereafter cited as *Parl. Deb. (C)*].
7. For further details see Akenson (1973), 185–8, and statements in *Belfast Newsletter,* 5 Dec. 1949.
8. *Parl. Deb. (C),* lxvi, 830 (2 May 1967).
9. O'Neill (1972), 92–3.
10. *News Letter,* 3 Apr. 1965.
11. Sources: Harbinson (1973), 188–209; Chubb (1970), 173.
12. Sources: Harbinson (1973), 188–209; Chubb (1970), 175; Punnett (1971), 97.
13. *Parl. Deb. (C),* xlvii, 1103 (13 Dec. 1960).
14. Ervine (1949), 372.
15. *Ibid.*, 562.
16. Harbinson (1973), 139.
17. O'Neill (1972), 42–3.
18. Faulkner (1978), 28.
19. Bleakley (1974), 64.
20. Harbinson (1973), 137.
21. Brookeborough Memoirs, *Sunday News,* 4 Feb. 1968.
22. *Belfast Newsletter,* 29 Apr. 1943.
23. CAB 4/711/7, 10 Mar. 1947.
24. CAB 4/690/24, 14 Nov. 1946.
25. O'Neill (1972), 40–1.
26. *Ibid.*, 70.
27. *Parl. Deb. (C),* lix, 255–75 (3 Feb. 1965).

28. *Ibid.,* 280.
29. O'Neill (1972), 84–5.
30. Faulkner (1978), 40–1.
31. Boyd (1972 a), 59.
32. O'Neill (1972), 150–4.
33. *Irish Times,* 12 Aug. 1970.
34. Brookeborough Memoirs, *Sunday News,* 4 Feb. 1968.
35. CAB 4/616/5, 21 Feb. 1945.
36. *Parl. Deb. (C),* xxxvi, 263 (5 Mar. 1952).
37. *Irish Times,* 21 Apr. 1969.
38. *Comm. Constitution: Govt Depts NI* (1969), 15–17.
39. O'Neill (1972), 71–3.
40. Wallace (1970), 80.
41. Bleakley (1974), 96–7.
42. *Parl. Deb. (C),* xxxvii, 494–5 (26 Mar. 1953).
43. Evidence of the Minister of Commerce, *Report of the Select Committee on Public Accounts for the Year 1962–63,* HMSO, Belfast 1964 (HC 1575), 253–6.
44. O'Neill (1972), 152.
45. Boyd (1972 a), 58.
46. Callaghan (1973), 77.

Chapter 3
THE STORMONT PARLIAMENT
(pp. 50–67)
Principal sources
Donaldson (1958, 1967); J. Kennedy (1967); Magill (1965); Newark (1972); Whyte (1973)

Standing Orders of the House of Commons: Public Business, HMSO, Belfast 1969 (HC 2013)

1. For details see *Standing Orders of the House of Commons: Public Business,* HMSO, Belfast 1969 (HC 2013).
2. The data for the tables in this chapter are taken from the Northern Ireland *Parliamentary Debates* (Commons and Senate) for selected years to give some overall impression of the work of parliament in the period 1921–72.
3. Donaldson (1967), 37.
4. See *Second Report of the Joint Select Committee on Consolidated Bills, Health Services Bill and Welfare Services Bill,* HMSO, Belfast 1970 (S 20), 73.
5. *Report of the Joint Select Committee on Opposed Bills on the Magee University College, Londonderry, Bill,* HMSO, Belfast 1969.
6. Harbinson (1973), 119.
7. The following examples are taken from the regular reports of the Select Committee on Public Accounts, HMSO, Belfast.

8. *Special and First Reports of the Select Committee on Public Accounts for the Year 1969–70*, HMSO, Belfast 1971 (HC 2107), 18.
9. *Ibid.*
10. *The Future Development of the Parliament and Government of Northern Ireland*, HMSO, Belfast 1971 (Cmd 560).
11. Donaldson (1958), 142.
12. *Ibid.*, 153.
13. Magill (1965).
14. Sayers (1955), 60.
15. Magill (1965), 354.
16. CAB 4/646/5, 3 Dec. 1945.
17. *Parl. Deb. (C)*, xxxiii, 1109 (14 Jun. 1949).
18. Whyte (1973), 104.

Chapter 4
DIRECT RULE: GOVERNMENT WITHOUT STORMONT
(pp. 68–89)
Principal sources
Devlin (1975); Ditch (1977); Fisk (1975); Kelly (1972); Maguire (1975); Windlesham (1973)

The Future of Northern Ireland: A Paper for Discussion, HMSO, London 1972
Northern Ireland: Constitutional Proposals, HMSO, London 1973 (Cmnd 5259)
The Northern Ireland Constitution, HMSO, London 1974 (Cmnd 5675)

1. Faulkner (1978), 83.
2. Kelly (1972), 51.
3. Faulkner (1978), 152.
4. *Political Settlement*, HMSO, Belfast 1972 (Cmd 568), 4–5.
5. Windlesham (1973), 269.
6. *Ibid.*, 264.
7. Darlington in *Fortnight*, 8 Jun. 1973.
8. Windlesham (1973), 264.
9. Darlington in *Fortnight*, 8 Jun. 1973.
10. *Northern Ireland: Financial Arrangements and Legislation*, HMSO, London 1973 (Cmnd 4998).
11. *Northern Ireland: Constitutional Proposals*, HMSO, London 1973 (Cmnd 5259).
12. *Northern Ireland Assembly: Official Reports*, 3 vols, HMSO, Belfast 1974.
13. For accounts of negotiations on the formation of the Executive and the Sunningdale Agreement see Faulkner (1978), 187–238, and Devlin (1975), 29–51.

14. *NI Assembly: Official Report*, iii, 1153–8 (22 May 1974).
15. *NI: Finance and the Economy* (1974), 20.
16. *NI: Constitutional Proposals* (1973), para. 88.
17. *NI Assembly: Official Report*, ii, 126 (24 Jan. 1974).
18. *Ibid.*, 761–2 (12 Feb. 1974).
19. Devlin (1975), 3.
20. R. Bradford, 'Decline and Fall', *News Letter*, 1 Apr. 1975.
21. See Fisk (1975), 225–48.
22. *Hansard*, cmxv, 2428–32 (23 Jul. 1976).
23. *First Special Report from the Joint Committee on Statutory Instruments*, HMSO, London 1978 (HC 169), 10.
24. *Northern Ireland Constitutional Convention: Report*, HMSO, London 1975.

Chapter 5
THE POLITICAL SYSTEM
(pp. 90–109)
Principal sources
Boal and Buchanan (1969); Elliott (1973); Graham (1972); Harbinson (1966, 1973); Knight (1974, 1975); Laver (1976 a); Lawrence and Elliott (1975); Lawrence *et al.* (1975); McAllister (1975 a, b, 1976 a, b, 1977; McAllister and Wilson (1977); Rutan (1967); Sayers (1955, 1969); Scott (1971); Wright (1973)

1. Source: Elliott (1973), 96.
2. For details see Lawrence *et al.* (1975), 56.
3. Lawrence *et al.* (1975), 3.
4. *Ibid.*, 5.
5. *Belfast Newsletter*, 13 Jul. 1927, quoted in Mansergh (1936), 133.
6. Lawrence *et al.* (1975), 76.
7. McAllister (1975 a), 18–19; Laver (1976 b), 218–24.
8. Heslinga (1971), 58.
9. Laird in *Fortnight*, 30 Nov. 1973.
10. Sayers (1955), 55.
11. Harbinson (1973), 213.
12. Sartori (1969).
13. Wallace (1971), 69.
14. For a classification of Ulster Unionism along these lines see Wright (1973).
15. McAllister (1975 b), 356.
16. B. White, 'The Unionist Party—Where Does the Power Lie?', *Belfast Telegraph*, 3 Mar. 1970.
17. McAllister (1975 b), 357.
18. Birrell (1972).
19. McAllister (1976 a).
20. Source: *Ulster Unionist Yearbook*, UUC, Belfast 1971, 112–13.

Chapter 6
PRESSURE GROUPS
(pp. 110–131)
Principal sources
Beckett (1957); Bell (1970, 1973)) Bleakley (1953); Bowden (1976); Boyd (1972 b); Coogan (1970); Corkey; Daly (1973); Dewar *et al.* (1967); Gray (1972); Griffiths (1975); Hurley (1970); Irish Council of Churches: Roman Catholic Church Group on Social Problems, *Violence in Ireland* (1976); D. Kennedy (1957, 1967); Macaulay (1970); McCarthy (1973); McDowell (1975); Roberts (1971); Sams (1964); Sibbett (1939); Weiner (1976)

Industrial Relations in Northern Ireland: Report of the Review Body, 1971–74, HMSO, Belfast 1974

1. For an account of the development of education policy see Akenson (1973).
2. For an account of the role of the United Education Committee see Corkey.
3. *Report of the Ministry of Education, 1925–26* HMSO, Belfast 1926 (HC 107), 9.
4. CAB 4/593/3, 20 Aug. 1944.
5. CAB 3/647/7, 3 Dec. 1945.
6. Kennedy (1971), 37.
7. CAB 4/647/6, 5 Oct. 1945.
8. See Annual Reports of the General Assembly of the Presbyterian Church, Belfast 1971–73.
9. See 'Catholics at the Crossroads', *Belfast Telegraph,* 11 Aug. 1975.
10. Daly (1973).
11. D. Wilson, 'Church and Conflict', *Hibernia,* 12 Dec. 1975; D. Kennedy (1967).
12. Callaghan (1973), 72.
13. Birrell *et al.* (1979), 493.
14. McAllister (1975 b), 356.
15. For a history of the Orange Order see Sibbett (1939) and Gray (1972).
16. See Dewar *et al.* (1967), 18.
17. Roberts (1971).
18. Dewar *et al.* (1967), 188.
19. Gray (1972), 221.
20. Birrell *et al.* (1979), 493.
21. Quoted in Wallace (1971), 70.
22. See Corkey.
23. *Belfast Telegraph,* 14 Dec. 1949.
24. Sayers (1955), 69.
25. Dewar *et al.* (1967), 196.
26. M. Smyth, 'The Orangemen March Forward to Defend Cherished Freedom', *Belfast Telegraph,* 9 Jul. 1976.

27. Bleakley (1953).
28. *Fifty-Eighth Annual Report, National Executive of the ICTUC,* Dublin 1952, 154.
29. *Parl. Deb. (C),* lii, 1233–4 (14 Nov. 1962).
30. Sams (1964), 269.
31. For a detailed account see Boyd (1972 b), Appendix 2.
32. Bleakley (1953), 163–4.
33. For a detailed study see Fisk (1975).
34. 'MacMoney' in *Fortnight,* 9 Jan. 1976.
35. *Ibid.*
36. *Comm. Constitution: NI* (1971), 147–61.
37. See Weiner (1976).
38. 'Glossary of Loyalist Organisations', *Irish Times,* 10 Jan. 1976.
39. Griffiths (1975).
40. Rose (1971), 344.
41. For details of newspaper readership see *Readership Survey of Northern Ireland,* Research Services Ltd, London 1971.
42. Windlesham (1973), 270.

Chapter 7
THE CIVIL SERVICE AND CENTRAL ADMINISTRATION
(pp. 132–154)
Principal sources
Birrell (1978); Donnison in *New Society,* 5 Jul. 1973; Freer (1953); Neill (1957); Oliver (1978 a); Ryan (1967); Northern Ireland Civil Service Alliance, *Annual Reports* (1968–71;) Northern Ireland Public Service Alliance, *Annual Reports* (1972–75)

The Civil Service Report of Sir R. R. Scott, HMSO, Belfast 1926 (Cmd 66)
Civil Service Regrading: Report of Departmental Committee, HMSO, Belfast 1930
Comm. Constitution: Govt Depts NI (1969)
Comm. Constitution: NI (1971)
Northern Ireland Parliamentary Commissioner for Administration, *Annual Reports* (1970–75)

1. Blake (1956), 11.
2. Neill (1957), 154.
3. CAB 4/558/12, 10 Sep. 1943.
4. *Parl. Deb. (C),* lviii, 350 (4 Nov. 1964).
5. *The Civil Service Report of Sir R. R. Scott,* HMSO, Belfast 1926 (Cmd 66); *Civil Service Regrading: Report of Departmental Committee,* HMSO, Belfast 1930.
6. Oliver (1978 a), 60.
7. *Comm. Constitution: NI* (1971), 9.
8. For details of the work of the Whitley Council see Annual Re-

ports of the Northern Ireland Civil Service Alliance, Belfast 1968–71, and the Northern Ireland Public Service Alliance, Belfast 1972–75.

9. [Hall Report] *Report of the Joint Working Party on the Economy of Northern Ireland*, HMSO, Belfast 1962 (Cmd 446), 56–7.

10. Northern Ireland Economic Council, *The Feasibility of State Industry in Northern Ireland*, HMSO, Belfast 1971.

11. [Burges Report] *Reorganisation of Secondary Education in Northern Ireland*, HMSO, Belfast 1973 (Cmd 574).

12. See *NI Development Programme, 1970–75* (1970), 2.

13. 'MacMoney' in *Fortnight*, 2 Apr. 1976.

14. Hall Report (1962), 57.

15. *Comm. Constitution: NI* (1971), 34.

16. *Report of the Select Committee on Public Accounts for the Year 1965–66*, HMSO, Belfast 1967 (HC 1953), 32–5, 170–85.

17. *NI Development Programme, 1970–75* (1970), 205.

18. *Ibid.*, 207.

19. Brett (1970), 273.

20. *Parl. Deb. (C)*, lxxxii, 186 (24 Jun. 1971).

21. *Comm. Constitution: NI* (1971), 44.

22. O'Neill (1972), 71–3.

23. Oliver (1978 a), 160.

24. *Ibid.*, 78–80.

25. Barritt and Carter (1962), 96.

26. Donnison in *New Society*, 5 Jul. 1973.

27. Statement of Ministry of Finance, Northern Ireland Office, Press Notice, 6 Jul. 1973.

28. Barritt and Carter (1962), 98.

29. O'Neill (1972), 39–40.

30. Annual Reports of the Northern Ireland Parliamentary Commissioner for Administration, HMSO, Belfast 1970–75.

31. Statement of Ministry of Finance, Northern Ireland Office, Press Notice, 6 Jul. 1973.

32. *Second Report of the NI Parliamentary Commissioner for Administration*, HMSO, Belfast 1971, 4.

33. Oliver (1978 a), 78.

34. *Ibid.*, 92.

35. See *Report of Progress in Reorganisation of Local Government*, HMSO, Belfast 1971, and Annual Reports of the NI Public Service Alliance (1972–75).

36. [Osmond Report] *Training in the Public Service* (unpublished), Belfast 1972.

37. *First Annual Report of the NI Public Service Alliance* (1972), 14.

38. Windlesham (1973), 263.

39. Devlin (1975), 28.

40. Fisk (1975), 218.

41. Faulkner (1978), 276–7.

42. Oliver (1978 a), 104.

43. For a discussion of the latter see Griffiths (1974).
44. Oliver (1978 a), 106.

Chapter 8
LOCAL GOVERNMENT AND LOCAL ADMINISTRATION
(pp. 155–190)
Principal Sources
Benn (1973); Booz-Allen & Hamilton Ltd (1972); Busteed (1970); Busteed and Mason (1971); Elcock (1972); Hayes (1967); Ilersic (1969 a); Jamison (1972); Johnson (1970); Lawrence (1965 b); Loughran (1965); Lynn (1967); Mackintosh (1971); Mansfield (1972); Queen's University, Belfast (Department of Business Studies), *The Reorganisation of Health and Personal Social Services*, Belfast 1976; *The Reshaping of Local Government: A Conference Report*, New University of Ulster, Coleraine 1969; Poole (1972)

Report of the Departmental Commission on Local Government Administration in Northern Ireland, HMSO, Belfast 1927 (Cmd 73)
Report on Health and Local Government Administration in Northern Ireland, 1938–46, HMSO, Belfast 1948 (Cmd 258)
[Nugent Report] *Report of the Committee on the Finances of Local Authorities*, HMSO, Belfast 1957 (Cmd 369)
The Reshaping of Local Government: Statement of Aims, HMSO, Belfast 1967 (Cmd 517)
The Reshaping of Local Government: Further Proposals, HMSO Belfast 1969 (Cmd 530)
The Administrative Structure of the Health and Personal Social Services in Northern Ireland, HMSO, Belfast 1969.
[Macrory Report] *Review Body on Local Government in Northern Ireland*, HMSO, Belfast 1970 (Cmd 546)
Northern Ireland Commissioner for Complaints, *Annual Reports* (1970–79)

1. *Report of the Departmental Commission on Local Government Administration in Northern Ireland*, HMSO, Belfast 1927 (Cmd 73).
2. CAB 4/267/17, 21 Aug. 1930.
3. CAB 4/248/18, 28 May 1929.
4. CAB 3/594/5, 5 Jun. 1944.
5. Hayes (1967), 82.
6. For a complete list see Ryan (1967) and *Northern Ireland: Discussion Paper: Government of Northern Ireland: A Society Divided*, HMSO, London 1975, Annex 5, pp. 36–52.
7. Loughran (1965), 38.
8. [Matthew Report] *Belfast Regional Survey and Plan: Recommendations and Conclusions*, HMSO, Belfast 1963 (Cmd 451), para 180.

9. For detailed discussion see Birrell *et al.* (1971), 133–61.
10. CAB 4/594/3, 19 Aug. 1944.
11. CAB 4/669/6, 17 May 1946.
12. *The Reshaping of Local Government: Statement of Aims,* HMSO, Belfast 1967 (Cmd 517), para 9.
13. [Nugent Report] *Report of the Committee on the Finances of Local Authorities,* HMSO, Belfast 1957 (Cmd 369), para. 224.
14. Ilersic (1969 a), 21.
15. *Ibid.,* 16.
16. Hayes (1967), 17.
17. Ilersic (1969 a), 49.
18. *Ibid.,* 11.
19. Research survey in progress at the New University of Ulster, Coleraine.
20. [Cameron Report] *Disturbances in Northern Ireland: Report of the Commission appointed by the Governor of Northern Ireland,* HMSO, Belfast 1969 (Cmd 532), para 229.
21. Barritt and Carter (1962), 97–100.
22. Busteed and Mason (1971), 316.
23. Cameron Report (1969), para. 138.
24. *Ibid.,* para. 139.
25. Rose (1971), 239.
26. Cameron Report (1969), para. 140.
27. Barritt and Carter (1962), 111.
28. Harris (1972), 215.
29. Loughran (1965), 35.
30. Lawrence (1965 b), 22.
31. Oliver (1978 a), 191.
32. Busteed and Mason (1971), 316.
33. Northern Ireland Economic Council, *Area Development in Northern Ireland,* HMSO, Belfast 1969, 35.
34. *The Reshaping of Local Government: Statement of Aims,* HMSO, Belfast 1967 (Cmd 517).
35. *The Reshaping of Local Government: Further Proposals,* HMSO, Belfast 1969 (Cmd 530).
36. *The Administrative Structure of the Health and Personal Social Services in Northern Ireland,* HMSO, Belfast 1969.
37. Interview, *News Letter,* 4 Feb. 1970.
38. *Northern Ireland: Text of a Communiqué issued after Discussions between the Home Secretary and the Northern Ireland Government,* HMSO, London 1969 (Cmnd 4178), para. 6.
39. [Macrory Report] *Review Body on Local Government in Northern Ireland,* HMSO, Belfast 1970 (Cmd 546).
40. *Ibid.,* para. 46.
41. *NI: Text of a Communiqué* (1969), para. 24.
42. N. Dugdale, 'The Restructuring of the Social Services' (Conference Paper, Portstewart, 5 May 1971).
43. Ilersic (1969 b), 15.

M

44. Johnson (1970), 21.
45. Interview, *Belfast Telegraph,* 10 Sep. 1974.
46. Civil Service Management Division, 'Northern Ireland Housing Executive: Senior Management Structure' (unpublished, 1978).
47. Queen's University, Belfast (Department of Business Studies), *The Reorganisation of Health and Personal Social Services: Second Report,* Belfast 1976.
48. [Cockcroft Report] *Department of the Environment, Review of Rural Planning Policy,* HMSO, Belfast 1978.
49. *Ibid.,* 4.
50. *The Role of District Committees: Explanatory Booklet,* Northern Ireland Health and Social Services Boards, Belfast 1974.
51. *The Northern Ireland Commissioner for Complaints* (leaflet), Belfast, Apr. 1970.
52. Source: Annual Reports of the Northern Ireland Commissioner for Complaints, HMSO, Belfast 1970–79.
53. *Ibid. (Report ... for 1975),* HMSO, Belfast 1976, 1.
54. *Ibid. (Report ... for 1972),* HMSO, Belfast 1973, para. 52.
55. Benn (1973), 11.
56. *Sixth Report of the NI Commissioner for Complaints,* HMSO, Belfast 1974, 22.
57. *First Report of the Fair Employment Agency for Northern Ireland,* HMSO, Belfast 1977, 9.
58. Unpublished research by one of the authors.
59. *Ibid.*
60. Lawrence *et al.* (1975), 30–1.
61. 'District Councils and Community Work', *Scope: A Review of Voluntary and Community Work in Northern Ireland,* No. 13 (1977), 14–20.
62. Cockcroft Report (1978), 17.

Chapter 9
SOCIAL POLICIES (1): PLANNING, HOUSING AND SOCIAL SECURITY
(pp. 191–234)

Principal sources

Birrell *et al.* (1971); Black (1960); Boal (1970); Boal *et al.* (1974); Compton (1978); Compton and Boal (1970); Darby and Morris (1974); Davies *et al.* (1977); Evason (1976); Evason *et al.* (1976); Hendry (1977); Jones (1960); Murie (1973, 1974 b); Murie *et al.* (1974, 1976); Ragg (1972); Rainsford (1973); Stevenson (1964); Weiner (1976)

[Hall Report] *Report of the Joint Working Party on the Economy of Northern Ireland,* HMSO, Belfast 1962 (Cmd 446)

[Matthew Report] *Belfast Regional Survey and Plan: Recommendations and Conclusions,* HMSO, Belfast 1963 (Cmd 451)

[Wilson Report] *Economic Development in Northern Ireland,* HMSO, Belfast 1965 (Cmd 479)

Ministry of Health and Social Services, *Financial and Other Circumstances of Retirement Pensioners in Northern Ireland,* HMSO, Belfast 1966

Northern Ireland Development Programme, 1970–75, HMSO, Belfast 1970

Northern Ireland Office, *Northern Ireland: Discussion Paper: Finance and the Economy,* HMSO, London 1974

Department of Housing, Local Government and Planning, *Northern Ireland: Discussion Paper: Regional Physical Development Strategy, 1975–95* HMSO, Belfast 1975

Northern Ireland Housing Executive, *Northern Ireland Household Survey, 1975,* NIHE, Belfast [1976]

Areas of Special Social Need, HMSO, Belfast 1977

1. See Compton (1978).
2. Compton and Boal (1970).
3. Department of Employment, *New Earnings Survey,* HMSO, London 1977, Pt D. The figures relate to men aged 21 and over and women aged 18 and over who work full-time and whose earnings are not affected by absence.
4. See, e.g., 'Labour Costs in Northern Ireland in 1968', *Employment and Productivity Gazette* LXXVIII, No. 10 (1970), 872–9; 'The Effect of Regional Employment Structures on Average Earnings', *ibid.* LXXVII, No. 3 (1969), 231–4. See also Department of Employment, *Time Rates of Wages and Hours of Work,* HMSO, London 1975; Marquand (1967).
5. Statistics on unemployment are regularly reproduced in *Department of Employment Gazette,* HMSO, London (monthly); see also *Northern Ireland Digest of Statistics,* HMSO, Belfast (bi-annual).
6. For a full discussion see Murie (1974 b).
7. Duff (1973). See also Spencer (1973); Boal *et al.* (1974); *Areas of Special Social Need,* HMSO, Belfast 1977.
8. Department of Finance, *Social and Economic Trends in Northern Ireland,* No. 2, HMSO, Belfast 1976, 25. The main sources are Central Statistics Office, *Regional Statistics,* HMSO, London (annual); Department of Employment, *New Earnings Survey,* HMSO, London (annual); Board of Inland Revenue, *Inland Revenue Statistics,* HMSO, London (annual); Department of Employment, *Family Expenditure Survey,* HMSO, London (annual); *Northern Ireland Digest of Statistics,* HMSO, Belfast (bi-annual); *Family Expenditure Survey: Report for Northern Ireland,* HMSO, Belfast (annual).
9. E.g. 'Labour Costs in Northern Ireland in 1968'.

10. See *NI: Finance and the Economy* (1974), 6–7; Department of Finance, *Social and Economic Trends in Northern Ireland*, No. 1, HMSO, Belfast 1975, 10–11.
11. *Ibid.*; see also Murie *et al.* (1974).
12. *NI Development Programme, 1970–75* (1970), 4–8, 63–4; see also *NI: Finance and the Economy* (1974), 6, 15.
13. Coates and Rawstron (1971), 9–42.
14. Figures on FIS from *Social and Economic Trends in NI*, No. 2 (1976). These also show that Northern Ireland accounts for 14.7 per cent of UK weekly expenditure on FIS and 17.2 per cent of the total number of people provided for by FIS. Northern Ireland Housing Executive, *Northern Ireland Household Survey, 1975*, NIHE, Belfast [1976], 177, provides an estimate of FIS eligibility.
15. *Ibid.*; see also Ministry of Health and Social Services, *Financial and Other Circumstances of Retirement Pensioners in Northern Ireland*, HMSO, Belfast 1966; Evason (1976), 30–6.
16. *NI Household Survey, 1975* This poverty line is based on the needs allowance used for rent rebates. This is closely linked to and slightly above the long-term supplementary benefit scale rate. The particular method of applying this to survey data led the authors of the report to argue that they could be understating the extent of poverty (pp. 175–7).
17. See *Family Expenditure Survey* and *Family Expenditure Survey: Report for NI;* see also Evason (1976), 28.
18. Compton (1978), 112.
19. McCrone (1969), 149–66.
20. See, e.g., Newman (1965) and Andrews (1970).
21. Wallace (1971), 123.
22. O'Neill (1972), 47.
23. OD Cars Ltd *v.* Belfast Corporation.
24. Hall Report (1962); Matthew Report (1963); Wilson Report (1965); *NI Development Programme, 1970–75* (1970).
25. Comparisons of inducements are presented in Murie *et al.* (1974). A comparison of the value of the inducements is presented in *NI Development Programme, 1970–75* (1970), Appendix IV.
26. Rose (1971), 98.
27. Department of Housing, Local Government and Planning, *Northern Ireland: Discussion Paper: Physical Development Strategy, 1975–95*, HMSO, Belfast 1975.
28. Cameron Report (1969), para. 142.
29. Planning (Northern Ireland) Order, 1972. For discussion see Murie (1973) and Hendry (1977).
30. *NI: Physical Development Strategy, 1975–95* (1975).
31. See Boal (1975).
32. Cockcroft Report (1978).
33. For a discussion see Davies *et al.* (1977).
34. Birrell *et al.* (1975).

35. [Quigley Report] *Economic and Industrial Strategy for Northern Ireland,* HMSO, Belfast 1976.
36. Moore *et al.* (1977); Davies and McGurnaghan (1975).
37. Davies *et al.* (1977), 56.
38. Simpson in *Fortnight,* 22 Oct. 1976.
39. Davies *et al.* (1977), 58–9.
40. Lawrence (1965 a), 127 ff.
41. See de Paor (1970), 67 and *passim.*
42. Black (1960), 36–71, 241–8.
43. Gilbert (1970), 139; see also Moorhouse *et al.* (1972), 134–6.
44. Murie *et al.* (1971).
45. Rutan (1964); see also Birrell *et al.* (1971), 133–61.
46. *Report of the Ministry of Home Affairs on the Administration of Local Government Services, 1937–38,* HMSO, Belfast 1938 (Cmd 200), 55.
47. *Housing in Northern Ireland: Interim Report of the Planning Advisory Board,* HMSO, Belfast 1944 (Cmd 224), 9–11.
48. CAB 4/594/3, 19 Jul. 1944.
49. See Buckland (1979), 173.
50. CAB 4/669/6, 17 May 1946.
51. O'Neill (1972), 31.
52. Birrell *et al.* (1971), 148–51; Cameron Report (1969), para. 139.
53. *NI Household Survey, 1975,* 20–6.
54. Kennedy and Birrell (1978), 102.
55. For example, Birrell *et al.* (1971) suggested a target of 20,000 dwellings per annum. *NI Development Programme, 1970–75* (1970) recommended that new completions should rise to 17,000 per annum by 1975 (75,000 in 1970–75). The Stormont government in *Northern Ireland Development Programme, 1970–75: Government Statement, 1970,* HMSO, Belfast 1970 (Cmd 547), accepted a lower target of 73,000 dwellings in 1970–75.
56. Kennedy and Birrell (1978).
57. *Parl. Deb. (C),* lxxvii, 74–192 (21 Oct. 1970).
58. For progress in dealing with older housing see *Digest of Housing Statistics for Northern Ireland,* HMSO, Belfast (monthly).
59. Figures in this section are taken from Compton (1978).
60. Murie *et al.* (1976), 135.
61. *Ibid.,* 120–7, 156–62.
62. Jones (1960), 172–206.
63. Northern Ireland Community Relations Commission, *Flight: A Report on Population Movement in Belfast during August 1971,* NICRC, Belfast 1971; Darby and Morris (1974).
64. See, e.g., Weiner (1976).
65. Evason *et al.* (1976), 23.
66. *Ibid.,* 6–29.
67. See Buckland (1979), 157–9; Farrell (1976), Chapter 6; Lawrence (1965 a), 161.
68. Evason *et al.* (1976), 26–7.

69. Farrell (1976), 126–30.
70. Evason *et al.* (1976), 24, 29.
71. *Interim Report of the Committee of Inquiry on Unemployment Insurance and Employment Exchanges,* HMSO Belfast 1922 (Cmd 2), para. 2; Buckland (1979), Chapter 7; Lawrence (1965 a), Chapter 9.
72. Source: Reports of the Supplementary Benefits Commission, HMSO, Belfast 1973–74.
73. Ministry of Health and Social Services, *Financial and Other Circumstances of Retirement Pensioners in Northern Ireland,* HMSO, Belfast 1966.
74. Murie (1974 a), 38–40.
75. *NI Household Survey, 1975,* 64, 177.
76. Rainsford (1973); but see also Ragg (1972) and Evason (1976), 35–6.
77. O'Hara (1976).
78. Lawrence (1965 a), 161.
79. *Ibid.,* 162–3.
80. Gilbert (1970), 69.
81. Buckland (1979), 151–2.

Chapter 10
SOCIAL POLICIES (2): EDUCATION, HEALTH AND SOCIAL SERVICES
(pp. 235–262)
Principal sources
Akenson (1973); Corkey; Donaghy (1970); Hood (1971)

The Existing Selection Procedure for Secondary Education in Northern Ireland, HMSO, Belfast 1971 (Cmd 551)
Ministry of Health and Social Services, *A Survey of General Practice in Northern Ireland in 1970,* HMSO, Belfast 1972
[Burges Report] *Reorganisation of Secondary Education in Northern Ireland,* HMSO, Belfast 1973 (Cmd 574)
Reorganisation of Secondary Education in Northern Ireland, HMSO, Belfast 1976
Department of Health and Social Services, *Legislation and Services for Children and Young People in Northern Ireland,* HMSO, Belfast 1977

1. Akenson (1973); Buckland (1979), Chapter 11.
2. Quoted in Akenson (1973), 46.
3. *Ibid.,* 52.
4. CAB 4/18/7, 2 Sep. 1921.
5. Akenson (1973), 52.
6. For this process see Corkey; Kennedy (1971).
7. See Buckland (1979), 252–6.

8. Akenson (1973), 87.
9. Buckland (1979), 266–7.
10. *Ibid.*, 260.
11. *Ibid.*, 267.
12. CAB 4/611/5, 16 Jan. 1945.
13. Akenson (1973), 177.
14. *Ibid.*, 188; see also O'Neill (1972), 47.
15. Akenson (1973), 193.
16. *Ibid.*, 117.
17. Buckland (1979), 263.
18. *Ibid.*, Chapter 11.
19. *Reorganisation of Secondary Education in Northern Ireland,* HMSO, Belfast 1976, 3.
20. *The Existing Selection Procedure for Secondary Education in Northern Ireland,* HMSO, Belfast 1971 (Cmd 574); Burges Report (1973).
21. *Reorganisation of Secondary Education in Northern Ireland,* HMSO, Belfast 1976.
22. *Reorganisation of Secondary Education in Northern Ireland: A Statement by Lord Melchett, Minister of State,* HMSO, Belfast 1977.
23. Statement by Mr Basil McIvor, *NI Assembly: Official Report,* iii, 299 (30 Apr. 1974).
24. Evason *et al.* (1976), 174–219.
25. *Ibid.*, 219.
26. *Ibid.*, 228.
27. *Ibid.*, 230.
28. [Lockwood Report] *Higher Education in Northern Ireland,* HMSO, Belfast 1965 (Cmd 475); *Higher Education in Northern Ireland: Government Statement on the Report of the Committee,* HMSO, Belfast, 1965 (Cmd 480).
29. Cameron Report (1969), para 142; see also *Parl. Deb. (C),* lv–lxi *passim.*
30. Evason *et al.* (1976), 68.
31. *Ibid.*, 80.
32. *Ibid.*, 68.
33. Lawrence (1965 a), 129.
34. *Ibid.*, 128.
35. *Report of the Irish Public Health Council on the Public Health and Medical Services in Ireland,* HMSO, Dublin 1920 (Cmd 761), quoted *ibid.*, 129.
36. *Ibid.*
37. Lawrence (1965 a), 131–2.
38. *Ibid.*, 133.
39. *Ibid.*, 138–9. It should be noted that the division of responsibility also applied in England.
40. Buckland (1979), 161.
41. *Ibid.*, 161–2.

42. *Report of the Departmental Committee on Sickness Visitation by Approved Societies*, HMSO, Belfast 1937, para. 17.
43. *Report of the Departmental Committee on Sickness Visitation by Approved Societies*, HMSO, Belfast, 1937, para. 17.
44. *Ibid.*
45. Stevenson (1964).
46. *Lawrence* (1965 a), 142.
47. White Paper on the health services and their development (Pr. 8665), quoted in Hensey (1968), 44.
48. *The Administrative Structure of the Health and Personal Social Services in Northern Ireland*, HMSO, Belfast 1969.
49. Evason *et al.* (1976), 98; see also Annual Reports of the General Health Services Board, HMSO, Belfast 1968–72, and Annual Reports of the Northern Ireland Health and Social Services— Central Services Agency, HMSO, Belfast 1973– .
50. *Ibid.* and Ministry of Health and Social Services, *A Survey of General Practice in Northern Ireland in 1970*, HMSO, Belfast 1972, 3.
51. Hood (1971); *NI Digest of Statistics*, No. 35 (1971), 36 and No. 52 (1979), 40.
52. Hood (1971); see also Wade and Hood (1972).
53. Evason *et al.* (1976), 119.
54. *Ibid.,* 121.
55. *Ibid.,* 125.
56. Ministry of Health and Social Services, *Memorandum on the Development of Services for the Elderly*, HMSO, Belfast 1966, para. 6.
57. Evason *et al.* (1976), 136–7.
58. For a fuller discussion see *ibid.,* 141–8.
59. Department of Health and Social Services, *Legislation and Services for Children and Young People in Northern Ireland*, HMSO, Belfast 1977.
60. *Social Service Teams: The Practitioner's View*, HMSO, London 1978, 231–2.
61. *Ibid.,* 235.
62. *Ibid.,* 225.
63. Social workers with CQSW from Evason *et al.* (1976), 162.
64. Ministry of Health and Social Services, *Guide to the New Structure for Health and Personal Social Services*, Belfast 1972, 2.
65. Department of Health and Social Services, *Strategy for the Development of Health and Personal Social Services in Northern Ireland*, HMSO, Belfast 1975, para. 104.

Chapter 11
SOCIAL POLICY AND DEVOLUTION
(pp. 263–302)
Principal sources

Barritt and Carter (1962); Birrell (1972); Birrell and Murie (1973,

1975); Boserup (1972); Buckland (1979); Busteed and Mason (1971); de Paor (1970); Farrell (1976); Lijphart (1975); McCrone (1969); Rutan (1964); Stephens and Glasscock (1970)

Kilbrandon Report, I (1973)
The Northern Ireland Constitution, HMSO, London 1974 (Cmnd 5675)

1. Carrier and Kendall (1973).
2. Johnson, editorial in *Public Administration* LII (1974), 1–12.
3. Buckland (1979), 278–9.
4. *Ibid.*, 280.
5. Kilbrandon Report, I (1973), 166–7.
6. *Ibid.*, 167–8.
7. *Ibid.*, 391–3.
8. Rolston in *Fortnight*, 1 Apr. 1977.
9. Kilbrandon Report, I (1973), 377–8.
10. Buckland (1979), 3.
11. Kilbrandon Report, I (1973), 379.
12. *Ibid.*, 378.
13. *Ibid.*, 380.
14. Lijphart (1975); see also Boserup (1972).
15. *NI: Finance and the Economy* (1974), 23–4.
16. Simpson in *Fortnight*, 20 Sep. 1974.
17. *The Northern Ireland Constitution*, HMSO, London 1974 (Cmnd 5675), para. 40.
18. For this and similar statements see *NI: Finance and the Economy* (1974), 8–9.
19. Boal *et al.* (1974); *Areas of Special Social Need* (1977); see also *NI Household Survey, 1975*.
20. See Jones (1960), 172–206; Boal (1970, 1971).
21. Poole in *Fortnight*, 6–31 Aug. 1971; NI Community Relations Commission, *Flight: A Report on Population Movement in Belfast during August 1971* (1971); Darby and Morris (1973, 1974).
22. Lijphart (1975), 86–91.
23. Boserup (1972), 166–78.
24. Birrell (1972), 326–31.
25. Boserup (1972), 171.
26. Budge and O'Leary (1973), 143.
27. Evason (1976), 4.
28. Barritt and Carter (1962), 109.
29. Rose (1971), 97.
30. *Comm. Constitution: NI* (1971), Appendix II.
31. For a fuller discussion see Birrell and Murie (1975).
32. Cameron Report (1969), paras 127–40.
33. Barritt and Carter (1962), 67–8.
34. Busteed and Mason (1971), 316.
35. Birrell and Murie (1973).

36. Akenson (1973), 39–48.
37. Sir James Craig, 14 Mar. 1922, quoted in Buckland (1979), 150.
38. Oliver (1978 a), 43.
39. *Ibid.*, 47.
40. Blake (1956); see also Titmuss (1950).
41. Oliver (1978 a), 69.
42. O'Neill (1972), 31.
43. *Ibid.*, 47.
44. Oliver (1978 a), 78.
45. *Ibid.*, 79.
46. Source: *NI: Finance and the Economy* (1974).
47. For a fuller discussion see Birrell and Murie (1975).

Chapter 12
POSTCRIPT: FUTURE FORMS OF GOVERNMENT
(pp. 303–311)
Principal sources

Administration (Special Issue: 'The Irish Dimension') XX, No. 4 (1972); Catherwood (1972); Gibson (1974); Kingston (1975); Lyons (1972); Molyneaux in *Belfast Telegraph*, 3 Feb. 1977; Oliver (1976, 1978 b); Rose (1976); Rose and McAllister in *Irish Times*, 16 Sep. 1975; Ulster Loyalist Central Co-ordinating Committee, *Ulster Can Survive Unfettered*, Belfast 1976; Wilson (1972)

The Future Development of the Parliament and Government of Northern Ireland, HMSO, Belfast 1971 (Cmd 560)
Northern Ireland: Discussion Paper: Constitutional Procedure, HMSO, London 1974
Northern Ireland: Discussion Paper: Government of Northern Ireland: A Society Divided, HMSO, London 1975
Northern Ireland Constitutional Convention: Report, HMSO, London 1975
Northern Ireland Constitutional Convention: Report of Debates, 2 vols, HMSO, Belfast 1975–76
Letter from Secretary of State, HMSO, London 1976 (Cmnd 6387)

1. See *Our Changing Democracy: Devolution to Scotland and Wales*, HMSO, London 1975 (Cmnd 6348); *Wales Bill*, HMSO, London 1978.
2. *NI Constitutional Convention: Report* (1975), 12.
3. *The Future of Northern Ireland: A Paper for Discussion*, HMSO, London 1972, 24.
4. See Alliance Party proposals, *NI Constitutional Convention: Report of Debates, February to March 1976*, HMSO, Belfast 1976, 954 (17 Feb. 1976).
5. *NI Constitutional Convention: Report* (1975).

6. *NI Constitutional Convention: Report of Debates . . . 1976* (1976), 950 (12 Feb. 1976).
7. See Oliver (1976).
8. Lijphart (1969).
9. For a detailed discussion see Rose (1976).
10. Lawrence and Elliott (1975), para. 9.
11. Dowling (1974), 57.
12. Rose (1976), 151–2.
13. See, e.g., Ulster Loyalist Central Co-ordinating Committee, *Ulster Can Survive Unfettered*, Discussion Document, Belfast 1976.

Bibliography

This bibliography is restricted to material relevant to government, administration and social policy in Northern Ireland. For a comprehensive bibliography covering conflict in Northern Ireland see J. Darby, *Conflict in Northern Ireland: The Development of a Polarised Community,* Gill & Macmillan, Dublin 1976

1. Books and articles

Administration (Special Issue: 'The Irish Dimension') XX, No. 4 (1972)

Akenson, D. H. (1973): *Education and Enmity: The Control of Schooling in Northern Ireland, 1920–1950,* David & Charles, Newton Abbot

Andrews, J. H. (1970): 'Geography and Government in Elizabethan Ireland' in Stephens and Glasscock (1970), 178–91

Barritt, D. P., and Carter, C. F. (1962): *The Northern Ireland Problem: A Study in Group Relations,* Oxford University Press

Beckett, J. C. (1957): 'Ulster Protestantism' in Moody and Beckett (1957), 159–69

Bell, J. B. (1970): *The Secret Army,* Sphere, London

Bell, J. B. (1973): 'The Escalation of Insurgency: The Provisional IRA's Experience', *Review of Politics* XXXV, No. 3, 398–411

Benn, J. (1973): *A Commissioner's Complaint,* Occasional Papers in Social Administration, New University of Ulster, Coleraine

Birch, A. H. (1956): 'A Note on Devolution', *Political Studies* IV, No. 3, 310–11

Birrell, W. D. (1972): 'Relative Deprivation as a Factor in Conflict in Northern Ireland', *Sociological Review* XX, No. 3, 317–43

Birrell, W. D. (1973): 'The Stormont–Westminster Relationship', *Parliamentary Affairs* XXVI, No. 4, 471–91

Birrell, W. D. (1978): 'The Northern Ireland Civil Service— From Devolution to Direct Rule', *Public Administration* LVI, 305–20

Birrell, W. D., Greer, J. E., and Roche, D. J. D. (1979): 'The Political Role and Influence of Clergy in Northern Ireland', *Sociological Review* XXVII, No. 3, 491–512

Birrell, W. D., Hillyard, P. A. R., Murie, A. S., and Roche, D. J. D.

(1971): *Housing in Northern Ireland*, University Working Paper, Centre for Environmental Studies, London

Birrell, W. D., Hillyard, P. A. R., Murie, A. S., and Roche, D. J. D. (1975): *Some Aspects of Labour Mobility in Northern Ireland*, Occasional Papers in Social Administration, New University of Ulster, Coleraine

Birrell, W. D., and Murie, A. S. (1973): 'Social Policy in Northern Ireland' in K. Jones, ed., *The Year Book of Social Policy, 1972*, Routledge & Kegan Paul, London, 134–55

Birrell, W. D., and Murie, A. S. (1975): 'Ideology, Conflict and Social Policy', *Journal of Social Policy* IV, Pt 3, 243–58

Black, R. D. C. (1960): *Economic Thought and the Irish Question*, Cambridge University Press

Blake, J. W. (1956): *Northern Ireland in the Second World War*, HMSO, Belfast

Bleakley, D. W. (1953): 'The Northern Ireland Trade Union Movement', *Journal of the Statistical and Social Inquiry Society of Ireland* XX (1953–54), 156–68

Bleakley, D. W. (1974): *Faulkner: Conflict and Compromise in Irish Politics*, Mowbray, London

Boal, F. W. (1970): 'Social Space in the Belfast Urban Area' in Stephens and Glasscock (1970), 373–93

Boal, F. W. (1971): 'Territoriality and Class: Two Residential Areas in Belfast', *Irish Geography* VI, No. 3, 229–48

Boal, F. W. (1975): 'Review of Plans and Studies', *Town and Country Planning* (Dec. 1975), 556–7

Boal, F. W., and Buchanan, R. H. (1969): 'The 1969 Northern Ireland Election', *Irish Geography* VI, No. 1, 78–84

Boal, F. W., Doherty, P., and Pringle, D. G. (1974): *The Spatial Distribution of some Social Problems in Belfast Urban Area*, Research Paper, NI Community Relations Commission, Belfast

Booz-Allen & Hamilton Ltd (1972): *An Integrated Service: The Reorganisation of Health and Personal Social Services in Northern Ireland* (management consultants' report), Belfast

Boserup, A. (1972): 'Contradictions and Struggles in Northern Ireland' in Miliband and Saville (1972)

Bowden, J. (1976): 'The IRA and the Changing Tactics of Terrorism', *Political Quarterly* XLVII, 425–37

Boyd, A. (1972 a): *Brian Faulkner and the Crisis of Ulster Unionism*, Anvil, Tralee

Boyd, A. (1972 b): *The Rise of the Irish Trade Unions*, Anvil, Tralee

Brett, C. E. B. (1970): 'The Lessons of Devolution in Northern Ireland', *Political Quarterly* XLI, 261–80

Brookeborough Memoirs, *Sunday News*, 4 Feb. 1968

Buckland, P. (1979): *The Factory of Grievances: Devolved Government in Northern Ireland, 1921–39*, Gill & Macmillan, Dublin

Budge, I., and O'Leary, C. (1973): *Belfast: Approach to Crisis—A*

Study of Belfast Politics, 1613–1970, Macmillan, London

Busteed, M. A. (1970): 'Reshaping Belfast's Government', *Administration* XVIII, No. 3, 256–61

Busteed, M. A., and Mason, H. (1971): 'Local Government Reform in Northern Ireland', *Irish Geography* VI, No. 3, 315–23

Callaghan, J. (1973): *A House Divided: The Dilemma of Northern Ireland,* Collins, London

Calvert, H. (1968): *Constitutional Law in Northern Ireland: A Study in Regional Government,* Stevens, London

Carrier, J., and Kendall, I. (1973): 'Social Policy and Social Change', *Journal of Social Policy* II, Pt 3, 209–24

Catherwood, Sir F. S. (1972): 'A Possible Political Settlement' in *The Ulster Debate: Report of a Study Group of the Institute for the Study of Conflict,* Bodley Head, London, 102–9

Chubb, B. (1970): *The Government and Politics of Ireland,* Oxford University Press

Civil Service Management Division (1978): 'Northern Ireland Housing Executive: Senior Management Structure' (unpublished)

Coates, B. E., and Rawstron, E. M. (1971): *Regional Variations in Britain,* Batsford, London

Compton, P. A. (1978): *Northern Ireland: A Census Atlas,* Gill & Macmillan, Dublin

Compton, P. A., and Boal, F. W. (1970): 'Aspects of Inter-Community Population Balance in Northern Ireland', *Economic and Social Review* I, No. 4, 455–76

Coogan, T. P. (1970): *The IRA,* Pall Mall, London

Cook, J. I. (1953): 'Financial Relations between the Exchequers of the United Kingdom and Northern Ireland' in Neill (1953 a), 18–44

Corkey, W., *Episode in the History of Protestant Ulster, 1923–47: History of the Struggle of the Protestant Community to Maintain Bible Instruction in their Schools,* privately published, Belfast, n.d.

Dallat, M., ed. (1971): *Aspects of Catholic Education,* St Joseph's College of Education, Belfast

Daly, C. B. (1973): *Violence in Ireland and Christian Conscience,* Veritas, Dublin

Darby, J. (1976): *Conflict in Northern Ireland: The Development of a Polarised Community,* Gill & Macmillan, Dublin

Darby, J., and Morris, G. (1973): 'Intimidation in Housing', *Community Forum* III, No. 2, 7–11

Darby, J., and Morris, G. (1974): *Intimidation in Housing,* Research Paper, NI Community Relations Commission, Belfast

Darby, J., and Williamson, A., ed. (1978): *Violence and the Social Services in Northern Ireland,* Heinemann, London

Darlington, R., 'Northern Ireland Legislation at Westminster', *Fortnight,* 8 Jun. 1973

Davies, R., and McGurnaghan, M. A. (1975): 'The Economics of

Adversity', *National Westminster Bank Review* (May 1975), 56–68

Davies, R., McGurnaghan, M. A., and Sams, K. I. (1977): 'The Northern Ireland Economy: Progress (1968–75) and Prospects', *Regional Studies* XI, 297–307

de Paor, L. (1970): *Divided Ulster,* Penguin, Harmondsworth

Devlin, P. (1975): *The Fall of the Northern Ireland Executive,* privately published, Belfast

Dewar, M. W., Brown, J., and Long, S. E. (1967): *Orangeism: A New Historical Appreciation, 1688–1967,* Grand Lodge of Ireland, Belfast

Ditch, J. S. (1977): 'Direct Rule and the Northern Ireland Administration', *Administration* XXV, No. 3, 328–37

Donaghy, T. (1970): 'A Study of Secondary School Systems in Northern Ireland' (unpublished MA thesis, Queen's University, Belfast)

Donaldson, A. G. (1955): 'The Constitution of Northern Ireland: Its Origins and Development', *University of Toronto Law Journal* XI, No. 1, 1–42

Donaldson, A. G. (1958): 'The Senate of Northern Ireland', *Public Law* (summer 1958), 135–54

Donaldson, A. G. (1959): 'Fundamental Rights in the Constitution of Northern Ireland', *Canadian Bar Review* XXXVII, 189–216

Donaldson, A. G. (1967): 'Law-Making' in Rhodes (1967), 31–41

Donnison, D., 'The Northern Ireland Civil Service', *New Society,* 5 Jul. 1973

Dowling, B. R. (1974): 'Some Economic Implications of a Federal Ireland' in Gibson (1974), 54–78

Duff, N. (1973): 'Community Self-Surveys: Unemployment in Turf Lodge and Andersonstown', *Community Forum* I, 19–21

'The Effect of Regional Employment Structures in Average Earnings', *Employment and Productivity Gazette* LXXVII, No. 3 (1969), 231–4

Elcock, H. J. (1972): 'Opportunity for Ombudsman: The Northern Ireland Commissioner for Complaints', *Public Administration* L, 87–93

Elliott, S. (1973): *Northern Ireland Parliamentary Election Results, 1921–1972,* Political Reference Publications, Chichester 1973

Ervine, St John (1949): *Craigavon, Ulsterman,* Allen & Unwin, London

Evason, E. (1976): *Poverty: The Facts in Northern Ireland,* Child Poverty Action Group, London

Evason, E., Darby, J., and Pearson, M. (1976): *Social Need and Social Provision in Northern Ireland,* New University of Ulster, Coleraine

Farrell, M. (1976): *Northern Ireland: the Orange State,* Pluto Press, London

Faulkner, B. (1978): *Memoirs of a Statesman,* Weidenfeld & Nicholson, London

Fisk, R. (1975): *The Point of No Return,* Deutsch, London
Freer, L. G. P. (1953): 'Recent Tendencies in Northern Ireland Administration' in Neill (1953 a), 57–85
Furness, N. (1975): 'Northern Ireland as a Case Study of Decentralisation in Unitary States', *World Politics* XXVII, No. 3, 387–404
Gibson, N. J. (1972): 'Note on Financial Relationships between Britain and Northern Ireland', *Administration* XX, No. 4, 136–9
Gibson, N. J., ed. (1974): *Economic and Social Implications of the Political Alternatives that may be Open to Northern Ireland: A Conference Report,* New University of Ulster, Coleraine
Gilbert, B. B. (1970): *British Social Policy, 1914–39,* Batsford, London
Graham, J. A. V. (1972): 'The Consensus-Forming Strategy of the NILP, 1949–68' (unpublished MSc thesis, Queen's University, Belfast)
Gray, Tony (1972): *The Orange Order,* Bodley Head, London
Griffiths, H. (1974): *Community Development in Northern Ireland: A Case Study in Agency Conflict,* Occasional Papers in Social Administration, New University of Ulster, Coleraine
Griffiths, H. (1975): 'Paramilitary Groups and Other Community Action Groups in Northern Ireland Today', *International Review of Community Development,* No. 33–4, 189–206
Harbinson, J. F. (1966): 'A History of the Northern Ireland Labour Party, 1891–1949' (unpublished MSc thesis, Queen's University, Belfast)
Harbinson, J. F. (1973): *The Ulster Unionist Party, 1882–1973: Its Development and Organisation,* Blackstaff, Belfast
Harris, R. (1972): *Prejudice and Tolerance in Ulster: A Study of Neighbours and 'Strangers' in a Border Community,* Manchester University Press
Hayes, M. N. (1967): 'Some Aspects of Local Government in Northern Ireland' in Rhodes (1967), 77–99
Hendry, J. (1977): 'Conservation in Northern Ireland', *Town Planning Review* XLVIII, No. 4, 373–88
Hensey, B. (1968): 'The Irish Health Services and their Administration and Financing', *International Review of Administrative Sciences* XXXIV, 39–47
Heslinga, M. W. (1971): *The Irish Border as a Cultural Divide: A Contribution to the Study of Regionalism in the British Isles,* 2nd ed., Van Gorcum, Assen
Hood, H. E. (1971): 'Disciplining Prescribing Data' (unpublished PhD thesis, Queen's University, Belfast)
Hurley, M., ed. (1970): *Irish Anglicanism, 1869–1969,* Figgis, Dublin
Ilersic, A. R. (1969 a): *Local Government Finance in Northern Ireland,* Association of Local Authorities of Northern Ireland, Belfast
Ilersic, A. R. (1969 b): 'Reshaping Local Government: Some Finan-

cial Aspects' in *The Reshaping of Local Government: A Conference Report,* New University of Ulster, Coleraine.

Irish Council of Churches: Roman Catholic Church Group on Social Problems (1976): *Violence in Ireland,* Belfast and Dublin

Isles, K. S., and Cuthbert, N. (1957): *An Economic Survey of Northern Ireland,* HMSO, Belfast

Jamison, P. (1972): Local Government in Belfast', *Local Government Review* (13 May, 3 Jun. 1972), 445–7, 493–4

Jennings, I. (1959): *The Law and the Constitution,* London University Press

Johnson, J. H. (1970): 'Reorganisation of Local Government in Northern Ireland', *Area,* No. 4, 17–21

Johnson, N. (1974): 'The Royal Commission on the Constitution' [editorial], *Public Administration* LII, 1–12

Jones, E. (1960): *A Social Geography of Belfast,* Oxford University Press

Kelly, H. (1972): *How Stormont Fell,* Gill & Macmillan, Dublin

Kennedy, D. (1957): 'The Catholic Church' in Moody and Beckett (1957), 170–81

Kennedy, D. (1967): 'Catholics in Northern Ireland, 1926–1939' in F. MacManus, ed., *The Years of the Great Test, 1926–1939,* Mercier, Cork, 138–49

Kennedy, D. (1971): 'Catholic Education in Northern Ireland, 1921–70' in Dallat (1971), 30–45

Kennedy, J. A. D. (1967): 'Parliament and the Executive' in Rhodes (1967), 26–40

Kennedy, S., and Birrell, W. D. (1978): 'Housing' in Darby and Williamson (1978), 98–116

Kingston, W. (1975): 'The Case for a Principality of Ulster', *Political Quarterly* XLVI, 255–76

Knight, J. (1974): *Northern Ireland: The Elections of 1973* Arthur McDougall Fund, London

Knight, J. (1975): *Northern Ireland: The Elections of the Constitutional Convention,* Arthur McDougall Fund, London

'Labour Costs in Northern Ireland in 1968', *Employment and Productivity Gazette* LXXVIII, No. 10 (1970), 872–9

Laird, J., 'Is the Party Over?', *Fortnight,* 30 Nov. 1973

Laver, M. J. (1976 a): 'Cultural Aspects of Loyalty: On Hirschman and Loyalism in Ulster', *Political Studies* XXIV, No. 4, 469–78

Laver, M. J. (1976 b): 'On Introducing STV and Interpreting the Results: The Case of Northern Ireland, 1973–75', *Parliamentary Affairs* XXIX, No. 2, 211–29

Lawrence, R. J. (1956): 'Devolution Reconsidered', *Political Studies* IV, No. 1, 1–17

Lawrence, R. J. (1965 a): *The Government of Northern Ireland: Public Finance and Public Services, 1921–1964,* Oxford University Press

Lawrence, R. J. (1965 b): 'Local Government in Northern Ireland;

Areas, Functions and Finance', *Journal of the Statistical and Social Inquiry Society of Ireland* XXI (1965–66), 14–25

Lawrence, R. J., and Elliott, S. (1975): *The Northern Ireland Border Poll, 1973,* HMSO, London (Cmnd 5875)

Lawrence, R. J., Elliott, S., and Laver, M. J. (1975): *The Northern Ireland General Elections of 1973,* HMSO, Belfast (Cmnd 5851)

Lijphart, A. (1969): 'Consociational Democracy', *World Politics* XXI, No. 2, 206–25

Lijphart, A. (1975): 'The Northern Ireland Problem: Cases, Theories and Solutions' [review article], *British Journal of Political Science* V, Pt 1, 83–106

Loughran, G. F. (1965): 'The Problem of Local Government in Northern Ireland', *Administration* XIII, No. 1, 35–8

Lynn, R. J. (1967): 'Revenue-Raising' in Rhodes (1967), 100–15

Lyons, F. S. L. (1972): 'The Alternatives Open to Governments' in *The Ulster Debate: Report of a Study Group of the Institute for the Study of Conflict,* Bodley Head, London, 25–47

McAllister, I. (1975 a): *The 1975 Northern Ireland Convention Election,* Occasional Paper No. 14, Strathclyde University, Glasgow

McAllister, I. (1975 b): 'Political Opposition in Northern Ireland: The National Democratic Party, 1965–70', *Economic and Social Review* VI, No. 3, 353–66

McAllister, I. (1976 a): 'Political Parties and Social Change in Northern Ireland: The Case of the SDLP', *Social Studies* V, No. 1, 75–89

McAllister, I. (1976 b): 'Social Influences on Voters and Non-Voters: A Note on Two Northern Ireland Elections', *Political Studies* XXIV, No. 4, 462–8

McAllister, I. (1977): *The SDLP,* Macmillan, London

McAllister, I., and Wilson, B. (1977): *Bi-Confessionalism in a Confessional Party System: The Northern Ireland Alliance Party,* Studies in Public Policy, No. 8, Centre for the Study of Public Policy, University of Strathclyde, Glasgow

Macaulay, A. (1970): 'Catholics in the North, 1870–1970', *Newman Review* II, No. 1, 21–32

McBirney, R. M. (1967): 'Stormont–Westminster Relations' in Rhodes (1967), 7–13

McCarthy, C. (1973): 'Civil Strife and the Growth of Trade Union Unity: The Case of Ireland', *Government and Opposition* VIII, No. 4, 407–31

McCrone, G. (1969): *Regional Policy in Britain,* Allen & Unwin, London

McDowell, R. B. (1975): *The Church of Ireland, 1869–1969,* Routledge & Kegan Paul, London

Mackintosh, J. P. (1971): 'The Report of the Review Body on Local Government in Northern Ireland, 1970', *Public Administration* XLIX, 13–24

'MacMoney', 'The CBI in Northern Ireland', *Fortnight,* 9 Jan. 1976

'MacMoney', 'All My Own Work', *Fortnight*, 2 Apr. 1976

Magee, J. (1974): *Northern Ireland: Crisis and Conflict*, Routledge & Kegan Paul, London

Magill, P. F. (1965): 'The Senate in Northern Ireland, 1921–62' (unpublished PhD thesis, Queen's University, Belfast)

Maguire, P. R. (1975): 'Parliament and the Direct Rule of Northern Ireland', *Irish Jurist* X, 81–92

Mansergh, N. (1936): *The Government of Northern Ireland: A Study in Devolution*, Allen & Unwin, London

Mansfield, F. (1972): 'Focus on Northern Ireland', *Municipal and Public Services Journal* (5 May 1972), 623–6

Marquand, J. (1967): 'Which Are the Lower-Paid Workers?', *British Journal of Industrial Relations* V, 359–74

Miliband, R., and Saville, J., ed. (1972): *The Socialist Register, 1972*, Merlin Press, London

Minar, D. W. (1961): 'Ideology and Political Behaviour', *Midwest Journal of Political Science* V, No. 4, 317–31

Molyneaux, J., 'Administrative Devolution for Ulster', *Belfast Telegraph*, 3 Feb. 1977

Moody, T. W., and Beckett, J. C., ed. (1957): *Ulster since 1800: A Political and Economic Survey*, BBC, London

Moore, B., Rhodes, J., and Tyler, P. (1977): 'The Impact of Regional Policy in the 1970s', *CES Review*, No. 1, 67–77

Moorhouse, B., Wilson, M., and Chamberlain, C. (1972): 'Rent Strikes—Direct Action and the Working Class' in Miliband and Saville (1972), 133–56

Murie, A. S. (1973): 'Planning in Northern Ireland', *Town Planning Review* XLIV, No. 4, 337–58

Murie, A. S. (1974 a): 'Family Income Supplement and Low Incomes in Northern Ireland', *Social and Economic Administration* VIII, No. 1, 22–42

Murie, A.S. (1974 b): 'Spatial Aspects of Unemployment and Economic Stress in Northern Ireland', *Irish Geography* VII, 53–67

Murie, A. S., Birrell, W. D., Hillyard, P. A. R., and Roche D. J. D. (1971): 'Housing Policy between the Wars: Northern Ireland, England and Wales', *Social and Economic Administration* V, No. 4, 263–79

Murie, A. S., Birrell, W. D., Roche, D. J. D., and Hillyard, P. A. R. (1974): *Regional Policy and the Attraction of Manufacturing Industry in Northern Ireland*, Research Paper, Centre for Environmental Studies, London

Murie, A. S., Hillyard, P. A. R., Birrell, W. D., and Roche D. J. D. (1976): 'New Building and Housing Need', *Progress in Planning* VI, Pt 2, Pergamon, London

Narain, B. J. (1973): *Public Law in Northern Ireland*, Appletree Press, Belfast

Neill, D. G., ed. (1953 a): *Devolution of Government: The Experiment in Northern Ireland*, Allen & Unwin, London

Neill, D. G. (1953 b): 'Some Consequences of Devolution in Northern Ireland' in Neill (1953 a), 86–99

Neill, D. G. (1957): 'Public Administration' in Moody and Beckett (1957), 148–58

Nelson, S. (1975): 'Protestant Ideology Considered: The Case of Discrimination' in I. Crewe, ed., *British Political Sociology Yearbook*, II, Crook Helm, London, 155–87

Newark, F. H. (1940): 'Parliamentary Freedom and the Government of Ireland Act, 1920', *Northern Ireland Legal Quarterly* IV, No. 2, 75–82

Newark, F. H. (1948): 'The Constitution of Northern Ireland: The First Twenty-Five Years', *Northern Ireland Legal Quarterly* VIII, No. 1, 52–66

Newark, F. H. (1953): 'The Constitution of Northern Ireland' in Neill (1953 a), 7–17

Newark, F. H. (1955): 'The Law and the Constitution' in Wilson (1955 a), 14–54

Newark, F. H. (1972): 'Legislation in Northern Ireland', *Northern Ireland Legal Quarterly* XXIII, No. 1, 95–100

Newman, C. F. S. (1965): 'A Short History of Planning in Northern Ireland', *Journal of the Town Planning Institute* II, No. 2, 47–53

Northern Ireland Community Relations Commission (1971): *Flight: A Report on Population Movement in Belfast during August 1971*, NICRC, Belfast

Northern Ireland Civil Service Alliance, *Annual Reports*, Belfast 1968–71

Northern Ireland Public Service Alliance, *Annual Reports*, Belfast 1972–75

O'Hara, J. (1976): 'Some Aspects of the Payment for Debt Act', *Quest* V, 9–16

Oliver, J. (1976): 'The Ulster Convention', *Blackwood's Magazine* CCCXX, No. 1930, 123–32

Oliver, J. (1978 a): *Working at Stormont*, Institute of Public Administration, Dublin

Oliver, J. (1978 b): *Ulster Today and Tomorrow*, PEP Broadsheet No. 574, London

O'Neill, T. (1969): *Ulster at the Crossroads*, Faber, London

O'Neill, T. (1972): *Autobiography*, Hart-Davis, London

Palley, C. (1972): *The Evolution, Disintegration and Possible Reconstruction of the Northern Ireland Constitution*, Institute of Irish Studies, Queen's University, Belfast

Poole, K. P. (1972): 'The Northern Ireland Commissioner for Complaints', *Public Law* (summer 1972), 131–48

Poole, M. 'Riot Displacement in 1969', *Fortnight*, 6–31 Aug. 1971

Presbyterian Church, General Assembly, *Annual Reports*, Belfast 1971–73

Punnett, R. M. (1971): *British Government and Politics*, Heinemann, London

Queen's University, Belfast (Department of Business Studies) (1976): *The Reorganisation of Health and Personal Social Services: Second Report,* Belfast

Ragg, N. (1972): 'Benefits in Northern Ireland' *Social Work Today* III, No. 13, 13–15

Rainsford, T. J. (1973): 'Supplementary Benefits in Northern Ireland', *Social Work Today* III, No. 23, 9–11

Readership Survey of Northern Ireland, Research Services Ltd, London 1971

The Reshaping of Local Government: A Conference Report, New University of Ulster, Coleraine 1969

Rhodes, E., ed. (1967): *Public Administration in Northern Ireland,* Magee University College, Londonderry 1967

Roberts, D. A. (1971): 'The Orange Order in Ireland: A Religious Institution?', *British Journal of Sociology* XXII, No. 3, 269–82

Robson, P. (1955): 'Standards of Public Expenditure in Northern Ireland' in Wilson (1955 a), 212–25

Rolston, Bill, 'Independence and the Dependent State', *Fortnight,* 1 Apr. 1977

Rose, R. (1971): *Governing without Consensus: An Irish Perspective,* Faber, London

Rose, R. (1976): *Northern Ireland—A Time of Choice,* Macmillan, London

Rose, R., and McAllister, I., 'Repartition and the Solution to Northern Ireland's Problems', *Irish Times,* 16 Sep. 1975

Rutan, G. F. (1964): 'Northern Ireland under Ulster Unionist Rule' (unpublished PhD thesis, University of South Carolina)

Rutan, G. F. (1967): 'The Labour Party in Ulster: Opposition by Cartel', *Review of Politics* XXVIII, 526–35

Ryan, J. L. (1967): 'The Role of the Statutory Bodies in Public Administration' in Rhodes (1967), 41–9

Sams, K. I. (1964): 'Government and Trade Unions: The Situation in Northern Ireland', *British Journal of Industrial Relations* II, 254–70

Sartori, G. (1969): 'Politics, Ideology and Belief Systems', *American Political Science Review* LXIII, 398–411

Sayers, J. E. (1955): 'The Political Parties and their Social Background' in Wilson (1955 a), 55–78

Sayers, J. E. (1969): 'The Legacy of O'Neill: Ulster Unionism, a New Course', *Round Table* LIX, No. 235 (Jul. 1969), 313–17

Scott, R. (1971): 'The 1970 British General Election in Ulster', *Parliamentary Affairs* XXIV, No. 1, 16–32

Sibbett, R. M. (1939): *Orangeism in Ireland and throughout the Empire* (1913), revised and enlarged ed., Thyme, London

Simpson, J. V. (1971): 'Regional Analysis: The Northern Ireland Experience', *Economic and Social Review* II, 507–29

Simpson, J. V. (1977): 'Public Sector Revenue and Expenditure in Northern Ireland', *Administration* XXV, No. 3, 338–48

Simpson, J. V., 'An Ulster Budget', *Fortnight,* 20 Sep. 1974.
Simpson, J. V., 'A Review of Economic and Industrial Strategy', *Fortnight,* 22 Oct. 1976
Spencer, A. E. C. W. (1973): *Ballymurphy: A Tale of Two Surveys,* Department of Social Studies, Queen's University, Belfast
Spencer, A. E. C. W., 'Integrated Schools: To Be or Not To Be?', *Fortnight,* 10 Jun. 1977
Stephens, N., and Glasscock, R. E., ed. (1970): *Irish Geographical Studies,* Queen's University, Belfast
Stevenson, J. (1964): 'Social Security in Northern Ireland' (unpublished PhD thesis, Queen's University, Belfast)
Titmuss, R. M. (1950): *Problems of Social Policy,* HMSO and Longmans, London
Ulster Loyalist Central Co-ordinating Committee (1976): *Ulster Can Survive Unfettered,* Discussion Document, Belfast
Wade, O. L., and Hood, H. E. (1972): 'An Analysis of Prescribing of an Hypnotic in the Community', *British Journal of Preventive and Social Medicine* XXVI, No. 2, 121–8
Wallace, M. (1967): 'Home Rule in Northern Ireland—Anomalies of Devolution', *Northern Ireland Legal Quarterly* XVIII, No. 1, 159–76
Wallace, M. (1970): *Drums and Guns: Revolution in Ulster,* Geoffrey Chapman, London
Wallace, M. (1971): *Northern Ireland: 50 Years of Self-Government,* David & Charles, Newton Abbot
Weiner, R. (1976): *The Rape and Plunder of the Shankill: Community Action: The Belfast Experience,* privately published, Belfast
Whale, J. (1970): 'Ulster Accepts London Domination', *Round Table* LX, No. 237 (Jan. 1970), 79–80
Whyte, J. H. (1973): 'Intra-Unionist Disputes in the Northern Ireland House of Commons, 1921–72', *Economic and Social Review* V, No. 1, 99–104
Wilson, H. (1971): *The Labour Government, 1964–1970,* Weidenfeld & Nicholson / Michael Joseph, London
Wilson, T., ed. (1955 a): *Ulster under Home Rule: A Study of the Political and Economic Problems of Northern Ireland,* Oxford University Press
Wilson, T. (1955 b): 'Devolution and Partition' in Wilson (1955 a), 183–211
Wilson, T. (1955 c): 'Devolution and Public Finance' in Wilson (1955 a), 115–36
Wilson, T. (1972): 'The Ulster Crisis: Reformed Government with a New Border', *Round Table* LXII, No. 239 (Jan. 1972), 37–54
Windlesham, Lord (1973): 'Ministers in Ulster: The Machinery of Direct Rule,' *Public Administration* LI, 261–72
Wright, F. (1973): 'Protestant Ideology and Politics in Ulster,' *European Journal of Sociology* XIV, 213–80

2. Government reports and papers

Hansard, 5th series
Parliamentary Debates (Northern Ireland House of Commons)
Northern Ireland Assembly: Official Reports, 3 vols, HMSO, Belfast 1974
Northern Ireland Constitutional Convention: Report, HMSO, London 1975
Northern Ireland Constitutional Convention: Report of Debates, HMSO, Belfast 1975
Northern Ireland Constitutional Convention: Report of Debates, February to March 1976, HMSO, Belfast 1976

Central Statistics Office, *Regional Statistics*, HMSO, London (annual)
Board of Inland Revenue, *Inland Revenue Statistics*, HMSO, London (annual)
Department of Employment Gazette, HMSO, London (monthly)
Department of Employment, *Family Expenditure Survey*, HMSO, London (annual)
Department of Employment, *New Earnings Survey*, HMSO, London (annual)

Northern Ireland Digest of Statistics, HMSO, Belfast (biannual)
Digest of Housing Statistics for Northern Ireland, HMSO, Belfast (quarterly)
Family Expenditure Survey: Report for Northern Ireland, HMSO, Belfast (annual)
General Health Services Board, *Annual Reports*, HMSO, Belfast 1968–72
Northern Ireland Parliamentary Commissioner for Administration, *Annual Reports*, HMSO, Belfast 1970–75
Northern Ireland Commissioner for Complaints, *Annual Reports*, HMSO, Belfast 1970–79
Northern Ireland Health and Social Services—Central Services Agency, *Annual Reports*, HMSO, Belfast 1973–
Supplementary Benefits Commission, *Reports*, HMSO, Belfast 1973–74

Interim Report of the Committee of Inquiry on Unemployment Insurance and Employment Exchanges, HMSO, Belfast 1922 (Cmd 2)
The Civil Service Report of Sir R. R. Scott, HMSO, Belfast 1926 (Cmd 66)
Report of the Ministry of Education, 1925–26, HMSO, Belfast 1926 (HC 107)
Report of the Departmental Commission on Local Government Administration in Northern Ireland, HMSO, Belfast 1927 (Cmd 73)
Civil Service Regrading: Report of Departmental Committee, HMSO, Belfast 1930

Report of the Departmental Committee on Sickness Visitation by Approved Societies, HMSO, Belfast 1932

Report of the Departmental Committee on Sickness Visitation by Approved Societies, HMSO, Belfast 1937

Report of the Ministry of Home Affairs on the Administration of Local Government Services, 1937–38, HMSO, Belfast 1938 (Cmd 200)

Housing in Northern Ireland: Interim Report of the Planning Advisory Board, HMSO, Belfast 1944 (Cmd 224)

Report on Health and Local Government Administration in Northern Ireland, 1938–46, HMSO, Belfast 1948 (Cmd 258)

'The Finances of Northern Ireland' in *Ulster Year Book*, HMSO, Belfast 1950, xix–xxxvi

[Nugent Report] *Report of the Committee on the Finances of Local Authorities*, HMSO, Belfast 1957 (Cmd 369)

[Hall Report] *Report of the Joint Working Party on the Economy of Northern Ireland*, HMSO, Belfast 1962 (Cmd 446)

[Matthew Report] *Belfast Regional Survey and Plan: Recommendations and Conclusions*, HMSO, Belfast 1963 (Cmd 451)

Report of the Select Committee on Public Accounts for the Year 1962–63, HMSO, Belfast 1964 (HC 1575)

[Wilson Report] *Economic Development in Northern Ireland*, HMSO, Belfast 1965 (Cmd 479)

[Lockwood Report] *Higher Education in Northern Ireland*, HMSO, Belfast 1965 (Cmd 475)

Higher Education in Northern Ireland: Government Statement on the Report of the Committee, HMSO, Belfast 1965 (Cmd 480)

Ministry of Health and Social Services, *Financial and Other Circumstances of Retirement Pensioners in Northern Ireland*, HMSO, Belfast 1966

Ministry of Health and Social Services, *Memorandum on the Development of Services for the Elderly*, HMSO, Belfast 1966

The Reshaping of Local Government: Statement of Aims, HMSO, Belfast 1967 (Cmd 517)

Report of the Select Committee on Public Accounts for the Year 1965–66, HMSO, Belfast 1967 (HC 1953)

The Constitution of Northern Ireland, HMSO, Belfast 1969

Commission on the Constitution: Written Evidence, 3: Government Departments of Northern Ireland, HMSO, London 1969

Standing Orders of the House of Commons: Public Business, HMSO, Belfast 1969 (HC 2013)

Northern Ireland: Text of a Communiqué and Declaration issued after a Meeting held at 10 Downing Street on August 19th, 1969, HMSO, London 1969 (Cmnd 4154)

Northern Ireland: Text of a Communiqué issued after Discussions between the Home Secretary and the Northern Ireland Government, HMSO, London 1969 (Cmnd 4178)

The Reshaping of Local Government: Further Proposals, HMSO, Belfast 1969 (Cmd 530)

[Cameron Report] *Disturbances in Northern Ireland: Report of the Commission appointed by the Governor of Northern Ireland,* HMSO, Belfast 1969 (Cmd 532)

[Hunt Report] *Report of the Advisory Committee on Police in Northern Ireland,* HMSO, Belfast 1969 (Cmd 535)

The Administrative Structure of the Health and Personal Social Services in Northern Ireland, HMSO, Belfast 1969

Report of the Joint Select Committee on Opposed Bills on the Magee University College, Londonderry, Bill, HMSO, Belfast 1969

Northern Ireland Economic Council, *Area Development in Northern Ireland,* HMSO, Belfast 1969

[Macrory Report] *Review Body on Local Government in Northern Ireland,* HMSO, Belfast 1970 (Cmd 546)

Northern Ireland Development Programme, 1970–75, HMSO, Belfast 1970

Northern Ireland Development Programme, 1970–75: Government Statement, 1970, HMSO, Belfast 1970 (Cmd 547)

Second Report of the Joint Select Committee on Consolidated Bills, Health Services Bill and Welfare Services Bill, HMSO, Belfast 1970 (S 20)

Commission on the Constitution: Minutes of Evidence, III: Northern Ireland, HMSO, London 1971

'The Links between the National Insurance Funds of Great Britain and Northern Ireland', *ibid.,* Appendix III

The Existing Selection Procedure for Secondary Education in Northern Ireland, HMSO, Belfast 1971 (Cmd 551)

The Future Development of the Parliament and Government of Northern Ireland, HMSO, Belfast 1971 (Cmd 560)

Special and First Reports of the Select Committee on Public Accounts for the Year 1969–70, HMSO, Belfast 1971 (HC 2107)

Report of Progress in Reorganisation of Local Government, HMSO, Belfast 1971

Northern Ireland Economic Council, *The Feasibility of State Industry in Northern Ireland,* HMSO, Belfast 1971

The Future of Northern Ireland: A Paper for Discussion, HMSO, London 1972

Political Settlement, HMSO, Belfast 1972 (Cmd 568)

Ministry of Health and Social Services, *A Survey of General Practice in Northern Ireland in 1970,* HMSO, Belfast 1972

Ministry of Health and Social Services, *Guide to the New Structure for Health and Personal Social Services,* Belfast 1972

[Osmond Report] *Training in the Public Service* (unpublished), Belfast 1972

Northern Ireland: Financial Arrangements and Legislation, HMSO, London 1972 (Cmnd 4998)

Northern Ireland: Constitutional Proposals, HMSO, London 1973 (Cmnd 5259)

[Kilbrandon Report] *Royal Commission on the Constitution, 1969–73,* Vol. I, HMSO, London 1973 (Cmnd 5460)

[Burges Report] *Reorganisation of Secondary Education in Northern Ireland,* HMSO, Belfast 1973 (Cmd 574)

The Northern Ireland Constitution, HMSO, London 1974 (Cmnd 5675)

Northern Ireland: Discussion Paper: Constitutional Procedure, HMSO, London 1974

Northern Ireland Office, *Northern Ireland: Discussion Paper: Finance and the Economy,* HMSO, London 1974

Industrial Relations in Northern Ireland: Report of the Review Body, 1971–74, HMSO, Belfast 1974

Northern Ireland: Discussion Paper: Government of Northern Ireland: A Society Divided, HMSO, London 1975

Our Changing Democracy: Devolution to Scotland and Wales, HMSO, London 1975 (Cmnd 6348)

Department of Employment, *Time Rates of Wages and Hours of Work,* HMSO, London 1975

Department of Housing, Local Government and Planning, *Northern Ireland: Discussion Paper: Regional Physical Development Strategy, 1975–95,* HMSO, Belfast 1975.

Department of Health and Social Services, *Strategy for the Development of Health and Personal Social Services in Northern Ireland,* HMSO, Belfast 1975

Department of Finance, *Social and Economic Trends in Northern Ireland,* No. 1, HMSO, Belfast 1975; No. 2, HMSO, Belfast 1976

Northern Ireland Housing Executive, *Northern Ireland Household Survey, 1975,* NIHE, Belfast [1976]

Letter from Secretary of State, HMSO, London 1976 (Cmnd 6387)

[Quigley Report] *Economic and Industrial Strategy for Northern Ireland,* HMSO, Belfast 1976

Reorganisation of Secondary Education in Northern Ireland, HMSO, Belfast 1976

Reorganisation of Secondary Education in Northern Ireland: A Statement by Lord Melchett, Minister of State, HMSO, Belfast 1977

Department of Health and Social Services, *Legislation and Services for Children and Young People in Northern Ireland,* HMSO, Belfast 1977

Areas of Special Social Need, HMSO, Belfast 1977

First Report of the Fair Employment Agency for Northern Ireland, HMSO, Belfast 1977

First Special Report from the Joint Committee on Statutory Instruments, HMSO, London 1978 (HC 169)

Social Service Teams: The Practitioner's View, HMSO, London 1978

[Cockcroft Report] Department of the Environment, *Review of Rural Planning Policy,* HMSO, Belfast 1978

Index